THE COMFORT WOMEN

WORLDS OF DESIRE
THE CHICAGO SERIES ON SEXUALITY, GENDER, AND CULTURE
A Series Edited by Gilbert Herdt

Also in the series:

THE COMFORT WOMEN

C. Sarah Soh

Sexual Violence and Postcolonial Memory in Korea and Japan

The University of Chicago Press | Chicago and London

The University of Chicago Press, Chicago 60637
The University of Chicago Press, Ltd., London
© 2008 by The University of Chicago
All rights reserved. Published 2008.
Printed in the United States of America

20 19 18 17 16 15 14 13 12 11   3 4 5 6 7

ISBN-13: 978-0-226-76776-5   (cloth)
ISBN-13: 978-0-226-76777-2   (paper)
ISBN-10: 0-226-76776-0   (cloth)
ISBN-10: 0-226-76777-9   (paper)

Library of Congress Cataloging-in-Publication Data

Soh, Chunghee Sarah.
   The comfort women : sexual violence and postcolonial memory in Korea
and Japan / C. Sarah Soh.
       p. cm. — (Worlds of desire) (American gay)
   Includes bibliographical references and index.
   ISBN-13: 978-0-226-76776-5 (cloth : alk. paper)
   ISBN-13: 978-0-226-76777-2 (pbk. : alk. paper)
   ISBN-10: 0-226-76776-0 (cloth : alk. paper)
   ISBN-10: 0-226-76777-9 (pbk.)
   1. Comfort women—Korea—History. 2. World War, 1939–1945—
Women—Korea. 3. Service, Compulsory non-military—Japan. 4. World
War, 1939–1945—Atrocities—Japan. I. Title.
   D810.c698s65 2008
   940.53'1—dc22

                                                    2008027222

for Jerry Boucher

Contents

Plates

Figure and Tables

Maps

Prologue | An Anthropological Analysis

ON THE WORK OF anthropology, James Peacock writes,

> The anthropologist seeks his [or her] subjects in a harsh light. . . .
> [T]he anthropologist shares a worldview sometimes termed "real-
> ism"—a way of seeing favored by natural science and certain kinds
> of literature, art, and philosophy, as well as by what we call common
> sense. Anthropology also favors a soft focus, in a certain sense. Lest
> they perceive too sharply any single object while missing its place in
> *context,* anthropologists gaze broadly, trying to glimpse foreground
> and background all at once, even including themselves in the picture.
> Aware that any object, any act is a convergence of myriad forces, they
> endeavor to capture the whole field, necessarily sacrificing precision of
> focus for breadth of vision. . . . Harsh light alludes to a no-nonsense
> realism grounded in detailed observation of life in raw circumstance,
> as well as a quest for the basic and elemental. Soft focus suggests an
> openness and a critical perspective, a holistic breadth of vision that in-
> cludes the world as well as the perceiver while embracing those shared
> understandings known as culture.[1] (Emphasis added)

Peacock's insightful photographic metaphor of the dual image of "harsh
light" and "soft focus" portrays an anthropological worldview as having two
complementary elements: a concern with the basic reality of the human
condition and a methodological holism that would enable a comprehensive
understanding of that condition. When I first encountered this metaphor
several years ago, I marveled at its felicity. In time I embraced it and have
used it to examine critically the dominant understanding of the comfort
women as "sex slaves" and a war crimes issue, which I refer to in this work
as a "paradigmatic story."

This book offers a critical anthropological perspective on the comfort
women phenomenon with a focus on the Korean case: Korean women constituted the great majority of the violated women, and the efforts of women

leaders and comfort women survivors in South Korea were essential in bringing this issue to the attention of the international community. The term "comfort women," an English translation of the Japanese euphemism *ianfu*,[2] refers to the tens of thousands of young women and girls of various ethnic and national backgrounds who were pressed into sexual servitude during the Asia Pacific War that began with the invasion of Manchuria in 1931 and ended with Japan's defeat in 1945. Estimates of the total numbers of Japan's comfort women range between 50,000 and 200,000.[3] Though these included small numbers of Japanese, Korean women constituted the great majority. It is believed that large numbers of Chinese women were also victimized.[4] The Japanese military also used women in Southeast Asia and the Pacific Islands, including the Philippines, Indonesia, Indochina, and Burma—then American, Dutch, French, and British colonies, respectively—which Japan occupied in the early 1940s.

Although I will not dwell on the horrid degradation of the women's lives as comfort women per se, using anthropology as cultural critique,[5] I will present a "person-centered," comparative perspective on their experiences and rethink the comfort women phenomenon in light of the specificities of colonial Korea and the post–cold war international politics of women's human rights.[6] In particular, I will consider the Korean comfort women issue partly as one important example of the massive exploitation of laborers, male and female, under Japanese colonial rule and so will be especially concerned with the tragedy of comfort women in its sociohistorical context. This approach is in stark contrast to the existing English-language literature, which defines the Japanese comfort system as sexual slavery and refers to the personal ordeals suffered by individual women as evidence of Japan's war crimes. This study of Korea's comfort women will cast new cultural-historical light on structural violence in patriarchal societies, especially against poor women who have customarily answered men's desire for nonprocreative, recreational sex outside the matrimonial bed, which I will call "public sex."

This is the first book-length treatment in any language to provide an anthropological interpretation of this victimization of young women in light of both Japan's colonial economy *and* the centuries-old sexual cultures of Japanese and Korean patriarchy. Korea's comfort women embody what I call "gendered structural violence" in the context of patriarchal colonial capitalism. Structural violence emanates from the economic, political, and cultural forces that are embedded in everyday life—notably gender, class, racial and ethnic inequality, and power imbalances. It is manifested in the abusive or demeaning exercise of power customarily practiced with impunity by one category of social actors or groups against others in situations of hierarchically organized social relations.[7] Korea's comfort women were thus victims of the mutually reinforcing convergence of sexism, classism, racism, colonialism, militarism, and capitalist imperialism. Accordingly, this study reveals that the wartime exploitation and lifelong suffering of Korean survivors arose not only within the comfort women system and the broader parameters of Japanese colonialism and fifteen years of war, but also within Korean patriarchy and its political economy under colonial rule.

By throwing a "harsh light" on the situational aspects of the tragic life trajectories of Korean comfort women and the organizational dimensions of the comfort facilities (or, in the bureaucratic language of imperial Japan, the "comfort station" [*ianjo*]), my goals in this book are (1) to move beyond the usually facile understanding of the women based on specific personal characteristics—in the language of modern social sciences, "de-essentialize"—and (2) to place Japan's wartime military comfort women from colonial Korea in a particular historical context—or "historicize"—thereby etching sharply their background and foreground. I will present individual life stories of former comfort women through a "soft focus" that blends their personal narratives of lifelong suffering—their often unhappy family lives, their very gloomy childhood experiences, and their horrid sexual ordeals as comfort women—into a holistic survey of the sexual cultural and historical contexts of Japanese and Korean societies.[8]

In light of the unprecedented and life-transforming impact of social reforms and capitalist industrialization that took place during the first half of the twentieth century, it is crucial that we consider the structural forces at work in late colonial Korea for a deeper understanding of the comfort women phenomenon; they not only contributed to the personal suffering of young women at home, but also inspired the risk-taking behavior that led to their fateful recruitment into the ranks of Japanese military comfort women. Some of these narratives have pointed to the oppression of patriarchal family relations that compelled young women to engage in acts of resistance. Their personal narratives paint quite a different picture from the canonized image of police or the military forcibly dragging them away from loving parents: They unwittingly interfere with the activists' paradigmatic story. In this study I take a deliberately unsentimental approach by "uncovering, reading, and making visible to others" the sexual and identity politics surrounding the comfort women in the ironic conjuncture between a transnational women's human rights perspective and South Korean ethnonationalism.[9] Both are invested in a paradigmatic story of Japan's comfort women as sex slaves who were forcibly recruited by the military. This critical anthropological approach, however, should not be construed as an absence of deep sympathy for countless dead and a very small number of officially registered surviving victims.

My research is committed to the exploration of inconvenient and unsavory social facts that have remained buried or unexplained in the major studies, including those by the most forceful critics of the comfort woman system in Japan, Korea, the United States, and elsewhere. The illumination of strategically "subjugated knowledge" surrounding Korea's comfort women tragedy is an indispensable first step in the journey toward truth and justice;[10] it means confronting the historicity of widespread trade in humans via indentured prostitution in prewar imperial Japan and in colonial Korea. It also calls for critical reflections on the historical and continuing exploitation and oppression of Korean (and Japanese) women, especially lower-class women engaged in public-sex work.

This study documents the collective complicity of Korean collaborators in the physical ordeals and psychological traumas visited on girls and young women forced into military prostitution and sexual slavery across the vast territories under Japanese occupation during the entire duration of the war. It further reveals that the lifelong social hardships and psychological sufferings of Korean survivors have been exacerbated by the traditional broad neglect in their society of victims of gendered structural violence—be they battered wives or women trafficked in the sex industry. Squarely confronting the crimes committed by Japanese soldiers and the colonial state, and neither denying nor diminishing the unspeakable ordeals these women endured, I significantly broaden the current understanding of Korea's comfort women beyond the familiar master narrative, or the feminist humanitarian paradigmatic story—the account of young girls forcibly recruited by the military into sexual enslavement.

Having struggled with the problems of conducting ethnographic field research on the multiple competing narratives in the sexual and identity politics over the comfort women issue, I maintain that the role of anthropologists in investigating national and international disputes over human rights politics is to provide "instruments of analysis," or "a topological and geological survey of the battlefield," rather than to engage in advocacy.[11] I agree with Jane Cowan and others who maintain that "An obligation to 'support human rights' unconditionally is misguided moralism."[12] I strongly believe the pluralism of anthropology (see the appendix) offers the most flexible approach to addressing the intractable problems of gendered structural violence in Korea before, during, and after the epoch of Japan's military comfort system. Anthropological engagement, I maintain, should result in nuanced ethnographic works that situate controversial issues—such as abortion, "female circumcision," minority rights, child prostitution, and the comfort women system—not only in the local social structure and cultural history, but also in international political and legal contexts, and reveal the diverse voices of the subjects themselves—in this case, those of Japanese as well as Koreans. By so doing, anthropological inquiry will contribute to a greater understanding of the complex dimensions of human behavior.[13]

Trying to "glimpse foreground and background all at once," as Peacock puts it, in the chapters that follow, I address a number of social structural, political, and psychological questions: in light of the politics of the contemporary redress movement, what significance do multiple contending representations of the comfort women have for understanding the truth about them? Why do South Koreans conflate the comfort women with the labor recruits called *chŏngsindae*? How was such large-scale victimization of Korean young women possible? What have we learned about the comfort women tragedy from individual survivors' life stories? What were the organizational characteristics of the Japanese military comfort system? How were comfort women remembered in Japanese and Korean popular memories prior to the redress movement? How are comfort women represented in the Japanese and Korean national history textbooks? What are we to make of the private countermemories of genuine affection and deep compassion toward individual Japanese soldiers in the reminiscences of Korean comfort women survivors? What have Japanese war veterans said about the comfort system? Finally, what explains the widespread—until recently—societal indifference to the plight of the comfort women not only in Japan, but also in Korea?

The book seeks to address the above questions by adopting a two-pronged approach in its investigation: a historiographic examination of the configuration and emergence of the paradigmatic representation of the comfort women and a critical review of survivors' life stories culled from both documentary sources and my own field research. A major aim of this study is to demonstrate the Korean comfort women tragedy as a prominent instance of gendered structural violence emanating from the social dynamics of power, resistance, and violence. My discussion thus intervenes in the transnationally dominant humanitarian paradigmatic story of the comfort women by shedding light on the variety of personal circumstances—within the larger social and historical conjuncture—that pushed these Korean women away from home and into the grossly exploitative comfort system. Their biographical narratives reveal not only the unbelievably wretched life conditions of the poor in colonial Korea, but also remarkable levels of agency, aspirations for autonomy, life-affirming perseverance, and resilience—characteristics that have been ignored or downplayed in most studies. Nonetheless, the lifelong suffering of survivors proves to be deeply rooted in the political economy and traditional culture alike. That is, the abuse and maltreatment of daughters and wives in the patriarchal system, with its long-standing masculinist sexual culture, contributed as much as did the colonial political economy to the ready commodification of these women's sexual labor. I challenge the categorical portrayal of Korean comfort women as victims *solely* of the Japanese military and colonialism, a view that ignores the complex historicity that entangled the lives of the men and women of colonial Korea and imperial Japan.

*   *   *

In light of the politically charged and emotionally explosive nature of the comfort women controversy, I think more than the usual caveats and disclaimers may be in order here. First, I in no way mean to somehow legitimize the comfort system by looking at it in context. By addressing the cultural and historical facts of state-controlled prostitution in prewar Japan and colonial Korea and during the total war against Allied forces, I present a critique of prevailing sexual cultures in patriarchal societies in general, and of military hypermasculinity in particular, which helped "normalize" sexual exploitation and violence against women during and after the war. As I will describe in chapter 6, for example, the Allied forces committed sexual violence against many Japanese women, and government policy led to the recruitment of destitute young women in postwar Japan to provide commercial sex to the occupation forces. In postcolonial Korea, the South Korean Army operated its own comfort stations during the Korean War (1950–1953). Moreover, for more than fifty years after the Korean War, hundreds of thousands of young South Korean women continued to endure sexual exploitation and violence as they labored in camptowns serving the U.S. military. The victimization of women in Japan and Korea received little societal attention, let alone sympathy, until the last decade of the twentieth century primarily because the prevailing sexual culture stigmatized these women even while regarding their services as "necessary." This pattern has persisted even into the twenty-first century, when, regrettably, even soldiers belonging to United Nations peacekeeping missions commit sexual abuse of women and girls, though not through an organized system.[14]

Second, my examination of the Japanese military comfort system focuses on the variegated organizational dimensions of the comfort station in the social and historical context of Japan's Fifteen-Year War, not just the last few years of World War II, which is generally the case with activists and the mass media reports. Hence, I introduce the selected testimonials of comfort women—from colonial Korea, as well as Japan, the Philippines, and the Dutch East Indies—seeking to cover the entire period of the existence of the wartime military comfort system to illustrate my theoretical analysis. Because data are often incomplete, rigorous *statistical* analysis of the survivors' narratives to make systematic comparisons would pose an almost impossible task for any researcher and is beyond the scope of this study.

Third, as a supporter of the transnational feminist movement for women's human rights and as an expatriate, I seek to transcend the ethnonationalist politics of "partial truths" by presenting a complicated picture that may disrupt the currently internationalized normative—though partial and partisan—understandings of the Korean comfort women's horrific experience. Examining the military comfort system (*gun ianseido*) as history inevitably reveals a range of unsavory social facts that should provide common ground through which warring camps can come to a basic agreement on the complex nature of the comfort system. This can perhaps improve the odds of an eventual reconciliation between Japan and Korea over the historical injustices perpetrated during colonial rule.

In short, I attempt to make an objective analysis of a controversial issue, so this study will probably offend everyone who takes sides in the sexual and identity politics of the opposing camps. Nevertheless, my study findings oblige me to take a critical stance against the simplified characterizations of Japan's military comfort stations as either "military brothels" or "rape centers." Defining the nature of Japan's military comfort system simply as commercial sex, sexual slavery, or war crime only serves the ends of the partisan politics being waged by adversarial ethnic nationalists and transnational human rights activists. Despite its important contributions to the international recognition of wartime sexual violence as a war crime, the Korean redress movement has employed "approximate truths" or strategic exaggerations that have effectively impeded deeper understanding of the comfort women issue and any real progress toward its resolution. That Japanese soldiers committed sex crimes during the war—not only the "usual" individual and/or mass rapes on the battlefield but also those that fall under the rubric of comfort stations—is beyond dispute.

But does this warrant sweeping categorical definitions such as "rape centers" for Japan's military comfort facilities comprising the diverse categories and subtypes of *ianjo* that evolved during the Fifteen-Year War? Is this a productive approach? Are the Japanese unique in providing systematically for their soldiers' sexual recreation? Is Korean society entirely innocent? I believe that we now need to ask these questions if we are to examine Japan's military comfort women system as a historical institution that was more complex than the competing categorical definitions of licensed prostitution versus war crime.

Finally, I must warn strongly against the rightists and militant nationalists in Japan and elsewhere who might abuse and take any portion of this book out of context to promote their own partisan positions. It is about time that they, as well as their domestic and foreign critics, acknowledged the whole complicated truth of historical facts about Japan's wartime military comfort system instead of continuing to cling to their own distorted partisan versions of "partial truths."

Acknowledgments

THIS BOOK IS the culmination of more than a decade of immersion in the study of the comfort women question. I owe numerous people and several public institutions thanks for their support of my multi-sited long-term research. First and foremost, I am immeasurably indebted to the courage and resilience of former comfort women in Japan, Korea, and elsewhere, who came out—in some cases decades prior to the international redress movement—to tell their stories of sexual violence and lifelong suffering and to be remembered as part of twentieth-century women's history. For their persistent hard work and passionate dedication to interrogating, redefining, and redressing the long-ignored problem of the comfort women issue as violence against women in war and crimes against humanity, I salute the women leaders and staff members of the Korean Council for Women Drafted for Military Sexual Slavery by Japan.

During the fieldwork I undertook between January 1995 and December 2006, I interviewed many people in Korea. I wish to acknowledge the cooperation and help I received from the Korean Council's founding co-representatives, Professors Yun Chŏng-ok and Lee Hyo-chae, whose instrumental role is further discussed in the appendix, and the former co-representatives Kim Yun-ok, Chung Chin-sung, and Shin Hye-su; the former staff member and current co-representative Yun Mi-hyang; the dedicated former and current researchers at the Korea Research Institute on Chŏngsindae, in particular Cho-Choi Hye-ran, Yŏ Sun-ju, and Professor Ahn Byungjik, as well as the director, Yi Sŏng-sun, for her warm hospitality during my visits to the institute. For their kind support, I am grateful to Professors Kim Doo-sub and Rhee Younghoon, as well as to the former director of the House of Sharing, the Buddhist monk Hyejin. I am also grateful to the several resident-survivors at the House of Sharing, including Kang Tŏk-kyŏng, Kim Sun-dŏk, Pak Ok-nyŏn, Pak Tu-ri, and Yi Yong-nyŏ, for their willingness to talk with me. I also wish to thank several other survivors, in particular Mun P'il-gi, Kim Ok-sil, Pak Pok-sun, Hwang

Kūm-ja (and Kim Chŏng-hwan of the Kangsŏ Ward Office for arranging the meeting), Yun Sun-man, and Sim Mi-ja, all of whom welcomed my visits with them at their homes; Kim Hak-sun, for agreeing to meet me and be interviewed at the office of Yujokhoe, whose staff members offered valuable reference materials for my research during my visits; and Kim Yun-sim, for opening up to me with her personal story, which countered the negative assessment of the truth of her testimony offered by the leadership of the nongovernmental organization. The officials at the Ministries of Foreign Affairs and of Health and Social Welfare who responded to my inquiries in a professional manner in the summer of 1997 and January 1999, respectively, deserve my sincere thanks.

As for personal contributions to my more-than-decade-long study, I have my two families across the Pacific Ocean to thank from the bottom of my heart.

As always, I could count on receiving my parents' loving care during my multiple research trips of varying length to Korea. They not only showed their abiding interest in my project but also offered help with translations of Japanese materials and mailed to me clippings of Korean media reports on the comfort women issue when I was back in the United States. My thanks are also due my three siblings for their warm encouragement and constant support. Myung-hee communicated her sisterly pride for my work in her own unique ways when her work schedule in a provincial town prevented her from traveling to Seoul to join the family gatherings during my research trips. I am thankful to Byung-hee for his insightful comments on an earlier chapter draft and for sending me a copy of important unpublished reference material. I owe special thanks to Yoon-hee for providing shelter and company during my field trips after our parents' move into an assisted living facility. In addition, I am deeply grateful for her generosity with her time in helping me obtain various reference materials for my project.

On this side of the Pacific, my ninety-four-year-old father-in-law, news of whose death reached me as I was completing the final manuscript, will be dearly missed and fondly remembered for his active interest in my work, which he expressed by mailing me clippings of a news report from a local paper in Modesto, California, for my reference. Most of all, I express my profound heartfelt appreciation to Jerry Boucher for his patient love and unwavering support for my seemingly endless project. Because of his generous and indispensable contributions in the form of editorial suggestions and technical assistance through all stages of my research, for which I can never thank him enough, I dedicate this book to him.

In Japan, where my primary fieldwork was carried out for over five months (in 1997 and 1998), followed by annual research trips for data collection and conference presentations until December 2006, I have met more people than I am able to acknowledge adequately in this limited space. They helped me collect much data (primarily on the politics of the comfort women redress movement), most of which remains to be mined for a future project. My memories of some of the many people I met have, after the lapse of more than a decade, dimmed under the shadow of "old-timer's disease" (to quote a self-excusatory phrase my beloved late mother-in-law used to cover up her embarrassment over occasional forgetfulness). My recent move into a new home has compounded the problem of locating all the memorabilia of my fieldwork in Japan that would have served as convenient memory joggers. I beg the forgiveness of all who have helped me for any unintended omissions of their personal contributions to my research.

I would like to express my sincere gratitude to Hirakawa Naomi (of the office of the Councilor Motooka Shōji) and her family for their hospitality and kind assistance, especially during the initial weeks of my fieldwork, when they helped me to settle in comfortably at the campus of the University of Tokyo International Lodge at Komaba. I am very thankful to the many professionals and activists and their supporters who graciously made time for me to interview them, including Arima Makiko, Arimitsu Ken, Aiko Carter, Chu Su-ja, Fukushima Mizuho, Harada Shinji, Hayashi Yōko, Heo Seon-ja, Hoshino-san, Ichikawa Ichirō, Ikeda Eriko, Itō Mutsuko and her two friends, Sam Jameson, Kanehira Teruko, Kawata Fumiko, Kim Il-myŏn, Kim Yŏng-hi, Matsui Yayori, Miki Mutsuko, Nakajima Shigeru, Nakazato Chiyo, Nishino Rumiko, Nobukawa Mitsuko, Shimizu Sumiko, the late So Chin-gŏ, Sŏ Kyŏng-sik, Song Sin-do (a Korean survivor-resident in Japan) and the members of her support group, Tagaki Ken'ichi, Maren Trosien, Uesugi Satoshi, Umemoto Ayako (and Hamada Tomoko for the introduction), Usuki Keiko, William Weatherall, Yamaguchi Yoshiko (a.k.a. Ri Kōran), Yi In-ha, and Dr. Yuasa Ken.

My sincere thanks are also due the following professionals and academics who helped me with thoughtful responses to my inquiries during our meetings, held at various places including coffeeshops, their offices, and their homes: Awaya Kentarō (kindly introduced in person by Yoshida Takashi), Fujioka Nobukatsu, Fujiwara Akira, Hashimoto Hiroko, Hata Ikuhiko, Andrew Horvat, Ishida Takeshi, Glenda Roberts, chief of the Foreign Ministry's Asia Policy Section Satō-san, Suzuki Yūko, Takasaki Sōji, Tanaka Hiroshi, Totsuka Etsuro, Utsumi Aiko, Yamashita Yŏngae, Yokota Yōzo, and Yoshimi Yoshiaki.

I thank my anthropology colleague Kuwayama Takami for providing me with an opportunity to talk about the comfort women issue with his students at Sōka University. My warm thanks are also due Ueno Chizuko, who graciously invited me to her seminar at the University of Tokyo, allowing me to meet with her students for a discussion of the controversial topic. I also note with deep appreciation the hospitality that Numazaki Ichiro, another anthropology colleague at Tohoku University, offered me during my visit to Sendai, where I met a local group of concerned citizens and supporters of Song Sin-do's lawsuit. I am indebted to the historian and director Wada Haruki for welcoming my affiliation with the Social Research Institute at the University of Tokyo. My special thanks are also due Mrs. Wada for the warm hospitality she extended to three advisees of her husband—two researchers from Korea and myself—with a memorable New Year's Japanese formal dinner at her home.

I very much appreciated the warm hospitality of Nitta Fumiteru and his wife Jean—whose untimely death is mourned by his friends and family—during my visit with them in Kurashiki on my way to Hiroshima. I was delighted Tomizawa Yoshiko not only helped me make an appointment but also took time out to accompany me when I visited the Kanita Women's Village, adding unexpected pleasure to the business of fieldwork.

With the advent of the Internet era, my home page on the comfort women project, which Jerry Boucher designed and created, has generated numerous inquiries, requests for help, and compliments. I diligently offered my responses in the earlier stages of my research. One such exchange resulted in my visit to Toyama, Japan. I thank Kakichi Shinji, a young journalist who sent me e-mail inquiries concerning my research on the comfort women issue and who invited me to stay with his family at his lovely home in June 1997.

In the Netherlands, I owe special thanks to Jan Ruff-O'Herne, Ellen van der Ploeg, and two other survivors, who will remain anonymous, for responding generously to my request for interviews. I am greatly indebted to Marguerite Hamer of the Project Implementation Committee in the Netherlands for her kind help in arranging my meetings with three survivors. I also received help and cooperation for my research from Professors Theo van Boven and Barend Cohen, retired General Govert L. J. Huyser, Rosemary Robson at the University of Leiden, Elly Touwen-Bouwsma at the Netherlands Institute for War Documentation, Connie Suverkropp, G. Jungslager, Mr. and Mrs. Lapré of the Foundation for Japanese Honorary Debts (Stichting Japanse Ereschulden), and Ikeda Tadashi, the Japanese ambassador to the Netherlands.

Back at my home institution of San Francisco State University, I received valuable assistance from several students, colleagues, and other professionals. In particular, I would like to thank Ann-Marie Guyot, Lim Soo-kyung, and Corie Tyson, who volunteered to help me in the early stage of my project with my literature review. Fujiu Keiko, Inagaki Naomi, Kim Miho, and Miko Yamamoto helped translate some Japanese-language materials. I thank Niels Teunis and Marguerite Hamer for their assistance with the Dutch texts and Ellen McElhinny for helping produce the maps.

Many interested students from various local, national, and international educational institutions, journalists at home and abroad, and the general public, most of whom had read the descriptions of my project on my Web site, sent me e-mail comments and various requests. Some people even mailed me interesting reference materials as well. Even though I am unable to acknowledge each of you by name, you know who you are, and I offer you my sincere thanks for your interest in my work. I should also like to offer my apologies and seek kind understanding for not having been able to respond to all the inquiries and requests that came to me in the later years of my project. I hope this book provides answers to some of these questions.

Generous support from the following institutions have been indispensable in my pursuit of field research and writing in Japan, the Netherlands, South Korea, and the United States: an Association for Asian Studies (AAS) Northeast Asia Council's (NEAC) Korean Studies Committee grant (1995); an AAS-NEAC travel grant (1996); a San Francisco State University (SFSU) Mini Grant (1997); a fellowship from the Japan Foundation (1997–1998); an SFSU summer stipend (1998); a senior visiting scholar award from the International Institute for Asian Studies of the University of Leiden (1998); an AAS-NEAC Japanese Studies Committee grant (1999); a John D. and Catherine T. MacArthur Foundation research and writing grant (no. 99-61141-GSS; 2000–2001); an SFSU sabbatical leave (spring 2003); and a research and writing grant from the Korea Social Research Center (2006).

For their collegial support in writing letters of strong support for my applications for research funding, I express my heartfelt gratitude to Phillip Bourgois, Karen Bruhns, Takie Lebra, and Bernard Wong. I also thank the Institute of Social Science of the University of Tokyo for the visiting fellowship (1997–1998) and the Institute for Research on Women and Gender at Stanford University for welcoming me as an affiliated scholar (2000–2001). I gratefully acknowledge Joel Kassiola, dean of the College of Behavioral and Social Sciences (BSS) at SFSU, for his hearty encouragement with several BSS conference travel grants and crucial support in the final stage of writing.

For providing helpful feedback on my earlier chapters, I thank Ann

Bodine, Sabine Frühstück, Jane Margold, Karen Offen, and Mark Selden. For their meticulous readings and valuable comments on the entire manuscript of earlier versions of this book, I would like to express my deep gratitude to Nancy Abelmann, Gail Bernstein, Bruce Cumings, John Lie, and Bernard Wong. For their skillful editorial assistance, I thank Terre Fisher and Joseph Parsons. For their interest in my research, kind words of encouragement, and practical help, I am thankful to Deborah Ahn, Michael Allen, Alexis Dudden, Dongwoo Lee Hahm, Chalmers Johnson, John Kim, John Lee, Meredith May, and Susan McEachern. For inviting me to give presentations on my research on comfort women, which enabled me to meet attentive audiences at institutions located across the country and abroad, I would like to express my sincere thanks to the many organizers, including Ruth Barraclough, Rose Bundy, Charles Burress, Im Ja Choi, Sera Choi, Deborah Davis, Germaine Hoston, Alan Howard, Sang Joo Kim, Mike Mochizuki, Gi-Wook Shin, and Wada Haruki.

This book contains materials that appeared in the following journals and edited volumes: "From Imperial Gifts to Sex Slaves: Theorizing Symbolic Representations of the 'Comfort Women,'" *Social Science Japan Journal* 3 (1): 59–76; "Aspiring to Craft Modern Gendered Selves: 'Comfort Women' and Chŏngsindae in Late Colonial Korea," *Critical Asian Studies* 36 (2): 175–198; "Women's Sexual Labor and State in Korean History," *Journal of Women's History* 15 (4): 170–177; "Teikokunippon no 'Gunianseido' ron: Rekishi to Kioku no Seijitekikattō," in *Sensō no Seijigaku,* pp. 347–380, vol. 2 of *Iwanami Kōza Ajia Taiheiyōsensō,* 8 vols. (Tokyo: Iwanami, 2005); and "The Korean 'Comfort Women' Tragedy as Structural Violence," in *Rethinking Historical Injustice in Northeast Asia: The Korean Experience,* edited by G-W. Shin, S-W. Park, and D. Yang (New York: Routledge), pp. 17–35.

On a much happier note, I am very pleased to acknowledge Funabashi Yōichi, a columnist for the *Asahi Shimbun,* for his kind assistance in helping me secure the permission to use a valuable "comfort bag" photograph in my book. Plates 0.1 and 4.2 are from the photocopies I obtained from the archival offices of Seoul Sinmunsa and Dong-a Ilbosa, respectively. Plates 1.1 and 1.2 are from photocopies I made with permission during my research at the National Archives in Washington, D.C. I acknowledge with gratitude Inagaki Naomi's research assistance for the past several years, in particular her recent strenuous but frustrated efforts to obtain, on my behalf, permission to use a couple of the late Dr. Asō's photographs (which have been a staple of activist brochures and are available on Internet sites, all apparently without permission): the doctor's daughter decided to refuse permission after reading the article I published in Japanese in 2005 (as cited above), concluding it was an example of Japan bashing.

At the University of Chicago Press, my special thanks go to Gilbert Herdt, the Worlds of Desire series editor; Douglas Mitchell and his team of highly skilled staff members (including Erik Carlson, Rob Hunt, Dustin Kilgore, Tim McGovern, and Christina Samuell); the copyeditor, Barbara Norton; and the university faculty board for their enthusiastic support for my project.

It would be extremely gratifying for me if my academic work could contribute to various partisan readers' deeper understanding of Japan's comfort women saga, which could help lead to the eventual discovery of a healing truth concerning the comfort women tragedy.

Note to the Reader

IN THIS BOOK, unless otherwise specified, "Korea" refers interchangeably to the Republic of Korea (South Korea) and to the one ethnic nation that existed prior to its postcolonial division into two political entities in 1948 during the cold war.

Except for certain familiar proper nouns, such as Seoul, and some personal names whose preferred romanization is known, the McCune-Reischauer system is used for Korean transliteration in the text and the Hepburn system for Japanese. Japanese and Korean names are given in the East Asian manner, with the family name first, followed by the given name, except when the individual follows the Western custom in his or her writings in a Western language. The two parts of the Korean given name are hyphenated, and the sound changes that may occur between them in given names are not observed.

This study speaks of the Asia Pacific War by adding "Asia" to the term "Pacific War" in order to underscore the sufferings experienced by the people of Asia. The term is not limited to the war between Japan and the United States over the Pacific after the attack on Pearl Harbor on December 7, 1941; rather, it refers to the duration of what some Japanese, such as the historian Ienaga Saburō, have called the Fifteen-Year War (from the Manchurian Incident in 1931 to Japan's defeat in 1945).

In transliterating the term for the Volunteer Labor Corps in the Korean language, I distinguish between the institution Chŏngsindae (capitalized and roman) and the term as a label for the members of the corps *chŏngsindae* (lowercase and italic). The translations of Korean and Japanese materials used in this book are my own unless otherwise noted. In conformance with the publisher's style, my quotation marks in the book's title, *The Comfort Women,* were not used.

The monetary units of Japanese yen and sen are rendered as wŏn and chŏn when used by Korean speakers. Regarding the monetary value of wartime yen, the historian Yoshimi Yoshiaki (Yoshimi 2000: 30) estimates the value of 300 yen during World War II to be the equivalent of 1.2 million yen today (about $10,000), which might be an underestimation as of 2008 but provides a useful approximation of the value.

THE COMFORT WOMEN

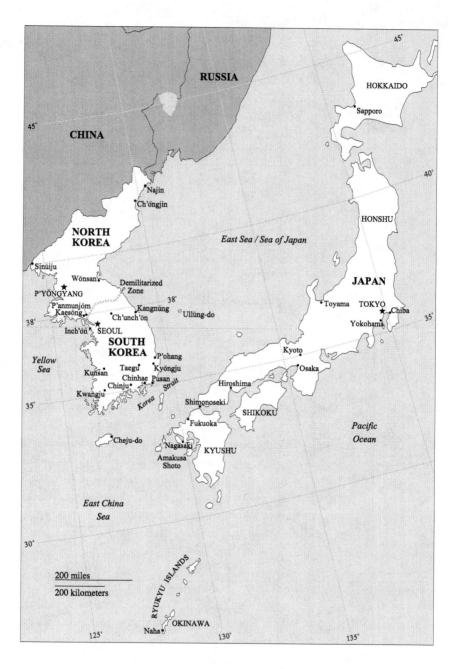

Map 1. The two Koreas and postwar Japan

Introduction | Gender, Class, Sexuality, and Labor under Japanese Colonialism and Imperialist War

> The issue of Japanese military "comfort women" resides at the point of convergence where the system of Korean patriarchy and the problems of colonized nation meet.
>
> —Han'guk Chŏngsindae-munje Taech'aek Hyŏpŭihoe-pusŏl Chŏnjaeng kwa Yŏsŏnginkwŏn Sentŏ Yŏn'gutim (War and Women's Rights Center Research Team), *Yŏksa rŭl Mandŭnŭn Iyagi,* 2004

MORE THAN SIXTY YEARS have passed since the end of World War II, but the wounds of Japanese colonialism and war still fester in several nations in East and Southeast Asia. In a number of countries—most notably South Korea, but to a lesser extent in China, Indonesia, and the Philippines as well—the plight of comfort women in particular has come to symbolize imperial Japan's "war crimes" (*chŏnjaeng pŏmjoe*, in Korean). Thanks to social movements that began in South Korea, Japan, and elsewhere in the early 1990s, comfort women survivors are now represented as "sex slaves" of wartime imperial Japan. Internationally prominent human rights lawyers and legal experts, progressive historians of Japan, nonfiction writers, novelists, and journalists worldwide have endorsed the political discourse condemning Japan's wartime "military sexual slavery."

Despite their historic contributions, the approach of South Korean activists and their supporters has obscured the continued ubiquity of grave human rights violations of women, especially those working in the sex industry in postcolonial South Korea. Although activists and their supporters have successfully publicized sexual violence and atrocities committed by the Japanese military, the way in which they have framed the story of comfort women as *exclusively* a Japanese war crimes issue has diverted attention from the sociocultural and historical roots of women's victimization in Korea, which Japan colonized from 1910 to 1945. The timely conjuncture of post–cold war transnational humanitarian feminism and South Korean ethnonationalism further obscures deeper understanding of the broader historical forces that were transforming colonial Korea from an agrarian male-oriented Confucian dynasty in which women's proper place was delimited within the confines of the family into a capitalist modern industrializing society that offered women unprecedented opportunities to seek autonomy and financial independence by working for wages in the public sphere. Some women freely left home to escape domestic violence, grinding poverty, familial strife, or an arranged marriage; some of these self-motivated women who made life-changing decisions in search of better life chances, however, were deceptively recruited by Japanese and Korean traffickers for the military comfort facilities of imperial Japan.

Listen, for example, to the voice of a Korean comfort woman survivor, Yi Sun-ok (b. 1921), who described the personal situation that made her aspire to go to Japan and make money by working at a factory in 1938:

> When I was about fifteen or sixteen, a distant kinsman moved from Kyŏngju to Yŏngdŏk, my hometown. He lived with his family just behind our house. Since he had been in prison for taking part in the independence movement against the Japanese occupation, the authorities kept a tight watch on us, on the grounds that he was our relative. When I was about seventeen, a rumor about *ch'ŏnyŏ kongch'ul* (literally, "maiden, or virgin, delivery" [as an obligation for official purposes]) floated around.[1] After consulting with the uncle and through his introduction, my father made an agreement with a divorced man, Mr. Pak, to have me registered, on paper only, as his new wife in October 1937. The man, whom I never met, agreed with my father to annul the marriage when I really got married later.
>
> Not long after that, my family moved to Yŏngch'ŏn County, and I began working for the Moritas, a kindly Japanese couple, washing their clothes and fetching water for them. I asked Mrs. Morita various questions about Japan and learned from her that there were many factories where girls could earn lots of money by working there. I told her that I wanted to go to Japan and earn money. The Moritas said that my father would beat me if he heard it and discouraged me from saying such things. One day, a Korean man, a Mr. O in his forties, visited Mr. Morita. I was there and listened to their conversation. Mr. O said that he had come to recruit girls to work in a new silk factory in Japan. Answering my questions, he even told me that I could quit

work anytime if I didn't like work there. Since I found it unpleasant and burdensome to pretend to be a married woman—with my hair up and wearing a kerchief—and because we were poor, I decided to go. My parents were against the idea but *I persuaded them* [emphasis added]. I was seventeen when I left home.

However, her desire to realize an autonomous self in the image of the self-supporting "new woman" (see below) was cruelly shattered when Mr. O delivered her in the early summer of 1938 to a military brothel in Guangdong, southern China, run by a Korean woman in her fifties from Chŏlla Province.[2]

* * *

For a critical understanding of the suppressed aspirations and daring personal agency revealed in testimonial narratives of my key informant, Mun P'il-gi (see chapter 2), and other Korean survivors (such as Yi Sun-ok) and their subsequent unspeakable ordeals, the late Eric Wolf's notion of "structural power" provides a useful analytical tool. In explaining Korea's comfort women phenomenon, Wolf would have suggested that the structural power of the political economy in the capitalist industrializing colonial Korea "shape[d] the social field of action so as to render some kinds of behavior possible, while making others less possible or impossible."[3] Here it is important to emphasize that industrialization and the modern capitalist economic system opened new doors for women into the public sphere when they found themselves subjected to domestic tyranny under battering fathers, bullying brothers, and/or unsympathetic mothers.

By drawing on ethnographic data collected during research conducted beginning in 1995,[4] I contend that the personal tragedies of Korean comfort women arose, in part, from the institutionalized *everyday* gender violence tolerated in patriarchal homes and enacted in the public sphere (including the battlefront) steeped in what I call "masculinist sexual culture" in colonial Korea and imperial Japan.[5] Notwithstanding South Korean nationalists' homogenizing rhetoric of the comfort women as sex slaves who were deceived as volunteer labor recruits or *chŏngsindae,* my research findings strongly suggest that most Korean comfort women survivors were not mobilized as *chŏngsindae.*

Whereas some Korean survivors stated having been kidnapped, others revealed that they were "sold" to human traffickers by their indigent parents. In fact, compatriot "entrepreneurs"—men and some women from colonial Korea who not only procured girls and women for the Japanese army but also, in many cases, managed or ran comfort stations—lured the majority of them. Furthermore, some chose to run away from home in order to escape domestic violence and maltreatment or the oppression of crushing poverty, fervently aspiring to become modern autonomous "new women." Their valiant acts of self-determination in pursuit of an education and autonomy to craft modern gendered selves deserve scholarly exposure and recognition in a more nuanced and postnationalist understanding of Korean women's tragic history of foiled aspirations and horrific ordeals under patriarchy, colonialism, and total war. Their leaving home represented a self-conscious act of personal resistance by daughters caught between the traditional paradigm of filial piety—inculcated by the Neo-Confucian gender ideology symbolized by "the rule of three obediences" (*samjong chido*)—and a modern individualist aspiration for autonomy and self-actualization.[6]

*   *   *

Here one might ask, How did runaway daughters come to acquire such modern aspirations in colonial Korea? To answer this question we must consider the far-reaching social consequences of the Korean modernization process of industrial and capitalist development under colonial rule. In particular, the modern education system and the transplanted system of licensed prostitution constituted the two most crucial public institutions in terms of the profound influence they had on many women's lives under Japan's colonialism.

MODERN EDUCATION AND THE "NEW WOMAN"

Perhaps the most revolutionary dimension of modernity Korean women encountered in the first half of the twentieth century was the opening of the formal public education system to young girls and women. As one of the leading institutions of modern society, formal education for girls at public schools and higher education for women helped bring about women's self-awakening and subsequent efforts to shake loose the yoke of patriarchy. The crucial significance of modern education as "cultural capital" in women's personal empowerment cannot be overemphasized in the historical context of Korean society.[7]

By contrast, during the Chosŏn dynasty (1392–1910), even the majority of men barely received any education beyond the local village schools, called *sŏdang,* where they learned the Chinese classics. The schools were theoretically open to all classes but were attended mostly by boys of the *yangban* (upper) class. In the capital city of Hanyang (today's Seoul), the head of the family was responsible for teaching the women and girls the principles of proper conduct. In the countryside, a learned and respected village elder was responsible for giving instruction to women.[8] Illiteracy was regarded as shameful for men, but not so for women, who were expected to stay in the inner quarters (*anch'ae*) and were strongly discouraged even from going outside the house. Most women could not read elementary Chinese letters or even the Korean alphabet, *han'gŭl,* which was invented to facilitate mass literacy for women and male commoners and promulgated under the reign of King Sejong (r. 1418–1450). Only one book was written in *han'gŭl* by a woman of Chosŏn, the memoir of Lady Hyegyŏng (1735–1815), a noblewoman who married Prince Sado (1735–1762) when both were nine years old in 1744. (Consummation did not take place until five years later.)[9]

Until the turn of the twentieth century, the scope of Korean women's education was limited to the cultivation of "wifely virtues," including obedience, chastity, and selfless service. "Guidebooks for womanhood" offered women instruction in everyday family affairs over their lifetime, teaching the qualities they needed to be filial daughters, faithful wives, and wise mothers. One such guidebook, *Naehun,* published in 1475, was written by Queen Sohye, the first daughter-in-law of King Sejo, the founder of the Chosŏn dynasty. It was adapted from a Chinese guidebook for women. Three more guidebooks for women, all of which were written by men, are extant.[10] Women in premodern Korea were taught to maintain their chastity when widowed and to become *yŏllyŏ* (exemplary, virtuous women) when faced with misfortune. Women of high learning were rare exceptions in Chosŏn. Astonishingly, those few with writing skills feared being mistaken for *kisaeng,*[11] or professional entertainers, who were better educated and "more active in intellectual life" than even upper-class women.[12]

The first school for girls, Ewha Haktang, was opened by the American missionary Mary F. Scranton in 1886 with the goal of spreading Christianity to Koreans by means of education. Even though tuition was free and the school provided food, clothing, and lodging, the missionary could not find a single student. Confucian mores simply did not allow girls to leave the house in order to receive an education. The school finally began when, on May 31, 1886, Mrs. Scranton engaged her first student, the concubine of a high official, after a year's patient waiting. She stayed only three months, but by the end of the year seven students had enrolled. In the beginning, students came mostly from the commoner class; very few upper-class girls attended the school. Ten years later, however, the school had 174 students.[13] A century later Ewha Womans [Women's] University and Ewha Girls' High School had become preeminent institutions of women and girls' education, respectively, and May 31 is celebrated as Ewha's founding day. Many South Korean women leaders, including Yun Chŏng-ok and Lee [Yi] Hyo-chae (who cofounded the Korean Council and helped launch the comfort women redress movement) and some others whose names are mentioned in this study, graduated from Ewha.

The social and political move toward reform in the Chosŏn dynasty began in the second half of the nineteenth century and culminated under Japanese pressure and sponsorship in the 1894 Kabo Reform.[14] The Ministry of Education promulgated ordinances that established public schools in 1895. At this point, however, no attention was given to women's education.[15] In contrast, the Meiji (1868–1912) state in Japan instituted a system of compulsory education of four years for both boys and girls in 1872. (Confucian proscriptions had traditionally prevented Japanese women—like Korean women—from receiving an education in subjects others than needlework and household tasks.)[16] By 1905 night schools, laborers' schools, and short-term training centers had opened in urban areas of Chosŏn Korea under a countrywide movement of "education for the nation."[17] The Korean government established the first public school for girls in 1908, and a college program for women was added at Ewha in 1910.[18] (In Japan, by contrast, the first tertiary institution for women's education—Tsuda College—was established in 1900, followed by another one—Tokyo Women's University—in 1901.)[19]

By the late 1910s and the 1920s, the fruits of modern education had given birth to the emergent social category of the "new woman" (*sin yŏsŏng,* in Korean; *atarashii onna,* in Japanese) in colonial Korea. As educated women sporting short hair and Western-style shoes and clothes, they participated in the public sphere as professionals. Some (such as Na Hye-sŏk [1885–1946]) became targets of harsh criticism for their unconventional lifestyles, advocacy of free love, and failed marriages.[20] These developments closely paralleled those in Japan, where "new women" emerged in the early 1900s as female poets (such as Yosano Akiko [1878–1942]) debated the meaning of individualism for women, including their own sexuality and desire. By 1912 the label "new woman" had accrued a negative image among the general Japanese public after the scandalous women of the Bluestocking Society attacked the existing family system and stressed the importance of women's economic independence.[21]

Meanwhile, the modern education system in colonial Korea continued to expand and began to reach the masses in the 1930s. By 1933, 20 percent of the Korean elementary school–age population was receiving a modern education, though wide discrepancies were evident in school attendance rates between the cities and the counties, as well as across the gender divide. Among the school-age girls in the countryside such as the case of Mun P'ilgi (described in chapter 2), only about 7.5 percent attended school.[22] By 1940, however, half of all school-age children—boys and girls—were attending elementary school.

*　　*　　*

Today the Korean people remember the first half of the twentieth century as a dark period of national humiliation and stagnation under Japanese colonialism. Any critical scholarly analysis of surviving comfort women's stories, however, must take into consideration the revolutionary changes in lifestyle that occurred under the burgeoning capitalism of colonial Korea, where magazines and newspapers carried "commentary cartoons" caricaturing the new lifestyles of "modern girls," "modern boys," and other resident consumers of modernity in the capital city, now called Kyŏngsŏng (Keijo, in Japanese; today's Seoul).[23]

When we turn to individual survivors' testimonial narratives, then, we should not be surprised to encounter a diverse and complex picture of their lives in late colonial modern period. This picture notably includes young women pursuing a place of their own in the evolving public sphere of Korea's industrial revolution and colonial modernity.[24] I use the term "colonial modernity" to capture a historical sense of that new age and the "modern" way of life experienced by individual Koreans living under colonial rule; it is also meant to highlight the structural and material transformations in political-economic institutions and social relations associated with that "modernity"—urbanization, industrialization, the broadening reach of capitalism, the intrusion of the state into everyday life, the emergence of a working class, increased occupational specialization, the expansion of public roles for women, and the capitalist commodification of women's sexuality.[25]

LICENSED PROSTITUTION IN KOREA

The modern system of licensed prostitution began in Chosŏn after Korea was pressured into signing the 1876 Kanghwa Treaty with Japan. It was first put into practice at the Japanese settlement in the port city of Pusan in 1881. With the subsequent outbreaks of the Sino-Japanese War (1894–1895) and the Russo-Japanese War (1904–1905), the burgeoning Japanese military presence in Korea had prompted the formation of pleasure quarters not only in the capital city and Pusan, but also in such port cities as Inchŏn, Wŏnsan, and Chinnamp'o. The first pleasure quarters in the capital, the Sinjŏng (Shinmachi, in Japanese), opened in June 1904, right after the start of the Russo-Japanese War. By the end of 1908, two years before Korea's annexation as a Japanese colony, the number of Japanese women working as "overseas prostitutes" in Korea was around 2,839.[26]

Japanese owners of the restaurant-*cum*-brothels recruited women from their homeland using the term "second-class *geigi*" (*geigi* is another term for geisha), which duped recruits into thinking that their work would be that of lower-ranked geisha, not outright prostitution. In Korea frequent scenes of tearful, angry Japanese recruits fighting their deceitful recruiters resulted in replacement of the ambiguous term "second-class *geigi*" with *shōgi* (licensed prostitute) in 1906.[27] That same year a Japanese entrepreneur (a Mr. Okabe) opened the first *okiya* (geisha house), called Ch'ŏngsusŏk, in the capital Kyŏngsŏng, which developed into the Kyŏngsŏng Kwŏnbŏn.[28] *Kwŏnbŏn,* the Korean appropriation of the Japanese *kenban,* or geisha registry office, combined the functions of *okiya* and the *kisaeng* union: it dispatched *kisaeng* to the special restaurants upon request, collected wages on behalf of the *kisaeng,* and charged the *kisaeng* fees for these services.[29]

Notably, Korean survivors such as Kim Hak-sun, Kim Ok-sil, and Kil Wŏn-ok were affiliated with local *kwŏnbŏn* to train as *kisaeng* in P'yŏngyang prior to becoming comfort women. Mun Ok-chu's mother sent her off to a *kwŏnbŏn* in Taegu about a year after her return home from Burma at the end of the war. She received her *kisaeng* training there for three years before starting to work at the pleasure quarters.[30] The personal stories of these survivors indicate not only the nationwide reach of the *kwŏnbŏn* system for *kisaeng* in late colonial Korea, but also its continued existence in the early years of postliberation Korea.

After Japan annexed Korea in 1910, the system of licensed prostitution became firmly entrenched, with a nearly 50 percent increase in the number of Korean prostitutes between 1910 and 1915 (from 1,193 to 1,768); tellingly, the number of Japanese prostitutes increased less than 20 percent (from 4,091 to 4,680) in the same period.[31] Out of ostensible concern with venereal disease, in 1916 the colonial government promulgated an ordinance that provided for centralized, nationwide regulation of prostitution in Korea.[32]

Because the colonial law did not recognize the Korean custom of allowing *kisaeng* to have husbands, known as *kibu,* a new term, *p'oju* (master or mistress of a brothel), came to be used.[33] Another important feature in the implementation of licensed prostitution in Korea was that, unlike Japan, prostitution was allowed *outside* the designated pleasure quarters, meaning the business of prostitution could seep into society as part of everyday life.[34]

The 1916 ordinance provided working conditions that were worse than the 1900 ordinance governing licensed prostitutes in Japan. The minimum age was set at seventeen (one year younger than in the Japanese system). Astonishingly, however, it is said that *thirteen*-year-old prostitutes were the most popular.[35] Korean women in the sex trade were generally younger than their Japanese counterparts. According to the records of 1930, Korean prostitutes twenty-five years and younger accounted for 86 percent of all prostitutes, while the figure for the Japanese was 67 percent. Most Japanese women (about 67 percent) had been in the adult entertainment industry before becoming licensed prostitutes, but the majority of the Korean women (about 60 percent) had had no such prior experience.[36] The historian Song Youn-ok contends, "[T]he majority of Korean prostitutes were married women who had fallen into difficult circumstances while their husbands were absent."[37]

The average advance a Korean woman received was 420 yen, compared to approximately 1,730 yen for a Japanese prostitute.[38] The fees for Korean prostitutes were set at between about one-third and one-half the rate for Japanese.[39] There was no mention of a woman's right to take time off work.[40] Not surprisingly, these regulations enforced discrimination between Japanese and Korean prostitutes, which were then mirrored in the operational rules of the military comfort system. Their ethnicity-based demographic and background differences were also replicated in the general profiles of Korean versus Japanese comfort women.

The first grassroots resistance to prostitution in colonial Korea surfaced in 1924.[41] This campaign started under the leadership of Korean Christians, who submitted to the governor-general a petition with 12,000 signatures requesting that prostitution be abolished, but it did not spread widely. As Pak

Chong-sŏng, a political scientist of the postcolonial generation, points out in his critique of the symbiotic relationship between the power elite and the prostitution industry, Koreans under colonial rule acculturated themselves to be participants in the transplanted prostitution system, whether out of political resignation, social frustration, or the hedonistic pursuit of carnal pleasure.[42]

By 1920 some Korean women had become "overseas prostitutes." Those who worked at a restaurant in Sapporo, Japan, became what Yun Chŏng-ok calls "industrial comfort women," serving Korean men who worked there.[43] When the adult entertainment business in Korea suffered as a result of the Great Depression of the 1920s, female workers and business owners migrated to China. By the late 1920s the capital of colonial Korea, Kyŏngsŏng, was home to four pleasure quarters, which employed a total of 4,295 prostitutes.[44] By the mid-1930s 45 percent of Koreans had become infected with syphilis, compared to 15 percent of the French.[45] Beginning in the early 1930s many Korean women were sold overseas to labor as prostitutes. *Dong-a Ilbo,* one of Korea's major daily newspapers dating from the colonial days, reported on December 2, 1932, that about a hundred women a month were sold for 40 to 50 wŏn to brothels in Osaka, Hokkaido, Sakhalin, and Taiwan; this report, in hindsight, seems to predict the large-scale mobilization of Korean women to serve the troops through the 1930s up to 1945. In fact, the survivors' testimonials amply illustrate that during the war Korean men and women actively collaborated in the recruitment of young compatriots to service the Japanese military and also ran comfort stations. For young, uneducated women from impoverished families in colonial Korea, to be a victim of trafficking became "an ordinary misfortune" in the 1930s.[46] Amid widespread complicity and indifference to young women's plight, the adult entertainment business in Korea began to recover after the start of the Second Sino-Japanese War in 1937, and it flourished until early 1940.

When the war effort intensified in the early 1940s, however, many adult entertainment establishments had to close down, and by 1943 it was practically impossible to run such a business. This encouraged some brothel owners to seek their fortune abroad, including in Taiwan and occupied territories in the Southeast Asia. As Song Youn-ok noted, had there not been a "widespread network of traffic in women used in the state-managed prostitution system, the mobilization of Korean comfort women would have been a very different process."[47] Under grinding poverty, working-class families in colonial Korea sold unmarried daughters for 400–500 wŏn for a contractual period of four to seven years. The parents received 60–70 percent of the money after various expenses involved in the transaction had been deducted, such as the mediator's fee, clothing, document preparation, transport, and pocket money.[48] Kim Sun-ok, who labored at a comfort station in Manchuria for four years, recalled:

> I had no childhood. I was sold four times from the age of seven. As soon as I returned to my home in P'yŏngyang from Sinŭiju after paying off my debt of 500 wŏn, I recall that procurers began showing up at my house, coaxing my parents. I declared to my parents that I was not going anywhere and begged them not to sell me again. However, I could sense that my parents were being influenced, and it appeared that I would be sold to Manchuria. I contemplated a variety of methods of killing myself. But my love of life and hope for a change in the future prevented me from committing suicide. My father entreated me and said: "It's not because of cruelty that your father wants to sell you. In comparison to your siblings, you have the attractive looks and the experiences of living away from home. It's your misfortune to have someone like me as a father. Go this one time. They promise to send you to a factory, which should be a good thing."
>
> Within a fortnight after my return home from Sinŭiju, I was sold for a fourth time and sent off to a military comfort station in Manchuria in 1941.[49]

EMERGENCE OF "WORKING-CLASS NEW WOMEN"

In the meantime, the historic paradigms of the "new woman" in Western-style clothes and the "modern girl" (called "*modan*" *kkŏl*—literally, "short-haired," hence modern, girl) had emerged in Korea during the 1920s,[50] when the number of factory girls (*yŏgong*) rose at an unprecedented rate (reaching millions by the end of the war under colonial industrialization).[51] Korea's first all-female union at the Kyŏngsŏng Rubber Factory in Seoul engaged in a collective action in 1923 by staging a strike to demand "higher wages and an end to sexual violence in the factories" (which constituted "two of the most prominent strike demands by [Korean] blue-collar women in the 1920s and early 1930s").[52] The November 3, 1929, issue of the *Dong-a Ilbo* published a letter from a young female factory worker under the title "A Factory Girl's Complaint" (*Ŏnŭ Yŏgong ŭi Hasoyŏn*), in which she states, among other things, "There was never a day when the male workers ceased waylaying us in their heavy hunger for sex."[53]

By the late 1920s women's occupations had diversified to include teachers, medical doctors, reporters, kindergarten teachers, midwives, nurses, radio announcers, telephone operators, and bank tellers, in addition to waitresses, factory workers, and a variety of wage earners in new modern service jobs. The "girl" (*gŏl*) became a new term to refer to young women in new types of service jobs such as *shob* (shop) girl, *depatŭ* (department) girl, *ba* (bar) girl, *bŏsŭ* (bus) girl, *ellibeitŏ* (elevator) girl, *helo* girl (telephone operator), *tiket* (ticket) girl, and *gaidŭ* (guide) girl. The "girls" were expected to be good-looking and sexually attractive.[54] Korean women of the younger generation found new opportunities to seek personal freedom and economic independence.[55]

By the 1930s the popular term *ero gŭro nŏnsensŭ* (erotic grotesque nonsense) came to stand for the essence of being "modern"—for not only "modern boys" but also urban residents.[56] It reflected, among other factors, the arrival of "mass society" with the expanding service industry, in which the commodification of women's sexuality developed in a variety of ways.[57] The enthusiasm for the erotic grotesque nonsense spread through the public space of the café, the "playground of the youth." It symbolized the arrival of the "era of stimulation craze" and heralded the coming of visually oriented modern society.[58]

It is in this social and historical context of late-colonial Korea that some aspiring daughters who left home as young women now remember, as elderly survivors, the pleasure of achieving the "modern girl" look when their recruiters had them dress in Western-style clothes and shoes and cut their hair short.[59] Pae Chok-kan (b. 1922), who left her home in a village in North Chŏlla Province to work at a cotton factory in 1938 and was taken, instead, to a comfort station run by a Korean man in China, stated, "Wearing Western-style dress and shoes for the first time in my life, I felt like I'd shed my deep-mountain village boorishness, which made me feel good."[60] Another survivor, Yi Yong-su (b. 1928), was sixteen years old when she left home without telling anyone in search of a better life. Yi came from a poor family in Taegu, the third largest city in Korea. Having worked in a cotton-batting manufacturing factory from the age of nine to thirteen and attended a night school for a short while under the Japanized name of Yasuhara Riyōshu, she vividly recalled—after the lapse of nearly half a century—the delightful moment of seeing a red dress and a pair of leather shoes in a packet the recruiter handed to her in the fall of 1944:

> At the time I was shabbily clothed and wretched. . . . [On the day I left home with my friend Pun-sun without telling my mother] I was wearing a black *t'ongch'ima* [Korean-style seamless one-piece skirt], a long-sleeved, buttoned-up cotton shirt, and *geta* [Japanese-

style wooden clogs, in Japanese] on my feet. . . . You don't know how pleased I was in my childlike mind when I received the packet. So without any further thought I readily followed him.[61]

*   *   *

The emergence of what I would call Korea's "working-class new women"— who labored at factories and in service jobs, including the adult entertainment and sex industry—in the first half of the twentieth century was itself the result of Japan's goal of modernization of colonial Korea via industrialization. When the Japanese occupation began in 1910, Korea had markets and light industry but little capital. The colonial government methodically set in motion a trajectory of modern capitalist development that began with land registration policies, which launched the rise of Japanese landlords. It also initiated a switch from the barter-based local economy to a monetary-based state economy that displaced almost the entire Korean farming population save for a small number of Korean landowners.[62] Unlike other colonial powers, Japan developed various heavy industries—steel, chemicals, and hydroelectric power—in its colonies. Japan also laid an extensive network of railways, which resulted in Korea's having "the most developed rail system in Asia outside of Japan" by 1945.[63] In fact, the railway system was in place by the early 1930s, when the survivor Yi Sang-ok—as a remarkably "fearless" (Yi's own word) nine-year-old girl from a town in North Kyŏngsang Province—was able to travel gratis to Seoul by herself, determined to satisfy her strong desire to receive an education.[64]

THE LAST DECADE OF COLONIAL RULE

As Korea's industrial revolution got underway during the last decade of colonial rule (1935–1945), peasants were uprooted from the land, a working class emerged, and population mobility contributed to a burgeoning urbanization.[65] The great drought of the spring of 1939, which left a huge number of agricultural workers and landless tenant farmers unemployed, led to a mass "rural exodus" to the industrial labor markets of Korea, Manchuria, and Japan.[66] By 1945 this exodus had resulted in 11.6 percent of the Korean population (close to 3.7 million Koreans) residing outside Korea, working either as free migrants or mobilized laborers in Japan and Manchuria.[67]

The social upheaval associated with the industrial revolution and the

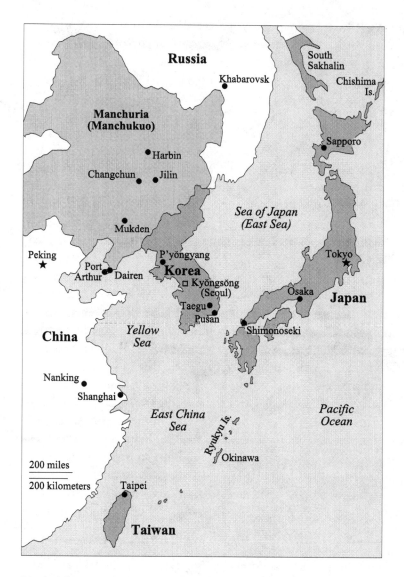

Map 2. The Japanese Empire in the 1930s: Japan, Korea, Manchuria, and Taiwan

war was most deeply felt among the rural working classes. With their husbands and/or sons mobilized for war, married women in the countryside, like their Japanese counterparts, had to bear the double burden of farming and their traditional duties of motherhood and housekeeping.[68] Middle-class housewives were urged to bear more children under imperial Japan's pronatalist policy with such slogans as "Let's give birth and multiply for the good of the country" ("Umeyo fuyaseyo okunino tameni"). In 1943 the

Greater Japan Women's Association in Korea presented awards to mothers who bore more than ten children.[69] For young unmarried women, the opportunities for employment in wartime industries multiplied. More than one million women migrated to the cities or overseas worksites.[70]

Of particular relevance to this study is the historic *conjuncture* of the Japanese system of licensed prostitution—transplanted and legalized in colonial Korea in 1916—and the emergent working-class labor market.[71] These two important factors of the colonial political economy—the legalized prostitution industry and wage work opportunities—largely defined the field of action for women workers in the theater of contractual, often indentured, labor. When many young women entered the market in late colonial Korea, their lives as working-class new women often directly intersected the institutional public spaces of wage labor in the adult entertainment industry, including licensed prostitution. By the mid-1920s the "dealers in human trade" (*saram changsakkun,* in the words of a Korean survivor)[72] often masqueraded as factory recruiters to pick up unsuspecting country girls at the labor exchange markets held at major provincial railway stations, whom they then sent to brothels.[73] By late October 1938, the year Yi Sun-ok was deceptively taken to a comfort station in China, Korean and Japanese civilian procurers could rather easily place an estimated thirty to forty thousand women, primarily Korean, at military brothels across China.[74]

The colonial government then enacted a law that required Koreans to "create [Japanese-style] surnames and revise given names" (*sōshi kaimei,* in Japanese; *ch'angssi kaemyŏng,* in Korean). The law went into effect on February 22, 1940.[75] Many Koreans even today feel the pang of humiliation for having been forced to adopt Japanese-style names during colonial rule. The memory of colonial occupation hurts Koreans deeply, especially because they had long prided themselves on being a neighboring nation that played the role of the "big brother" to Japan in the premodern history of the latter's cultural development.

Reflecting on the subtly different but equally unpleasant Korean and Japanese affective responses to the title word "lost" in *Lost Names: Scenes from a Korean Boyhood,* the Korean American author Richard Kim wrote in 1998:[76]

When *Lost Names* was translated and published in Korea and also, to my pleasant surprise, in Japan, the title word *lost* was translated in both languages as "violently, forcibly taken away." The Korean version implied that "someone took my name away violently," whereas the Japanese one suggested—passively it seemed to me—that "I had my name violently taken away." Neither rendition pleased me. If any-thing, I had wanted *lost* to mean, simply, lost. . . . What displeased me, though, was that the Korean title bristled with a condemnation that was nevertheless aflutter with pathos, while the Japanese translation shrouded the title with benign sympathy. Neither would do.[77]

Lost Names is a fictional account of a Korean family's life under Japanese colonial rule. The first-person narrator is a boy born in 1932, which is also the year the novelist was born, contributing to the view of most readers that the novel is a memoir.[78] A memorable scene the boy in the novel narrates concerns a historically based event, from which the novel's title comes: The boy is eight years old when his father adopts a new, Japanese name (Iwamoto) for the family in accordance with the colonial government's cultural assimilation policy for colonized Koreans. After describing the sorrowful and deeply ashamed reactions of the father and other grown-ups to the humiliation of losing their Korean names, the boy's narrative ends the "Lost Names" chapter as follows: "Today, I lost my name. Today, we all lost our names. February 11, 1940."

Notably, Richard Kim finds neither the South Korean condemnation nor the Japanese sympathy acceptable when he encounters the two contrasting emotional reactions of his publishers in Korea and Japan to the word "lost" in the process of translating the novel for the Korean and Japanese editions. He underscores his dispassionate use of the term "lost" when describing an event that took place more than half a century ago. A vast majority of the Korean population today, however, may not share his calmly detached attitude.

Nevertheless, we should be reminded here that in the nonfictional world of colonial Korea, some Koreans did adopt Japanese names—perhaps to reflect their new sociopolitical identity as the subjects of imperial Japan—even before the law required them to do so. The most notable examples include Song Pyŏng-jun (1858–1925), who assumed his Japanese name, Noda Heijirō, when he worked as an interpreter for the Japanese military during the Russo-Japanese War (1904–1905), founded a new pro-Japanese reformist organization called Ilchinhoe (Unity and Progress Society), and became a high government official who actively supported Japan's annexation of Korea.[79] A pioneering modern novelist and prominent cultural critic, Yi Kwang-su (1892–1950) is another well-known figure who voluntarily adopted a Japanese name (Kayama Mitsurō), declaring, "Koreans should completely forget being Korean."[80] Two former presidents, Park Chung Hee and Kim Dae Jung, also adopted Japanese names during the colonial period.

Not surprisingly, I have come across multiple examples of Koreans with Japanese-style names in the published testimonial narratives of Korean comfort women survivors. This is because the testimonials of most Korean survivors are focused on the period between the second half of the 1930s and the early 1940s, when the Korean people had to deal with the Japanese colonial government's cultural assimilation policy for imperial subjects and their eventual mobilization into the war. The last decade of colonial rule was also the period when many young Korean women were mobilized under deceitful promises of well-paying factory jobs. Many young women and girls who responded eagerly—or reluctantly, depending on their particular individual situations—to such enticements offered by compatriot human traffickers ended up at the Japanese military comfort stations established throughout China, Taiwan, and Southeast Asia under the Japanese occupation.

The colonial government began the general labor conscription of Koreans under the national registration system in November 1941. Both men (between sixteen and forty) and unmarried women (between sixteen and twenty-five) were required to enroll as a potential labor supply. Only men, however, were ever officially drafted: The Japanese government "merely 'urged' women to work in industry" and "remained ambivalent about the place of female labor in the war economy" until 1943.[81] Japanese female work patterns contrasted greatly with those in the major Western nations involved in World War II. In the United States, for example, the total number of working women increased by 50 percent. In Japan the increase was less than 10 percent between 1940 and 1944.[82] As the historian Thomas Havens has suggested, the state's pronatalist policy, in addition to traditional notions of women's place in the domestic sphere, may help explain this relatively low rate of women's participation in the labor force in wartime Japan. Because of imperial Japan's "family-state ideology" (*kazoku kokkakan*, in Japanese), the government's pronatalist policy generated a dichotomized view of women's reproductive versus productive roles, leading to a failure to utilize women's labor effectively in arms production.[83]

However, a more crucial factor in the underutilization of Japanese women in the wartime labor force may have been the ready availability of Japan's colonial labor force.[84] Imperial Japan in fact used the Korean peninsula as its supply base for human and material resources throughout the war. Japanese mobilization of Korean labor was carried out in three stages: recruitment (1939–1941), government-led arrangements (1942–1943), and forced labor drafts (1944–1945).[85] By the end of the war, Koreans made up a third of Japan's industrial labor force.[86] It was predominantly farmers and resident Koreans in Japan who were forced to work under conditions of near slavery in constructing airfields, harbors, mines,[87] roads, and large civilian projects for such well-known companies as Mitsubishi, Sumitomo, and Suzuki. Indeed, Japan's war machine rested squarely on the contributions of Korean migrant laborers overseas; this took various forms, such as conscripted troops, forced labor, civilian and military employment, and sex slavery abroad.[88]

WOMEN'S VOLUNTEER LABOR CORPS

In January 1944 Prime Minister Tōjō announced the plan to create the Women's Volunteer Labor Corps (Joshi Rōdō Teishintai, in Japanese) to support efforts in aircraft manufacturing and other essential industries. Unmarried females (twelve to thirty-nine years of age) were "eligible" to join the corps. The period of service was to be a full year; the term was later extended to two years. The ordinance for a Women's Volunteer Labor Corps was promulgated in August 1944.

Under the emergency guidelines and procedures announced for student labor mobilization in April 1944, students from elementary schools to colleges in both Japan and Korea were also mobilized to produce food and munitions and to build military facilities, and more than 200,000 young Korean men were drafted between 1944 and 1945.[89] A former student at Kyŏnggi Girls' High School—the nation's most elite educational institution for girls, located in Seoul—remembered how all of her classmates were mobilized to labor in the last year of the war, which was her senior year:

> They converted the entire top floor of Mitsukoshi [today's Sinsegye] Department Store into a factory, and all of my classmates worked there every day. The floor was arranged with alternating rows of sewing machines and ironing boards. Those at the machines sewed certain seams of a uniform and handed them over to those at the ironing boards. We never saw a finished uniform. It was a very monotonous and mechanical work that lasted all day long. Those who came late were slapped on the cheek by the teachers who were supervising us.
>
> There was no class at all during the semester from April to August 1945. We were told that we were being paid nominal salaries for the work. But the principal said because we were all such patriotic students, we would gladly donate our salaries to the country. We never knew how much the salary was nor saw a penny of it. So we

Plate 0.1. Korean *chŏngsindae* laboring in a factory for Japan's war project. (Source: *Seoul Sinmun.*)

were triply being deprived, our schoolwork, our tuition, and our salaries. If we complained, we were told to shut up. From time to time good students were mobilized to go to local government offices to do some paperwork that had been piling up because of the shortage of manpower.[90]

The precise scale of the mobilization of Korean women as the Volunteer Labor Corps (Kŭllo Chŏngsindae) is an unknowable, thorny question, and several conjectural figures have been given in the past. The Japanese historian Takasaki Sōji (b. 1944),[91] an active supporter of the comfort women redress movement, estimates that no more than 4,000 Korean women were sent to Japan as *chŏngsindae*.[92] In a 1981 essay published in a national daily newspaper (*Han'guk Ilbo*), however, Yun Chŏng-ok, then a professor of English literature, claimed that 200,000 *chŏngsindae* aged twelve to forty were recruited from 1943 to 1945, and between 50,000 and 70,000 of the volunteers aged eighteen to twenty-three were selectively sent as comfort women to the front lines in northern China and the Pacific Islands.[93] Yun did not reveal the source of the figures given in her essay.

By contrast, the reporter Kim Tŏk-sŏng, who had used exactly the same figures a decade earlier than Yun, drew a very different picture of Chŏngsindae that included more Japanese than Korean women. His article was published in 1970 in *Seoul Sinmun,* another Korean national daily. Kim wrote, "From 1943 to 1945 approximately two hundred thousand Korean *and* Japanese women were mobilized as *chŏngsindae.* The estimated number of Koreans among them is between fifty and seventy thousand" (emphasis added).[94]

In other words, Korean women made up a substantial *minority* in the Volunteer Corps. Between a quarter and a third of the *chŏngsindae* recruits were Korean women, while Japanese women made up between two-thirds and three-quarters of the total figure. Further, Kim's article asserted that the majority of the Korean *chŏngsindae* were sent to the front lines in the Pacific and northern Manchuria as "'playthings' of starved soldiers." It is clear that in the case of the Korean recruits the reporter has conflated *chŏngsindae* with comfort women.

Oddly, the *Seoul Sinmun* article made no mention of those who had become comfort women prior to 1943, which makes one wonder: Was the reporter unaware of any earlier recruitment? Or did he regard them in a different light from the "forcibly drafted *chŏngsindae*-turned-comfort-women"—that is, as "merely" prostitutes—and therefore did not consider them victims of imperial Japan? I wonder what his response would have been had he been informed that a great majority of South Korean comfort women survivors were recruited prior to 1943.

THE DUTCH CASE AND ITS IMPLICATIONS

One of the major obstacles in the quest for "the truth" and justice for Japan's comfort women is that there is no documentary evidence to determine either the total number of the women or the methods of their recruitment—except in the case of the Dutch. Notably, in January 1994 the Dutch government made available an English translation of the "Report of a Study of Dutch Government Documents on the Forced Prostitution of Dutch Women in the Dutch East Indies during the Japanese Occupation" (the Dutch government report, hereafter), which stated:

> Forcing women into prostitution was regarded by the government of the Dutch East Indies as a war crime and material on the subject was therefore collected by the various government bodies concerned [to help reach] a number of judgments . . . of the temporary war tribunal at Batavia. . . . [I]n recruiting European women for their

brothels in the Dutch East Indies, the Japanese occupiers used force in some cases. Of the two hundred to three hundred European women working in these brothels, sixty-five were most certainly forced into prostitution.[95]

The Dutch government report further notes that one of the forcibly recruited women, a sixteen-year-old girl, was "sent back to the camp as she was considered to be too young."[96] It also acknowledges, "Organized force was no longer used to any extent by the army or military government" on Java from mid-1944.[97]

The use of forcibly recruited Dutch women at the comfort stations was abruptly banned in April 1944 by order of the 16th Army Headquarters, leading to the closure of such facilities. The Dutch women were then returned to internment camps. The sudden order to shut down some of the comfort stations in Semarang came about after a staff officer in the Ministry of War in Tokyo, Colonel Odajima Tadashi, met, during his inspection trip to Java, one of the Dutch internment camp leaders, whose daughter had been taken away. Colonel Odashima, who was in charge of the supervision of both the civilian and prisoner-of-war camps, had come to Java in April 1944 to inspect the internment camps there.[98] The colonel promptly informed Batavia, Singapore, and Tokyo of his findings and recommended the immediate closure of the Semarang brothels that had been involved in forced recruitment of European women from internment camps. As a result, four military brothels in Semarang, which had been in operation for about two months, were immediately closed.[99] The Dutch government report elaborated:

> The remaining military brothels had to recruit European women from privately-run brothels or other procurers. . . . Altogether, more than a hundred women [including Jan Ruff-O'Herne, whom I first met in Tokyo in 2000] were transferred from brothels to these [internment] camps. According to two women who had worked in the brothels at Magelang and Semarang only thirty to thirty-five of these women, in addition to the three from Pekalongan and Malang, had been forced to work as prostitutes.[100]

Among other factors, the prompt official response indicated that Japanese authorities were aware that forcible recruitment of women for the purpose of prostitution was a violation of international law. In fact, the Japanese government signed international treaties banning traffic in women and girls in 1925; however, a provision in the international treaties permitted the signatories *not* to apply the laws in their colonies.[101] That explains in part why the Semarang incident did not affect the operation of other comfort stations in Indonesia using trafficked women from Korea and Taiwan as well as local women.[102]

After Japan's defeat, the military officers and brothel operators involved in the Semarang incident were tried and punished in the Dutch Ad Hoc Military Court in Batavia—today's Jakarta.[103] One officer was executed by firing squad. The harsh punishment, I suggest, was not only for the sexual violence against women, but also for racial transgression, the sexual abuse of bourgeois "white" women by "yellow" men. It is significant to note that those interned Dutch women who were forcibly taken belonged to the colony's "respectable bourgeoisie," who, in the prevailing colonial discourses of sexuality, were above "lower-class immorality."[104] These bourgeois Dutch women, in fact, constituted an anomaly in the social characteristics of the vast majority of Japan's comfort women. Just as imperial Japan ruthlessly exploited the sexuality of women of its colonies for the military comfort system, the colonial racism of the Dutch state—reflected in the Batavia military court—prioritized the abuse of bourgeois Dutch women by Japanese men; it completely overlooked the ordeals suffered by the women of its own colony in East Indies, today's Indonesia. Whereas China's war crimes tribunals did put the Japanese on trial for "forcing women to become prostitutes,"[105] the rest of victimized Asian women's search and claim for justice had to wait until early 1990s, which ushered in the post–cold war era of the global politics of women's human rights.

One important, and rather remarkable, aspect of the Dutch government report is, however, that it not only acknowledges the inability to ascertain whether the Japanese authorities applied "physical force" to the majority of Dutch or European women in procuring their services as prostitutes: it also concedes, based on the examination of available data, that "the conclusion must be drawn that the majority of the women concerned does not belong to the group of women forced into prostitution."[106]

By stark contrast, in South Korea, where women activists first defined the Japanese comfort system as a war crime in the early 1990s,[107] the media portray all comfort women as victims of forcible recruitment by imperial Japan's military or police. After the comfort women issue was internationally sensationalized, South Korean comfort women survivors were redefined as "sex slaves" who were deceptively mobilized as wartime labor recruits, or *chŏngsindae*. It is worth noting here that leaders of South Korean women's organizations have been galvanized by a strong dose of postcolonial ethnic nationalism and have turned the redress movement into a righteous battle against Japan, demanding truth and justice for the latter's historical wrong-doings perpetrated during its colonial rule. Although the comfort women issue constitutes only one of four major contemporary controversies in South Korea's relations with Japan, it has commanded the greatest attention in the world media.[108]

THE NUMBERS QUESTION

The total number of wartime comfort women will never be known for sure. The estimates range widely between 20,000 and 400,000. Given the wide-ranging, multiple, competing figures, which should the reader believe to be closer to the unknowable truth?

The guesswork figures regarding comfort women were published in the last three decades of the twentieth century and come primarily from eight individuals of three ethnic backgrounds: three Koreans (a journalist, a writer, and a professor of English literature), four Japanese (a journalist and three historians), and one Chinese historian. The varying figures demonstrate the "situatedness" and resultant "partiality" of anyone's knowledge claim. As Donna Haraway and other feminist scholars have noted, "situated knowledges" derive from one's social and historical location and reflect the researcher's interest in gender, class, race, and nationality.[109] It is not surprising, then, that the figures asserted by the Korean and Chinese researchers tend to be much larger than those estimated by the Japanese. The figures advanced by the Japanese historians, however, are diverse, and it is noteworthy that one of them (Hata Ikuhiko) chose to revise his earlier estimation, arriving at a much smaller figure in reaction to increasing international pressure on Japan to compensate comfort women survivors. But from a moral standpoint, even the smallest number is huge.

When trying to find out which among the estimated figures for comfort women would be closer to "the truth," we must consider not only the social and political positionality of individual writers, but also the time period of their work, that is, whether it was carried out prior to or after the emergence of the international redress movement. In this regard, it is remarkable that the figures given by the early 1990s by the two Japanese—whose positions represent opposing political camps—were rather close: 80,400, according to the sympathetic reporter Senda Kakō (in 1978), and 90,000, given by the conservative historian Hata Ikuhiko (in 1993). The chronopolitical change in Hata's figures—from 90,000 to 20,000—must be considered in the developmental context of the redress movement. When Hata's earlier work came out in 1993, the Korean comfort women movement had just begun. Hata's revised smaller figure is one of the consequences of his political alignment with the conservative anti-redress camp in Japan that emerged in the latter half of the 1990s.

What, then, would be an impartial number to quote in writing about Japan's comfort women? Given the varying estimates and the impossibility of ascertaining the exact number, it would seem that "tens of thousands" is rather vague but does not involve any purposeful exaggeration. Perhaps one might suggest 50,000 as a base number to quote, given the fact that this is the lowest number in the estimations of both the 1970 Korean newspaper article and the Japanese historian Yoshimi Yoshiaki (whose pioneering research and political support provided pivotal ammunition for the activists of the transnational redress movement).[110]

CONCLUSION

There can be no denial of the tragic victimization of forcibly recruited women who suffered slavery-like conditions. Nevertheless, as South Korean critical feminist researchers have trenchantly noted, the postcolonial Korean public discourse of the comfort women in terms of forcible recruitments of helpless young virgins by the Japanese military would arbitrarily exclude the personal experiences of sexual violence suffered by other individual victims such as Kil Wŏn-ok, who had been sold multiple times to earn money in brothels.[111] For sure, it was Japan's colonialism that undoubtedly facilitated the large-scale victimization of tens of thousands of Korean women who suffered an unspeakable sexual ordeal and ethnic discrimination. However, the causes of surviving victims' lifelong sufferings are often more complex and divergent than the nationalistic and transnational discourse of Japan's comfort women phenomenon would suggest.

In the following pages I attempt to add a new layer of understanding to activists' discourses on Japan's comfort women phenomenon. In chapter 1, I present my theoretical analysis of the multiple ideologies undergirding the competing representations of the comfort women, the transnational English-language template of the "paradigmatic story" of the comfort women and its fictional constructions as well as Korean activists' inflection of it, academic writings on the subject, Japan's domestic cacophony over its postwar responsibility to comfort women survivors, and the political symbolism of naming the victimized women. Chapter 2 analyzes the testimonial narratives of several Korean survivors, focusing on their prerecruitment family lives and personal agency in the historical context of Korean patriarchy under Japan's colonialism; I discuss the diversity in the officially registered survivors' responses to the ongoing redress movement and take a comparative perspective on the performative quality in the process of bearing witness, in particular, the "truth" of some individual Korean survivors' testimonial narratives regarding a crucial issue of the method of their recruitment. In chapter 3, I present a historical view of the comfort system, which encompassed both commercial *and* criminal sex, by portraying the organizational diversity and evolving nature of Japan's military comfort system in the milieu of Japanese sexual cultural history, colonialism, and the imperial war of expansion, and describe some Korean, Dutch, and Filipina survivors' recalled experiences at three different categories of military comfort facilities. In chapter 4, I investigate the postwar and postcolonial public memories of the comfort women in Japan and Korea, and I discuss some surprising private memories of Japanese war veterans and Korean and Dutch comfort women survivors in chapter 5. Chapter 6 delineates the historical role of the state in considering the generalized societal indifference to and denigration of stigmatized women laboring in the sex industry and the prosperous "customary business" of providing public sex for heterosexual men's "needs" in the context not only of the continuous phenomenon of military prostitution in postwar Japan and postcolonial Korea, but also of the newly emergent trade in sex tourism for foreign—primarily Japanese—male visitors. The epilogue presents my concluding thoughts on the issues of truth, justice, and reconciliation between Korea and Japan over Korea's comfort women tragedy. The appendix discusses the methodological stance of my present work as belonging to a genre of "expatriate anthropology."

Part 1

Case studies of individuals reveal suffering, they tell us what happens to one or many people; but to explain suffering, one must embed individual biography in the larger matrix of culture, history, and political economy.

—Paul Farmer, "On Suffering and Structural Violence," in *The Anthropology of Politics,* 2002

Structural violence—the violence of poverty, hunger, social exclusion and humiliation—inevitably translates into intimate and domestic violence. . . . Violence can never be understood solely in terms of its physicality—force, assault, or the infliction of pain—alone. . . . Rather than *sui generis,* violence is in the eye of the beholder. . . . Depending on one's political-economic position in the world (dis)order, particular acts of violence may be perceived as "depraved" or "glorious." . . . Perhaps the most one can say about violence is that like madness, sickness, suffering, or death itself, it is a human condition. Violence is present (as a capability) in each of us, as is its opposite—the rejection of violence.

—Nancy Scheper-Hughes and Philippe Bourgois, "Introduction: Making Sense of Violence," in *Violence in War and Peace,* 2004

GENDER AND STRUCTURAL VIOLENCE

Chapter 1

From Multiple Symbolic Representations to the Paradigmatic Story

They were beaten and tortured in addition to being repeatedly raped day after day by officers and soldiers. . . . When they were brought to the comfort stations, they were healthy in body and spirit. They left the comfort stations, diseased in body and crippled in spirit.

—Adama Dieng, Secretary General, International Commission of Jurists, preface to U. Dolgopol and S. Paranjape, *Comfort Women,* 1994

The Japanese comfort woman who became the mistress of my boss at the Navy hospital lived in a very nicely decorated place with pretty dolls. I am ashamed to admit it, but one of the reasons I befriended her was her ample supply of tasty and hard-to-obtain sweets, such as *yōkan* [a traditional Japanese sweet made from azuki beans, agar-agar, and sugar and served with tea]. She generously shared them with me. Once I had my picture taken wearing a beautiful kimono she let me borrow from her.

—Nakazato Chiyo, a Japanese wartime military nurse, 1997

WHEN NAKAZATO CHIYO graduated from school on March 25, 1944, she received from the Japanese Red Cross a draft card—what was then commonly referred to as the "red paper" (*akagami,* in Japanese)—to serve as a military nurse. When I interviewed her at her home in Kawasaki, outside Tokyo, in November 1997, she said that the Red Cross call was purportedly voluntary but was in fact "semimandatory." On April 1, 1944, she reported for three months of training at the Second Navy Hospital in Meguro, Tokyo, then left Japan aboard a navy ship.

Before joining the staff at the Japanese Navy hospital on Hainan Island—off mainland China, where she worked until the end of the war—Nakazato spent about three months in Taiwan during the American attack on the Japanese colony. Her monthly salary was nine yen and sixty sen, but she does not remember having received any money after the situation worsened. "I hate the ships," she told me. For Nakazato, ships have come to symbolize the tools of war. She recollected that the Japanese comfort woman who became the mistress of the navy hospital director had played a leadership role among comfort women of Japanese nationality. The Japanese women who served the officers lived in a wooden house with fourteen rooms that was named Kainansō and functioned as the comfort station. When one of the women who served the assistant director of the hospital as his "only" (Japanese slang for a mistress) was brought to the hospital for her extrauterine pregnancy, Nakazato was scolded for expressing to the officer her distaste for taking care of the woman. The man shouted, "What? Don't you forget that you owe your personal safety to these people who are here with us out of the spirit of sacrifice." Nakazato further observed that the Korean comfort women, who were housed in primitive makeshift shacks constructed of tropical plant leaves, served not only Japanese soldiers but also Korean and Taiwanese employees of the military.

Nakazato's observations reveal that the degree of sexual violence and abuse the comfort women suffered varied with geographical and chronological factors as well as with the ethnicity of individual women. Some Japanese comfort women apparently led relatively secure lives as imperial "gifts," serving only officers and being charged with taking care of their needs, both physical and psychological. One may surmise that Nakazato, not to mention the wartime military, did not and would not think of the Japanese comfort woman she described as a sex slave. Rather, ordinary people in both wartime and postwar Japan were—and remain—most likely to regard their lives as cases of traditional gendered patterns of women's contractual obligation to take care of men's sexual "needs"; in other words, this was a quite conventional lifestyle of a financially dependent woman performing her expected role as a mistress in the historical context of Japan's masculinist sexual culture.

In stark contrast, the picture of the life of comfort women drawn by Adama Dieng of the International Commission of Jurists (ICJ) is alarming and horrid. A nongovernmental organization comprising distinguished jurists from around the globe founded in 1952, the ICJ proclaims that its task is to "defend the Rule of Law throughout the world and to work towards the full observance of the provisions in the Universal Declaration of Human Rights."[1] The Geneva, Switzerland–based ICJ routinely consults such international organizations as the United Nations Economic and Social Council. In 1994 the organization exerted a significant influence at an early stage of constructing the newly dominant paradigmatic story of the comfort women by producing an important mission report on the issue.

As the two epigraphs to this chapter demonstrate, Japan's wartime comfort women have been represented in multiple and conflicting ways, underscoring our need to consider the social significance and political implications of the diversity. A fuller understanding of the phenomenon of comfort women requires that we move beyond the facile explanations of the phenomenon that have been dominant in the past. To do so, we must probe the competing ideologies to get at the multifarious categorical terms that various people—primarily people other than the women themselves—have deployed to symbolically represent Japan's wartime comfort women.[2] Four principal groups are implicated and intertwined in characterizing categorically the social identity of young females of diverse ethnic backgrounds and social circumstances who were pressed into sexual labor at various types of comfort facilities during the Asia Pacific War (1931–1945): the wartime state, the troops, and contemporary activists of two distinct strands, one of feminist humanitarian fervor and another of self-righteous ethnonationalist convictions. I will call the four underlying ideologies "fascistic paternalism," "masculinist sexism," "feminist humanitarianism," and "ethnic nationalism."

For the Japanese wartime state the comfort system embodied a paternalistic state policy. Based on fascistic statism, racism, and sexism, it regarded the comfort women as considerate "gifts" to the emperor's warriors for recreational sex. The state and military leadership conceived of the *ianjo* (comfort station) as a facility where Japanese servicemen could obtain a quick commercial service for public sex and psychic "comfort" from a young woman who would satisfy their presumably uncontrollable libidos. Accordingly, the state endorsed the military's recruitment of young females from its colonies (Korea and Taiwan), with the expectation that the comfort system would, among other benefits, raise military morale. The perspective of the troops (and apparently some government officials of contemporary Japan and many conservative Japanese citizens as well) conceived of the comfort system simplistically, as a military version of licensed prostitution available in imperial Japan and its colonies.

The ideological perspectives of contemporary activists are bifurcated into those fighting for and those working against the redress movement. Feminist humanitarianism is backed by the concept of "women's rights as human rights," which is revolutionizing the centuries-old patterns of gender discrimination in patriarchy.[3] It conceives of the comfort system as military sexual slavery enforced by state power, resulting in gross violations of women's human rights and requiring state compensation to the survivors. Ethnic nationalism, whether on the part of the aggressor nation or aggrieved nations, is characterized by blind emotional devotion to upholding the honor of one's own nation at the expense of recognizing the complex history of the comfort system, straddling military prostitution and sexual slavery. The emotional contents and ideological contours of ethnic nationalisms energizing contemporary activists diverge depending on one's nationality and political stance toward imperial Japan's wartime comfort women.

These disparate ideological conceptions of the comfort system are directly reflected in the symbolic representations of the women who toiled as sexual laborers for the military. Thus, the specific terms and images deployed to refer to them vary significantly, from statist euphemisms such as "comfort women," through the paternalistic metaphor of imperial "gifts" and the documentary classification of the women as military "supplies," to the coarse and objectifying *pi* (vagina; pronounced "pea") and the crude metaphor of public "toilet,"[4] as well as the ethnic nationalists' reactive representations of the women as either licensed "prostitutes" (primarily by the Japanese) or deceived labor recruits called *chŏngsindae* (by the Koreans), to the prevailing feminist label of "sex slaves."

The boundaries of these disparate symbolic representations, however, are fuzzy and permeable. The paternalistic "gifts," when received and unwrapped by the troops, turned into the commercial and communal *pi*. The living conditions of the *pi* in some cases resembled those of licensed prostitutes, while in other cases the women were treated as veritable sex slaves (see chapter 3).

Similarly, the ideological boundaries of fascistic paternalism, masculinist sexism, and contemporary Japanese neonationalism overlap. The fascistic paternalism of wartime Japan—to say nothing of the ethnic nationalism of contemporary Japan—encompassed masculinist sexism. That is, both the wartime and contemporary statist and nationalist perspectives, as well as the generalized masculinist perspective of the military and civilian populace, share a common understanding of the ultimate function of the comfort system as a recreational amenity for the troops.

Further, the masculinist representation of comfort women as prostitutes does not necessarily preclude humanitarian recognition or sympathy for the women because of the conditions of near-slavery in which many of them were held captive. Some of the survivors bear witness to the decency of a few soldiers at comfort stations (see chapter 5). Those who subscribe to feminist humanitarianism, however, appear unwilling to acknowledge the local sexual-cultural contexts of the comfort system or the multifarious living conditions and life experiences of individual comfort women, both Japanese and non-Japanese. In the politics of the redress movement and the compensation issue, fuzzy boundaries between ideologically based symbolic representations have solidified into "prostitutes" versus "sex slaves," strengthening the positions of particular interest groups.

The feminist humanitarian representation of comfort women as sex slaves achieved its ascendancy in the context of the post–cold war politics of human rights. The contemporary paradigm for the comfort women as sex slaves solidified after the precedent-setting 1992 U.N. debates on the comfort women issue in general and, more specifically, after the 1993 Vienna Human Rights Conference with the slogan "Women's rights are human rights." The systematic rape of Bosnian women by Serb forces in the Balkan conflict beginning in the spring of 1992 also contributed to raising feminist consciousness about sexual violence against women during armed conflict,[5] generating a surge of keen interest in the Korean comfort women movement and sympathetic support for the survivors by the international community. In the United States, the National Organization for Women (NOW), for example, has said that the Korean comfort women issue constitutes wartime violations of women's human rights, just like the Bosnian case of mass rape, and invited a representative of the Korean Council to participate in a large-scale public demonstration held in Washington, D.C., on February 24, 1993, to protest mass rape in Bosnia. South Korea was, notably, the only Asian country invited to participate in the international protest rally organized by NOW.[6]

It is not surprising that the prevailing transnational discourse, or the paradigmatic story, adopts the activists' theme of forcible recruitment by the military and ensuing sexual slavery. Although the feminist humanitarian representation of comfort women as military sex slaves has finally thrown light on their abject victimization, we should be aware that seeing them *only* as sex slaves denies—however unintentionally—the marked human agency enacted by some former comfort women against gendered oppression (as witnessed in the Korean survivors' narratives and private counter-memories of their life experiences discussed in this study).

We must also note that, in the highly politicized discussions of the comfort women, both progressive scholars and human rights activists today seem to regard the use of the term "sexual slavery" rather than "prostitution" as a shibboleth, no doubt in reaction to the claim by Japanese neonationalist activists that comfort women were simply prostitutes following Japan's military.[7] In this regard, it is interesting to note the wartime U.S. military assessment of the comfort women as prostitutes. The 1944 U.S. military's "Japanese Prisoner of War Interrogation Report No. 49" on twenty Korean "comfort girls" (who were captured near Myitkyina in Burma on August 10, 1944) stated, "A 'comfort girl' is nothing more than a prostitute or 'professional camp follower' attached to the Japanese Army for the benefit of the soldiers. The word 'comfort girl' is peculiar to the Japanese."[8] Not surprisingly, Japanese conservatives have used the report as evidence to support their one-dimensional argument that "comfort women" were prostitutes working in "legal, privately operated brothels established in the war zone."[9]

The report also observed that the interrogations revealed the average Korean "comfort girl" to be "about twenty-five years old, uneducated, childish, whimsical, and selfish" and that "in an average month a girl would gross about fifteen hundred yen," half of which she turned over to the house "master."[10] It noted, "The girls were allowed the prerogative of refusing a customer. This was often done if the person were too drunk," and added, "In the latter part of 1943 the Army issued orders that certain girls who had paid their debt could return home. Some of the girls were thus allowed to return to Korea."[11] Concerning their "living and working conditions," the report states:

> They lived in near-luxury in Burma in comparison to other places. This was especially true of their second year in Burma. They lived well because their food and material was not heavily rationed and they had plenty of money with which to purchase desired articles. They were able to buy cloth, shoes, cigarettes, and cosmetics to supplement the many gifts given to them by soldiers who had received "comfort bags" from home. While in Burma they amused themselves by participating in sports events with both officers and men, and attended picnics, entertainments, and social dinners. They had a phonograph, and in the towns they were allowed to go shopping.[12]

The report noted that they were found to be in "good" health because they had been "well supplied with all types of contraceptives."[13] The photo of three Korean "comfort girls" (plate 1.1) seemed to corroborate the U.S. military report concerning their health conditions.

*   *   *

Plate 1.1. Three Korean "comfort girls" (captured in Burma), photographed while being interrogated by Capt. Won Loy Chan (San Francisco, California), Tech. Sgt. Robert Honda (Hawaii), and Sgt. Hirabayashi (Seattle, Washington), all of the G-2 Myitkyina Task Force of the U.S. Army; photo dated August 14, 1944. (Source: U.S. National Archives, SC-262580.)

By comparison, a photograph captioned "Prisoners of War—Japanese Women" (plate 1.2), which had been released for publication by the Bureau of Public Relations of the U.S. War Department, showed four miserable-looking "JAP Girls." Captured by troops of the Chinese 8th Army at a village on Sung Shan Hill on the Burma Road when Japanese soldiers were killed or driven from village, the four were photographed by a U.S. serviceman (a Private Hatfield) in September 1944. Notably, it is this same photo that the South Korean Ministry of Gender Equality and Family Web site exhibits in the English section of its Japanese Military Comfort Women Victims e-Museum, which opened in August 2005.[14] The pregnant girl on the right has been identified as Pak Yŏng-sim (1921–2006; see plate 1.3), who

Plate 1.2. "Prisoners of war—Japanese women": photo released for publication by Bureau of Public Relations, U.S. War Department; the grinning soldier guarding the women was of the Chinese 8th Army; photo dated September 3, 1944. (Source: U.S. National Archives, SC-230417.)

participated in the Women's International War Crimes Tribunal on Japan's Military Sexual Slavery in Tokyo (see below) as a representative of North Korean survivors.[15]

The four women in plate 1.2 appear clearly to be in worse condition than the three Korean "comfort girls" shown in plate 1.1, supporting the point of the present study that underscores the wide range of situations concerning the comfort facilities and personal conditions of individual comfort women.

*　　*　　*

Plate 1.3. Two North Korean survivors (with Pak Yŏng-sim on the left) at the Women's Tribunal, Tokyo, December 2000. (Photo by the author.)

MULTIPLE IDEOLOGIES AND SYMBOLIC REPRESENTATIONS

Fascistic Paternalism and Imperial "Gift"

The concept of "fascistic paternalism" highlights the interventional magnanimity of the imperial state, which provisioned its troops with the considerate "gift" of regulated access to recreational sex. This paternalism became manifest from the second stage in the history of the comfort system after the Nanking (Nanjing) massacre, when a large number of women began to be recruited from colonized Korea.[16]

When imperial Japan promoted ultranationalism by molding the indigenous folk belief system of Shinto into a national religion and coaxing absolute loyalty from its subjects to the emperor as a living god,[17] it simultaneously extended its nationalist projects to the colonized. For instance, beginning in 1937, Koreans as imperial subjects had to recite "the Pledge of the Imperial Subjects," hoist the Japanese national flag, worship the emperor, and attend Shinto ceremonies. Further assimilation policies, which required, among other things, the changing of Korean names into Japanese-style ones, helped forge a new national identity for the colonized Koreans as the subjects of imperial Japan, the process of which was referred to as the "imperialization" of subject peoples, or *kōminka* (in Japanese).[18]

After the Japanese government enforced all-out systematic mobilization of Koreans of both sexes for the war effort in 1939, it sent Korean laborers to Japan, Sakhalin, and other parts of Asia.[19] As the Second Sino-Japanese War escalated into the so-called Greater East Asian War after the December 7, 1941, attack on U.S. forces at Pearl Harbor, the drafting of Korean men as soldiers and laborers and women as laborers became both compulsory and better organized. Nonetheless, Japan's recruitment of young females from colonial Korea to support the war effort was nominally voluntary participation in the Volunteer Labor Corps. It is undeniable that Korea's status as Japan's colony facilitated the large-scale conscription of many young unmarried Korean women, especially those from destitute families. Further, the Korean cult of female virginity, which strictly enforced the norm of girls' premarital chastity, unwittingly served as an important contributing factor in rendering Korean unmarried women desirable recruits in the eyes of the Japanese authorities. Indeed, Asō Tetsuo (1910–1989), an army doctor, concluded in his report—written after his medical examinations of the women—that unmarried Korean women, rather than Japanese prostitutes, would make better "gifts for the Emperor's warriors."[20] The indigenous sexual culture, with its emphasis on what I call "virginal femininity," thus helped render colonial Korea a prime source of young "virgins" to satisfy the needs of the Japanese military comfort system.

For imperial Japan, the comfort system was an institutionalized "gift," rewarding the emperor's warriors—in a spirit of paternalistic *omoiyari* (consideration)—with a regulated liberation from their battlefield duties: the gift of brief moments of rest and recuperation in the comforting company of young and healthy *ianfu* from colonial Korea. From the paternalistic state's perspective, Korean comfort women were merely performing their "gendered duties as imperial subjects," helping the soldiers relax and rededicate themselves selflessly to winning the "Sacred War." Some Korean survivors confessed that they had prayed for Japan's victory and remembered their disappointment at its defeat. Others acknowledged that while laboring as comfort women they themselves had employed the statists' gendered discourse of women's duty to "comfort" when they had to confront abusive soldiers.[21]

Gradually, comfort women and condoms came to be seen as essential supplies for the imperial troops. In fact, when the military transported comfort women, the paperwork listed them simply as military matériel (*heitan busshi*), with no record of their personal identities. It is notable that military transport regulations covered soldiers and animals—such as horses—but not women.[22] Upon their arrival at comfort stations, however, non-Japanese comfort women typically were either given a Japanese first name by the management or commanded to adopt one. Jan Ruff-O'Herne (b. 1923), the first Dutch woman to give public testimony, for example, recalled that she was given a Japanese name. She wrote that although she could not remember her Japanese name exactly, she knows it was the name of a flower.[23]

Forcing non-Japanese women to adopt new Japanese-style feminine personal names was an expression of fascistic paternalism, putting the psycholinguistic comfort of Japanese soldiers above the integrity of the personhood of the women. These name changes functioned as an important symbolic wrapping of non-Japanese comfort women with culturally familiar "professional" names suitable for imperial gifts to the troops. We might presume here that as recipients of such gifts the soldiers, in whom a deep sense of loyalty to the nation was inculcated, may have felt psychologically even more obligated to return the favor of the paternalistic state by doing their best to win the war.

Masculinist Sexism and the *Pi*

The androcentric euphemism *ianfu,* coined by wartime Japanese officials, masks the harsh reality of military prostitution and sexual slavery. The soldiers themselves used cruder terms. The Chinese slang term *pi* was coined by the soldiers stationed in China. It is a "very ugly word and hurts the ears of anyone who is not used to hearing gutter language."[24] "Cunt" would be an appropriate English translation, one that carries the connotations of *pi,* as uttered by those soldiers in reference to their imperial "gifts."

The use of slang phrases such as *pi-kankan* (*pi* viewing) and *pi-mai* (*pi* purchase) by Japanese soldiers stationed in China unequivocally reveals their perceptions of comfort women as prostitutes and hence the soldiers' objectification and commodification of these women's sexuality.[25] Conscious of their ethnic differences, the soldiers would identify the ethnicity of comfort women by referring to them, for example, as Korean *pi* or Chinese *pi.*[26] In the case of Korean comfort women, the Japanese soldiers had two versions of the phrase, *Chōsen pi* ("Korean *pi*") and its still more derogatory abbreviation, *'sen pi. Pi* eventually became a common term throughout the Japanese imperial forces. Mun Ok-chu, a South Korean survivor, remembered having been constantly denigrated as a *Chōsen pi* by the soldiers stationed in Burma.[27]

The soldiers also used the graphically objectifying term "public toilet" (*kyōdō benjo*) to refer to comfort women, symbolically underlining the dehumanization and objectification of women as sexual receptacles. The use of *kyōdō benjo* in reference to comfort women seems to have originated with Asō Tetsuo, who not only conducted physical examinations of comfort women, but also drafted the rules and regulations for comfort stations. Asō wrote, among other things, that "the special military comfort station must not become a place of hedonistic pleasure; rather, it ought to be a hygienic public toilet."[28]

Asō's conception of the military comfort station as a "hygienic public toilet," in fact, was not original: it reflected the common viewpoint of prewar government officials who regarded the licensed pleasure quarters (*yūkaku*) as a "public latrine" that needed to be isolated under tight regulations.[29] The toilet as a Japanese sexual metaphor has, in fact, a long cultural history. It reflects a generalized male contempt for prostitutes, rooted in the conventional attitude of male superiority and the right of men to public sex; it was not limited to government officials and wartime military men. People in Japan used such terms as *shomben* (toilet) *geisha* to refer to low-class geisha available for prostitution. Even male college students in postwar Japan, up to the 1970s, used the term *toire* (toilet) to refer to women with whom they had recreational sex.

It is significant in this context that "Liberation from the Toilet" was the title of a 1970 manifesto for the group called Fighting Women (Tatakau Onna) in the women's liberation movement in Japan.[30] The young Japanese feminist Tanaka Mitsu, author of the manifesto, condemned the conventions of masculinist sexual culture that divides women into the binary categories of mothers and whores: "As far as men are concerned," she wrote, "a woman is split into two images—either the expression of maternal love: a 'mother,' or a vessel for the management of lust: a 'toilet.'"[31]

A male-centered, "hydraulic" model of sexuality is certainly not limited to Japanese sexual culture but seems to be prevalent across the globe in patriarchal societies.[32] It perceives females as repositories for semen. In premodern agrarian patriarchies such as Korea, women's sexual function had conventionally been symbolized as that of the "field" (*pat,* in Korean) into which men cast their "seed" (*ssi,* in Korean). In the Korean agrarian metaphor,[33] then, the sexual act is accomplished unilaterally by a man's scattering of his "seed" into the womb, which is metaphorically likened to the motionless "field" mutely receiving male discharge. This stark, emotionless imagery of the sex act is, in fact, congruent with the masculinist construction of male sexuality as biologically grounded in physical needs.

It is notable that the American writer W. E. B. Griffin, in his 1990 novel about the U.S. Marine Corps, used the term "seminal sewer" to describe a woman who might have been placed in a "Japanese Army comfort house."[34] I was struck by the description for two reasons. First, it was perfectly matter-of-fact. Second, the book was published before the issue of the comfort women became internationalized. Both the use of the term and the timing of the publication indicate that knowledge about the Japanese military comfort system was available to non-Japanese men, especially men who served in the military or had connections with it. The American fictional account reinforces my argument that, from the masculinist perspective, whether in the East or West, sex acts are commonly perceived as acts of bodily relief, akin to urination and bowel movements. It is no surprise, then, that Asō and the Japanese soldiers also regarded comfort women as receptacles for male sexual energy.[35] The doctor's conception of the comfort station as a "hygienic public toilet" merely epitomizes an essentialist and phallocentric view of male sexuality as a natural force or energy that needs to be released or controlled—a widely prevalent perspective in masculinist cultures.

Feminist Humanitarianism and Sex Slaves

From the perspective of feminism, sexual violence against women is a violation of human rights, and rape by the military in wartime is a war crime. Feminists have argued that rape is a crime of violence against women's bodies, autonomy, and integrity, comparable to other cruel and inhumane treatment.[36] In contrast, the Geneva Convention has characterized rape as a crime against the "honor" and dignity of women. As Catharine MacKinnon points out, the common kinds of dehumanization directed explicitly toward women, such as rape and battery, were not until recent years defined by the international community as human rights problems unless they were directly linked to political acts of the state.[37] The end of the cold war, the consequent emergence of human rights as a defining value in the emergent new world order, and the media attention to mass rape in the Balkan conflict in 1992 have come together to contribute to the dramatic paradigm shift from regarding the comfort women issue as part of a Korea-Japan bilateral dispute to seeing it as a global issue of sexual violence against women in situations of armed conflict.[38]

The participants in the International Symposium on Violence against Women in War and Armed Conflict resoundingly endorsed the feminist position on the topic during the 1995 Beijing World Conference on Women.[39] The idea that human rights include a woman's right to her bodily integrity came to be integral to feminism in the post–cold war world order of the late twentieth century. Feminist humanitarianism, which derives from the revolutionary woman-centered—sometimes known as "gynocentric"—discourse of the 1990s transnational women's human rights movement,[40] demands a radical reinterpretation of the sexual politics in gender power relations. It calls into question many patriarchal patterns of behavior and value judgments that have made women's oppression seem "normal."

Radical feminism, for example, contends that "female sexual slavery" applies not only to "women in prostitution who are controlled by pimps but also to wives in marriages who are controlled by husbands and daughters who are incestuously assaulted by fathers."[41] Feminists seek to transform the gender inequity of the traditional masculinist sexual culture and lend full support to activists' demand for punishing perpetrators and providing redress for the victim-survivors of Japan's wartime military sex crimes. Accordingly, the leaders of three women's organizations—from Japan (Matsui Yayori of the NGO Violence against Women in War, known by its acronym VAWW-NET Japan), South Korea (Yun Chŏng-ok of the Korean Council), and the Philippines (Indai Sajor of ASCENT)—collaborated to organize the Women's International War Crimes Tribunal on Japan's Military Sexual Slavery (hereafter, the Women's Tribunal), which was held in Tokyo in December 2000 and drew several thousand participants: although the attendees were overwhelmingly female and Japanese, more than 150 nongovernmental organizations in Asia sent representatives and a total of 64 survivors from South Korea, North Korea, the People's Republic of China, Taiwan, Indonesia, the Philippines, the Netherlands, and East Timor attended.[42]

The feminist activists organized the Women's Tribunal because the International Military Tribunal for the Far East held in Tokyo in 1946 failed to prosecute and punish those responsible for establishing the military comfort system or committing mass rape during the war. The Women's Tribunal prosecutors recognized survivors' stories as evidence to establish Japan's military comfort system as an institution of slavery that violated the antislavery conventions and international treaties of the time. The Japanese feminist historian Fujime Yuki, who testified as an expert witness, argued that Japan's prewar system of licensed prostitution was itself a system of sexual slavery and that the military comfort system was an extension of that system.[43] The Women's Tribunal then categorically embraced many Japanese women as victims of sexual slavery by declaring that those comfort women who had been licensed prostitutes before their conscription into the military comfort facilities were victims of "crimes against humanity." The judgment given in The Hague a year later found guilty the late Hirohito (r. 1926–1989)—posthumously named Emperor Shōwa—of Japan.[44]

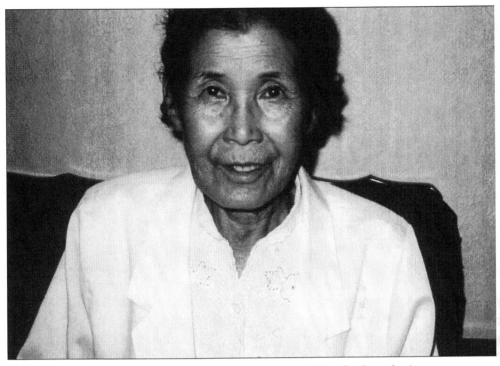

Plate 1.4. Kim Hak-sun in the office of Yujokhoe, Seoul, 1995. (Photo by the author.)

Ethnic Nationalisms and Contentious Memories

On December 6, 1991, just before the fiftieth anniversary of Japan's attack on Pearl Harbor, Kim Hak-sun (1924–1997) riveted the attention of both Japan and the world community by appearing in person as a former comfort woman and a plaintiff in the Korean class-action suit against the Japanese government, shedding bitter tears during a Tokyo press conference. The plaintiffs were members of the South Korean Association of the Pacific War Victims and Bereaved Families and included two other comfort women survivors (who chose to remain anonymous). The lawsuit demanded 20 million yen for each of the thirty-five South Korean war victims and their bereaved families, who were represented pro bono by the attorney Takagi Ken'ichi and his team of Japanese lawyers.

*   *   *

A month later the comfort women issue exploded in Japanese media and society. On January 11, 1992, *Asahi Shimbun*, one of Japan's oldest and largest national daily newspapers, with a nationwide circulation of 12 million, reported on the research of the Japanese historian Yoshimi Yoshiaki, who found at the Library of the National Institute for Defense Studies in Tokyo six official documents that clearly implicate the Japanese government in the establishment and maintenance of the military comfort system.[45] The newspaper account compelled the Japanese government to acknowledge the state's involvement in the wartime comfort system, and on January 13, 1992, Tokyo issued an apology. Four days later, during a state visit to South Korea that had been planned prior to the *Asahi* report, Miyazawa Kiichi became the first Japanese prime minister to apologize to the Korean people for the comfort women issue in a public speech.[46]

Soon thereafter, both Seoul and Tokyo investigated the matter and issued their first reports in July 1992. The Japanese government then conducted more research on the matter, which included a fact-finding trip to Seoul, where the investigators listened to the testimonies of South Korean comfort women survivors. On August 4, 1993, Kōno Yōhei, then chief cabinet secretary, announced the findings of the government study on the comfort women issue. The announcement, known as the Kōno Statement, acknowledged the direct and indirect involvement of the wartime Japanese military in the establishment and management of the comfort stations and the transfer of comfort women. It also noted that in many cases the women were recruited against their own will and that "[t]hey lived in misery at comfort stations under a coercive atmosphere."[47] The subsequent pressure from the advocates, both at home and abroad, which included the ICJ recommendations, resulted in the Japanese government cabinet's approval in August 1995 of the establishment of a hybrid national public organization, to be called the Asian Women's Fund, to fulfill Japan's "moral responsibility" for the survivors. In spite of severe criticism from redress advocates for shirking "legal responsibility," the disbursement of the fund's "atonement money" donated by the Japanese people and the implementation of their government's money for medical welfare project for the survivors began in August 1996.[48]

In the meantime, however, a wave of strong resistance arose among conservative Japanese who were opposed to compensating comfort women survivors. (It is notable here that the Japanese public debate on the comfort women has generally conjured up the survivors as women of Korean ethnicity.) During my interview with Takagi Ken'ichi, the Japanese lawyer in charge of the legal team for the 1991 South Korean lawsuit,[49] he suggested three causal factors for this Japanese resistance. First, stunned by the

Plate 1.5. Takagi Ken'ichi in his Tokyo office, 1997. (Photo by the author.)

compensation lawsuit, some Japanese immediately assumed that Korean comfort women survivors were motivated by economic gain. Second, they pointed out that everybody had suffered during the war, and that Japanese women had also worked as comfort women. (In other words, it was gendered labor that a certain class of women of imperial Japan had offered in order to help their nation-state win the war.) Finally, many Japanese backed their government's position that the 1965 agreement for normalization of diplomatic relations between Japan and South Korea had settled all reparation issues.

Nevertheless, the feminist humanitarian perspective seemed to dominate the Japanese public discourse on the comfort women issue until 1996, when another major controversy concerning history textbooks began in Japan that sharply polarized Japanese civil society into pro– and anti–comfort women camps.[50] By contrast, South Korean public discourse on the comfort women, which has been fueled by strong postcolonial ethnonationalism, has unquestioningly endorsed the media's, as well as activists', representation of Korean comfort women as victims of deceptive recruitment by the state agents under the guise of *chŏngsindae*.

As Christa Paul perceptively suggested in her preface to the 1996 Japanese translation of her work on forced prostitution in wartime Nazi Germany,[51] postcolonial and/or postwar ethnic nationalisms, steeped in a strong antipathy toward Japan, have played a pivotal role in launching and sustaining the "radical"—to use Paul's word—Asian women's movement for comfort women survivors. The Asian advocates' nationalist representation of the comfort women fundamentally revolves around the issue of "forced recruitment by the state power." The ethnic nationalisms of afflicted countries, especially the two Koreas and Taiwan as former colonies of Japan, have fully embraced the feminist humanitarian perspective, framing the comfort women issue as a war crime, while conservatives in Japan have angrily contested it as "not [supported by] the historical facts."[52] Contentious representations of the comfort women, which have been constructed by interested parties dealing with Japan's postwar responsibility, have rendered the chances rather dismal for some reasonable resolution of the matter, in the ongoing conflict over international identity politics and history war that has raged between conservatives in contemporary Japan and activist-survivors and their advocates in Japan's former colonies and adversaries.

THE PARADIGMATIC STORY

Before the South Korean comfort women movement was internationalized in the early 1990s, virtually nothing had been published about the issue in English. Alice Y. Chai's 1993 article in *Korean Studies* reported on the emerging comfort women movement as "Asian-Pacific feminist coalition politics" and Watanabe Kazuko's 1994 article in *Bulletin of Concerned Asian Scholars* dealt with the comfort women issue as forced sexual labor for Japanese soldiers.[53] Then, two former comfort women published their autobiographies. The first one that appeared in 1994, *50 Years of Silence,* was by Jan Ruff-O'Herne, a Dutch-born Australian. As a young Dutch colonist interned in a Japanese prisoner-of-war camp together with her mother and two younger sisters in Java, Dutch East Indies (today's Indonesia), in 1942, she was forcibly recruited to labor as a comfort woman for about two months at a military brothel in Semarang in February 1944. Her book is a description of her privileged prewar life followed by a moving narrative of her desperate struggle to resist forced prostitution in the face of Japanese military occupation of the Dutch East Indies.

In 1996 Maria Rosa Henson published her autobiography, *Comfort Woman: Slave of Destiny.* A Filipina, Henson's life history included her humble origins and impoverished life as an illegitimate daughter of a wealthy landlord and his poor housemaid as well as her abduction and sexual enslavement at a Japanese military barracks. The autobiography was accompanied by her own illustrations of the family members and major events of her life.

Influential reports by legal specialists were also published.[54] The authors were often affiliated with international organizations (such as ICJ and the United Nations), and their works contributed to the transformation of the discursive paradigm for the comfort women in the international community by employing the concept of "sexual slavery."

In general, there is hardly any dispute in the international discourse on the comfort women issue. What the great majority of the published works I discuss below have in common is the replication of the advocates' paradigmatic story line and the monolithic representation of the comfort system as sexual slavery. Such portrayals understandably have emanated from their authors' sympathy for the plight of the comfort women analyzed exclusively through the lens of Japanese military and state exploitation, without taking into account the wide range of varying experiences of victimized women and of the organizational diversity of the comfort stations found across the vast territories under Japanese occupation over a period of more than thirteen years. Although it is unquestionable that some women victims were "diseased in body and crippled in spirit" and some even lost their lives in the battlefield, others (such as Ruff-O'Herne, Henson, and other survivors I have met), to their credit, were able to move on with their lives and courageously came out to tell their stories.

Transnational English-Language Template

The first report put out by an international organization was *Comfort Women: An Unfinished Ordeal,* the 1994 product of an ICJ mission that consisted of Ustinia Dolgopol (an Australian lecturer of law) and Snehal Paranjape (an Indian and advocate of the Bombay High Court). The ICJ report is based on reviews of documents and interviews with about forty victims (including Filipinas as well as North and South Koreans); three Japanese former soldiers; representatives of not only the governments of Japan, North Korea, South Korea, and the Philippines but also nongovernmental organizations; lawyers; academics; and journalists.[55] The mission found that life in the comfort stations for the women was a "living hell" of beating, torture, and rape. After setting up what has since become the paradigmatic story (of forcible recruitment by the military into sexual violence and enslavement), the ICJ report recommended, among other things, that "the sum of US$40,000 for the rehabilitation of each woman who has come forward" be granted.[56]

Two years later, in January 1996, Radhika Coomaraswamy, the U.N. special rapporteur on violence against women, its causes, and consequences, submitted her report on a mission to North Korea, South Korea, and Japan on the comfort women issue. The Coomaraswamy Report further helped the human rights activist community by characterizing the issue as "military sexual slavery," which Coomaraswamy claimed more accurately (than the term "comfort women") reflects the suffering, "such as multiple rapes on everyday basis and severe physical abuse in wartime."[57]

Gay J. McDougall, another special rapporteur, upped the ante in 1998 by using the terms "rape centers" and "rape camps" to refer to the Japanese military comfort stations—which she also calls Japan's "comfort women stations"—in a final report on contemporary forms of slavery submitted to the United Nations. Because rape and forced prostitution were prohibited under international law before the first comfort stations were established, McDougall wrote, the individual comfort women have a right to adequate compensation for the damages they suffered at the hands of Japanese government and military officials.[58]

Other significant books on the comfort women issue for nonspecialists published during the first half of the decade include George Hick's *The Comfort Women: Japan's Brutal Regime of Enforced Prostitution in the Second World War* and Keith Howard's edited volume, *True Stories of Korean Comfort Women,* the first—and the only translated—volume in the Korean Council's publication series of collected testimonials of South Korean former comfort women.[59] The nongovernmental organization Asian Women Human Rights Council published the Filipino comfort women case.[60] In addition, scholarly journal articles dealt with the issue under the rubrics of "militarism, colonialism, and the trafficking of women," the Korean comfort women movement, and the role of the "state as pimp."[61] Finally, the 1997 special issue of *positions: east asia cultures critique,* edited by Chungmoo Choi, was devoted to the comfort women issue in the context of the larger issues of colonialism, war, and sex.[62]

Publications that came out during the second half of the decade brought more voices of Japanese scholars as well as Korean American writers to English-language readers. For example, Yoshimi Yoshiaki's pioneering study on the topic (*Comfort Women: Sexual Slavery in the Japanese Military during World War II*) and the feminist sociologist Ueno Chizuko's critical pieces on nationalism, comfort women, and the politics of memory (including *Nationalism and Gender*) have been translated and published in North America and Australia.[63] It is remarkable that the subtitle of Yoshimi's English translation contains the term "sexual slavery," whereas the original

Japanese title was simply *Jūgun Ianfu* (Military Comfort Women). I tried, without success, to find out whether the inclusion of the term in the subtitle reflected the author's wishes or a decision on the part of the translator or an executive of the press, or a combination of the three.[64] In any case, in his new introduction to the English edition Yoshimi clearly notes that the Japanese military comfort system was "a system of military sexual slavery."[65] Tanaka Yuki, another Japanese historian, initially dealt with the comfort women issue as "part of a larger pattern of how war makes women victims" in his *Hidden Horrors: Japanese War Crimes in World War II.*[66] Tanaka's later work, *Japan's Comfort Women: Sexual Slavery and Prostitution during World War II and the US Occupation,* discusses the victimization of not only non-Japanese women for the Japanese military but also Japanese comfort women for the Allied occupation forces that landed in vanquished Japan in September 1945.[67]

The books published by Korean American women such as Dae-sil Kim-Gibson and Sangmie Choi Schellstede have offered further personal life stories and testimonial narratives of Korean survivors.[68] Notably, Kim-Gibson's *Silence Broken: Korean Comfort Women* is an accompaniment to her docudrama of the same title, which was aired on public television in the United States.[69] Schellstede's edited volume, *Comfort Women Speak: Testimony by Sex Slaves of the Japanese Military,* contains brief personal stories of nineteen Korean former comfort women, seven of whom had already had their testimonials published in *True Stories of Korean Comfort Women.* Dongwoo Lee Hahm, the founding president of the Washington-based nongovernmental organization Washington Coalition for Comfort Women Issues, interviewed the survivors. The book's front matter contains two full-size photographs of Korean comfort women as prisoners of war (including the one with the pregnant Pak Yŏng-sim). It also carries the contemporary black-and-white full-page photographs of all the featured South Korean survivors (except for "Ms. K," who has immigrated to the United States). A young woman photographer of Korean ethnicity, Soon Mi Yoo not only took these pictures but also translated and edited the testimonies of the Korean "rape camp survivors" (in Schellstede's words). The book's appendices include excerpts of the reports on the comfort women issue put out by ICJ and the United Nations as well as the December 1996 news release by the U.S. Justice Department announcing the placement of sixteen suspected Japanese war criminals on the "watch list" of excludable aliens. (These Japanese citizens either were members of "Unit 731"—the infamous secret biological warfare unit set up in northeast China following the Japanese invasion[70]—or had been involved in the operation of the military comfort stations.)

A volume coedited by two Georgetown University faculty members, Margaret Stetz and Bonnie Oh, and titled *Legacies of the Comfort Women of the World War II* grew out of the International Symposium on Comfort Women held at Georgetown in September 1996. It contains academic essays as well as activist writings and artistic responses.[71] David A. Schmidt's *Ianfu—The Comfort Women of the Japanese Imperial Army of the Pacific War: Broken Silence* is based on his research in Japan. An American scholar, Schmidt stumbled on the comfort women issue when he found himself in Tokyo in December 1991 and read a short article about a news conference held for the Korean plaintiffs (including Kim Hak-sun) bringing suit against the Japanese government. He opines, "[T]he *ianfu* issue remains one of the least understood atrocities of the Twentieth Century."[72] The focus of his work is on the "chronological treatment of the issue as a political and historical issue."[73]

Journal articles offered more focused analyses of a variety of such problems as

- the competing symbolic representations of the comfort women from "imperial gifts" to "sex slaves"
- the meaning of "human rights" for the survivors
- the "imaginative power" of the comfort women's story to inform various contemporary debates over social identity and women's human rights
- the significance of the mock tribunal organized by the transnational civil society
- Japan's responsibility toward comfort women survivors
- the controversy surrounding Japan's National/Asian Women's Fund
- the postnationalist understanding of Korean comfort women's tragic stories of foiled aspirations and horrific ordeals under patriarchy, colonialism, and total war
- a comparative perspective on postwar reproductive health and infertility among comfort women survivors
- the Korean comfort women tragedy as structural violence
- the role of nongovernmental organization trials in the "resignification" of the comfort women.[74]

Significantly, postcolonial and/or postwar ethnic nationalisms of the people in former colonies (such as South Korea) and enemy countries (such as China) have fostered vigorous support for the emerging paradigmatic story of the comfort women issue.[75] Advocates of the comfort women redress movement have forcefully expressed their righteous anger over Japan's "national amnesia" concerning the brutalities committed by its soldiers during Japan's war of aggression and colonial exploitation of forced labor. This criticism, however, overlooks the substantial number of published works on the topics by progressive writers, academics, and pacifist activists in postwar Japan. (In fact, as we shall see in chapter 4, several historiographical works and confessional memoirs became best sellers in the 1970s and 1980s and made crucial contributions to the construction of the new transnational paradigmatic story of the comfort women issue.)

*   *   *

I turn now to the manner in which three fictional accounts of the comfort women in the English language, published in the latter half of the 1990s, have helped to artfully add flesh and blood to the media representations of the paradigmatic story.[76] It is especially notable that these were written by two women and one man, all of whom have Korean ancestry and reside in the United States. Nevertheless, the subtle differences in the specific personal circumstances of the individual writers (such as their parentage, national origin, and gender identity) have clearly affected their authorial standpoints as well as their artistic imaginations and the degree of pedagogical inclinations. Given the enormous impact literary works can exert in shaping the images and memories of the past, it is worthwhile for us to examine the three novels in some detail here.

Therese Park, a native of South Korea who immigrated to the United States in 1966, dedicates her 1997 novel *A Gift of the Emperor* to "all victims of forced sex-slavery in the Japanese military brothels during World War II," which places the military comfort system only in the less-than-four-year period of World War II in Asia and the Pacific rather than the total period beginning in the early 1930s. Although Park's novel received much less media attention than the other two, it is the most historically factual about Korean life under colonial rule. Nevertheless, its narrow focus on the personal story of one young woman fails to offer a larger historical picture of the military comfort system in the sociocultural context of colonial Korea.

Park's perspective is unmistakably that of an ethnic Korean nationalism. The protagonist Soon-ah (also known by her Japanese name "Keiko Omura") is a seventeen-year-old "high school"–educated girl, very uncommon in light of the data on South Korean comfort women survivors. Soon-ah is forcibly drafted by Japanese soldiers—rather than civilian traffickers or local functionaries, as revealed in the majority of the survivors' stories—in 1942 after her father, a Presbyterian minister, is murdered by "Japanese policemen" and her mother is raped by a "Japanese soldier" (in a rather unconvincing episode). On the day after the first rape, Soon-ah publicly yells to an officer who slapped her face, "Kill me now! You are going to kill us anyway! It's better to die now than to be used as your sex slaves!"[77] Although today's (Western) readers may fully sympathize with Soon-ah, it is doubtful that a young woman could have made such a bold statement, using the term "sex slaves," in 1942. Not long afterward, however, Soon-ah falls in love with a Japanese war correspondent despite her initial intention to reject his affections because of his ethnicity. The two then decide to escape together in a boat and are rescued by an American ship that takes them to Honolulu, where they become separated. The novel ends with Soon-ah returning home after the end of the war and reuniting with her mother.

As a 1997 Kirkus review notes, Park describes war crimes against women memorably, but her characters seem "more like one-dimensional witnesses than vibrantly complex fictional creations."[78] However, another review posted on the Internet by an anonymous reader states that the book is "the only novel that truly shows in great detail what atrocities these women suffered, and the strength and grace they showed in the face of the enemy. . . . I also met Therese Park when she was on a book tour in California, and was very impressed with her passion and dedication toward creating more awareness for victims and survivors of war crimes."[79]

Nora Okja Keller's first novel, *Comfort Woman,* also published in 1997, conjures up the double memoirs of two protagonists, the obituary writer Beccah and Akiko, the Japanese name by which Beccah's Korean-born mother was known as a comfort woman. Early in the story, Soon Hyo (Akiko's Korean name) is "sold" at age twelve by her oldest sister, who needs money for her dowry, and yet Keller writes that the Japanese "soldiers," rather than the ubiquitous traffickers, came to take her on their proverbial truck.[80] During her two years as a comfort woman at the "recreation center," Akiko became pregnant. She has an abortion, then manages to escape and is eventually taken to a missionary house. Akiko, by now just fourteen, is then forced to marry a much older American missionary. After the war is over, she gives birth to Beccah in Hawaii. *Comfort Woman* received much media attention and literary praise for mingling "the Asian past and the American present" with sensitivity.[81]

Born of Korean and German ancestry in Seoul, Keller moved to the United States with her family when she was four and settled in Hawaii when she was seven. In an interview conducted by a staff reporter of the *Korea Times,* Keller stated that growing up in the United States, she "rebelled" against her mother "who was also rebelling against" American culture. She said, "Common to a lot of Asian American writings in the U.S. is that we struggle with what it means to be, in my case, Korean American, and we try to resolve it with writing. It's such an irony. I do feel like I'm very drawn to Korean culture and yet I can't even speak the language. And that's a lot of conflict. And because of the conflict, I try to write about it."[82]

Notwithstanding its literary merit, Keller's novel offers very few concrete depictions of the life of a comfort woman and is ultimately unsatisfying. The cryptic, fragmented personal memories of Akiko, who is portrayed as a mentally unstable woman given to shamanic mysticism, are difficult to read. In her review posted on the Amazon.com page on *Comfort Woman,* C. Joan Villanueva noted, "[T]he book focused less on what happened to the mother during the war and more on her shamanism and on mysticism . . . all of the spookiness . . . was a bit far-fetched."[83] For her part, Keller has stated that she regards her novel as both "a story of the comfort camp" and "a story about inter-generational conflict and type of pain that continue from generation to generation."[84]

Keller's transliterations of Korean and Japanese terms, unfortunately, are lax, and some of her descriptions and statements are incredibly imaginary and factually incorrect. Drying cow dung for fuel,[85] for example, is not a Korean custom. The Japanese did not use the term *Jungun* [sic] *Ianfu,* or military comfort women, for the women "at the camps."[86] (Keller's term refers to a terminology used in postwar Japan.) Keller also writes of the "P" and misrepresents it as the Korean vernacular term for the female genitalia (*poji*), when in fact it stands for the Chinese slang *pi.* Some of Keller's descriptions of the scenes of the March 1 Independence Movement of 1919 are so unbelievably lacking in any understanding of the history and cultural context of the period that they can only belong to the realm of fantasy born out of the present-day American cultural lens. Keller writes how Soon Hyo's mother, who was a student of "Ewha College" (which came into being in 1925), participated in the street "parade" (rather than serious political march that it was) and "stole glances at lovers stealing kisses behind their flags."[87] (Even in today's South Korea, it would be most unlikely that participants in a serious political march would steal glances at some young lover participants kissing each other in public.) Keller identifies the planned gathering place for the independence "celebration" (instead of grassroots uprising that it was) as the "Chang Duk Palace" (rather than the famed Pagoda Park).[88]

Some of Keller's descriptions of life at what she calls the "recreation camp" belong to the realm of literary license, not to creative work based on careful research. She talks of "the name and number stenciled" across the jacket Akiko and other comfort women wore, bringing up glum images of uniformed prison inmates.[89] Indeed, Japanese names were often given to Korean women at the comfort stations. Some Korean survivors also reported that they were given numbers rather than Japanese names, but none of them spoke of wearing uniforms or having their names or numbers stenciled on their clothes. Rather, the markers of their new forced identity were often displayed on the wall in the entry area of the comfort stations or on the doors of their rooms. I winced to read an Amazon.com review by an admiring reader who felt Keller's book was "almost the perfect introduction" to the "history" of comfort women.[90]

It is not surprising that some unsatisfied readers' commentaries posted on the Internet include a complaint that the book does not deal with Korea or the comfort women.[91] Others fault Keller for rehashing the mother-daughter themes "that run through almost all Asian American Lit written by female authors."[92] Another reader pronounces under the title "Orientalist Mumbo Jumbo":

> So much of Asian American feminist fiction writes from an American sensibility. . . . Despite the fact that Keller . . . testifies that she has done "research" for this book, she obviously knows very little about Korea or shamanism. . . . Sloppy transliterations from Korean language and ridiculous scenes like the waving of a chicken over the head made me want to cringe. . . . Although I appreciate the fact that this book raises awareness about the comfort women issue, the contrived, Orientalist rendering of the Korean woman/immigrant as schizophrenic outsider detracts too much attention away for me. This is NOT about Korea at all, but about a Korean American author trying to image and construct a Korea she knows very little about.[93]

An even sharper criticism charges Keller with "exploit[ing] the nightmare of the 'comfort women' by making it a convenient backdrop for an otherwise tired rehash of the slew of Asian Woman Writer novels . . . of the hackneyed mother-daughter tear-jerkers hyped by the mega-publishing house PR mill."[94] An Asian American academic, Kandice Chuh, is critical of Keller's novel for the dichotomous presentation of Akiko as a victim and Soon Hyo as a heroic figure of successful survival, "leaving us little space to ascribe the ordinary complexities of human life to either Akiko or Soon Hyo. . . . What we are left with is the distinct sense that the novel's interest in 'comfort woman' is finally less about that history or the persons who lived it, and is rather more driven by the needs of the present."[95]

Finally, in *A Gesture Life,* published in 1999, Chang-rae Lee, the American-educated son of Korean immigrant parents, approaches the topic of comfort women obliquely through the long-repressed personal memories of his protagonist, Franklin Hata, a Korean adopted by a Japanese family who immigrated to the United States after the end of the war. "Doc" Hata's memories of his tragic relationship with "K," an unusually intelligent and beautiful "volunteer" (i.e., *chŏngsindae*) from Korea, are disclosed gradually but vividly and sometimes mystically, along with the personal stories of his postwar life as a Japanese American lifelong bachelor running a surgical supply store and an adoptive father struggling over a strained relationship with Sunny, his rebellious mixed-blood daughter whose birth parents are presumed to be a Korean woman and an American GI.

In contrast to the two women writers, Park and Keller, whose first novels similarly conjure up feminist portrayals of extremely self-possessed, strong, courageous young Korean women who eventually escape comfort stations in Palau and China, respectively,[96] as a male writer Lee presents a grim war story from the point of view of the male protagonist, who served in the Japanese army during the war.[97] Hata's flashback describes the perspectives and sexual behaviors of the military men stationed in a far-flung outpost in Burma. Hata's memories of his days as a paramedical officer, Lieutenant Kurohata Jiro, in the Japanese army poignantly remind us how "wartime and soldiering . . . is the grimmest business of living."[98] Hata confesses that "like everyone else" he "appreciated the logic of deploying young women to help maintain the morale of officers and foot soldiers in the field."[99] Until the night when the convoy arrived with five women "volunteers," he assumed that it was a "familiar modality" in a wartime camp. He realized how mistaken he was when the day finally came and tragic incidents ensued involving both soldiers and the young women. The meticulously recalled dramatic scenes are powerfully disturbing, awash with bloodshed and violence—an officer's savage brutality toward his men, the camp commander's accidental killing of a sentry, the suicide of a comfort girl and K's sister, and the tragic demise of K herself.

Despite its literary finesse, Lee's characterization of K (including her unlikely Korean name Kkutaeh, given the noble background Hata attributes to her) pushes the envelope of literary license. Lee's fictional story of Korean comfort women and Japanese soldiers unforgettably, and unquestioningly, endorses the South Korean nationalist discourse of the comfort women as abused *chŏngsindae:* Lee has acknowledged at the end of the book that he received help from Korean women activists, including Yun Chŏng-ok of the Korean Council, as well as survivors, for background research for his novel. Through Hata's narrative, Lee notes that Korean comfort women were referred to as "volunteers" who "had unwittingly enlisted or been conscripted into the wartime women's volunteer corps, to contribute and sacrifice as all did."[100]

Lee's overall representation of the comfort women issue, however, comes across as introspective, nuanced, and suggestive. He distances himself from the ethnonationalist rhetoric of victimization, which apparently "disappoints" some readers of Korean descent. An online reviewer named "Korean reader," for example, notes:

> While the content is realistic enough, it is not truthful. . . . [W]hile writing with the assumed authority of a Korean-American, he has once again upheld the stereotype of Asian immigrants as being emotionally impenetrable, duplicitous and damaged. . . . The awkward weaving of the "back-story," that of the comfort women, is really pitiful. . . . As far as the tragedy of comfort women themselves, I can only say that I've read better and more moving accounts of what comfort women went through in textbooks.

Lee's descriptions of the gory violence in the barracks, which involved the deaths of comfort women, may have contributed to the negative reviews by some Japanese-descended readers of *A Gesture Life*. A reviewer named "Kazuo," for example, states, "I was very disappointed with his use of bad history to write a novel based on total hearsays [*sic*]."

By contrast, another reviewer, "a reader from L.A., CA," praised the fiction as a "carefully crafted work of art" and cautioned:

> This kind of novel must be treated with care however. Issues surrounding the "comfort women"—those Japanese, Korean and other Asian women recruited to work in Japanese frontline brothels during WWII—has been hugely politicized and sensationalized. The issues, and books/films about them, have been used not only as legitimate guide into this tragic event in history but also as a way to vent prejudice and hate against today's Japan and Japanese people. We must not succumb to the temptation of racially-charged Japan-bashing again. We must, however, ensure to keep "comfort women" part of our historical remembrance and vow to respect the human rights of every individual at all times—even during the most bitter and bloody war.[101]

South Korean Nationalist Inflection

In 1990, when South Korean women leaders formed two new organizations for the comfort women issue, they chose to adopt the wartime fascist term *chŏngsindae,* and not the masculinist euphemism *wianbu* for prostitutes, in naming two new nongovernmental organizations. Chŏngsindae Research Association (Chŏngsindae Yŏn'guhoe, in Korean) was formed in July 1990 under the leadership of Yun Chŏng-ok, then a professor of English at Ewha Womans [Women's] University in Seoul. It began as a small study group consisting of all women—mostly of the younger generation, with the exceptions of Yun Chŏng-ok, who was nearing her retirement and Ahn Byung-jik (An Pyŏng-chik), the senior and sole male historian, who was affiliated with Seoul National University. The group's purpose was to conduct scholarly research and disseminate information on the comfort women issue. The group later revised its name to Korean Research Institute for Chong-shindae (Han'guk Chŏngsindae Yŏn'guso, in Korean [KRIC]).[102] The other nongovernmental organization, Chŏngsindae-munje Taech'aek Hyŏpŭihoe (commonly referred to by its acronym, ChŏngTaeHyŏp), was formed four months later, in November 1990, as an activist umbrella organization that brought together thirty-seven women's groups, the majority of which were associated with Christian churches. Its English name is the Korean Council for Women Drafted for Military Sexual Slavery by Japan (or, for short, the Korean Council).[103]

In light of the fact that the founding corepresentatives (Yun Chŏng-ok and Lee Hyo-chae) of the Korean Council had lived through the war as young women,[104] it is significant that the names of the two nongovernmental organizations contain the term *chŏngsindae* rather than *wianbu*. The choice of names reflects a generalized Korean perception that identifies the comfort women with *chŏngsindae*. In her undated manuscript entitled "*Jungshindae*—Korean Military 'Comfort Women,'" Yun in effect equated Korean comfort women with *chŏngsindae*. (*Jungshindae* is an alternative romanization of *chŏngsindae*.)

The three-syllable term *chŏng-sin-dae* is the Korean pronunciation of wartime imperial Japan's officialese *tei-shin-tai*. The literal translation, "volunteering [*tei/chŏng*] body [*shin/sin*] corps [*tai/dae*]," conjures up the spirit of patriotic sacrifice. A South Korean–English dictionary notes that *chŏngsin* is a "military" (*kunsa*) term and translates it as "volunteering."[105] Remarkably, KRIC's English-language Web site defines *chŏngsindae* as a "Korean term for the women drafted for military sexual slavery by Japan during the Japanese colonial period,"[106] appropriating wartime imperial Japan's fascist terminology *teishintai* as a native term.

In colonial Korea, the term Chŏngsindae was used from about early 1941 to refer to a variety of ad hoc "patriotic" organizations of students, farmers, housewives, and other ordinary citizens whose members were mobilized to support the war efforts of imperial Japan. From late 1943, however, usage tended to be limited to women's groups (as in *yŏja* [female] *chŏngsindae* or *yoja kŭllo* [labor] *chŏngsindae*), and after the August 1944 ordinance for a Women's Volunteer Labor Corps the term's usage appears to have been confined to women mobilized for the war effort.[107]

Testimonial evidence supporting South Korean nationalist discourse of comfort women as abused *chŏngsindae* has been scant. Among the more than one hundred cases of Korean victim-survivors I have examined,[108] five claimed to have been recruited as *chŏngsindae* labor recruits and sent to Japan or China to become comfort women. Only two cases appear to qualify as having been "real" *chŏngsindae*-turned-comfort women. Kang Tŏk-kyŏng (1929–1997) described how she had actually worked as a real *chŏngsindae* before she escaped from the airplane plant in Toyama, Japan. She was soon caught by a military policeman, raped, and delivered to a comfort station. Kang, however, was regarded as an "exceptional" (*yeoejŏk*) case.[109] For one thing, she was the only woman who had completed primary school among the nineteen survivors whose testimonials were published in 1993. Kang stated:

> I was born in Chinju, South Kyŏngsang Province in 1929. My father died when I was young. After my mother remarried, I was physically separated from her, growing up in the household of my maternal grandparents. They were rather well off. In June 1944, when I was enrolled in the first year of the high school section of Yoshino Primary School, I went to Japan as a member of the first group of Women's Volunteer Labor Corps. This happened because my Japanese teacher visited my family and encouraged me to go as *chŏngsindae* by saying that one could "learn and earn money" as well. After the teacher left, I decided to go even though my mother strongly objected to my decision and made a terrible scene, crying and pleading with me.[110]

It is difficult to determine how Kim Ŭn-jin (pseudonym; b. 1932) became a comfort woman after having worked as a *chŏngsindae* at a factory in Toyama Prefecture in 1944.[111] She stated that she was taken to a "whore's den" (*ch'angnyŏgul*) in Aomori Prefecture after American bombers destroyed the Fujikoshi factory in Toyama.

In two other cases the women (Kim Pok-tong and Pak Sun-i) appear to have been fraudulently recruited by procurers who were assisted by local civil servants, including a teacher.[112] Even though Kim Pok-tong (b. 1926) stated that her recruiters urged her mother to send her daughter to the Teishintai in 1941 and that she was forcibly drafted, activist researchers have not classified Kim Pok-tong as a *chŏngsindae* case.[113] Pak Sun-i (b. 1930) was in the sixth grade in August 1944 when she volunteered to go to Japan upon hearing from the teacher at her primary school about an opportunity to study there. Together with two other students from her school, Pak was taken to Toyama Prefecture in Japan, where she became a comfort woman. The fifth case involved a local policeman who coercively mobilized a woman to join the Women's Volunteer Labor Corps in September 1944. Along with about thirty other girls her age "Ms. K" was sent to China, where they separated the girls into different groups. Ms. K and a few other girls were taken to a military camp to labor as comfort women.[114]

No documentary evidence exists that proves the Chŏngsindae were used as comfort women. Nevertheless, some South Korean researchers believe that there must have been good grounds for the widespread perception that Chŏngsindae meant comfort women.[115] Notably, Chung Chin-sung (Chŏng Chin-sŏng), a sociologist of the postcolonial generation and a former corepresentative of the Korean Council, continues to endorse the popular nationalist discourse about the comfort women as abused *chŏngsindae*.[116]

At first, the positions of South Korean activists (such as the Korean Council's founding corepresentatives) may have reflected the depth and strength of lingering suspicions Koreans had about the Chŏngsindae as a formal mechanism for deceptively recruiting comfort women. Nevertheless, nationalist activists' vigorous campaign since the early 1990s also has resulted in solidifying the South Korean popular belief into a virtual historical "fact." One wonders when South Koreans will come to terms with the facts of the historical truth and finally abandon the ethnic nationalist mythology of *wianbu* = *chŏngsindae* that has produced preposterous headlines such as "the Netherlands also had the Chŏngsindae."[117] If South Korean activists and the media are serious about uncovering the truth about the comfort women, as they have long demanded Japan do, it is also important that they self-critically reflect on their unthinking promotion of a comforting nationalist mythology.

Significantly, what is conspicuously absent from South Korean public discourse on the comfort women as *chŏngsindae* is the difference that one's socioeconomic class position made in the wartime mobilization of women for manual and sexual labor. Nearly all women laborers came from the lower classes. There were no elite women "volunteer" groups in which college-educated members of privileged classes participated in the war effort. Almost all of more than two hundred survivors in South Korea who have come out since 1991 and who have officially registered as former military comfort women come from very poor families. Very few of them received any formal education. By contrast, among about 370,000 Korean men "pressed into war duty" (primarily as hard laborers or civilian employees of the military) was an exceptional group of 4,385 young college students who became the Special Student Volunteer Soldiers in 1944.[118] After liberation this group produced prominent members of the political leadership class: one became prime minister, another a cardinal, and others served as professors, ambassadors, or corporate chairmen.[119]

We must note here that the two founding corepresentatives of the Korean Council (Yun Chŏng-ok and Lee Hyo-chae) were the age mates of the surviving comfort women. A major difference between them and the survivors is that they came from urban middle-class families, whose daughters were educated at not only the primary school level but, in some cases, all the way up to the graduate school. It is unnecessary to point out that no family members or classmates of Yun or Lee had served as *chŏngsindae* or as *wianbu*. My interviews with other professional women who came of age during colonial period further underscored the factor of social class in the mobilization of women for manual and sexual labor for imperial Japan's war efforts.

A prominent businesswoman who has actively led and wholeheartedly supported—using her personal funds—the lawsuit filed jointly by former "real" *chŏngsindae* and several comfort women survivors residing in the Pusan area, Kim Mun-suk (b. 1927) has published several books on the topic, including one in Japanese.[120] Kim stated that she never heard any rumors about the abuse of the Chŏngsindae as comfort women during the colonial period. She further stated that the reason many people tried to avoid becoming a Chŏngsindae labor recruit and work at factories producing military supplies was because they feared being killed by enemy bombings that targeted military support facilities. She recalled that after the attack on Pearl Harbor the state and school authorities encouraged the students in her fourth (senior) year class at the elite Kyŏngbuk Girls' High School in Taegu to apply to be military nurses upon graduation. Only one student applied, and she was highly praised as a "patriot"; those who did not were referred to as unpatriotic *hikokumin* ("traitors"; literally, in Japanese, "nonnationals"). At the commencement ceremony, this student was given the honor of being the valedictorian instead of Kim Mun-suk, who, having achieved the highest scholastic record, would traditionally have been accorded the honor. (The "patriotic" nurse applicant, according to Kim Mun-suk, returned safely to her home in Taegu after the war.)

Another case of professional women who came of age during colonial rule concerns Nah Young-gyun (Na Yŏng-gyun; b. 1929). A retired professor and author of the memoir *As to My Family in the Era of Japanese Empire* (*Ilchesidae, Urikajokŭn*), Nah provides numerous interesting descriptions of the "labor service" (*kŭllo pongsa*, in Korean) in which she and her classmates engaged during the last two years of the war.[121] From their third year on at Kyŏnggi Girls' High School in Seoul (in 1944, based on the ordinance for student labor), Nah and her classmates attended class for only two hours each morning; the rest of the day was devoted to flaking off pieces of mica with the tips of sharp knives. According to Nah, the work itself was not difficult, and at first the students enjoyed the release from study and paid no attention to the purpose of their labor—providing the material for manufacturing airplane bodies, according to their teacher's explanation. As the war progressed, however, weekends and vacations disappeared under a new wartime week, starting with "double Mondays" and ending with "double Fridays." Every day Nah and her friends wearily engaged in the same labor service.

My interview with Nah in July 2005 revealed an episode in which one of her classmates, as a form of personal protest against her unfaithful father, volunteered to serve as a *chŏngsindae* and left home. A daughter of a wealthy man, the student found out by accident that her father kept a mistress and that her half sister was attending the same school. Her father had to chase his rebellious daughter all the way to Pusan, where he successfully persuaded her to return home to Seoul.

To be sure, deceptive recruitments under the guise of Chŏngsindae work may have been commonplace. We should remember, however, that the term's usage tended to be limited to women's groups from late 1943 and that it was only after the August 1944 ordinance for women's volunteer labor was promulgated that it seemed to be confined to women mobilized for the war effort.[122] Moreover, colonial period use of the term *chŏngsindae* or *teishintai* in the sense of both manual laborers and comfort women was apparently limited among people with some education.[123] In fact, Kim Yun-sim, an activist-survivor whose testimonial was solicited once again by the KRIC researchers to be preserved on video in December 2004, stated, "I never knew the term *chŏngsindae* until recently."[124] Kil Wŏn-ok (b. 1928), another activist-survivor, observed her terminological ignorance of both *chŏngsindae* and *wianbu:* "I now know because I heard about them, but at the time I never knew what *chŏngsindae* was or what *wianbu* was because I never heard those terms."[125]

Moreover, statistical analyses of the data on 190 cases of surviving Korean comfort women, deriving from a research project sponsored by South Korean Ministry of Gender Equality (Yŏsŏngbu) and published in 2002, showed that less than a quarter (23.2 percent, or 44 cases) had been recruited between 1943 and 1945.[126] The majority of them, 76.8 percent (146), were recruited between 1930 and 1942.[127] This analysis unequivocally reveals that the great majority of Korean survivors could not have been recruited as *chŏngsindae.* Because comfort stations existed almost from the start of the Asia Pacific War and the majority of South Korean survivors became comfort women before 1943, one may seriously question the validity of the South Korean assertion and belief that *all* Korean comfort women were initially recruited as *chŏngsindae* and then taken to military comfort facilities.

More important, one may suggest that the Korean usage of the term *chŏngsindae* to refer to comfort women proved to be a sociopsychologically as well as a politically effective decision on the part of activists in order to highlight the deceptive and/or coercive methods used in the recruitment of Korean comfort women. Furthermore, the term *chŏngsindae* symbolically sets wartime comfort women apart from contemporary *wianbu* satisfying the sexual desires of members of the American military stationed in South Korea. In this sense, the term *chŏngsindae* functions as a South Korean "nationalist euphemism" born out of cultural sensitivity for the survivors: it helps avoid the negative image of prostitutes evoked by the term *wianbu.*

Remarkably, the South Korean conflation of comfort women with *chŏngsindae* is not replicated in the North Korean official discourse, nor does it find a counterpart in Taiwanese public discourse on the subject. North Korean officials have consistently employed the term *chonggun wianbu* (military comfort women) in their strident critique of Japan's colonial wrongdoings. The Taiwanese, who lived under Japanese colonial rule for fifty years (1895–1945), were also drafted into Japan's war efforts with the outbreak of the Second Sino-Japanese War in 1937 under the national mobilization policy. Nevertheless, there has been no mention of the Volunteer Labor Corps in the reports on Taiwanese comfort women survivors. The historian Zhu Delan, an advisory member of the nongovernmental organization Taipei Women's Rescue Foundation—the only organization involved with the comfort women issue in Taiwan—has revealed the patterns of close cooperation among the government, the military, and industry leadership in the construction of comfort stations on Hainan Island during the war. During her interview, Zhu confirmed that no suspicion or rumor exists among the Taiwanese about deceptive recruitment of comfort women as Teishintai, or the Volunteer Labor Corps, there.[128] This, however, is not to say that Taiwan lacks an anti-Japanese nationalist discourse about the comfort women issue; ethnonationalist sentiments seem to run high especially among mainlanders—who had fought against Japan and fled from mainland China after losing their battle against the communists at the end of the civil war—as well as younger generations who do not share older people's benign, even nostalgic, memories of the Japanese colonial period.

Japan's Domestic Cacophony

The question of wartime "forced" recruitment of Korean women as "military comfort women" (*jūgun ianfu,* in Japanese) was first raised formally in the Japanese National Diet in June 1990, after the state visit by South Korean President Roh Tae Woo, whose official inquiry into the matter came about as a result of the demands made by the leaders of South Korean women's organizations. When Motooka Shōji, a Socialist Party member of the upper house of the Japanese Diet, demanded at a budget committee session on June 6, 1990, that government investigate the *jūgun ianfu* issue, the government refused, insisting on its official position of regarding the wartime military comfort station as private enterprise. Angry leaders of South Korean women's organizations sent an open letter to Prime Minister Kaifu Toshiki prior to his visit to South Korea in October 1990 demanding an admission, an apology, and compensation by his government for the sexual enslavement of Korean women. Receiving no response, South Korean leaders of various women's organizations formed the Korean Council as an umbrella organization to handle the comfort women issue in November 1990. In April 1991 the Japanese government replied to the Korean open letter that there was no evidence of forced drafting of Korean women as comfort women and therefore no question of any apology. Tokyo's denial of the wartime state's involvement in the military comfort system stopped finally, and promptly, after the January 11, 1992, *Asahi Shimbun* report on Yoshimi's discovery of official documents supporting the charge against Japan.[129]

Since then, public discourse on the issue as a war crime has increased in Japan. The *Asahi Shimbun* report also prompted the active participation of a number of human rights lawyers, progressive historians, and public intellectuals in dealing with the issue as part of Japan's postwar responsibility. The progressive leaders of civil society felt dismayed when the Japanese government tried to put an end to the comfort women issue by stating that it would do "something in lieu of compensation" by the end of 1992 and that there was "no evidence found that proved" coercion by the wartime state or the military in the recruitment of the comfort women. They pointed out that non-Japanese victims of the Asia Pacific War included not only comfort women but also numerous victims of other war crimes and crimes against humanity committed by Japan. They objected to their government's attempt to make temporary "political settlements" to war victims and argued that "the government and the National Diet need to be pressured into finding the truth regarding foreign war victims and to start a thorough examination of war compensation based on their findings."[130]

Concerned historians and lawyers then formed an executive committee in September 1992 to hold the International Public Hearing Concerning Japan's Postwar Compensation (Nihon no Sengo Hoshō ni Kansuru Kokusai Kōchōkai; International Public Hearing, hereafter) in Tokyo on December 9, 1992. Comfort women survivors and victims of forced manual labor in Japanese mines in Sakhalin and of prisoner-of-war camps in Southeast Asia traveled to Tokyo (from North Korea, South Korea, the Philippines, the People's Republic of China, Taiwan, and the Netherlands) and testified onstage, recounting their stories in great detail. As the only non-Asian woman, Ruff-O'Herne, for example, gave her testimonial narrative by reading a prepared text, which moved many participants to tears when she vividly described the fear and humiliation she experienced and the desperate resistance she put up against Japanese military officers, to no avail, at the comfort station in Semarang. In closing, she stated, "It was my deep Faith in God that helped me survive all that I suffered at the brutal, savage hands of the Japanese. I have forgiven the Japanese for what they did to me, but I can never forget."[131] (Since then her contribution to globalizing the comfort women issue has been immeasurably huge, actively supporting the Korean comfort women redress movement. During my interview in The Hague in 2001, she stated with a smile that some Korean activists have called her their white "angel.")

The executive committee also invited a delegation of legal experts from foreign countries such as the Netherlands, Canada, the United States, and South Korea, as well as the Japanese human rights lawyer Totsuka Etsurō and historian Yoshimi Yoshiaki, to participate in the International Public Hearing. The experts' analysis of survivors' life stories deployed the language of international law and human rights. The historic significance of the International Public Hearing lies in the momentum it helped generate in ushering in what may be called "the era of the survivor" that constructed the new transnational paradigmatic story of Japan's comfort women.

After the event the executive committee established the Center for Re-

Plate 1.6. Jan Ruff-O'Herne in the Hague, 2001, wearing a medal awarded for her human rights activism by the Dutch government. (Photo by the author.)

search and Documentation on Japan's War Responsibility (JWRC, hereafter) to continue fact-finding research and to support the redress movement. The JWRC received the ICJ mission in April and released its first research report on the comfort women issue on June 26, 1993, which it submitted to the government in July. In a press release the JWRC proclaimed that its research report served as "one factor" in Tokyo's acknowledgment of the forced nature of the mobilization of comfort women in the Kōno Statement issued on August 4, 1993.[132] The JWRC also submitted its research reports to the United Nations Commission on Human Rights (UNCHR) in March and May 1994 and supplied "crucial" information on the comfort women issue to the U.N. special rapporteur, "contributing to the Coomaraswamy Report," which recommended, among other things, state compensation for the survivors.[133] The JWRC established a committee to collect a petition in support of the Coomaraswamy Report in February 1996.

The progressives appeared to hold sway in the domestic public debate in defining the comfort women issue and Japan's postwar responsibility toward comfort women from January 1992 to mid-1996, apparently because conservatives regarded the comfort women redress activism through a small number of nongovernmental organizations as "noise" that over time would fade away. Totsuka Etsurō, who first reported on the comfort women issue to the United Nations in February 1992, noted that the bureaucrats in the Japanese government were misinformed about the concern of the UNCHR for the comfort women issue. They thought that "only a small number of nongovernmental organizations are involved. Things will quiet down sooner or later."[134] The Coomaraswamy Report submitted to the United Nations in January 1996, however, set off an urgent wakeup call to Japan's conservatives.

In particular, the mention of comfort women in new history textbooks for the middle school, which reflects one of the United Nations' recommendations, sparked a strong wave of masculinist neonationalism across the country in 1996, resulting in what the feminist historian and activist Suzuki Yūko (b. 1949) called an "anti–comfort women campaign."[135] Senior politicians, prominent journalists, and public intellectuals, including university professors, have joined forces to argue that the comfort women were nothing more than licensed prostitutes and that there is no evidence of their forced recruitment by the state or the military. At a Tokyo press conference on June 5, 1996, Okuno Seisuke, a former justice minister and a senior member of the ruling Liberal Democratic Party, said that foreign women had volunteered to be sent to the Japanese troops and did it as a "commercial activity" for money. He added, "The Japanese Army may have arranged the transportation for them to go to the war-fronts for their work, but it didn't force them to go."[136] Since mid-1996 the cartoonist and social critic Kobayashi Yoshinori has published best-selling cartoon books that have influenced many young Japanese—such as Kakichi Shinji, mentioned in the acknowledgments—to see the comfort women as participating in a commercial activity (shōkōi).[137] Kobayashi then joined, as a founding member, the Society for History Textbook Reform (Atarashii Rekishi Kyōkasho o Tsukuru Kai; hereafter, Tsukuru Kai) in December 1996. The production of a new history book by Tsukuru Kai generated another international controversy over Japanese history and public memory of the Asia Pacific War in 2001.[138]

The comfort women debate heated up again in Japan after Mike Honda, a Democratic congressman from California, submitted to the House Committee on Foreign Relations a nonbinding resolution calling on the government of Japan to formally apologize and accept historical responsibility "in a clear and unequivocal manner for its Imperial Armed Forces' coercion of young women into sexual slavery" (HR 121) on January 31, 2007. The

House Subcommittee on Asia, the Pacific, and the Global Environment subsequently held a public hearing at which three former comfort women (two South Korean and one Dutch-born Australian) gave testimonies on February 15. The stories of the three individual survivors clearly illustrated the range of recruitment methods. One Korean woman (Yi Yong-su) was deceptively recruited by the Japanese proprietor of a military brothel in Taiwan. The other Korean woman (Kim Kun-ja) was "sold" to a trafficker by her foster father. The Dutch-born woman (Jan O'Herne) was forcibly mobilized into prostitution by the military but was returned after about two months on orders from headquarters (as discussed earlier).

When the Japanese Prime Minister Abe Shinzō denied the "coercive" recruitment of comfort women by the Japanese military at a press conference on March 1, 2007, the world media reacted swiftly and critically. In Japan, however, the conservative newspapers *Yomiuri* and *Sankei* did not cover the comfort women issue much, whereas the March 6 *Asahi* and March 8 *Mainichi* carried, respectively, editorials entitled "Refrain from Comments That Invite Misunderstandings" and "Kōno Statement Must Stand."[139] By contrast, Sakurai Yoshiko, a nationally known former television news anchor and current freelance journalist, resolutely critiqued both the 1993 Japanese government statement announced by the chief cabinet secretary, Kōno Yōhei (known as the Kōno Statement) and American media such as the *New York Times* and the *Washington Post* for distorting the truth about the comfort women. Sakurai, who had interviewed Kōno previously, stated that the Japanese government had bowed to South Korean pressure to acknowledge the forcible recruitment of wartime comfort women based solely on hearings involving sixteen South Korean survivors, who were not questioned and who presented no documentary evidence. Referring to the sudden closure of the Semarang military brothels, Sakurai argued that the case of the former Dutch comfort women, in effect, serves as "counterproof" against the accusation that the Japanese military "coercively" recruited women for comfort stations.[140] Historian Hata Ikuhiko also notes that the comfort women issue is "a political problem raised by forces (both domestic and foreign) with multiple, diverse agendas" and that "the absence of bloodshed notwithstanding, the facts have been shoved aside."[141] Hata wished that his fellow countrymen would break the postwar habit of "apologizing or shrugging when criticized" and stand up to "issue a rejoinder to an unjust accusation."[142]

*   *   *

A fundamental fault line in Japanese society, I suggest, originates with the self-critical progressive versus ethnocentric conservative interpretations of Japan's modern history as an empire that colonized neighboring countries and waged war against China and the United States. More than one and one half decades after Yoshimi's "bombshell" (to use Hata's term) compelled Tokyo to acknowledge and apologize for the comfort women issue,[143] polarized Japanese society continues its cacophonous reactions to the newly constructed and globally dominant paradigmatic story of the comfort women as military sexual slavery and a war crime. Japanese progressives (represented by the founders and members of the JWRC and human rights lawyers such as Takagi and Totsuka) believe that their embrace of the globalizing human rights culture and their active advocacy for the comfort women and other victims of the Asia Pacific War will contribute to the creation of a new, peaceful world order, which in turn will enhance the moral status of Japan in the international community. Conservatives (represented by the proponents and members of Tsukuru Kai and ruling party politicians such as Okuno Seisuke), however, find it hard to accept the charges that Japan was the aggressor in World War II and that the comfort system was anything other than a form of licensed prostitution. Japan lobbied hard against Honda's "comfort women resolution," placing a full-page paid public comment entitled "The Facts" in the June 14, 2007, issue of the *Washington Post*. The comment stated that another advertisement, "The Truth about Comfort Women," which had appeared in the *Washington Post* in April 2007, made claims that were not factual but "the products of 'faith.'" The five facts presented in the public comment reflected the Japanese conservative nationalist perspective on the comfort women issue. Supporters of the advertisement included Diet members, professors, political commentators, and journalists, including Sakurai Yoshiko.

This assertive action on the part of prominent conservative leaders of Japan backfired.[144] The U.S. House of Representatives unanimously approved the resolution on the comfort women in July 2007, calling on Japan to formally apologize and take responsibility unequivocally for its wartime sex slavery, thereby "irritating" Prime Minister Abe and other nationalist conservatives.[145] Thanks to a concerted campaign mounted by the Korean Council and its international supporters such as Amnesty International, by November similar resolutions had passed in the lower houses of the national legislatures of the Netherlands and Canada. These legislative actions were followed in December 2007 by similar ones in the European Parliament (Resolution B60525/2007).[146]

THE POLITICAL SYMBOLISM OF NAMES

In the context of identity politics that surrounds the comfort women issue, the dynamics of naming the women and the resultant multiple designations for them may appear obvious, but their underlying meanings at times are more subtle and complex than has been assumed. Particular designations are crucial if an interested party is to frame the comfort women issue to its own political advantage. Hence it is imperative that we examine both the political connotations and the sociolinguistic denotations of key official and popular terms that have been used in postwar Japan, South Korea, and elsewhere in reference to both wartime comfort women and today's elderly survivors.

From "Comfort Girls" to "Comfort Women"

Since the issue was internationalized, "comfort women" has become the standard English translation of the Japanese euphemism *ianfu*. Previously, however, Dutch- and English-speaking soldiers and writers alike had translated the term as "comfort girls." In fact, the Dutch term *troostmeisje* (*troost* for comfort and *meisje* for girl) has been coined to refer to the women forced into prostitution for the Japanese military, whereas the Dutch call other women sex workers *prostitué* or *hoer,* both of which are much more degrading terms.[147] The 1978 English translation of the Japanese historian Ienaga Saburō's work stated that prostitutes for the military were euphemistically called "comfort girls."[148] "Comfort women" may generally sound more respectful than "comfort girls," although the latter is more accurate in the cases of many teenage *ianfu*. Notably, a Korean sociologist translated the euphemism as "comfort lady" in his 1996 work on colonial Korea.[149]

Analysis of the compound term *ian-fu/wian-bu* (Japanese/Korean) reveals that it reflects the views of a paternalistic state. It referred to an adult female (*fu/bu*) who provided sexual services to "comfort and entertain" (*ian/wian*) the warrior, affording him rest and relaxation and thereby boosting his morale, which in turn enables him to fight fiercely in order to win the "sacred war." Ironically, Korean government of the Chosŏn Dynasty (1392–1910) had the same masculinist rationale for providing "comfort women" (*wianbu*) for its troops as did wartime imperial Japan.[150]

The state and military of wartime Japan also used other terms, such as *shakufu* (sake pourer, or waitress) and *tokushu* (special) *ianfu* to refer to the comfort women,[151] and the comfort women who served the navy in Palau, as noted in the life story of Shirota Suzuko, or Yoshie-san (see chapter 6), were referred to as "special personnel" (*tokuyōin,* in Japanese). Neither the wartime government nor the military appears to have used the term "military comfort women" (*jūgun ianfu*), however, even though this term has come into common use in the public discourse on the subject in postwar Japan.

"Military Comfort Women"

In postwar Japan, the term *jūgun ianfu* (comfort women who followed or accompanied the troops) appears to have prevailed over the unmodified euphemism *ianfu,* the official wartime lingo. Some researchers suggest that the term came into common usage after Senda Kakō (b. 1924) published a book entitled *Jūgun Ianfu* in 1973,[152] although a reference in Kim Il-myŏn's book reveals that the term was used in the title of a 1971 article.[153]

Advocates of the redress movement in Japan and Korea, however, have become sensitized to the connotations of the term *jūgun,* giving the impression that comfort women were *voluntary* camp followers. Accordingly, they have come up with alternative terms such as *Nihongun* and *Ilbon'gun* (Japanese military, in Japanese and Korean, respectively). The English translation of *jūgun ianfu* as "military comfort women" loses the connotation of "following" (*jū* in Japanese, *chong* in Korean) the military (*gun*) owing to one's occupation (such as a nurse, journalist, photographer, clergy, and so on). Some Korean women—such as Kim Hak-sun and others—who served front-line soldiers in remote battlefields were indeed forced to *jūgun/chonggun,* or "follow" the movements of military units, whereas those who labored in settled and/or urban areas such as Shanghai and Singapore had no need to do so.

Ironically, it is not only comfort women supporters in Japan and Korea but also ultranationalist critics of the comfort women redress movement that are opposed to attaching the term *jūgun* to Japan's wartime *ianfu.* The right-wing objection to the term *jūgun ianfu* is twofold: whereas this term implies *official* affiliation with the military, the term was not used, nor did it even exist, during the Asia Pacific War. It is a postwar neologism that clearly implicates the close connection between the military and the comfort women, which is one reason Japanese neonationalists object to its usage in reference to wartime comfort women.

By contrast, the official South Korean term for comfort women, used in the Government Interim Report of July 1992, is "military comfort women under Imperial Japan" (*ilcheha kundae wianbu*). Like *chonggun wianbu,* discussed here, *kundae wianbu* is translated as "military comfort women" in English. However, *kundae* refers to the military as a category, without the connotation of voluntarily "following" the military as in *chonggun*. Also, the official phrase (*ilcheha kundae wianbu*) unequivocally denotes the wartime *wianbu* who serviced the Japanese imperial forces. This clarification is sociopsychologically as well as politically significant because it describes comfort women survivors as victims of Imperial Japan, thereby placing responsibility for them on the Japanese government and also clearly differentiating them from postliberation South Korean *wianbu* laboring in camp towns for the U.S. troops.[154]

We should note here the additional connotation of "obedience" in the characters for *jū/chong* in *jūgun/chonggun* (in Japanese/Korean). When the sociolinguistic force of this term *jū/chong* overlaps with imperial Japan's mandate for the 1944 ordinance for the Women Volunteer Labor Corps, for instance, the specter of the modern nation-state's new powerful claim to women's obedience to the nation-state looms metalinguistically. Traditionally, the rule of "three obediences" applied to females throughout their lives within the context of the patriarchal family structure: obedience to the father as a daughter, obedience to the husband as a wife, and obedience to the son as a widow.

What is notable about the new "nationalization of women" in wartime Japan is that women as gendered subjects of the empire were expected to differentially enact this new extrafamilial, "fourth rule of obedience" in accordance with their ethnicity, marital status, and personal location in the social and economic class structure.[155] "For the good of the country" (a country that under fascistic military leadership was bent on territorial expansions through wars of aggression), females—from as young as twelve to thirty-nine years of age—of the Japanese empire were exhorted to voluntarily join the women's labor corps for factory work, whereas other unmarried, nubile ones, primarily from indigent families in colonies, were coaxed into providing sexual services to soldiers so as to help raise their morale and win the war. As noted earlier, however, no married women from middle-class families regardless of their ethnicity were expected to work outside the home; rather, they were encouraged to help strengthen the manpower of the nation by giving birth to as many children as possible.

"Sex Slaves," Not "Comfort Women"

As the internationalization of the redress movement has progressed, some South Korean survivors and their advocates have felt compelled to declare that they were not "comfort women," especially after Ruff-O'Herne's forceful criticism. She strongly condemned the media's use of Japan's euphemism "comfort women," declaring it "an insult." She insisted that she and fellow surviving women were "war-rape victims, enslaved and conscripted by the Japanese Imperial Army."[156] Victim-survivors in other Asian countries have also voiced their objections to the Japanese euphemism. A 1997 book that presented a collection of non-Japanese survivors' testimonies, for example, was entitled *I Am Not a Comfort Woman* (*Watashi wa Ianfu Dewanai*, in Japanese). When *War Responsibility That Japan Does Not Know* (*Nihon ga Shiranai Sensō Sekinin*, in Japanese), written by Totsuka Etsurō, was translated, the Korean title became *[They Are] Not "Comfort Women" but "Sex Slaves"* (*"Wianbu" ga Anira "Sŏng Noye" Ida*, in Korean).

Though some survivors have chosen to use the term "sex slaves," others apparently are uneasy about its degrading connotation and dislike it as well. Psycholinguistic sensitivity to the problematic aspect of the different designations has led a Dutch nongovernmental organization representative to eschew the use of either "comfort women" or "sex slaves" when speaking in public. Instead, she refers to survivors as "victims of forced prostitution."[157]

It is of some interest that the English name of the activist nongovernmental Korean Council for Women Drafted for Military Sexual Slavery by Japan initially contained the term "sexual service," not "sexual slavery." When Lee Hyo-chae sent a petition dated March 4, 1992, to the U.N. Commissioner on Human Rights, the letterhead of the petition identified her as a corepresentative of the Korean Council for Women Drafted for Sexual *Service* (emphasis added) for Japan, even though she uses the term "slave" in the text.[158] In fact, Kim Il-myŏn had already described Korean comfort women as "sex slaves" (*sekkusu no dorei*) in his 1976 book on the topic.[159] Nonetheless, the categorical representation of comfort women as "sex slaves," and the term's international acceptance and common usage, would emerge only in the 1990s in the post–cold war world politics of human rights.

From "Virgins" to Non-kin "Grandmothers"

The general public in South Korea, whose singular image of Korean comfort women is firmly fixed as a "virgin" mobilized coercively or deceptively as a labor recruit *chŏngsindae*, initially reacted negatively to the use of the term "sex slave" (*sŏng noye*, in Korean translation) in reference to surviving comfort women because the image of their being in abject slavery was hurtful to their self-esteem. For example, a Korean graduate student in history, who regards the English term "sex slave" as "not so good," posed a critical question concerning the usage of the term. It was included in an English-language pamphlet produced by visiting Japanese students at a meeting in Seoul on September 26, 1998, which was attended by eleven students and three professors of Tongguk University, a Buddhist-funded institution.

There they exchanged views on topics of mutual interest with nine Japanese students visiting from Dōshisha University led by Asano Ken'ichi, a Dōshisha professor of journalism. One Japanese student who produced the pamphlet defended her use of the term "sex slave" by saying that the term "military comfort women" connotes voluntary commercial activity and does not reflect reality. Asano Ken'ichi, who took his seminar students to Nanum ŭi Chip (House of Sharing, a Buddhist-supported shelter for South Korean comfort women survivors located in the outskirts of Seoul) to meet with several residents there the following day so they could learn about Japan's war responsibility by listening to the stories of Korean survivors,[160] supported his student's argument and pointed out that "sex slave" is the new designation for the comfort women that the United Nations has endorsed.[161]

The sociolinguistic sensitivity to the term "comfort women," which conjures up the image of prostitutes, has also forced advocates to search for a respectful way to refer to and address the survivors. As a result, South Koreans have adopted the term *halmŏni,* or "grandmother." They address the survivors as "grandmother" and make a collective reference to them as *chŏngsindae halmŏni* or *wianbu halmŏni.* Conventionally, Koreans use fictive kin terms such as "uncle," "aunt," "grandfather," and "grandmother" as a polite form of addressing strangers in accordance with relative ages of the actors involved and their gender differences. The Korean usage of the term *halmŏni* to refer to the comfort women with respect has influenced Filipino and Taiwan activists to adopt a similar linguistic convention. As a result, they use the terms *lola* and *ama* as the Filipino and Taiwanese counterparts of the Korean term *halmŏni,* respectively.

In contrast to the widespread public use of *halmŏni,* which denotes a two-generation age difference from the speaker, Sŏ Kyŏng-sik, a second-generation male *zainichi* (Korean resident in Japan) writer, has used the term *ŏmŏni* (mother) to express his respect and sympathy to surviving comfort women.[162] By contrast, Kim-Gibson, a Korean American filmmaker and author, declares that she calls her research subjects—Korean comfort women—"grandmas" because she feels "as if they are [her] own grandmas,"[163] which, nevertheless, disregards the generational strata: the survivors are basically of the same generation as her own mother, some being even a few years younger.

It is interesting to note that Yamazaki Tomoko, Japanese author of the nonfiction bestseller *Sandakan Hachiban Shōkan (Sandakan Brothel No. 8),* wrote that once she had come to know a former "overseas prostitute" (*karayuki-san*) named Osaki[164]—during her research stay at the latter's home in Amakusa, Kyūshū. In the course of the subsequent four-year exchange of letters with her, Yamazaki came to call Osaki-san "'Mother' from the depths of [her] heart."[165] Arguably, it makes good sense for Yamazaki and other middle-aged persons to identify surviving comfort woman and/or *karayuki-san* as "mother": in their cases "mother" more accurately reflects the generational distance between speaker and addressee than does "grandmother."[166]

In my observations of South Korean discourse on comfort women survivors for over a decade, I have noted that many people comfortably prefix the term *halmŏni* with the term *chŏngsindae,* but not with *wianbu.* When referring to comfort women survivors, a majority of South Koreans seems to prefer *chŏngsindae halmŏni* to *wianbu halmŏni* because of the connotation of prostitution in the term *wianbu.* This discursive practice, I suggest, embodies the Korean Council's successful political strategy to represent comfort women as forcibly recruited *chŏngsindae*—a highly debatable assertion and far from the factual truth disclosed in South Korean survivors' testimonials. It seems to me that the Korean government's official term, *ilcheha kundae wianbu* (Imperial Japan's military comfort women), or, more simply, *ilbon'gun wianbu* (Japanese military comfort women), may formally represent Korean comfort women as a social category of the particular historical cohort. In personal and private interactions with survivors, South Koreans might like to use either of the two fictive kinship terms, *halmŏni* or *ŏmŏni,* depending on the speaker's own feelings and perceived generational distance from the one spoken of. When writing or talking about comfort women survivors individually, however, perhaps one should use their full names followed by the honorific suffix *-ssi* or *-nim.*

*   *   *

We might remember here that at comfort stations, many Korean women had to adopt new Japanese names, thereby losing the Korean names that had constituted an important part of their personal identities. Perhaps it is high time South Koreans helped them reclaim their personal names for individual identification in their everyday life—a fundamental human right that most of us take for granted. In this regard I note with interest what Yi Yong-su—the survivor whose recollections of the red dress and her journey to a comfort station in Taiwan I have described earlier—is reported to have said to the audience gathered at Harvard University to hear her story in April 2007. According to the news report, "Yi Yong-su *halmŏni*" said, "The

Japanese called me *wianbu*, but my name is Yi Yong-su, which my parents had given me."[167] (Her published testimonial says that she was known as "Toshiko," a Japanese name given her by a Japanese soldier soon after her arrival at a military brothel in Taiwan.)[168]

Here I should also observe the curious nonuse, or rather, the conscious avoidance of the use, of the term *halmŏni* as a polite term for some women who are of the same age cohort as the survivors. Why, for example, do South Korean supporters of the comfort women movement never address Yun Chŏng-ok or Lee Hyo-chae, the founding corepresentatives of the Korean Council and retired professors, as *halmŏni,* even though they are of the same generation as surviving comfort women, whereas the latter are routinely called *halmŏni?* The fictive kin term *halmŏni,* while meant to be polite among strangers, is also perceived to be both awkward and inappropriate, if not downright insulting, when used to address older professional women with a high social status. Neither the survivors nor their advocates, therefore, would consider addressing or referring to Yun and Lee as *halmŏni.* Instead, they invariably address the two leaders either as *kyosu-nim* or *sŏnsaeng-nim,* attaching the honorary suffix *-nim* to their professional title *kyosu* (professor) or to the more generic term *sŏnsaeng* (used for teachers or social elders). The different address terms used, respectively, for comfort women survivors and the Korean Council representatives (even though they are of the same age cohort) functions as paralingual markers that symbolically distinguish and reconfirm the inequality in social status between the two categories of older women.

From the perspectives of gender, sexuality, and personhood, the indiscriminate usage of fictive kin term *halmŏni* for the survivors is problematic. A major underlying issue in the comfort women debate is the privileged status of men and their customary right to indulge in public sex, in paradoxical contrast to the social stigmatization to which women sex workers are subjected for serving men's carnal desires. What the common usage of the fictive kinship term "grandmother" for comfort women survivors achieves paralinguistically is their social relocation and reclassification into gendered but sexually inactive beings, highlighting their current status of being twice removed generationally from the period of ordeals that their bodies—cast as sexual commodities—endured during their adolescence and/or young adulthood. The cultural symbolism of the term "grandmother" conveniently erases the actual feminine sexuality of former comfort women, whose suffering was rooted in the very exploitation and violation of their youthful sexual bodies. Their personal identity as individuals, which had been obliterated under the euphemism *ianfu,* is once again masked under the term *halmŏni,* albeit with the good intention of expressing respect. Names classify and individuate and, as such, function as important tools for expressing one's personhood. As anthropologists have reported, however, in some societies (such as traditional China as well as Korea) women essentially lose their names when they marry and become known (in reference and address) by a series of kinship terms, teknonyms, or category terms such as "old person" (*noin,* in Korean).[169] Women in such societies recede into general anonymity when they marry.

The collective appellation of survivors as *chŏngsindae halmŏni* likewise obscures their individual personhood. Use of this term ignores their diverse social backgrounds prior to their mobilization as comfort women, and their disparate postwar life stories. As Kandice Chuh has thoughtfully noted, we need to recognize the "gross inadequacy" of any term of identity—be it "comfort woman" or "grandmother"—to "account for the lives of the people referenced by it." Such acknowledgment of the limitation of representation might help us "offer a kind of justice" to these individual survivors by "critically recognizing their irreducibly complex personhood."[170] Feminist projects should help rescue them not only from a gendered anonymity and sociological marginality but also from an activist collectivism.

We ought to also become sensitized to the connoted desexualization as one of the insidious effects of ageism—especially for women—in our conventional usage of the fictive kin terms such as "grandmother" and "grandfather" to address mature adult strangers. I remember clearly how taken aback I was, albeit pleasantly, when I saw the picture of one South Korean survivor shown to me in New York City in March 1999 when I interviewed her Korean American activist attorney (John Kim) about her case. The survivor, who immigrated to the United States at the invitation of her sister and was suffering from poor health by the time of my request for an interview, in the photo was youthful and refined in appearance, wearing a stylish pair of eyeglasses. Having become accustomed to the South Korean practice of referring to a survivor as "grandmother" by then, I had not imagined her to be an attractive, fashionable middle-aged woman. The picture delivered a refreshing jolt to my mind that had stereotypically expected to see an elderly woman wearing an angry or mournful expression on her deeply wrinkled face, as has been often the case with the published photos of a number of comfort women survivors, especially those that are posted on the home pages of the Internet sites of advocacy organizations such as KRIC and the Korean Council.

CONCLUSION

For the ideological combatants, rendering dominant in the public discourse their own representational version of the comfort women is crucial, not only to achieve legal victories but also for the social, cultural, and sexual dimensions of their national identity and survivor's individual self-concept. Both legal battles over Japan's postwar responsibility and the culture war between masculinist sexism and human rights feminism carry symbolic implications for a variety of other issues, such as the international image of Japan, the social meaning of the sufferings endured by survivors in several patriarchal nation-states in Asia, and the political agenda of promoting the feminist humanitarian perspective in order to help protect women from sexual violence, in war and at home, all over the world. It is to the credit of the Korean Council and their international allies (including the novelists) that advocates' decontextualized, transnational version has emerged as the "paradigmatic story," overriding the competing symbolic representations of the comfort women in the world community such as the United Nations.

Of the four ideologies I have discussed as undergirding the symbolic representations of the comfort women, the fascistic paternalism of wartime Japan and the masculinist sexism of the troops derive from the same roots of masculinist sexual culture, with its long history of licensed prostitution. Their customary Janus-faced discursive practices have dealt with the comfort women by means of public formalism (coining euphemisms such as *ianfu* to refer to the women) and private informalism (objectifying the women as the *pi*). In contrast, contemporary feminist humanitarian discourse belongs to the post-Holocaust human rights culture in general, and to an emergent post–cold war culture of women's rights as human rights in particular. In addition, mutually hostile ethnic nationalist discourses (of the perpetrator nation versus the afflicted) reveal the stakes involved in the ongoing transnational social movement for comfort women survivors, especially in the case of Japan against Korea as its former colony. The political symbolism of the variety of the terms used to refer to the comfort women in the Japanese and Korean languages, which I have analyzed in this chapter, underscores the significance of both individual and collective social psychology in dealing with the gross social injustice inflicted on young women of colonial Korea whose suffering was embedded in the context of particular sexual cultures and everyday violence practiced in the context of the entangled historical relationship of the disparity in political and economic power between Korea and Japan.

Chapter 2

Korean Survivors' Testimonial Narratives

Since it was my *han* for a lack of education that made me leave home, I urged in my letter that my parents do everything in their power to send my younger siblings to school.

—Mun P'il-gi, a comfort woman survivor, 1993

NOW THAT THE SUFFERINGS of comfort women survivors as a social and historical category have been established in various ways, including the publications of their "testimonial narratives," in order to better understand the social, cultural, psychological, and economic forces that shaped the circumstances of individual Korean survivors prior to their recruitment we can, and should, direct our attention to their individual testimonial narratives. I use the term "testimonial narratives" (*testimonio*),[1] rather than the more legalistic "testimonies," to refer to survivors' published personal accounts, which anthropologists would call "life stories." Whereas South Korean public discourse of comfort women as Japan's war crime has been crucial to the success of the redress movement both domestically and internationally, it has had the unfortunate effect of silencing, or at least ignoring, subaltern voices of the women as historical actors, which might compromise postcolonial Korean nationalist discourse.

Significantly, a number of the testimonial narratives of individual survivors, for example, unexpectedly reveal their strikingly proactive personal responses to the expanding public sphere in modernizing Korea and the Japanese Empire. What then motivated Kang Tŏk-kyŏng, Mun P'il-gi, Yi Sun-ok, and Yi Yong-su, to name a few survivors, to behave the way they did when they decided to leave home? Readers may recall that Kang Tŏk-kyŏng left home to become *chŏngsindae* over her mother's tearful objection. Yi Sun-ok persuaded her parents to let her go with the recruiter. Mun P'il-gi and Yi Yong-su left home promptly, without their parents' knowledge, when a friend and/or the recruiter came calling. It is important for us to acknowledge and understand the unprecedented pattern of independent decision-making and risk-taking behaviors found among the survivors when they were still young unmarried women in colonial Korea.

The life stories I present in this chapter will focus on the formative years, before their recruitment, of several relatively well-known survivors. (Individual recollections of life at comfort stations and idiosyncratic personal stories as comfort women will be discussed in chapters 3 and 5.) The Korean survivors' testimonial narratives analyzed below show how the intersection of gender, class, and labor in the colonial capitalist system that commodified and exploited working women resulted in the confluence of forces that produced, and victimized, young women who, as aspiring youthful subjects, chose to boldly pursue financial independence and individual autonomy with intention of crafting modern gendered selves.[2]

DAUGHTERS' *HAN* NARRATIVES

The contemporary South Korean mass media often characterize the lives of surviving comfort women by stock phrases such as "a life filled with much *han*" (*han manŭn salm*) or "a life knotted (or bound) in *han*" (*han maetch'in salm*). These clichés are a conventional Korean mode of telling stories of hard, unfulfilled lives. "The closing of a life knotted in *han*" (*han maetch'in salm magam*), for example, was the headline of a national daily that reported the death of Kim Hak-sun in 1997.[3] It is not surprising, then, that the survivors themselves frequently use the term *han* in their testimonial narratives and everyday personal accounts to tell their life stories, as exemplified in Mun P'il-gi's statement quoted in the epigraph of this chapter.

In the Korean ethnopsychological imagination, *han* takes the form of a painful, invisible knot that an individual carries in her heart over a long period of time, made of a complex of undesirable emotions and sentiments such as sadness, regret, anger, remorse, and resignation. In the Korean language, *han* has several homonyms, whose distinct meanings may be represented by different Chinese characters.[4] The concept of *han* is not unique to Korean language and culture; it is represented in the languages of China, Korea, and Japan by the same Chinese ideograph. Nevertheless, the socially constructed meaning and linguistic usages of the term appear incomparably prominent in the Korean culture and society in terms of the psychological weight, the frequency of use, and the richness of the emotional vocabulary containing the concept.

The feelings of *han* permeate the survivors' narratives, but there is no single word in English that can adequately convey its complex meaning. Even though the concept of *han* is a key emotional term widely used by Koreans, it has until recently received scant scholarly attention.[5] Researchers dealing with Korean culture and society have translated *han* variously as "unrequited resentments," "bitterness and anger," and *ressentiment.*[6] *Han* is widely recognized as a major affective characteristic that many Koreans are said to harbor not only as individual actors but also as members of the Korean nation (*Han minjok*). One might say that *han* constitutes a core characteristic of the traditional Korean *habitus,*[7] formed through its long history of suffering numerous foreign invasions, seasonal famines, and social discrimination (justified by the hierarchical status system, including slavery under autocratic dynastic rulers) in the premodern, monarchical systems, as well as in the tumultuous twentieth-century political upheavals that resulted in the division of the country.[8]

The *han* complex may be formed through subjective experiences of social injustice, unfulfilled aspirations, and/or tragic misfortune.[9] A variety of social and/or psychological causal factors can generate the feeling of *han* in the mind of a subject. Once generated, *han* is usually suppressed over a long period of time, developing into a complex of many negative psychopathological feelings. Because those afflicted with it typically lack the social resources and political power to resolve or remove its cause, *han* generally tends to fester.

Specifically, gender, class, and sexuality have been regarded as the major factors that generate *han* in individuals. Thus, more women than men, and more poor people than rich, tend to suffer from this complex;[10] traditionally, people have also believed that it afflicts the souls of young men and women who died before being able to consummate a marriage.[11] The women's literature of the Chosŏn dynasty (1392–1910), for example, is replete with the themes and emotional undercurrents of *han* felt by women as they suffered through their duty-bound, constricted lives as mothers, daughters-in-law, concubines, and/or widows.[12]

By comparison, the *han*-filled testimonials of some surviving comfort women show paradoxically how, in the historical context of modern Korea, their negative and painful *han* complex, in part, derives from women's exercising agency as youthful risk takers. That is, their stubborn resistance against domestic oppression and their eventual active pursuit of personal emancipation in the larger world signaled their determination to forestall the lifelong *han* that earlier generations of women had suffered, with no recourse to remedy. To their crushing chagrin and bitter sorrow, however, the consequences of such valiant efforts would practically destroy their chances for fulfilling personal aspirations to become New Women.

The life story of Mun P'il-gi provides a clear example of an exercise of personal agency leading unexpectedly to tragedy. I first met her on a wintry Wednesday in January 1995 during a weekly protest rally held in front of the Japanese embassy in Seoul.[13] A small, frail-looking woman with a courteous demeanor and gentle smile, Mun had labored at a military brothel in Manchuria for two years starting in late 1943; she had formally registered as an ex–comfort woman in June 1992. I present below a portion of her *han*-filled testimonial narrative, which examines her family life during her childhood in a harsh light and at the same time places her reasons for running away from home in soft focus.[14]

Mun P'il-gi and Her Daughterly *Han*

I was born in 1925 into a small shopkeeper family with two boys and nine girls. Three of the girls died when they were very young, and the older of the two boys was a half brother born of my father's concubine. My mother, who had suffered my father's anger for not producing a son, finally gave birth to a boy when she was forty-one. During my childhood I was called Miyoko [Japanese female name]. The one thing that stands out about my childhood memories is my fervent desire to go to school and study. My father, however, was adamantly opposed to the idea of a girl studying, saying that educated girls turn into "foxes."[15] When I was nine years old, my mother secretly sold a bag of rice to provide tuition for my enrollment at a primary school. My father found out within a week that I was attending school despite his injunction. He dragged me out of the classroom and burned all my books. His anger did not subside with that. He beat me severely and threw me out of the house. I had to take refuge at my uncle's for a while. I was allowed to return home only after I promised that I would never go to school again.

I harbored *han* for being unable to receive any education. I thought that I would somehow put myself through school and lead a proper life as a learned person. I so much wanted to go to school and learn. I believe I could have been able to study to my heart's content had I been born a boy. Since my elder sisters died young, I played the role of the eldest daughter. From the age of nine, for example, I did housework at home and helped with farming chores such as raising vegetables, picking cotton, spinning, and weaving. I also helped my mother in the shop by boiling sweet potatoes to sell. Our family hired day laborers for the rice paddy work, and it was my duty to cook meals for them each day. It was hard work. All that work of mine was for the *choe* [sin or crime, in Korean] of having been born as a daughter who had to play the role of the eldest.

On an autumn day in 1943 a man in his fifties who lived in our village and worked as an agent for the Japanese approached me and told me that he could introduce me to a place where I could both earn money and study. His proposition was very attractive to me, an eighteen-year-old girl whose heart was filled with *han* over being denied an education. I decided to leave without telling my parents because I feared that my father would beat me if I told him about my plan. When the man came to see me a few days afterward and asked me to follow him for a brief visit to some undisclosed place, I left home without saying anything to my parents. The man took me to a secluded spot, not far from my house, and there was a truck parked there. A Japanese policeman, Tanaka, who worked at the neighborhood police stand, was also there. The two men told me to get on the truck and took me to Pusan, where they took me to a beauty salon to have my long hair cut short despite my resistance. Afterwards, the man from my village left me with the policeman, telling me to be obedient to him since he would help me receive an education. The policeman brought a Western-style maroon dress for me to wear. He said my *ch'ima* and *chŏgori* [a Korean-style long skirt and a short blouse] were too dirty and I should change into clean and pretty clothes. The next day, after breakfast, I was put on a train, together with four young women, in the compartment reserved for the military, and we were taken to Manchuria.

What is significant about Mun's case is that she was neither abducted by the military nor forced to leave home for economic reasons, unlike many other women who came from destitute families and sought to make a living when they left home. Rather, it was the patriarchal and abusive power relations under which she chafed that drove her away from home in pursuit of self-fulfillment, in particular her burning desire for an education. In fact, other testimonial narratives have disclosed that she was not alone in yearning to study (*kongbuhada*), although not all of these frustrated girls necessarily ran away from home. The amazing strength of her yearning to craft a modern educated self is strikingly revealed in the one and only communication she sent to her parents after leaving home. Mun stated:

I sent a letter to my parents just once during my time in Manchuria. Since I was illiterate, I asked my best friend, Kiyoko [a Japanese female name], to write it for me. She was a good-looking Korean woman from P'yŏngyang, where she had been trained and worked as a *kisaeng* [professional entertainer]. Since it was my *han* for a lack of education that made me leave home, I urged in my letter that my parents do everything in their power to send my younger siblings to school. The letter did not have the sender's address, nor did I tell them that I had become a comfort woman. I simply said that I was doing well. I was able to send it by secretly asking a Chinese boy who worked at the place to post it.

By the time I first met her in 1995, her testimonial—together with those of eighteen other survivors—had already been published. At the weekly rally in front of the Japanese embassy, and later over lunch, I sought to know her as a person, rather than pressing her to recollect the painful minutiae of her life as a comfort woman and possibly traumatizing her anew in the process. I hoped to gather more information on her childhood and postwar life and present situation. While walking with me to a restaurant for the weekly group lunch, Mun spontaneously reminisced—perhaps because of the freezing temperatures that day—about living conditions in Manchuria, such as how cold it was there, and yet how the (Russian-style) *pechika* wall kept her room warm enough to do without long underwear. In response to my questions about her postwar life, she told me of her constant fear and anxiety that somebody might find out she had been a comfort woman. She then lowered her voice and related the following incident, which took place after the war when she was living as a common-law wife:

> One day my husband's legal wife showed up at my house and assaulted me physically for luring him away. To be frank, when she was breaking my furniture and dragging me by my hair, I was most concerned about whether the angry woman somehow knew about my past life in Manchuria. The material damage and my physical pain were of secondary importance to me at that time!

This psychological reaction to the attack, which clearly reflected the conventional unequal relationship between the legal (primary) wife and a mistress (a secondary wife), made a deep impression,[16] yet what was especially striking was how her behavioral response also followed from the anxiety that her past might be known and revealed.[17]

Plate 2.1. Mun P'il-gi at her home, Seoul, 1999. (Photo by the author.)

Another significant moment in my conversations with Mun later illuminated her own understanding of what brought about her lifelong suffering. During one visit in 1999, Mun, in a rueful, reflective mood, said quietly: "I have not visited my father's gravesite to this day. I really have no intention of doing so in the future." This simple statement was an unforgettable revelation. Her unsolicited, soulful confession of deep resentment toward her father pointed to perhaps the most significant act of censure an abused daughter could take against her abusive father, if only posthumously. In a culture where filial piety continues to be regarded as the highest moral value and is expressed ritualistically in ancestor-worship ceremonies at parents' gravesites during national holidays such as New Year's Day and Chusŏk (Korea's thanksgiving holiday),[18] Mun's self-conscious refusal to visit her father's grave and make a *kŭnjŏl* ("big bow") in front of it shows a complete disavowal of any filial love and respect.[19] This indictment of her father derives from his violent reaction to his daughter's desire to go to school. Unlike many surviving comfort women, Mun did not leave home out of economic necessity. Her father apparently suffered from a sense of guilt after his daughter left. When she returned at the end of the war, her mother told her that he used to complain of recurring nightmares in which he ran for his life, away from his angry daughter.

More Daughterly *Han* Narratives

Mun is not alone in voicing this deeply felt daughterly *han*. Other survivors resented their parents for depriving them of an education, in line with the traditional discrimination against girls. Their testimonials reveal that they, too, had fled this sort of patriarchal oppression and related gender-based mistreatment at home. It was their fervent desire to live as independent, educated persons that motivated Yi Tŭk-nam and Yi Sang-ok, for example.[20] But their acts of resistance and determined pursuit of autonomy, like Mun P'il-gi's, only led them into the world of military brothels instead of the factory or service jobs that uneducated young women typically took.

Yi Sang-ok (1922–2004) grew up in Talsŏng County of North Kyŏngsang Province where her father was *myŏnjang,* or head of the township. Like Mun, she was faced not with poverty but with traditionally sanctioned prejudice:

> My family was well-off enough to afford hiring a *mŏsŭm* [farmhand] and a wet nurse for my younger siblings. Yet, when I started going to school at the age of nine, my older brother strenuously objected to it, saying it was useless to educate a girl. He burned my books, threatening to kill me if I attempted to go to school again. I was extremely envious of the tall girl next door who went to school.
>
> Later that year, I left home for Seoul without telling even my mother. As a child I was able to ride the train [the hallmark of industrial society] and the streetcar for free and arrived at my aunt's house. My aunt was a widow who ran a fabric shop with difficulty. So she urged me to return home, while making me work for my keep. With the understanding and support of my older cousins, however, I was able to go to school again in the following year. I remember my teacher stroking my long hair and saying I had a good brain. There were some Japanese students at the school and a lot more boys than girls. When my aunt visited Talsŏng, my brother reportedly pestered her for sending me to school and urged her to stop doing so. My aunt paid the school tuition for me for four years before she told me to go home since she could not support me any more. I could not return home because I was afraid my brother might beat me to death.
>
> Instead, I found an employment agency for women near my aunt's place and the woman proprietor took me in as a "foster daughter." I spent about a year there, cooking and doing laundry. Women job applicants continued to gather at the agency. Some girls came there

because their fathers sold them. One day when I asked the older girls where they were going, they told me they were going to a factory in Japan with the Japanese employee of the military who brought them to the agency. I asked them, "Shall I join you?" (*Nado kalkka?*) They invited me to do so, and the Japanese man agreed to take me as well. When I told the agency owner of my desire, she was willing to let me go.

I was fifteen, the youngest among the ten women when we left Seoul for Pusan, where we boarded a ship to go to Shimonoseki, Japan. There I was told to have my long hair bobbed so as to avoid being recognized as Korean. A week later, we boarded another ship that took us to Palau. The Japanese man who traveled with us delivered us to a Korean couple who spoke the Chŏlla dialect and were known by the Japanese surname Hayashi: they were the owners of the brothel. They paid the Japanese man. The amount he paid for each girl determined the period of labor, such as one and a half years, two years, three years, etc. Mine was one and a half years, but I never received any advance for that. Each of us was given a Japanese name, and mine was Nobuko. At first there were only ten of us, but more women came later. Some of them were *kisaeng,* including one that had been famous in P'yŏngyang. Some *kisaeng* danced, others played the *kayagŭm* [the Korean twelve-string long zither]. The *kisaeng* also had to serve the "customers" [*sonnim,* in Korean].[21]

Remarkably, after laboring for about six years as a comfort woman Yi Sang-ok unexpectedly reaped a small reward for having been educated: in recognition of her ability to speak Japanese, the Japanese military surgeon who took care of her stab wounds from a violent soldier helped her work in the hospital after her recovery. Her job there was to examine once a week the sexual organs of more than a hundred women from both a Japanese brothel and a Korean brothel in Palau. About half of the women were Korean. Her salary of fifty chŏn (half a wŏn) per month, however, did not leave much after she bought cigarettes. In comparison, her monthly income as a comfort woman was a fixed rate of thirty wŏn, sixty times that of her salary as a medical assistant. However, the proprietor deducted expenses for her clothes, cosmetics, and other personal belongings from the monthly income, so, Yi recalled, she never actually held money in her hand. (Yi's and some other survivors' similar accounts regarding remuneration reveal the type of the comfort station to which they had been taken.) When the American bombing raids started in March 1944, the military doctor made special arrangements for her to return to Korea. Unfortunately, the ship was bombed on the eve of her departure, and she had to wait until the end of the war to return.

The *han*-filled life stories of Mun and Yi both highlight the tragedies brought about by customary practices in traditional patriarchal societies, where social discrimination against females led to nonrecognition and violation of the basic human rights of girls and women—such as the right to an education. It was against their culturally enforced subservience in the domestic sphere that Mun P'il-gi, Yi Sang-ok, and other young women made their daring decisions to venture into the public sphere in pursuit of autonomy, unaware of the pitfalls. The actions of these women signaled, among other things, that, by the last decade of colonial rule (1935–1945), even uneducated young girls in the countryside were aspiring to create modern selves in an unprecedented age of expanding public space for unmarried women.

Another survivor who carries a profound sense of *han* toward her parents is Yi Tŭk-nam (b. 1918), who labored as a comfort woman for six years (three years in China, beginning 1939, and another three years in Sumatra, until the end of the war). She recounted a similar story: her abusive gambler-drunkard father prevented her from going to school and assaulted her "for no reason." Yi Tŭk-nam remembered, "I hated being at home more than dying." When she was seventeen, her parents began talking about arranging her marriage, which made her feel as though she was being sold off, so she quietly left home with a friend in search of a paying job and boarded a train to a textile factory in Inch'ŏn.[22]

Kim Ok-sil (b. 1926; now known as Kim Ŭn-rye), who labored as a comfort woman in China for three years from 1942, told a similar story of an abusive, sexist father whose severe physical punishment put an end to her repeated attempts to pursue an education:

> I was born in the outskirts of P'yŏngyang. My mother died of an illness when I was seven. My father was the eldest son and had four brothers. We all lived together in an extended family of twelve. When I was about eleven years old, a neighborhood friend told me that there was a place where we could learn Han'gŭl [the Korean alphabet] and songs and suggested that we go there together. That's how I came to attend a primary school for a few days without my father's knowledge. When Father found out, he was furious and bellowed, "To what use will a girl put her literacy? You're planning to write love letters, aren't you?" He chased after me threatening to break my legs. I hid behind my grand-

mother, who defended me by saying, "I told her to go. I did! Don't you have pity for your only daughter who has no mother? The world has changed and she should also learn Han'gŭl. How can a father behave like that?" Yet my grandmother could do no more than that to persuade my father.[23] I yearned to go to school and make friends, too. Later, I once again went to school secretly for a few days before my father learned about it. I half died from his assault. From then on, I hated seeing my father. I disliked being at home and wished to leave.

One day, I overheard neighborhood women talk about *kisaeng*. They said it was best to be *kisaeng* in P'yŏngyang. I heard them say that *kisaeng* learn how to sing, play music, and dance. Given the oppressive atmosphere in my home, where I was forbidden to learn anything, I began to feel a strong desire to be *kisaeng* so that I could wear pretty clothes and ride in the palanquin. I quietly left home thinking that once I became *kisaeng*, I would help my grandmother live in comfort. I walked all the way to downtown P'yŏngyang, which was about an hour's walk, and managed to find a school for *kisaeng*. There I told the teachers about my desire and passed their test by impressing them with my singing ability. They told me that I would make an excellent *kisaeng* after three years' training. I was taken in as a foster daughter on the spot. I made a quick adjustment to my life as an apprentice, doing such chores as cleaning and washing dishes, while learning to sing by observation.

Before a week passed, however, father and grandmother showed up. My father shouted with rage, "This girl is bringing shame to the ancestors and the neighborhood." My grandmother tearfully entreated me to come home. What could I do? Grabbed by my father, I had to return home.

Kim Ok-sil soon applied for and got a job at a sock factory, where she worked for three years. She then moved on to a better-paying job at a tobacco factory, where she had to pack the tobacco powder into packages of Changsuyŏn ("Longevity Smoke").[24] Kim Ok-sil was forced to join the ranks of the comfort women when police traffickers visited her home:

After I had worked for nearly four years, my family started talking about marrying me off. I was sixteen, and I detested the idea of getting married to a man from another poverty-stricken family. All I wanted was to continue earning wages at the factory job and live with my grandmother. It was around this time when two policemen, a Japanese and a Korean, visited my house and notified my grandmother that I had to "be sent to a textile factory in Japan" and that I could "earn a lot of money if I worked there for only three years." They told my grandmother, "We will come back in a few days and make sure that Ok-sil stays home. If she flees, all the family will be shot to death." My grandmother was in tears when she reported this to me when I returned home from work. She declared that she would never let me go. So, I told her, "Grandma, don't worry too much. I doubt I will die there. I will go and work for three years to return with a lot of money." I was scared but I pledged to myself, "I will work hard and help my grandma lead a pampered life."

A few days later, the policeman visited us again in the morning with a girl of my age from the neighborhood. Everybody was in tears when I left home. The policeman took us to a train station—I don't know the name of the station, maybe P'yŏngyang—where a woman took charge of us. We rode the train the whole day and arrived at a harbor. There was a big group of girls, about sixty I think. The woman who had brought us there disappeared. A thin woman and several men in civilian clothes then ordered us around when we boarded a ship. We sailed on the ship for a fortnight before arriving in Nanking in the spring of 1942.[25]

Kim Ok-sil spent three years in China as a comfort woman. When she returned from Nanking to Pusan after the war, she was unable to fund the trip all the way home to P'yŏngyang. She was approached by another trafficker, this time a woman from Ch'ungch'ŏng Province who advised her to first make some money before returning home. The woman then introduced her to a man:

They sold me to a drinking place for two years' contract. I worked there for half a year before a rich client paid my debt off and made me his second wife. I suffered enormously from the legal wife's mistreatment. After my husband's accidental death at sea, I fled and worked at drinking places before marrying a thirty-three-year-old farmer, a widower with three daughters. I gave birth to a daughter when the Korean War (1950–1953) broke out. I had been married for two years when my second husband was shot to death by the North Korean People's Army. "I've been so unbearably unlucky. . . . " Once again I was on my own. As a single mother, I worked hard at odd jobs to raise my daughter. However, I could not afford to educate her beyond the first few years of primary school. This has become the major reason for my lifelong *han.*[26]

Some survivors' indelible personal *han* derived from, and was directed toward, their self-centered, abusive, and/or remarried mothers. For example, Kim Hak-sun, the first Korean woman to give a public testimonial as a former comfort woman, did not get along with her remarried mother and went to live with a man who took on the role of foster father and trained her to become a *kisaeng.* Song Sin-do (b. 1922), a survivor who spent seven years as a comfort woman and has resided in Japan since the end of the war, provides another example of a daughter mistreated by her biological mother. I met her first at a hearing of her lawsuit held at the Tokyo District Court and interviewed her at a posthearing meeting of her support group in Tokyo in October 1997. Song Sin-do was sixteen years old when she started working at odd jobs to make a living. She decided to go to China at the urging of a neighbor, who deceived her with the promise of a good job. Although Song harbors intense resentment toward her mother, she has fond memories of her father, a religious leader who died when she was twelve. During our interview Song remembered:

My mother was a very cold-hearted woman who maltreated me just for being a girl! When I was sixteen, my mother married me off. This was not only against my wishes; it was also against my deceased father's advice to keep my younger sister and me at home until twenty years of age. At the time I was completely ignorant of sexual matters. Besides, I had the personality of a tomboy. On my wedding day, I fled from the nuptial bed to return home wearing only my underwear. When I showed up at my mother's place in the wee hours of the morning, my mother scolded and beat me. I had to take refuge at a friend's place and began working at odd jobs such as babysitting and washing clothes. One day, a Korean woman in her early forties approached me. She introduced herself as an acquaintance of my mother since they were both "from the north," although I had never met her before. She urged me to go to the *senchi* [battlefield, in Japanese]. Saying nice things about the *senchi,* she stated that my going there would be "for the sake of the country." She assured me that I could make a living there without getting married. Without really knowing what the *senchi* was about, I accepted this offer. I naively trusted this woman, who took me to an employment agency [*sogaeso,* in Korean] in Sinŭiju. Then, a Mr. Ko, a Korean, took me and seven or eight other girls to Hankow, China. There I worked as a comfort woman from 1938 to the end of the war in 1945. Since I did not want to return home where nobody would welcome me back, I accepted a marriage proposal from a Japanese soldier named Ōta and arrived in Japan in spring of 1946. Ōta deserted me after our arrival in Japan. I had to face a whole new series of hardships to survive in a foreign land as a single woman.

Thanks to the help of a group of dedicated supporters (consisting not only of Japanese men and women but also Korean residents in Japan), Song filed a lawsuit against the Japanese government in April 1993. It was dismissed by the Tokyo District Court in 1999 and by the Tokyo High Court in 2000.

Pae Chok-kan (b. 1922), whom the reader met in the introduction, left home in 1938 feeling happy to wear, for the first time in her life, Western-style dress and shoes upon being deceitfully recruited. She was taken to a comfort station run by a Korean man in China. Prior to her departure from home, she suffered physical abuse from her mother and sexual abuse from the Buddhist monk who was her mother's lover.[27] She had felt little attachment to her parents and attempted suicide before leaving home "nonchalantly" (sŏnsŏnhi) when the village headman made an offer—which turned out to be fraudulent—to get her work at a cotton factory. Pae reminisced, "My mother and stepfather did not even bother to see me off when I left with the man."[28]

After laboring at three different comfort stations in China for eight years, Pae returned to Korea in 1946. When she arrived at her family home, her parents showed no interest in her return. Because of her deep resentment, she refused to go to her mother's deathbed, even after her mother had sent for her. Pae now has bittersweet stories to tell of her experiences with the soldiers and a philosophical perspective on the comfort woman issue, to which I will return in chapter 5.

REGISTERED SURVIVORS AND THESPIAN TESTIMONIALS

More than two hundred South Korean elderly survivors have come out since 1991. They registered as former comfort women with the Ministry of Health and Social Welfare until 2000, when the newly created Ministry of Gender Equality took charge of the comfort women cases. The great majority of them live in South Korea, but some live abroad, in China, Japan, Thailand, Cambodia, and the United States. A little more than a hundred of them are still living. The South Korean survivors may be divided into four clusters based on their accessibility and participation in communal activities. The great majority have completely stayed out of the limelight. They are the largest but an invisible and silent cluster.

A second cluster, the most visible and accessible, is composed of the several survivors who have become permanent residents of the Buddhist-supported social welfare facility called House of Sharing (Nanum ŭi Chip). Since its establishment in 1992, the House of Sharing has provided permanent shelter for a number of needy survivors, who have received numerous, continual visitors, including foreigners such as Japanese students and tourists who come to show their remorse and support for the survivor-residents with gifts and monetary donations. When I first visited it in January 1995 and met the survivor-residents (including Kang Tŏk-kyŏng, Kim Sun-dŏk, Pak Tu-ri, Pak Ok-nyŏn, and Yi Yong-nyŏ), they were living in a rather dilapidated traditional-style rental house located in Hyehwa-dong in Seoul. The 1995 documentary *The Murmuring* (*Najŭn Moksoriro*, in Korean)—which won the director Byun Young-joo (Pyŏn Yŏng-ju) the Ogawa Shinsuke Award at the 1995 Yamagata International Documentary Film Festival in Japan and the 1996 Film Critics' Special Award in Korea—portrays the lives and stories of six survivor-residents in the Hyehwa-dong house.

After raising enough funds from private sources in Korea and Japan and obtaining a generous donation from the Buddhist businesswoman Cho Yŏng-ja of her private land, located in Kwangju County, on the outskirts of Seoul, the construction of a spacious, modern compound was completed in December 1995. The survivor-residents moved to the brand-new House of Sharing in February 1996. The facility contains two residential wings and two more buildings for the office, recreation room, Buddhist sanctuary, and education and training activities. It also houses the first Japanese Military Comfort Women History Museum (Ilbon'gun "Wianbu" Yŏksakwan, in Korean), which was built with private funds donated by individual Koreans as well as Japanese citizens and opened in August 1998.[29]

The survivor-residents of the House of Sharing have been the most regular participants in the weekly Wednesday demonstrations in front of the Japanese embassy in Seoul since 1992. Cho Yŏng-ja and a Buddhist monk, Hyejin, were recognized by the prime minister for their support of the survivor-residents' welfare in June 1996.[30] Almost from the beginning of the House in 1992, Hyejin energetically worked to help support the redress movement, raised funds from private donors in Korea and Japan to build the museum, and participated actively in the activists' project to repatriate several Korean survivors residing in China by offering them residence at the House of Sharing. He published a collection of essays entitled *Na, Naeil Demo Kandei* (I'm Going to the Demonstration Tomorrow) in 1997, depicting with humor his experiences of living with the "Japanese military comfort women grandmothers" as a young bachelor monk and director of the House. In the process, he reveals frankly the conflicts of interest between the residents and himself and the quarrels among the survivor-residents, describing the issues presented by communal living for a group of survivors with diverse personalities.[31] (The monk resigned after his sexual scandal involving staff members of the House was revealed in 2001.[32] In March 2001 a Buddhist nun, Nŭngkwang, became the new director of the House of Sharing.)

In 1999, as a sequel to *The Murmuring,* Byun Young-joo produced *Habitual Sadness: Korean Comfort Women Today* (published in Korean as *Najŭn Moksoriro 2*), the second in the documentary trilogy on Korean comfort women. The film shows the transformative impact the social support of the international redress movement had on comfort women, as well as the salutary influence of communal living on the strengthened sense of self-respect of the featured survivors, eight of whom live at the new House of Sharing and two of whom live in Ulsan and Taegu. The film functions as a precious humanitarian tribute that places the elderly survivors at center stage. Despite its English title, *Habitual Sadness* is primarily a peaceful portrayal of the everyday life of eight survivors in the comfortable and well-cared-for communal environment of the House of Sharing, nestled in a rather idyllic setting where the residents can grow vegetables in the adjacent fields. As I have noted in my review of the film elsewhere, viewers come to know the survivors as individual characters as they go about their quotidian lives caring for and bickering with each other. Viewers also come across some unexpectedly humorous and playful scenes and observe the survivor-residents engaging in a collective action to resolve their grievance against the authoritarian management style of the young monk-director of the House. Pak Tu-ri, a tall and outspoken survivor-resident, for example, reprimands him by bluntly asking rhetorically, "Do you ever consult us on anything?" The film closes with the symbolically hopeful scenes of survivor-residents planting seeds in the spacious vegetable garden behind the House.[33]

A third cluster of about twenty survivors lives independently, mostly in government-owned rental apartment buildings in the metropolitan areas of Seoul, Inchŏn, Sŏngnam, and Taegu.[34] Several survivors who used to reside in Seoul, including Mun P'il-gi, Kim Ok-sil, and Hwang Kŭm-ju, also became active participants in the redress movement by staying in close

Plate 2.2. Kim Sun-dŏk standing next to her painting, Berkeley, 2000. (Photo by the author.)

contact with the Korean Council and showing up regularly at the weekly demonstrations.

Some of the survivors belonging to the two accessible clusters described above have acquired a level of media fame of their own—"stars," as Hyejin called them.[35] They have been interviewed multiple times by reporters from the major newspapers, magazines, and television stations, both domestically and internationally. In the earlier years of the movement, Kang Tŏk-kyŏng and Kim Sun-dŏk received a great deal of attention with their unique paintings, which told the story of the comfort women in graphic and colorful terms. After Kang's death, Hwang Kŭm-ju emerged as a prominent representative. Since 2004 Yi Yong-su has become one of the most energetic and visible activist survivors; in 2007 she presented public testimonies in the United States and Japan. These "star" survivors have traveled to Japan, the United States, Canada, several countries in Europe, and Australia, where they have given their testimonials to social groups and legislative bodies as part of an effort to generate support for the redress movement.

A fourth cluster of survivors consists primarily of the members or associates of the Korean Association of Pacific War Victims and Bereaved Families (T'aep'yŏngyang Chŏnjaeng Hisaengja Yujokhoe), which is commonly referred to in South Korea as Yujokhoe, or the Association of Bereaved Families. Except for Kim Hak-sun, Pak Pok-sun, and Sim Mi-ja, all of whom are plaintiffs in the 1991 class-action lawsuit against Japan brought by Yujokhoe, the other survivors affiliated with Yujokhoe have, by and large, remained obscure until recently, when a few of them started closely associating themselves with the Korean Council after the latter began operating its own communal shelter Urijip (Our House). And Yujokhoe member-survivors were implicated in the incident involving the seven "turncoats" who were severely criticized for accepting the "atonement money" offered by Japan's Asian Women's Fund (AWF) in 1997.[36]

One of the most maligned survivor-recipients in the AWF saga, Pak Pok-sun (1921–2005) became the target of death threats and hate calls for going against the Korean Council's adamant opposition to the AWF atonement project. For eight years until her death, she led a bitter life of social isolation from fellow Koreans. She was fortunate, however, to find a sympathetic confidante in Usuki Keiko. A representative of the Japanese nongovernmental organization Hakkirikai (Association to Clarify Japan's War Responsibility), Usuki had once been barred from entering South Korea for her intermediary role in the 1997 AWF controversy. Pak Pok-sun formed a strong bond with Usuki, on whom she relied like a daughter. She would often fly to Japan to stay with the Japanese activist, who acted as a devoted caretaker of the frail, ailing, and lonesome Pak. When Pak died in 2005, Usuki flew from Japan to attend her funeral. Political leaders in Seoul and Tokyo expressed their condolences by sending huge wreaths with their names inscribed on them, but no one from Pak's family was in attendance. It was Usuki who carried the urn holding Pak's ashes at the crematory.

Pak, as a plaintiff in Yujokhoe's class-action lawsuit, is also known to her supporters by her Japanese name, Kaneda Kimiko.[37] After multiple attempts, I finally received Usuki's approval to visit and interview Pak in April 2000 at her government-owned rental apartment in Puch'ŏn. Understandably, Pak was extremely critical of the way the Korean Council has conducted the redress movement. She stated that in addition to hate calls and death threats, she had also received offensive mail from irate supporters of the Korean Council's position. Pak, whose testimonial narratives are not included in the Korean Council's publication series, also asserted with anger and disgust that some of the registered victim-survivors are "imposters" and that they are telling "lies" about life at comfort stations.

Some other Yujokhoe members have also complained about the Korean Council's position. Notably, a researcher who interviewed Sŏk Pok-sun (pseudonym; b. 1921), another survivor affiliated with Yujokhoe, reported that she not only expressed sympathy toward her friends for receiving the AWF money but also divulged her "strong" dissatisfaction with the Korean Council's position.[38] During our interview Sim Mi-ja (b. 1924), another plaintiff in Yujokhoe's suit and the founding representative of the Hibiscus Club, composed of the survivors, discussed in detail her unhappy relationship with both the Korean Council and the House of Sharing from the mid-1990s.[39] Sim and the members of her Hibiscus Club have charged the two organizations with a lack of transparency about the funds they have raised on behalf of the survivors. Sim has also asserted that 80 percent of South Korean comfort women survivors had been prostitutes, a figure she based on a private investigation she conducted by talking to the fellow survivors individually. The Korean Council meanwhile has deemed her testimonial narrative as unconvincing and has not included it in the multivolume series of collections of survivors' testimonials.

Pak Pok-sun's charges of "untruthful" testimonies and the Korean Council's negative assessment of the veracity of Sim's story point to the problems of ascertaining the truth about Japan's comfort women issue by relying on individual survivors' testimonial narratives alone as historical sources of factual truth. Their memories are now at a remove of more than sixty years from their days at comfort stations, and yet in colonial studies such oral histories, with their strong emotional resonance, are often invoked to counter official versions of documented history.[40]

Here it is useful to introduce the four different kinds of "truth" that South Africa's Truth and Reconciliation Commission (TRC) distinguished in its 1998 report on the apartheid-era killings and other violations of human rights that took place between March 1960 and May 1994. In addition to "factual truth," the TRC recognized "personal or narrative truth," "social or dialogue truth," and "healing or restorative truth." These three truths are all remarkably victim-centered. Victims were given a chance to narrate the truth from their personal point of view (personal or narrative truth). The truth of a victim's experience was to be established through social interaction and debate (social or dialogue truth). Finally, healing or restorative truth places facts and their meanings "within the context of human relationships, both among citizens and between the state and its citizens."[41]

The significance of the TRC's distinction between different kinds of truth is that full and public acknowledgment of personal, social, and healing truths is critical to the restoration of dignity to victims. Nevertheless, the TRC's restorative-justice approach to healing the nation by means of reconciliation through truth has been criticized for ignoring popular ideas of justice as retribution.[42]

Moreover, in the contemporary politics over historical injustices and the search for justice, sympathy for the personal sufferings of victims appears to have often translated into an unwritten rule of not questioning or contradicting their narrative testimonials. Activists seeking justice for the victims of historical injustice, it seems, tend to prioritize the personal truth in victims' testimonials over the factual truth of historical events or the social truth established through social debate. Alongside the capitalist motto of "the customer is king!" the social and political activists' taboo against contradicting victims seems to have generated a similar motto: "The victim is king (or queen)!" Nobody would dare to gainsay him or her.

An example may be drawn from a nationally sensationalized controversy in February 2004 in South Korea over a commercial project: "comfort women nude photographs." Alarmed by the harsh criticism of the project, when the actress Yi Sŭng-yŏn, a former Miss Korea, visited the Korean Council to apologize to the survivors for her participation in the controversial commercial project, a seventy-six-year-old comfort woman survivor, Yi Yong-su, declared to the tearfully apologetic actress, "I was dragged away from my sleep by the Japanese military."[43] Her statement—declared to a sympathetic nation under the flashes of the cameras of the mass media—may be called her "thespian truth," and it fit perfectly into her role as a representative of the surviving victims. However, the problem is that it was not her own personal truth: it differed from the presumably truthful account she gave in her original testimonial narrative, published as part of the first volume of South Korean survivors' stories in 1993.

The discrepancy reminded me of an international controversy debunking the truthfulness of the testimonial that Rigoberta Menchú, the Guatemalan native rights activist and recipient of the 1992 Nobel Peace Prize, narrated to the anthropologist Elisabeth Burgos-Debray.[44] On the basis of his ethnographic field research, the anthropologist David Stoll revealed several inaccuracies in Menchú's claim to have been an eyewitness to atrocities committed against her people, including her brother.[45] Stoll's critique was primarily directed toward poorly informed outside supporters of the guerrilla movement for their romanticization of the nature and consequences of such resistance, which has inflicted much pain and suffering on the people it purportedly represented. Menchú's supporters were outraged at the anthropologist's charge, while her critics jumped to discredit her as a liar.[46] As Ana Douglass notes, Stoll's research forces not only a rereading of Menchú's testimony but also a rethinking of "the primarily Western readers' assumptions *about* [emphasis original] the witness—the notion that the witness is necessarily innocent, truthful, and above conscious manipulation in the telling of his or her story."[47]

"Stories That Make History"

In South Korea, some well-known Korean survivors (such as Kim Hak-sun, Pae Pong-gi, and, most recently, Yi Yong-su) have given different versions of testimonial narratives,[48] which both Japanese and Korean researchers, as well as conservative activists and the right-wing nationalists in Japan, have noted and discussed.[49] For example, Ko Hye-jŏng, the director of the Korean Research Institute on Chŏngsindae, perceptively underscored the interactive and multilayered performative quality of bearing witness in her preface to the 2001 volume of the collected testimonials of Korean survivors. She wrote that interviews are not monologues but dialogues and, accordingly, the "*halmŏni*'s stories" change in the level of language and the points that are emphasized about a specific matter depending on the identities of the listeners.[50]

In particular, the stories of some Korean survivors have varied regarding a crucial issue of the method of their recruitment. In the case of Yi Yong-su—whose remarkable zest for life and outgoing personality have propelled her into the limelight of the world media as a dramatically effective representative of fellow survivors—the published account states that she left home at dawn when her age-mate and neighborhood friend Pun-sun knocked on her window and whispered, "Come out quietly." Yi recalled: "I tiptoed out and furtively followed Pun-sun to leave home. Without letting my mother know, I simply left home by following my friend."[51] Her published testimonial narrative included a description of what she was wearing at the time. The reader will recall her reminiscence of the delightful moment of seeing a red dress and a pair of leather shoes in a packet the recruiter handed to her in the fall of 1944, when she could not think anything else except to follow him "readily" (*sŏnttŭt*).[52]

By contrast, Yi's recently devised imaginative statement of having been "dragged away by the Japanese military during sleep" dovetails with the activists' paradigmatic discourse on the comfort women issue. Such a statement given by a publicly recognized individual survivor is apt to have a very potent emotional impact, creating an indelibly horrid image that serves to legitimate the generalized Korean nationalist rhetoric. In comparison, her published—and presumably truthful—statement of "following a friend without telling her mother" lacks the dramatic and infuriating scene that the general public expects to hear, based on the activists' familiar and paradigmatic story. Instead, Yi Yong-su's original testimonial has rather confoundingly revealed a profile of a determined young woman eagerly and fearlessly following her friend in search of a better chance in life.

Notably, Yi further developed the theme of forcible recruitment when she gave testimonies in the United States and Japan in 2007. At the February 15, 2007, hearing conducted by the U.S. House of Representatives Subcommittee on Asia, the Pacific, and the Global Environment in Washington, D.C.—the entirety of which I witnessed live on the Internet—Yi Yong-su again dramatized her recruitment story. She said that she was sleeping at night when a Japanese (presumably male; the Korean term did not indicate the person's gender) and a girl came and, covering her mouth, dragged her away. Notably, I found that the written version of the testimonial the activists submitted to the subcommittee on her behalf was basically the same as her original story, minus her recollection of the pleasure of receiving the dress and the shoes. At the hearing, she did mention having received the packet containing the dress and the shoes, but, understandably, without talking about her positive emotional response to the personal items. In addition, she made her "torture" story sound as if she herself had suffered it at the hands of the military, whereas she did clarify in her original story that the brothel owner, not the troops, inflicted much physical violence— including electric shocks—on her.[53]

A week later, the February 22, 2007, issue of the *Japan Times* article reported on Lee (an alternative transliteration of Yi's surname) Yong-su's oral testimony at Japan's House of Councilors Building in Tokyo the previous day: "On an evening in 1944, Japanese soldiers forced their way into fourteen-year-old Lee's home and dragged her out by the neck." At the Foreign Correspondents' Club of Japan (FCCJ) in Tokyo on March 2, 2007, she repeated her untrue story of forcible recruitment by the Japanese military, adding a newly concocted detail of the time of the forced draft to be "about two or three in the morning" and dramatic stories of violence, "torture," and "electric shocks" she suffered at the hands of Japanese soldiers,[54] all of which were absent from her original testimonial narrative. She also made it sound as though she spent four years (instead of less than a year) at the comfort station in Taiwan by stating that she was taken at the age of fifteen (instead of sixteen) and that she was nineteen when she came home in 1946.[55] The March 6, 2007, issue of the *New York Times* article then reported: "Japanese soldiers had dragged her from her home, covering her mouth so she could not call to her mother."

Remarkably, Kim Kun-ja, the other Korean survivor who also gave testimony before the House subcommittee, touched up her recruitment story as well. Kim stated that she was "captured" in front of the railroad station and taken away to China at the age of seventeen and that there were many soldiers and women on the train. In contrast, her original testimonial, published in 1999, revealed that her foster father "sold" her.[56] In an interview conducted by a Korean woman scholar in October 2003, Kim reportedly stated that she "hated the father more than the Japanese military."[57]

It may be a fine line, but in light of the continuing controversy concerning the issue of "coercion by the military" in the recruitment of women, a clarification ought to be made for accuracy's sake regarding the manner in which Korean comfort women survivors were recruited. In the cases of Yi Yong-su and Kim Kun-ja, their original published testimonial narratives told very different stories from the current, paradigmatically established image of all former comfort women having been drafted by the Japanese military.

One may also note here that in stark contrast to the dramatic but untruthful exaggerations some survivors have recently added to their original and published stories in order to live up to the paradigmatic story of the forcible recruitment by the Japanese military, some other South Korean survivors have firmly refused to be further interviewed after the initial investigation for the government certification process. Some kept their silence out of fear of making "speech errors" that might lead to the cancellation of their registration and hence the cessation of their welfare support money.[58]

* * *

We may ask here what caused the survivors to present such dramatically untruthful versions of their recruitment when they were placed under a spotlight on the political stages in the United States and Japan. A clue may be found in South Korean activists' rhetoric of "forcible recruitment," which has been formalized since 1993 under the published title *Kangjero Kkŭllyŏgan Chosŏnin Kunwianbudŭl* (Forcibly Dragged Away Korean Military Comfort Women) in the multivolume series of collections of South Korean survivors' testimonial narratives.[59]

Notably, Ahn Byung-jik (An Pyŏng-chik), who worked as the sole male historian participant in the team research project on the nineteen Korean survivors whose stories were published in the first volume in 1993, discussed in a preface to the volume that his motive for participating in the investigation was simple: as a researcher specializing in Korea's modern history, including the colonial period, he wished to know the reality of the military comfort women and was also concerned that the general public might be dealing with the issue without grasping the reality properly. Ahn also discussed some of the difficulties of conducting the research, especially when the researchers sensed that facts had been intentionally distorted in the survivors' testimonials. Despite the diverse attitudes and methodological approaches among the researchers in the initial stage, Ahn stated that they all agreed to the most important principle of revealing the truth as it is found.[60]

During my interview with him in Seoul in December 2005, Ahn also revealed how strongly he objected to and criticized the nationalist stance of some researchers who assiduously constructed the paradigmatic story by giving volume series the title they did. Ahn stated that he left the research group after three years of collaborative investigation because he found the members to be more interested in fighting against Japan than in learning about the historical facts.[61] For him such a fight was pointless and contradictory when many *wianbu* existed in privately run prostitution enclaves in South Korea.

Kang Man-gil stated in 1997 that it was no exaggeration to say that there was little concern about the comfort women issue among Korean historians.[62] Ten years later, Ahn Byung-jik reflected critically on the responsibility of historians for the lack of progress in the resolution of the issue.[63] Indeed, few reputable historians or nationally known scholars in the field of social science have involved themselves in the task of sorting out the truth in the comfort women controversy, mired as it is in politics. In contrast, Ahn, now a professor emeritus at Seoul National University, made a forthright scholarly statement in public during an interview on MBC television—a major Korean network—in Seoul in December 2006. While readily acknowledging the "possibility" of coercive recruitments, Ahn nevertheless insisted that no objective data existed on forcible recruitment of Korean women under Japanese colonial rule and added that Koreans made up more than half the people who recruited comfort women and ran the brothel business. He was, of course, severely criticized for his "pro-Japan" statement.[64]

Remarkably, it took more than a decade before the Korean Council's publication project finally dropped the title "Forcibly Dragged Away Korean Military Comfort Women." The sixth volume, published in 2004, is entitled "Stories That Make History: Experiences and Memories of Japanese Military *Wianbu* Women" (*Yŏksa rŭl Mandŭnŭn Iyagi: Ilbon'gun "Wianbu" Yŏsŏngdŭl ŭi Kyŏnghŏm kwa Kiŏk*). The anthropologist Kim Myŏng-hye, who headed the research team that produced the sixth volume, wrote how her team wrestled with the methodological task of interpreting the multiply layered meanings of Korean survivors' narratives.[65] The team sought to overcome the dichotomous perspectives of nationalism and feminism and underscore the subjectivity of individual survivors' experiences, thereby "deconstructing from below" the formal public discourse on the comfort women, which has been constructed in a manner different from the experience of individuals.

Accordingly, the researchers who interviewed Kil Wŏn-ok (b. 1928) frankly discussed their shock at hearing her story: Kil had received training to be *kisaeng* and had been to the comfort stations in China twice, with her friends and to make money. They realized that Kil's voice as a former comfort woman could never be heard without its breaking down the dominant South Korean public understanding of "forcibly dragged away Korean military comfort women." Her personal history, one may note, was "thoroughly stained with humiliation" "if spoken about in the dominant language of patriarchy."[66] In this sense the inclusion of Kil Wŏn-ok's story in the South Korean survivors' testimonial narratives amounts to a revision of the nationalist history, or at least an acknowledgment of the "stories that make history" (*yŏksa rŭl mandŭnŭn iyagi*) of the previously marginalized or silenced subaltern voices of survivors. This is why the researchers felt a "moral responsibility" to include her story in the volume even though they were wary that Japan's right wing would use it to attack the redress movement.[67] It is remarkable here that since the publication of her story, Kil has been able to actively participate in the redress movement, traveling to Europe and giving her testimony at the European Parliament's hearing on the comfort women issue in Brussels in November 2007. (The Parliament passed the comfort women resolution in the following month.)

CONCLUSION

This chapter has demonstrated that in colonial Korea it was not only girls and young women from poor backgrounds, but also those from middle-class families, who chose to leave home to escape unhappy, dysfunctional, and/or oppressive situations and to seek employment in a modern industrializing society. Nevertheless, the voices of working women—such as the runaway daughters who labored at the forefront of the industrial revolution as factory workers and other young women who were trafficked in the capitalist system of licensed prostitution—have been conspicuous by their absence from the historiography of colonial Korea. It is in this social context that attention to personal narratives of Korean comfort women survivors allows us to discern subaltern voices that speak, repeatedly and insistently, of domestic violence and gender discrimination at home, as well as of an irrepressible desire for self-improvement, self-reliance, and socioeconomic mobility promoted by the modern industrializing economy and the emergent popular culture imported from the West via Japan, the colonial master.[68] These were the principal sociological factors that pushed some of young women in colonial Korea to voluntarily leave home and aspire to become educated, autonomous modern gendered selves. If we are to reach a more comprehensive understanding of the historic process in which Korean women struggled to become modern gendered selves within industrializing colonial society under imperial Japan, the life stories of both collective ordeals *and* personal aspirations and the individual experiences of working women in colonial Korea must be recovered.

There is no question that some girls and young women, especially those in occupied territories in China and the Southeast Asian countries, were seized by the military and brutally raped in or near the battlefield and/or taken to the barracks for sexual slavery, as testimonials of surviving victims in China, the Philippines, and elsewhere have revealed. We have also noted that in some cases individual survivors have exaggerated their testimonial narratives influenced by the dominant public "discourses valued by society at the moment [they] tell their stories."[69] The fact that some individual survivors and their advocates have given accounts that are exaggerated or only partially true, however, does not warrant the assertion by conservative leaders in Japan that Japan is being "condemned based on propagandistic accounts of things that simply did not happen."[70] On their part, transna-

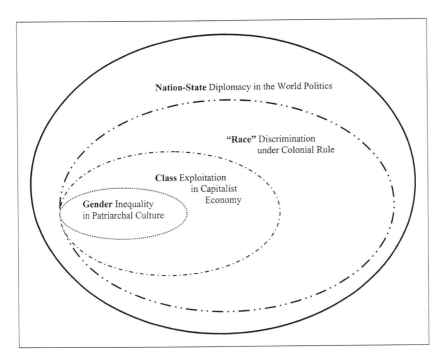

Figure 2.1. Power dynamics of structural violence against comfort women

tional advocates of the redress movement and the world media that have helped construct the paradigmatic story of Japan's comfort women need to acknowledge the uncomfortable fact of diversity in the personal situations of Japan's wartime comfort women as young individuals, whereas their collective suffering of sexual ordeals at military comfort stations must, of course, be formally recognized, with a shared goal of preventing violence against women.

✻   ✻   ✻

Figure 2.1 illustrates diagrammatically my analysis of Korea's comfort women tragedy. The lifelong suffering of South Korean survivors, I maintain, has been entrenched in the concentric structural conjuncture of (1) gender inequality in masculinist sexual culture and patriarchal abuse of power against wives and daughters at home; (2) class exploitation in society under capitalist economy; (3) "race" discrimination under colonial rule of

Imperial Japan; and (4) Korea's unequal diplomatic relations with Japan (during *and* after colonial rule) and with the United States after the war in the nation-state power dynamics to redress historical wrongdoings.

Furthermore, the conjuncture of various social structural axes contributed not only to the wartime victimization of Korean comfort women but also to the continuous *societal indifference* to them after the end of the war in postcolonial Korea, which must be further contextualized in the genealogy of Korean women's stigmatized but customary professional labor to provide men with public sex for over a millennium, an important topic to which I will return in chapter 6. The comfort women survivors' *han* narratives discussed in this chapter, one might add, represent unfortunate—but not uncommon—tragedies that countless women seekers of autonomy have encountered in patriarchal capitalist societies around the globe. The systemic violation of women's human rights in many patriarchies is a centuries-old practice that continues to challenge conscientious policy makers and committed social activists.

In closing, let me note here that Koreans afflicted with the *han* complex have traditionally turned to healing rituals of *kut,* performed by shamans, in order to experience the cathartic effect of unleashing the knotted emotions suppressed in their heart.[71] It is both remarkable and unsurprising, therefore, that the first public commemorative event (organized by a women's organization and held in July 1990) to console the "angry wandering souls" of deceased comfort women was a performance of the *"chŏngsindae haewŏn kut"* (a shamanistic ritual *kut* to help release the rancorous *han* of Korean comfort women [euphemistically referred to as *chŏngsindae*]).[72] The *kut* ceremony included prayer-like propitiatory narrative songs, which the shamans sang to posthumously and collectively console the souls of numerous deceased comfort women and help resolve their knotted *han* so that they may rest in peace. I quote below the lyrics of the shaman song:

> Pitiable are angry souls with hungry tummies and plentiful *han.*
> Accept This World's offerings and
> Borrow the power of the shaman so as to
> Unbind your mountainous and river-like *han* and
> Open your heart's door.
>
> In the Other World,
> Put on your *yŏnji* [rouge] and
> *Konji* [the red dot painted in between the bride's eyebrows].[73]
> Give birth to sons and daughters. . . .

Chapter 3

Japan's Military Comfort System as History

When the Japanese army advances, the officers' primary concern is the transportation of the "girl army." The reason Japanese troops don't rape Chinese women is precisely because they have the "girl army." So they are not merely prostitutes!

—Nakayama Tadanao, director of the Nakayama Institute of Japanese-Chinese Medicine, June 1933, in Yoshimi Yoshiaki, *Comfort Women*, 2000

The logic of male privilege that declared that a man who hadn't had sex was not a man and that life was futile supported the licensed prostitution system at home and in the colonies, as well as the military comfort station system in war zones.

—Yoshimi Yoshiaki, *Comfort Women*, 2000

SOUTH KOREAN ACTIVISTS defined the Japanese military comfort system as a "war crime" in the early 1990s; these activists considered the comfort women to have been forcibly and deceptively recruited *chŏngsindae* and abused by the Japanese Imperial Army.[1] Here we should note, however, that "war crime" is *not* a special conceptual category.[2] A war crime may take place *during* war, facilitated by the chaos and confusion of the time, but it is in fact a type of criminal act committed in everyday life under another name, such as murder, torture, rape, forced prostitution, or theft. Testimonials of surviving Korean comfort women encompass a wide range of situations that complicate the picture; they include cases of destitute families selling daughters into indentured prostitution, runaway daughters deceptively recruited into forced prostitution by Japanese and Korean traffickers, abduction by civilian thugs, and forcible recruitment by agents of the colonial state.

Internationally, after publication of a 1996 U.N. report, pro-redress activists, the mass media, and also scholarly publications in English routinely began to use the term "military sexual slavery" with reference to the Japanese comfort system. By the end of the decade, Japanese, South Korean, and Filipino activists had organized the 2000 Women's International War Crimes Tribunal on Japan's Military Sexual Slavery, which indicted Japan—and the late emperor in particular—for wartime sexual violence against women.[3]

We should also note that most activists—in both the pro- and the anti-redress movements—have neither lived experience nor personal memories of the historical period under discussion (the early 1930s to 1945) by which to understand the sociocultural and political economic context of the widespread "commerce in women" and the nature of the Japanese military comfort system. Nevertheless, the vigorous redress movement, spearheaded by Korean and Japanese activists and their international supporters, has by now constructed something that may be called a "transnational memory" of the comfort women's experience as sexual slavery.[4] This has been possible, in part, because of the global post–cold war politics of human rights.

Faced with conflicting memories from those who experienced the war (the veterans and surviving comfort women) and this newly formed transnational memory, we must address the question of how one goes about probing into "the truth" about the nature of Japan's military comfort system and the slavery-like conditions many women endured to "comfort" Japanese soldiers. This question goes to the heart of the comfort women controversy, that is, the multiple dimensions of truth as remembered and asserted by disparate individuals and agents with competing personal, national, and feminist political interests and perspectives.

In this chapter, I attempt to compile a broader, better integrated historical view of the comfort system than the ahistorical binary representation of commercial sex versus war crime commonly asserted by the activists of opposing camps. My primary aim is to fully expose the fact that the comfort system encompassed both commercial *and* criminal sex, a point often conveniently lost in the heated international memory wars waged for and against the redress movement. In this regard it is imperative that we take a historical overview of the cultural legacies of traditional Japanese institutions of public sex for a deeper understanding of the wartime military comfort system. Institutionally, Japan's comfort women system was rooted in the country's long history of a system of state-sanctioned prostitution.

PROSTITUTION AND THE STATE: JAPAN'S HISTORY IN BRIEF

Prostitution is commonly regarded as the world's oldest profession. However, feminist scholars have underscored its exploitative nature by contending that pimping, "the living off of the earnings of a prostitute," is the oldest profession across the globe.[5] As the histories of Korea and Japan demonstrate, the most powerful pimps have sometimes been none other than the state itself. Prostitutes may be of either sex, but historically the majority of them have been young women. Prostitution as a social institution was widespread in both preindustrial and industrial societies.[6] The ancient Babylonians, for instance, worshiped fertility and believed that the generative influences of human sexual activity promoted fertility in nature. They maintained a class of women attached to temples whose role was to "civilize the wild man."[7] In medieval Europe many cities maintained public houses of prostitution for the benefit of young unmarried men. Some of these institutions were subsidized by municipal governments, and others generated profits for their host cities. The prostitutes in these establishments were not marginalized or criminalized; they were legally free and socially eligible for marriage.[8]

In contrast, sexual landscapes in modern times have been characterized by stringent moralistic social control of private sexual conduct, on one hand, and provision of regulated prostitution in the public sphere, on the other. Modern societies have produced a profusion of social discourse on sex to which scientific knowledge about human sexuality has often lent a kind of moral weight; these developments constitute the effects of "polymorphous techniques of power" employed in modern nation-states.[9] Licensed prostitution in imperial Japan, for instance, was a commercial system composed of state-regulated "pleasure quarters" (yūkaku) in delimited districts where prostitutes' bodies were confined; this system, which fell under state surveillance, controlled virtually every aspect of these women's lives.[10]

Japan's officially condoned institutions of public sex have a long history. The state has played a pivotal role in generating the particular organizational forms, the specific rules and regulations, and the various euphemistic terms for the highly stigmatized women's sexual labor performed for both civilians and servicemen.[11] The establishment in 1193 (Kamakura period, 1185–1333) of an official post (yūkun bettō) to deal with prostitutes recognized a loosely organized system of prostitution that provided traveling men with access to female sexual services. Under the shogun Yoshiharu (r. 1521–1546), a new bureau (keisei kyoku) was established and began levying a tax on the houses of prostitution in 1528.[12]

The Pleasure Quarters
A forerunner of the pleasure quarters appeared in Kyoto in 1589. It had the support of the warlord Toyotomi Hideyoshi (1536–1598), who saw such facilities as necessary to the welfare of men in his service who had been

separated from their wives.[13] The Yoshiwara, the first pleasure quarters in Edo (today's Tokyo), were granted an official license in 1617. The Yoshiwara is just the best-known among hundreds of prostitutes' quarters that existed in pre–World War II Japan. International fame came to the Yoshiwara with the forced opening of Japan to the West toward the end of the Tokugawa shogunate (1600–1868). The Yoshiwara stunned Commodore Matthew C. Perry and his men when they first landed in Japan in July 1853.[14] Visitors could buy guidebooks to these pleasure quarters (*Yoshiwara saiken*), which was a world unto itself, with its own rituals, its own seasonal observances, even its own private language.[15]

> The basic fee (which was doubled on festival days) [for high-ranking courtesans] ranged from the equivalent of $450 to $750 in 1993 American money, and this included none of the tips that had to be paid to the *hikitejaya* [teahouse], the entertainers, and the courtesan's attendants. . . . [Lower-ranking courtesans] . . . had to sit on public display in a custom known as *harimise*. . . . [They sat] behind their cage-like windows on full view to passersby.[16]

One of the rules at the brothels was that samurai had to leave swords and daggers with attendants to prevent them from wielding their weapons while intoxicated.[17] Most of the women in the brothels had been sold by destitute parents and were virtual prisoners. But according to Donald Jenkins, curator of Asian art at the Portland Art Museum and author of *The Floating World Revisited,* the terms of their captivity resembled indentured servitude more than slavery, and "life in the brothels was not excessively harsh by the standards of the time."[18]

During the 1850s and 1860s, Japan underwent a period of rapid social and political change in response to economic distress, the onslaught of Western demands that it open its doors, popular unrest, and finally the civil war that ended the Tokugawa shogunate.[19] Japan was pressured to sign unequal treaty agreements with the Americans, the British, the Russians, and the Dutch. Foreign traders began to settle in large numbers around the harbor of Yokohama. Based on an agreement with the American consul-general Townsend Harris, who had arrived in Japan 1856, pleasure quarters were established for foreigners in Yokohama to ward off disputes over the rape of Japanese women by resident foreigners.[20] With the "commerce in foreigners and women" prospering in Yokohama, the government approved the Yoshiwara brothel owners' request to build a special red-light district for foreigners in Tokyo in 1868.[21] This was the same year the new Meiji ("enlightened rule") state was born. Japanese society at that moment was reeling from the effects of "foreigner shock," the civil war, and the pauperization of the people. There was a surfeit of prostitutes, most whom were the wives and daughters of more than a million and a half samurai who had been freed from their masters and forced to seek new livelihoods. More than thirty thousand women in Edo alone lost contact with their samurai husbands and had to make a living on their own.[22]

The Meiji State and Modern Prostitution System
The Meiji state (1868–1912), which revolutionaries helped establish by ending the shogunate and restoring imperial rule under the fourteen-year-old emperor, pledged in its "charter oath" to seek knowledge "throughout the world in order to strengthen the foundations of imperial rule."[23] Japan's effort to modernize and strengthen the nation included legislating a series of new laws and ordinances concerning the prostitution system, and from the 1870s on the Japanese sex trade modeled itself after European systems of regulated prostitution.[24] For example, in 1868 the new government established a syphilis clinic in Yokohama at the suggestion of a Dr. Newton, a medical doctor in the British Royal Navy, and placed it under British jurisdiction inside the licensed pleasure quarters.[25] In 1871 the Meiji state issued a directive to local governments to set up examination centers for syphilis; these came to be known as "prostitute hospitals."[26]

The licensed prostitution system of Meiji Japan was qualitatively different from the system of the Tokugawa era in three respects.[27] First, following a European (French) practice,[28] it required prostitutes to submit to compulsory venereal disease examinations, in effect holding the women responsible for infection. Many Japanese regarded this program as "a gift from foreign countries," and government leaders believed that its introduction was consistent with the Meiji's enlightened policies.[29] Second, the government levied a monthly licensing fee on brothel owners and prostitutes. Third, it prohibited and criminalized unlicensed prostitution. The Japanese historian Fujime Yuki characterizes these state policies as an attempt to monopolize the traffic in women for sex.[30] The American historian Susan Burns, by contrast, interprets it as the state-led production of a new social and political discourse on human sexuality. This discourse engaged the Japanese public in rethinking the nature of the body, the public implications of disease, and notions of female social roles and sexuality in the construction of an emergent concept, the "national body" (kokutai).[31]

Most significant for this study, the first human rights controversy over Japan's licensed prostitution erupted as an aftereffect of lawsuits involving the Peruvian ship *Maria Luz,* which entered Yokohama harbor for repairs in June of 1872.[32] On board were 231 Chinese under transport from Macao to Peru. So desperate were conditions on the ship that a man who had been deceptively recruited by traffickers in the "coolie trade" risked his life by jumping ship to seek help. He was rescued by the crew of an English battleship. The resident British chargé d'affaires contacted the Japanese Ministry of Foreign Affairs and asked to be allowed to intervene in the mistreatment of the Chinese passengers, among whom were thirteen children. At the recommendation of British and American diplomats, the Japanese government set up a special court. The Japanese judge ruled that the captain was innocent and his ship was allowed to leave. The judge refused, however, to return the Chinese to the ship. The captain filed a civil suit, and his lawyer, F. V. Dickens, an Englishman residing in Yokohama, argued that if the Chinese laborers were to be regarded as slaves from a humanitarian perspective, the tens of thousands of women trafficked as prostitutes in Japan were in fact slaves, too. High officials in the courtroom as well as the judge were deeply disturbed at the charge. Judge Ōe responded in the end that the Japanese government was in fact considering emancipation of prostitutes.[33] The Japanese informed China of the incident, and a special envoy arrived from China to convey his countrymen home on September 13. Less than a month later, on October 2, 1872, the Japanese government promulgated Ordinance No. 295, the "prostitutes liberation law" (*shōgi kaihō rei*).[34]

In fact, this new law amounted to little more than a political declaration meant to save face with the international community. The tearful joy of the emancipated prostitutes lasted less than a month. Most of them were unable to find other means of support after returning to their hometowns; consequently, they either engaged in unlicensed prostitution or returned to the pleasure quarters.[35] The government had no intention of eradicating prostitution, but it was painfully aware that the institution drew sharp criticism from foreign powers. The face-saving regulations resulted in a host of euphemisms that disguised the customary trafficking practices in new contractual language; technically the women now enjoyed the status and rights of autonomous agents.

The *yūkaku* became "rented banquet or drawing rooms" (*kashi zashiki*), where prostitutes "voluntarily" entertained customers; brothel owners merely rented out the rooms and served food. The wording of regulations for the "rental room business" represented relations between brothel owners and prostitutes as fair commercial transactions. The conventional term "human trafficking" (*jinshin baibai*) was replaced by "human mortgage" (*jinshin teitō*), and the "body price" (*midaikin*) was changed to "advance wage" (*maegari*). Within two years, the business of prostitution had adjusted to its new terms and went on with little substantive change.[36]

The first grassroots prostitution abolitionist movement began in 1880 when members of the Gumma Prefectural Assembly, including Yuasa Jirō, an advocate of Christian civil rights, submitted a petition to the local government to end prostitution. Members of the industry fought back by forming a national association that supported licensed prostitution. The battle between these groups lasted for more than a decade before the abolition ordinance was adopted in Gumma Prefecture in 1891. The ordinance eliminated the *shōgi* (licensed prostitutes), but it did not stop privately run prostitution. Gumma Prefecture continued to levy taxes on prostitution businesses and perform venereal disease examinations.[37]

Gumma's success in abolishing licensed prostitution encouraged the Japan Women's Christian Temperance Union (Nihon Kirisutokyō Fujin Kyōfūkai) and the Salvation Army to engage in a nationwide abolitionist movement. The objectives of the movement were to save the nation's dignity, criminalize those involved in prostitution, and spread the social ethic that prostitution was a vice and a "shameful or indecent occupation" (*shūgyō*) that made prostitutes *shūgyōfu* (women of indecent occupation).[38] For the abolitionists, licensed prostitution "sullied the dignity of the empire."[39] Thus, the Christian women's society referred to prostitutes working abroad not by the euphemistically ambiguous term *karayuki-san* (literally, "China-bound person"),[40] but as *kaigai* [overseas] *shūgyōfu*.

"Overseas Prostitutes" and Military Prostitution

While advocating the establishment of a disease-free "Pure Japan," however, prostitution abolitionists overlooked the transplantation of regulated prostitution in colonial Korea and Manchuria. In supporting the militarist project of territorial expansion for the greater Japanese Empire, they were actively concerned with programs for the prevention of venereal disease and urged the Japanese government to emulate the military prostitution policies of other imperialist nations. When the military comfort policies were instituted, their effect was to connive with the Japanese army in the massive exploitation of lower-class women, especially those of colonial Korea and other countries.[41]

As Japan continued to militarize in the late nineteenth century, military bases sprang up across the country. Because bases meant local financial gain from increased spending on public works projects and other patterns of consumption, the prefectures competed for such installations, and local authorities tried to lure the military by establishing red-light districts and amusement areas. The establishment of military bases and the institution of licensed prostitution by local governments went hand in hand.

The demand for military prostitutes and for red-light districts in both Japan and the colonies increased as Japan engaged in imperialist aggression and territorial expansion in the first Sino-Japanese War (1894–1895) and the Russo-Japanese War (1904–1905). Nearly twenty thousand Japanese women were laboring as *karayuki-san* by 1910.[42] The term *karayuki-san* initially referred to migrants who went to China or Southeast Asia in search of work, but it gradually came to refer to the destitute women of prewar Japan who worked abroad as prostitutes. These women came from impoverished rural areas and coal-mining towns, especially in northwestern Kyūshū,[43] and had been sold into overseas prostitution. *Karayuki-san* labored at the many Japanese-owned brothels that flourished in Korea, Manchuria, China, Southeast Asia, and North America between the 1860s and 1930s.[44]

J. Mark Ramseyer, an American scholar of Japanese legal studies, has pointed out that most scholars tend to explain Japan's prewar prostitution by repeating journalists' accounts of "naïve women tricked by usurious brothel owners" into a life of "thinly disguised slavery."[45] While recognizing that the slavery argument was "not all fiction," he has cautioned scholars "not to let the brutality of prostitution blind them to the effective ways peasant women and men make the most of bad situations."[46] Ramseyer notes that the women who became licensed prostitutes were "not women with many attractive alternatives" and that "prostitution did pay well."[47] His study concludes that women in prewar Japan became licensed prostitutes by signing six-year indenture contracts, and "most prostitutes did *not* become slaves" (emphasis in original).[48] Instead, most of them quit when their contracts expired, and some were able to quit earlier by repaying their debts in three or four years.

The lived experience of some Korean comfort women has corroborated Ramseyer's research findings, but their personal histories have remained a part of strategically "subjugated knowledge" in contemporary politics. Nevertheless, a vocal minority of feminist leaders and human rights activists, in prewar as well as in contemporary Japan, have pointed out that even those who became "prostitutes"—in the sense that they "voluntarily" entered *ianjo* without overt physical coercion and received money for their services—were also often under economic and social compulsion. The fundamentally clashing views of prostitution as commercial sex versus sexual slavery, in fact, constitute a crucial axis in the competing public discourses and conflicting memories over the comfort women in Japanese society.

In any case, the customary use of red-light districts by the military undoubtedly served as a model for the military comfort stations established at the front as well as in urban centers during the Asia Pacific War. Moreover, the *karayuki-san* provided a concrete model for the comfort women system.[49] The similarities between the *karayuki-san* and the *ianfu* include the sources and methods of their recruitment. Both *karayuki-san* and *ianfu* came mainly from impoverished families and were sold or deceptively recruited into indentured prostitution. Some were simply abducted.

There were major differences, however, in their labor patterns and living conditions. For one thing, *ianfu* labored exclusively for the military, which meant for some women living near or on the battlefront. Furthermore, military authorities and other state agents became systemically involved in the management of military brothels. Finally, compared to *karayuki-san* with civilian clients, *ianfu,* especially non-Japanese women, were more likely to suffer physical violence at the hands of hypermasculine soldiers and also ran a higher risk of being killed by virtue of their proximity to the battlefront.[50]

THE JAPANESE MILITARY COMFORT SYSTEM

In order to get beyond the nationalistic-versus-human-rights discourses, I portray below in broad strokes imperial Japan's military comfort facilities by throwing a harsh light on them to reveal the diverse categories and types of the facilities, which purported to provide troops with regulated access to sexual recreation during the war. I suggest three major categories of the comfort facilities—the concessionary, the paramilitary, and the criminal—to help sort through the ambiguities and complexities of the historical reality surrounding them, which have been nearly uniformly referred to as "comfort stations" (*ianjo,* in Japanese) in the activist discourse as well as in scholarly publications. In this discussion I use the terms *ianjo,* "military comfort facilities," and "comfort stations" interchangeably.

The general contours of the comfort facilities sketched below underscore the fact that the sexual behavior of Japanese troops and the quality of life at comfort facilities varied enormously across time and locale. The reconstruction here of three organizationally diverse categories of the *ianjo* will help illuminate the nature of the comfort system and place it in a comparative historical and cross-national perspective. Analytically, I approach the comfort system as a historical institution deriving from the dynamics of capitalism, militarism, and a sexual-cultural order acted out in a "structure of the conjuncture," to use the anthropologist Marshall Sahlins's terms, in which "cultural categories are actualized in a specific context through the interested action of the historic agents and the pragmatics of their interaction."[51] In other words, in the conjuctural structure of imperial Japanese society the paternalistic state and its military leaders realized the comfort women system by instructing low-level local functionaries to enlist the help of profit-seeking entrepreneurs in Japan and colonial Korea who, in turn, unscrupulously recruited with false promises young women in search of wage-paying jobs.

To construct a theoretically useful classification of the *ianjo,* then, we first need to situate the military comfort system within the social and historical structures of modern imperial Japan. Only then can we probe its "actualization" in the participation of men and women as individual "historic actors," relying on their own language to reveal personal motivations and circumstances. To do this we must undertake a "double engagement of culture with history."[52] Cultural influence manifests not only in speech and activities in social and public life, but also in customs pertaining to intimate private acts. The concept of sexual culture must be considered "a cultural lifeway" involving notions of personhood, proper gender relations, and theories of human nature as part of a conventionalized and shared system of sexual practices.[53]

For example, the euphemism "comfort women" epitomizes a naturalized masculinist sexual culture. In masculinist sexual culture (a shared feature of patriarchal societies, including Japan and Korea), people believe that men have biologically based sexual "needs" that must be met by access to the female body. This sexual cultural belief, which I shall call "normative heterosexual masculinity," has traditionally been a principal component of what R. W. Connell calls the "heterosexual sensibility" underlying hegemonic or dominant social practices that construct idealized masculinity and femininity and customary gendered power relations between men and women in patriarchy.[54] In both Japanese and Korean patriarchies the state-sanctioned systems of public sex emblematically represented the cultural practice of normative heterosexual masculinity, which encompassed the traditional institutions of professional women entertainers, the geisha and *kisaeng* (in Japan and Korea, respectively). They were trained formally in the arts of literature, music, and dance to entertain male clients in the so-called customary trade in adult amusement. The boundary between "entertainment" and "prostitution" became fuzzy in the lives of traditional geisha and *kisaeng,* especially the low-ranking ones.[55]

In short, in Japanese history the state-regulated system of prostitution recognized what might be called the rule of male sex right,[56] that is, the right of men to have orderly access to commercial, public sex outside marriage, and which presumably helped to protect virtuous respectable women from rape. It is not surprising, then, that the wartime fascist state of imperial Japan endorsed the military comfort system as an extension of licensed prostitution for its armed forces engaged in prolonged warfare.

VARIETIES OF THE MILITARY COMFORT FACILITIES

Let us now turn to the organizational diversity of the *ianjo,* bearing in mind their starkly opposed categorical representations as "rape centers" rather than "comfort stations." Here it is important to ask, What criteria can one employ to effectively differentiate among the variety of *ianjo* described by victim-survivors?

Earlier researchers have asked who managed the comfort stations and where and how long they ran them. Yoshimi Yoshiaki, for example, classified military *ianjo* into three categories: (1) those directly run by the military for the exclusive use of military personnel and civilian military employees; (2) those managed by civilians but supervised and regulated by the military for the exclusive use of the troops or civilian military employees (the most numerous type); and (3) facilities, including restaurants, open to the general public but designated as comfort stations, where military personnel were given special priority.[57] Tanaka Yuki, however, classified them differently, as (1) "permanent" *ianjo* located in major cities; (2) "semipermanent" *ianjo* attached to large army units; and (3) "temporary" *ianjo* set up by small units near the front lines. Tanaka notes that the permanent and semipermanent types were managed either by private proprietors under the military control or by the military forces themselves, while the temporary type is believed to have been run by individual units.[58]

This study, however, considers the *motives* behind running, supporting, and/or patronizing these facilities to better explain the nature of the comfort system. I therefore pay special attention to the "organizational" motives of the diverse categories of *ianjo.*[59] The motives, which can be inferred from narratives of surviving comfort women (and former soldiers), ranged from commercial profit (by civilian entrepreneurs), to paternalistic accommodation (by the state and military leaders), to criminal self-gratification (by soldiers on the battlefield), both individually and collectively. These varying foundational motives must be recognized when we discuss the different operational factors that underlay the concessionary, the paramilitary, and the criminal categories of *ianjo* considered here.

I use the term "concessionary" to refer to commercial houses of assignation and prostitution run by civilian concessionaires to make money; they were generally located in urban areas. The relationship between civilian proprietors of concessionary *ianjo* and the military authorities sanctioning such enterprises was contractually regulated: the former, as concessionaires, offered the commodities (i.e., sexual services and entertainment) desired by the military; the latter possessed the power to dictate the terms of operation and regulate behavior at the comfort stations. Nakasone Yasuhiro, who became prime minister after the war, mentioned in his memoirs how he, as the chief accounting officer for the 2nd Construction Corps in the navy, permitted the building of an *ianjo* on the island of Borneo to be used by over three thousand men under his command, some of whom had attacked local women.[60] Nakasone provides no operational details, but his *ianjo* probably falls into the paramilitary category, which was installed and managed directly by local units of the military.

A fundamental difference between the concessionary and the paramilitary *ianjo* lay in the fact that the former was run by civilian—mostly Japanese and Korean—entrepreneurs for profit, although this does not necessarily mean they always made money. The paramilitary *ianjo,* by contrast, were operated as not-for-profit recreational facilities, run by the paternalistic military to control the troops through regulated access to sex, though those run under the ticketing system might have been financially profitable. Although both categories seemed to have largely relied on civilian traffickers to procure women, the military was at times directly involved as evidenced by the case of interned Dutch women such as Ruff-O'Herne. Whether concessionary or paramilitary, the articulated aims of the *ianjo* were the same: boosting the morale of the troops, checking the spread of venereal disease, and preventing sex crimes against local women.[61]

By contrast, the most vicious category of the comfort stations, what I call the criminal *ianjo,* came into being primarily *as an outcome* of sex crimes committed by individual troops against local women. Criminal *ianjo,* which were run by soldiers themselves in the battlefield, confined women in enemy territory in sexual enslavement after either rape and abduction or coercive procurement. Soldiers gratified their sexual "needs" at will and for free. The criminal category of *ianjo* appears to have emerged primarily during the final years and months of the war.[62]

Here we must note that, in practice, ambiguities and underlying similarities existed among the different categories of *ianjo.* The lives of comfort women featured elements of coercion in the recruitment and slavery-like conditions in incorporation processes. Moreover, it was not only soldiers, but also the civilian managers and owners, who inflicted physical violence against the women, as many survivors have described. Despite the common underlying brutality of the system, however, the criminal category appears to have been an anomaly of vicious and hypermasculine lechery, distinct from the state-endorsed and regulated *ianjo* of the concessionary and paramilitary categories that catered to cultural assumptions about normative heterosexual masculinity. The criminal *ianjo* constituted a battlefield embodiment of aggressive and violent military heterosexual hypermasculinity.[63]

The Concessionary *Ianjo*

The concessionary *ianjo* may be further divided into two subtypes: the "house of entertainment," which served primarily officers, and the "house of prostitution," which catered to the rank and file. The former offered a more comprehensive range of recreational activities, as exemplified in the case of the Military Center described below, whereas the latter was operated simply as a brothel.

1. The House of Entertainment

The "house of entertainment" refers to relatively comprehensive comfort facilities run by civilians in cooperation with the military. Like establishments in the pleasure quarters of imperial Japan, the entertainment house often resembled a special type of restaurant called *ryōtei* (*yojŏng,* in Korean) that were known under ordinary business names. For example, the Silver Moon Loft (*Gingetsurō,* in Japanese; *Ŭnwŏllu,* in Korean) and the Abundant Sea Loft (*Hōkairō,* in Japanese; *P'unghaeru,* in Korean) are the names of comfort stations set up exclusively for the Japanese navy in Ch'ŏngjin, a port city in North Hamkyŏng Province in northern Korea. These were established in the mid-1930s and 1938, respectively,[64] and all the comfort stations in Taiwan, Saipan, Truk, and Palau that the Japanese comfort woman survivor Shirota Suzuko recalled in her autobiography had normal business names.[65] The entertainment house usually served food and alcoholic beverages, as well as heterosexual entertainment and prostitution, exclusively for military men and for civilian military employees. Detailed regulations for the operation of comfort facilities issued by the Japanese army in Shanghai on April 1, 1932, reveal that the authorities were most concerned with the prevention of venereal disease. They stipulated a weekly medical examination of the "female receptionists" (*sekkyakufu*). The regulations set business hours and hourly fees for sexual services on the basis of the women's ethnicity: 1.5 yen for Japanese women, 1 yen for Korean and Chinese women.[66] Notably, Korean women's status in the ethnic hierarchy appears to have improved toward the end of the war, which, presumably, reflected a conscientious implementation of imperial Japan's "one body" (*naisen ittai*) policy of the forced assimilation of Koreans.[67] For example, comfort stations in Manila around 1943 or 1944 charged the same rate for Korean *ianfu* as for Japanese.[68]

The Military Center (Kunin Hoegwan, in Korean) in Manchuria was an example of upscale modern military recreational facilities. According to the testimonial of Mun Myŏng-gŭm (1919–2000), the Military Center was a huge two-story building that also housed the general headquarters of the 123rd Unit of the 4th Army of the Kantōgun.[69] The east wing of the building held a big cinema, and the first floor contained a huge banquet hall, a restaurant, and a public bath. Mun, who was deceptively recruited at age eighteen by a Korean man in his fifties, recalled her room at the Military Center, the second floor of which was used as the business as well as residential quarters for comfort women:[70]

> The room assigned to me was simple but clean. When I first entered it, I saw a Japanese-style tatami floor on which military bedding for two people had been placed, with two pillows. I thought naively that I might be sharing the room with another woman. What surprised me most, however, was that the room had its own bathroom. It was equipped with a huge mirror, a bathtub, a sink, a towel, and a bar of soap. Remembering the hard labor involved in getting water in my rural hometown, I was further amazed to find that not only cold water but also hot water was instantly available upon turning the knob. Everything in the bathroom looked new. The daily necessities we had to buy were toothpaste and personal cosmetics.[71] For me and other colleagues who did not have money, the manager of the comfort station entered these purchases as part of our individual debts. "What work would they have us do to allow us such fine accommodation?" My mind was full of questions then. After we had rested for a few days, I came to learn that we were placed at a military comfort station.[72]

Another entertainment house in Manchuria is mentioned in the testimonial of Kim Sun-ok (b. 1922). Kim labored at a comfort station that housed about forty women and was located in a place called Tongnyŏnghyŏnsŏng, near the Chinese-Russian border, from 1941 to 1945.[73] Some Japanese women also labored there, but Koreans were more numerous. Kim was told that her comfort station admitted only those women who had been educated at *kisaeng* schools or had had comparable training.[74] Parties for senior officers were frequently held there to celebrate victories and other events. Japanese geisha in kimonos or Korean *kisaeng* in *ch'ima* and *chŏgori* (Korean dress) played music and danced to entertain the officers at these parties.

Another account of an entertainment house comes from Southeast Asia. In Rangoon, Burma, an officer's club called Suikōen hired only Japanese women, who served military officers exclusively. The Suikōen was a special branch of a famous, high-class restaurant of the same name in Kurume, Japan.[75] Entertainment houses such as Suikōen served primarily high-ranking officers from the beginning to the end of the Asia Pacific War in areas where large contingents of the Japanese military were headquartered. According to a former infantryman named Honda (b. 1914), however, some "officers' clubs" in China offered sexual services to all military men, dividing service hours among different ranks and reserving the overnight service for officers only.[76]

2. The House of Prostitution

The second type of the concessionary *ianjo* was owned and managed by civilians but was closely supervised and regulated by the military. Ichikawa Ichirō (b. 1920), a former military policeman turned supporter of the redress movement,[77] stated during our interview that it is "not incorrect" to argue, as some former soldiers and antiredress activists have, that military comfort stations were run by civilian entrepreneurs. Conscripted in 1943, Ichikawa served as a *kempei* (military policeman) in Manchuria for about a year and half. After the war ended, he was held for five years in Siberia as a prisoner of war and a war criminal prior to his repatriation in 1950. During the war Ichikawa's main duty as a *kempei* was to supervise two military comfort stations. He recalled that when he was assigned he hardly knew the term *ianfu*:

> I thought vaguely that *ianjo* was a place where soldiers went to relax and enjoy themselves. In addition to the two military *ianjo* I supervised, there were *minkan ianjo* [private or civilian comfort stations] as well as many special restaurants where prostitution took place. The military customers there were almost exclusively officers. However, officers also went to military *ianjo,* since they were cheaper than civilian ones.

A notable difference between civilian and military *ianjo,* according to Ichikawa, was that as a security precaution managers of the military *ianjo* under his supervision had to provide information on the personal identity of

Plate 3.1. Ichikawa Ichirō with the author, Tokyo, 1997. (Source: the author.)

each comfort woman and submit to the military police a daily report on the names of customers and of the women who served them.[78] As a matter of fact, the practice of systematic record keeping at brothels and state surveillance of the adult entertainment industry were nothing new to the Japanese authorities. The policies of the Meiji (1868–1912) government, for example, had included a set of regulations that supervised and taxed the five categories of workers in the pleasure quarters. Houses of assignation and banquet halls, for instance, were required to record and report daily on the identity of all customers and the amounts of money they spent on the premises.[79]

Kim Sun-dŏk (a.k.a. Kim Tŏk-chin),[80] a Korean survivor who developed an intimate relationship with a high-ranking officer named Izumi during her three-year (1937–1940) ordeal as a comfort woman, recalled that the military regularly inspected her comfort station—located outside Shanghai and later in Nanking (Nanjing) and run by the Korean man who recruited her—to check the food and the cleanliness of the house. Kim also mentioned a regular medical examination conducted by the military doctor. By comparison, Yi Yong-su, who arrived in Taiwan in January 1945, stated that there was no regular medical examination at her comfort station, which was run by a Japanese man who had recruited her from Taegu (as described in the introduction). When Yi contracted a venereal disease, the proprietor gave her an injection known as "No. 606," which contained mercury and contributed to her later infertility. The area had no hospital or health clinic.[81]

In general, the houses of prostitution catered primarily to noncommissioned officers and enlisted men but reserved overnight services as a privilege exclusive to officers. Some brothels, by contrast, served only officers. One such example was the House of the Seven Seas in Java, described in detail by Ruff-O'Herne.[82] It was set up in a large Dutch colonial–style house with nicely furnished rooms for each woman, a storeroom for food, servants' rooms, a large garden with several trees, and a pen for fowl. The front veranda of the house was used as a reception area, where the officers could lounge and purchase tickets for the girls or women of their choice, whose pictures were displayed on a bulletin board. The army doctor who conducted weekly medical examinations of the women was one of the regular "customers." An Indonesian housemaid and a houseboy served meals and did various household chores for the Dutch comfort women, who included married "volunteers."

The majority of the Korean survivors appear to have labored at these houses of prostitution, where they were identified by their newly given "professional" Japanese names such as "Nobuko" for Yi Sang-ok and "Mi-chan" for Mun P'il-gi, a short version of Mun's childhood Japanese name, Miyoko. Many claim not to have received any money. Among the very few who acknowledged payment for their sexual labor, Ha Yŏng-i (pseudonym; b. 1922) stands out for her detailed recollections of her nearly seven years as a comfort woman. Ha received 10 percent of the 1.5-yen fee until after 1940, when upon the order of a military leader her cut jumped to 60 percent.[83]

On weekdays the women sat in the hallway for customers to view before picking their chosen ones. This practice of "sitting in public display" (*hari-mise*) had been common in licensed brothels of Japanese pleasure quarters since the seventeenth century.[84] Mun P'il-gi recalled that on weekdays they served about ten soldiers, usually during evenings because the men were out fighting during the day. Yi Yong-su, by contrast, stated that she served on average four or five soldiers a day when she labored in Taiwan in 1945. According to many Korean survivors, weekends at the comfort stations were hectic. They often did not have time to eat, let alone sit in the hallway. On Saturdays and Sundays, Mun P'il-gi had forty to fifty soldiers who would come from eight in the morning until seven in the evening, after which only officers could visit. Mun recalled that soldiers lined up outside the door, waiting their turn and sometimes quarreling when someone jumped the queue, while other survivors such as Pak Pok-sun insisted that such descriptions of queuing and quarreling were untrue. In any case, generally, each soldier was allowed thirty minutes but most left after about five minutes of sexual contact, according to Mun and others. Some brought their own condoms, but a few would refuse to use them. Mun would then insist, threatening to report them to their superiors or pleading with them to comply so they would not catch a disease.

Houses of prostitution were usually located in clusters,[85] both in big cities and in isolated areas where the military units were stationed. The experiences of Yi Ok-sŏn (b. 1927)—who was abducted by a Japanese man and a Korean man on her way home after shopping at a department store in Ulsan and taken to Manchuria, where she was held from 1942 to 1945— reveal that some brothel operators received substantial assistance from the military when they set up comfort stations. The brothel where Yi Ok-sŏn labored was first located inside the military camp, and during those several months the women were fed in the canteen after the soldiers had finished their meals. After the Japanese civilian proprietor moved the establishment outside camp and settled it near the market, it became a "regular military comfort station" with a big sign on the gate. Yi (also known by the Japanese female name Tomiko) was forced to wear makeup and participate in *harimise* for the soldier-customers.[86]

Brothels in urban centers served not only troops stationed in the city, but also those passing through. In addition, some women were made to travel from one camp to another. For example, Hong Kang-rim (b. 1922), who labored at an urban *ianjo* in Hunan Province in China from the early 1940s until 1945, recalled that the most difficult time of her life as an *ianfu* was when she and her colleagues had to take turns traveling on foot to outposts, where they would stay for a month at a time to provide sexual services to the men stationed there.[87] Proprietors of the houses of prostitution located in isolated areas followed the military unit they were servicing, as Kim Hak-sun's account reveals (see below). Kim Sun-dŏk also recalled moving several times along with her fellow *ianfu* whenever her Korean recruiter-proprietor decided to do so; they started somewhere near Shanghai and ended up in Nanking (Nanjing) before she returned home.[88]

The Paramilitary *Ianjo*

The paramilitary *ianjo* may also be subdivided into two types, in chronological order of their emergence. The *ianjo* I call the "maidens' auxiliary" was embedded with a particular military unit that directly managed the facility for its own exclusive use. It was typically located in a remote frontline area, where the *ianfu* played multiple feminine gender roles, performing both manual and sexual labor. In contrast to the maidens' auxiliaries, which constituted an *embedded* "girls' army" kept within the military compound, the second type of the paramilitary *ianjo,* the "quasi-brothel," was located outside the military compound and generally did not perform manual labor. The quasi-brothels operated by the military worked much like the civilian-run houses of prostitution but were not motivated by profit. The testimonials of victim-survivors suggest that civilian traffickers procured women for both types of paramilitary *ianjo.*

1. The Maidens' Auxiliary

The embedded maidens' auxiliary units seem to have been set up in the early 1930s, not long after the September 1931 Manchurian Incident (see the testimonial of Ch'oe Il-rye below). One may assume that the maidens' auxiliaries became more numerous after war with China began in earnest in 1937. The Japanese army used a variety of euphemistic terms, such as the "special platoon" (*tokushu shōtai*) and the "girls' army" (*jōshigun*) to refer to groups of the *karayuki-san*.[89] These prostitutes were regarded as an essential part of the army; the women were transported along with provisions when the army advanced. Navy documents referred to comfort women as *tokuyō-in* (literally, special-necessary-personnel) and sent them to Southeast Asia and the Pacific region as a matter of practical policy during the final phase of the war.[90] Nakayama Tadanao, whose 1933 comments on the "girls' army" after his visit to the Japanese Imperial Army headquarters in Jinzhou, Manchuria, are excerpted in the chapter epigraph, also observed that comfort women became "nurses as tender as wives" to the wounded soldiers.[91]

Notably, some survivors in South Korea, such as Yi Tŭk-nam (b. 1918) and Mun Ok-chu (1924–1996), testified that they indeed played the role of nurses in Indonesia and Thailand, respectively, during the last few months of the war.[92] In addition, the Korean survivor Ch'oe Il-rye provides uniquely significant evidence of a prototypical embedded maidens' auxiliary. Ch'oe's testimonial is extremely valuable for several reasons.[93] First, although documentary evidence for the establishment of the first confirmed comfort station in Manchuria is dated March 1933,[94] Ch'oe Il-rye's testimony dates the establishment to 1932. Second, her case reveals that the military played an active role in setting up comfort stations of the paramilitary category from the start of the Asia Pacific War rather than after the Nanking massacre in 1937, which official documents may suggest.[95] Third, because she labored as a comfort woman for the same military unit for thirteen years, covering roughly the entire period of the comfort system, her testimonial narrative, summarized below, reveals the deteriorating changes in living conditions at comfort stations during the final phase of the war and supports the hypothesis of a three-phase evolution of military comfort facilities. Ch'oe Il-rye recalled:

> My family lived in the remote countryside in South Chŏlla Province where one could hardly see a car pass by. I did not know about schools or studying. My father was an agricultural laborer. My mother died of an illness after she gave birth to my younger sister. We were very poor, and I worked as a maid for a neighbor. It was in 1932, when I

was sixteen years old, that two men in military uniforms [believed to be Japanese] abducted me from near a village well. The soldiers took me to a nearby city [possibly Kwangju], where we stayed for about a month so that they could gather more women. When we set out on the road, there were about thirty women riding in several trucks passing through Taejŏn, Seoul, and P'yŏngyang.

Upon the arrival of my group of five girls at a remote unpopulated battlefront in Manchuria on a very cold winter day, I watched the soldiers build their barracks using plywood and tent materials. A few yards away from their own large barracks, they built separate living quarters for us women. Metal wire fences surrounded the buildings, and two sentinels stood at the entrance to guard the barracks. At first, my group of five women was accommodated in one room, but later we were assigned to individual rooms. They also gave us new names. Mine was Haruko, and all five of us got along very well. The military provided us with meals and seasonal clothing.

A month or so after our arrival, a soldier came to conduct medical tests on us by drawing blood from the ear. After the test, a high-ranking officer summoned me to have sex. Until then I had no knowledge about the male sexual organ, let alone about coitus. The officer raped me, and I tried to accept everything as my fate. I recall that about thirty of us women resided scattered across the huge military compound. We gathered together for weekly medical examinations on a weekday when we did not serve soldiers.

For thirteen years, from 1932 to 1945, I labored as *wianbu,* serving only officers most of the time. Officers sent their men to fetch me to their places. My colleagues and I also worked as nurses and washerwomen for the soldiers. We would send off soldiers to battle, tend the wounded, and attend the funerals of those killed in combat, wearing black hats and kimonos. Sometimes, some of my colleagues and I became "serving women," which afforded us an opportunity to consume alcoholic drinks with the soldiers. There was no regular payment, but I was able to save a very large amount of money (about 1,000 yen) by accumulating the occasional tips of 2 to 3 yen given by some officers.

Toward the end of the war, when life became harder, without enough food to go around, an officer whom I served regularly told me to flee without telling the other women. He provided me with three white identification cards and explained to me in detail how to run away. I followed his instructions and was able to make it. By the time I arrived in Seoul, Korea was liberated. Then I returned to my hometown right away.[96]

2. The Quasi-Brothel

The quasi-brothel appears to have also existed in relatively remote areas close to the front lines, and it sometimes served multiple units. With the commanding officer's permission, unit members visited the *ianjo* of the quasi-brothels on specified days for an allotted amount of time. Extant official documents reveal these characteristics and record that this type of comfort stations were established "in rapid succession" in central China after 1938.[97]

Kim Hak-sun's description of her experiences highlights the characteristics of the quasi-brothel. Kim was seventeen years old when her foster father took her and another girl to China to find jobs for them. Both girls completed their training to become *kisaeng* but were unable to work in Korea because they were minors. Kim's accounts—as others have noted—vary as to the procedure whereby the two girls were taken to a comfort station, as well as the exact place.[98] Her testimonial narrative for the 1991 lawsuit stated that the foster father took the girls to a small village called Ch'ŏlpyŏkjin (Tiebizhen, in Chinese) and left them there. In her 1993 published version of the story, on their arrival in Beijing, the girls were separated from Kim's foster father by the Japanese military and were then forcibly taken to a house being used as a comfort station. In contrast, I learned from Yun Chŏng-ok, the founding corepresentative of the Korean Council, that Kim's original unpublished story given to Yun included a quirky twist: her foster father apparently worked as the manager of the comfort station until he disappeared one day,[99] though her published testimonial narrative states that no one managed the women directly in the house where she stayed. This sort of variation in circumstantial details should not detract from the fundamental value of her account. In light of the historical significance of her being the first Korean woman to come out and of her having helped ignite the redress movement, I provide the relatively detailed narrative of her life below, from her birth in Manchuria to her life as a comfort woman in 1941, ending with her successful escape from the comfort station and her return home as a married woman in 1946.[100]

I was born in Manchuria in 1924 and had the misfortune of losing my father soon after my birth, depriving me, among many other things in my wretched life, of the opportunity to receive the traditional celebration of the one-hundredth-day feast [*paegil chanch'i*] for newborn babies. My mother apparently came to regard my birth as an omen for her own hard life ahead. When I behaved in an unruly manner, for example, my mother would bewail her *sinse* [personal circumstances], accusing me of having brought on the death of my father. Mother would also berate me for being troublesome, "just like" my deceased father, who had pestered her so much. After returning to Korea, Mother remarried when I turned fourteen. I did not get along with the stepfather, and I felt estrangement in my *chŏng* [affect] toward mother. She then pawned me as a foster daughter to a man who changed my name to [the more feminine-sounding] Kŭm-hwa and gave me formal *kisaeng* training in singing and dancing.

When I finished my training, I was seventeen years old and my minor status prevented me from working as a *kisaeng*. My foster father then decided to find a job for me in China. After receiving permission to do so from my mother, he left for China with me and another girl (who had also been trained to be a *kisaeng*) in 1941. After we arrived in Beijing, we ran into Japanese soldiers and an officer, who asked my foster father if we were from Korea. They then took him away under charges of being a spy. Other soldiers hustled me and the other girl along a back street to where a truck was parked. About forty to fifty soldiers were on board. When we refused to board, the soldiers simply lifted us into the truck. Shortly afterward, the officer who had taken my foster father returned, and the truck sped away immediately. During the journey, when shooting was heard, everyone got off and crouched underneath the truck. We were given balls of cooked rice for food during the ride. At dusk the following day we got off the truck and were taken to a house. Later in the evening, the officer came to take me to an adjoining room, divided only by a curtain. He forced himself upon me. During the night, he raped me again.

The following day, soldiers brought two wooden beds they made for my companion and me. As we learned later, the red brick house had been abandoned by fleeing Chinese and turned into a comfort station. Next to the house was a military unit. I learned later from the soldiers that the place was called Ch'ŏlpyŏkchin. There were five Korean women in the house. They all had Japanese names. The twenty-two-year-old Shizue was the oldest. She gave my friend and me Japanese names, Emiko and Aiko, respectively, to be used at the comfort station. The soldiers brought us rice and other groceries, and the five women took turns cooking and doing laundry. As the youngest, I ended up doing the most cooking and washing. If I asked the soldiers for cooked rice occasionally, they would bring me the cooked rice and soup that they had prepared for their own consumption. Sometimes they would also smuggle me snacks such as dry biscuits.

Regarding fees, Shizue once told me that the rank and file should pay the women 1.5 yen a visit and the officers 8 yen to stay overnight. When I asked who received the money, all she replied was that we were the ones who should be paid. But I never received any money at the comfort station, and I wondered what made Shizue say such things. [It is conceivable that Shizue and others had entered into contracts of indenture with the civilian traffickers who delivered them to the paramilitary comfort station.]

If we wished to go out, the sentinel of the military unit located next to the house would check us. Each room had a bed covered by a blanket and a basin by the door. We wore cotton underwear that had been discarded by the soldiers. From time to time, they would bring us clothes acquired from abandoned Chinese houses. When the soldiers came to the house, they chose the rooms of the women they fancied. As a result, each of us had regular customers. They varied in the way they treated us. While some would knock me out [with exhaustion] at the end of the thirty minutes, others would be quite gentle. One ordered me to suck his sexual organ while holding my head between his legs. Another asked me to wash his sexual organ after intercourse. Sometimes when I resisted out of disgust, I would end up being roundly beaten.

The women at my place were not furnished with condoms. Instead, soldiers brought their own. And once a week, a military doctor from the rear would come with an assistant to conduct routine medical check-ups. When he was busy, he would sometimes miss a visit. We had no set holidays and had to serve soldiers even during menstrual periods. After a month, I began to realize that the same men kept coming back, and that there were no new soldiers. Usually, they would come in the afternoon for about half an hour, but when they had been out on punitive expeditions, they would visit us in the morning. On such days, they would return in the early hours of the morning, singing as they marched, and we had to be up early to serve them, usually at about seven or eight. Soldiers who came in the afternoon would stay for about thirty minutes each. When they visited us in the evening, they would often come drunk and demand that we entertain them by singing or dancing.

After about two months, the military unit moved in a great hurry one morning. We were told to ride in the truck with the soldiers. The new place was not too far away, but it seemed to be further out in the countryside. We could hear much more shooting than in the previous location. The house was smaller, and fewer soldiers came. The military doctor seldom visited the new place. Soldiers went on expeditions more frequently than before, and quite a few of them brought bottles of alcohol with them when they visited us in the morning after such trips. Life seemed more miserable than before, and I continued to look for ways to escape as I did before the move.

One day a Korean itinerant merchant of about forty years of age managed to sneak into my room. Upon confirming that he was a fellow Korean, I appealed to his sense of ethnic solidarity, begging him to take me with him. After servicing his sexual desire, I desperately pleaded again with the rather reluctant compatriot before I was able to flee with him. We became man and wife, and I gave birth to a daughter and a son before our return to Korea in 1946.

On first reading Kim Hak-sun's published testimony, prior to meeting with her in September 1995, I felt the primary tone of her narrative was fatalistic resignation tinged with a sense of *han*. In fact, the bitter memories she did not wish to "even recollect" included not only the four traumatic months at the two comfort stations in China, but also her childhood resentment toward her remarried mother and her own unhappy marital life. She concluded sadly that her "dirty lot" (*tŏrŏun p'alcha*) had started with her unlucky relationship with her parents, which led to her unfortunate young adulthood at the comfort station and marriage to an abusive husband. Most of all, as a mother she suffered dreadfully from the premature deaths of her children.

The Criminal *Ianjo*

Unlike the categories of *ianjo* described above, makeshift facilities that can only be called criminal appear to have sprung up during the final years and months of the war. They seem to have been improvised by combat soldiers on the battlefronts of occupied territories such as the Philippines. Life at the criminal *ianjo* bore little resemblance to those where commercial sex was provided, nor did these operations observe health regulations or hygienic considerations insisted on by the military authorities.

A general picture of the criminal *ianjo* may be drawn from the testimonials of Filipino victim-survivors who lived in provincial towns near the battlefronts after the Japanese invasion in December 1941. Their personal ordeals included being caught by soldiers and raped in the field before being brought to a garrison, where they were forced into sexual slavery. Among the twenty-two Filipino women whose testimonials have been published, the majority had been held between one week and a few months, but five stated they had been held for more than a year. Most managed to escape when they were not being watched or when the American military started bombing.[101]

The situations these women endured contrast sharply with that of comfort women in Manila, where Japanese nationals (then including Koreans and Taiwanese) operated dozens of concessionary *ianjo,* including special restaurants and what U.S. army intelligence reports translated as "houses of relaxation" for the military.[102] They employed not only Japanese, Koreans, and Taiwanese "geisha" or "prostitutes," but also Filipinas; however, none of the Filipinas who worked at these urban comfort stations are included among the litigants suing the Japanese government.

Maria Rosa Henson (1927–1997), who in 1992 became the first Filipina to come out as a former *ianfu,* described the criminal type of *ianjo* in some detail in her autobiography.[103] Henson was carrying food and medicine to help the Filipino guerrilla movement when a Japanese soldier at a checkpoint took her at gunpoint to a comfort station in April 1943. That *ianjo,* which was operated as a sort of "impromptu rape camp," was located on the second floor of the building that had been the town hospital but had been turned into the "Japanese headquarters and garrison."[104] Henson found six other women there. Henson was given a small room, which had a bamboo bed and a curtain but no door. Soldiers stood guard in the hall outside the rooms. The next day, a soldier entered her room and pointed his bayonet at her chest. He used his bayonet to tear her dress open before he raped her. When he was finished, other soldiers took turns.

The criminal *ianjo* Henson described, at least on the surface, resembles the "rape centers" of the Serbian forces during the Balkan conflict, except in one respect: the subjective and underlying motives to rape seemed to have fundamentally differed. Despite the claims of Korean activists that the Japanese use of Korean comfort women was a "genocidal act," rapes at the Japanese camps, from the viewpoint of soldiers, were committed for sexual release and satisfaction.[105] The Serbian military, however, used rape as a weapon intended to help carry out "ethnic cleansing" in the Balkan war.[106] Women held in rape centers in Bosnia-Herzegovina were subjected to "deliberate impregnation" and public display.[107] Some rapes were turned into "sexual spectacles" that were filmed for mass consumption as war propaganda.[108]

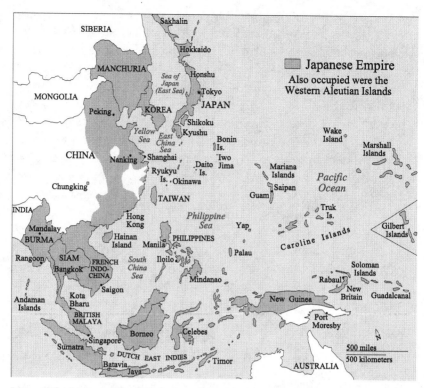

Map 3. The Japanese Empire, circa 1943

The Japanese *ianjo* of the criminal category, however, was rooted in centuries-old masculinist sexual culture and represented an embodiment of aggressive and violent military hypermasculinity. Soldiers at the criminal *ianjo* seem to have raped in private for personal sexual recreation. This point is driven home when we learn from Henson that one officer who raped her said "Arigatō" (thank you) before he left her room.[109] In addition, condom use was an important behavioral requirement at the Japanese comfort stations, even though some men ignored the regulation, as survivors' testimonials have disclosed.

EVOLVING PHASES OF THE *IANJO*

It is important to emphasize that the multiple categories and varying types of *ianjo* discussed above were created in the context of Japan's fifteen-year war—from their first appearance in 1932 in China (primarily in Shanghai and Manchuria) to their proliferation in number and variety during more than thirteen years across the vast expanse of the Japanese wartime empire, which included not only the Japanese archipelago, the Korean peninsula, Taiwan, and major parts of the mainland China, but also the Pacific Islands and Southeast Asian countries under Western colonial rule. These comfort stations represented the militarized behavioral practice rooted in Japanese masculinist sexual culture that regarded prostitution as among the "customary businesses" (*fūzokueigyō* or *p'ungsokyŏngŏp*, in Japanese and Korean, respectively) requiring licenses for the provision of "adult entertainment."[110] The starting point for the creation of comfort facilities for the Japanese military in China was commonsense recognition of normative heterosexual masculinity, tacitly acknowledging Japanese men's customary sex-right to seek and enjoy heterosexual entertainment and coitus outside matrimony. A theoretical model I am positing to explain the phenomenon of the Japanese military comfort station system and its evolutionary transformation across time and place is encapsulated in table 3.1.

The model postulates that the historical evolution of the comfort station system roughly coincided with three pivotal events in the trajectory of

Table 3.1. Three-phase evolutionary model of Japanese military comfort stations (MCS), 1932–1945

MCS category	Phase			Means of wartime liberation from MCS
	Post–Manchurian invasion, 1932–1937	Post–Nanking massacre, 1938–1941	Post–Pearl Harbor attack, 1942–1945	
1. Concessionary	Houses of entertainment (urban areas)			Payment of debt or officers' personal intervention
		Houses of prostitution (ubiquitous)		
2. Paramilitary	Maidens' auxiliaries (front lines)			Officers' special favor or (rarely) escape
		Quasi-brothels (ubiquitous)		
3. Criminal			Rape camps (battlefronts)	Escape or outside intervention

the war: the Manchurian Incident of 1931, which launched Japan's military aggression in China; the Nanking massacre (from December 1937 to early 1938), which intensified the Second Sino-Japanese War; and the Pearl Harbor attack in December 1941, which expanded the continental war into the Pacific.

Working with this periodization, I posit that the diversification of the concessionary and the paramilitary *ianjo* roughly coincided with war's escalating phases as follows: following the Manchurian invasion, houses of entertainment and the maidens' auxiliaries predominated in urban areas and at remote front lines, respectively. After the Nanking massacre, however, new types of comfort stations of both the concessionary and paramilitary *ianjo* categories, which I call houses of prostitution and quasi-brothels, respectively, emerged and mushroomed in response to the rapidly increasing numbers of troops. Finally, the criminal *ianjo* that embodied violent military hypermasculine sexuality emerged after Pearl Harbor, when the fighting raged in a total war of massive destruction of human lives in enemy territory until Japan's unconditional surrender.

In the post–Manchurian Incident phase (circa 1932–1937), facilities of the entertainment house type existed in urban centers as civilian-run special restaurants or exclusive clubs for military personnel, offering commercial sexual entertainment supplied by predominantly Japanese female employees or Japanized Korean women who wore kimonos and were identified for professional purposes by Japanese first names.[111] In addition, as shown in the case of Ch'oe Il-rye, maidens' auxiliaries were embedded with military units at the front, which directly managed the women for the exclusive use of their troops. Official documents reveal that in Shanghai, at the end of 1936, there were ten special restaurants, seven of which were comfort stations reserved exclusively for naval personnel. Official records show 102 Japanese women and 29 Korean women worked as *shakufu* (barmaids or women serving sake, in Japanese) at these restaurants.[112] There are no records on their recruitment methods, which makes it impossible for us to know whether Korean women were forcibly recruited by the state agents or had been *shakufu* when they arrived in Shanghai accompanied by their recruiters, who put them to work at houses of entertainment. Korean survivors' testimonial narratives, however, have revealed that liberation from the concessionary category of *ianjo* was possible when they paid their debt or a military officer intervened on their behalf.

In addition, official records kept by the Japanese Consulate General in Shanghai have revealed that, from the mid- to late 1930s, some Korean residents in Shanghai became business owners and managers in the "customary trade," and that five comfort stations with capital of more than 20,000 yen were run by Koreans.[113] In the particular case of Pak Il-sŏk (also known by his Japanese name, Arai Hakuseki), who served as an officer in the Shanghai Korean Association, the increase in scale of his business between 1937 and 1940 was spectacular. Pak began his Café Asea with capital of 2,000 yen in 1937, but when he turned his business into a comfort station in October 1939, his officially recorded capital was 30,000 yen, which quickly doubled to 60,000 yen in 1940. One may surmise that the Korean entrepreneur undoubtedly succeeded in making a great deal of profit by operating the comfort station for the military during the post–Nanking massacre phase (approximately 1938–1941).[114]

Indeed, it was after imperial Japan engaged in all-out war against China in July 1937 and expanded its occupied territories that the need for a great number of *ianfu* arose. The army was more systematically involved in building *ianjo* of the prostitution house and the quasi-brothel types during the second phase of the military comfort station system. The authorities believed such facilities would help prevent soldiers from committing random acts of sexual violence against women of the occupied territories—a greater concern after the infamous Nanking massacre, during which tens of thousands of Chinese women were raped.[115] In addition to safeguarding its own reputation, military authorities were concerned with the health of their troops, which prompted close supervision of hygienic conditions in the comfort stations. As noted previously, the gynecologist and army doctor Asō Tetsuo submitted a report in 1939 that suggested unmarried Korean women with no prior history as sex workers would be free of venereal diseases and thus more appropriate than Japanese prostitutes as "gifts for the imperial troops."[116] This report was based on his examination of Korean and Japanese women ready to be dispatched to an army comfort station in Shanghai in 1938. The Japanese military authorities soon began to look to colonial Korea as a preferred source of comfort women.

Here it is noteworthy that "comforting" the Japanese soldiers became a national project of wartime Japan in the late 1930s. As shown in plate 3.2, Mitsukoshi Department Store in Nihonbashi, Tokyo, for example, sold a range of "comfort bags" (*imon bukuro*) priced between 3 and 5 yen, to be sent to soldiers, in July 1938, the first anniversary of the Second Sino-Japanese War, and it offered shipping services to Shanghai and Manchuria. By 1939 "adolescent boys and girls in the cities" in Japan were mobilized to perform patriotic service through labor once every three days.[117] Their main activities included writing letters of encouragement to soldiers and making *imon bukuro* and shoulder straps for military uniforms.

Plate 3.2. Mitsukoshi Department Store advertisement of the "comfort bag" sale. (Source: *ASAHI-GRAPH,* July 13, 1938 special edition commemorating the 1st anniversary of the Second Sino-Japanese War. Courtesy of Asahi Shimbunsha.)

A Japanese woman who participated in the patriotic mobilization as a schoolgirl and made comfort bags reminisced:

> The majority of the students' fathers and brothers were in the military. We made efforts, on a school basis, to make *imon bukuro* and write compositions of comfort. We were not allowed to write our individual names on our compositions but only our school name. . . . We made face cloths, folding them in two and putting them in bags. We used a writing brush to write the word *imon*, or "comfort," on each bag. Daily groceries, medicines, loincloths, and letters of encouragement were already in the bags. It was a must that a letter of encouragement be in each bag. On those bags we wrote our names and addresses. The soldiers soon wrote back to us. Most of them asked us to send them our photographs. They sent theirs first, and because we admired the soldiers as the equals of the gods, we were all busy writing letters.[118]

Remarkably, these comfort bags from the Japanese people apparently were distributed not only to soldiers, but also to comfort women. A Korean survivor who labored in China from 1938 to 1945 and is a complainant in a class-action lawsuit against Japan, recalled that receiving a comfort bag about once a month was one of the exceptional moments of pleasure during her life at the comfort station.[119] According to the 1944 U.S. military intelligence report (on twenty Korean "comfort girls" who were captured in Burma),

> [The soldiers] also mentioned the receipt of "comfort bags" filled with canned foods, magazines, soap, handkerchiefs, toothbrush, miniature dolls, lipstick, and wooden clogs. The lipstick and clogs were definitely feminine and the girls couldn't understand why the people at home were sending such articles. They speculated that the sender could only have had themselves or the "native girls" in mind.[120]

*   *   *

After the attack on Pearl Harbor, 400,000 troops were dispatched south. After March 1942, the Ministry of War took charge of building comfort stations for enlisted soldiers and cooperated with the army in sending to overseas troops "hygiene sacks" (condoms) that were regarded as necessities for soldiers in the field. The September 1942 newsletter from the welfare section of the ministry indicated that a total of four hundred "permanent" comfort facilities had been established.[121]

One can only surmise the possibility of an increase in the number of criminal *ianjo* during the final phase of the war, when about one million Japanese troops occupied the Philippines, the Dutch East Indies, French Indochina, British Malaya, Singapore, and Burma, Thailand, and various islands in the Pacific.[122] Testimonials of Dutch and Filipina survivors prove that during the post–Pearl Harbor phase of the war not only Japanese subjects (including colonial Koreans and Taiwanese), but also local women, were recruited into compulsory sexual labor. As in the Korean cases, some women were recruited by local collaborators with false promises of well-paying jobs, while others were forcibly abducted by the military.[123]

COLLABORATION, COMPLICITY, AND COERCION

One must note here that, in the social history of colonial Korea, it was pimps, as well as state administrators, especially petty functionaries in rural areas, who became complicit in the systemic exploitation of the most

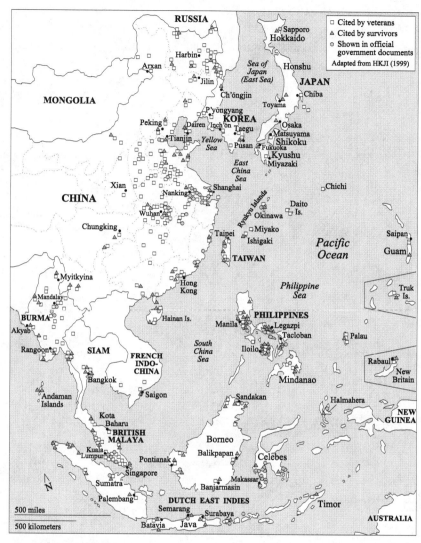

Map 4. Major military comfort stations

vulnerable and powerless. Local elites in colonial Korea entered into relationships of collaboration with the state in order to continue to exercise power in their locality under the pressure produced by the presence of the Japanese colonial occupiers.[124] One of the most salient examples of this Korean collaboration took place in 1941 when the Japanese army was preparing to invade the Soviet Union. The Japanese Kwantung Army requested that the colonial Government-General of Korea assist in the recruitment of twenty thousand Korean women.[125] The Government-General responded by enlisting the assistance of Koreans, such as the *myŏnjang* (head of the township), who visited and persuaded indigent families with many children to send their unmarried daughters to work in Japan. The only recourse for such indigent parents was to marry off their daughters, even if on paper only, because married women were exempt from the draft. This does not, however, mean that all Korean comfort women were unmarried. The statistical data on Korean survivors shows that slightly more than 10 percent of the survivors were married, divorced, widowed, or cohabiting at the time of their recruitment.[126]

The colonial government's collaboration resulted in the speedy assemblage of about eight thousand young girls and women who were sent as comfort women to the northern regions of Manchuria, where seven hundred thousand troops had mobilized along the Chinese-Russian border.[127] It is remarkable that the colonial Government-General of Korea could recruit less than half the requested number, which suggests that large-scale abductions in the manner of Yoshida Seiji's discredited confessional story of "slave raids" in Chejudo (discussed in chapter 4) could not, and probably did not, take place. It showed that, without the use of physical force, the organizational power of the local administration and the effectiveness of the collaborators proved to be limited.

In fact, the statistical analysis of the data on Korean survivors, which was jointly published by the Korean Council and the Ministry of Gender Equality (MOGE), reveals that most were recruited by either Korean (64) or Japanese (35) civilian procurers, whereas police (45) and soldiers or civilian employees of the military (45) also played significant roles as recruiters.[128] Some of the respondents listed multiple agents as their recruiters, including local administrative heads (17), teachers (4), and family members and relatives (2).[129] The MOGE collection also reveals that at the time of recruitment more than one-third of 172 cases worked as maids (26), factory workers (20), employees at restaurants or *kisaeng* houses (9), farmers (5), students (5), or merchants (1).[130] Further, statistical records on 181 cases showed that more than a quarter (48) were already living away from their families when they were taken to military brothels and that the majority (112) were taken to China, including Manchuria and Taiwan.[131] These figures illuminate the contours of the personal ordeal facing individual Korean comfort women. They highlight the depth of structural violence—that is, institutionalized gendered social injustice—inflicted primarily upon working-class women. The data not only confirm the criminal role played by the wartime military government of imperial Japan in the exploitation of colonial subjects, but also reveal the significance of local collaboration. It is striking that according to the accounts of survivors, Koreans actually outnumbered civilian Japanese among those seeking profit by human trafficking, forcing prostitution and sexual slavery upon young female compatriots.

It is now instructive to consider the recollections of a Korean man whose father had worked as a *myŏnjang* during colonial rule.[132] In an interview with the Japanese journalist and writer Senda Kakō he explained that out of fear for his and his family's security, his father carried out the recruitment order and managed to recruit two young women in the township by visiting indigent households and encouraging parents to send their daughters to work in Japan. He concluded tearfully, "One might say that my father was weak. But few Koreans at that time could do otherwise. [Because of his collaboration] my father had to vanish from his hometown after liberation, and I think this was his bad luck. I think it was his tragic fate to be appointed *myŏnjang* then."[133]

CONCLUSION

The Japanese military comfort system must be characterized as fundamentally rooted in a masculinist ideology that privileged men's presumably uncontrollable "biological need" for sex. The paternalistic Japanese state methodically assisted in the system's implementation and development, especially from 1938, after the Nanking massacre, believing that it would help maintain the morale of the troops and prevent rapes of local women. Although the system may have contributed to restraining and pacifying the troops' "savage feelings and lust," it is not surprising to learn that it did not in fact prevent rapes.[134] Reporting on 610 crimes committed by troops after they had invaded countries in Southeast Asia and the Pacific Islands in 1942, an army document noted the prevalence of rapes, a situation caused both by "insufficient comfort facilities and insufficient supervision."[135]

In addition to the lack of comfort facilities, however, one might further consider financial factors that contributed to battlefield rape. Problems cropping up at comfort stations in China in 1938, for example, included soldiers not paying for services rendered. A variety of survivors also mentioned this problem. Mun P'il-gi, whose deceitful recruitment into a comfort station in Manchuria was described in chapter 2, related that she would sometimes take pity and send a soldier away without having been paid.[136] Yi Sang-ok, who labored in Palau, first receiving 30 yen a month as a comfort woman and later only 50 sen as a medical assistant, stated that some soldiers stole her personal belongings when she left her room to wash.[137]

The monthly salary of an enlisted man was only 6 to 10 yen, depending on rank, so the service charges at the *ianjo* were not cheap for rank-and-file soldiers. The entries in the "Battlefield Diary" of an Imperial Army unit in central China dated March 3, 1938, for example, listed the service charges for the various ethnicities of women: Chinese (1 yen), Korean (1.5 yen), and Japanese (2 yen) an hour, with added warning that "Money must be paid without fail."[138] As mentioned above, Korean comfort women could earn the same rate as Japanese in Manila, where the comfort station rates were 1.5 yen for a thirty-minute service by either. This equal valuation was an improvement over the situations that prevailed in China, where the rates for Korean women ranked below those for their Japanese counterparts. This improvement arguably reflected the greater assimilation of Koreans as the subjects of imperial Japan at this point in the war and signified a formal endorsement of the official *naisen ittai* policy. The rate for Chinese women in Manila remained at 1 yen, the same as it was in China.[139]

In the experience of many Korean comfort women, however, their ethnicity was only a source of social discrimination. For instance, according to the ethnic hierarchy followed in Okinawa, Korean women were used by enlisted men, while Okinawans were reserved for officers. Furthermore, as Japanese nationals, Okinawan women were remunerated, while Korean women, being despised colonial subjects, had to supply the same services for no pay. Although local Okinawans were cruelly mistreated by mainland soldiers, natives of Okinawa in their turn were contemptuous of Koreans as colonial subjects.[140] Ethnic discrimination by the Japanese military was most transparently exercised at the end of the war, when soldiers informed *Japanese* comfort women of Japan's defeat and fled with them. Many Korean comfort women were simply abandoned, and it has been reported that in some extreme cases the retreating Japanese army killed the women by driving them into trenches or caves where they bombed, burned, or shot them, creating mass graves on the spot.[141] The massacre of Korean comfort women at the end of the war by retreating Japanese troops may have reflected the military's fears about the revelation of atrocities. But it was also likely rooted in the generally disdainful, ethnocentric, and sexist attitude of the Japanese military toward Korean comfort women. As colonial subjects reduced to sexual objects for the troops, these women were seen as expendable military supplies, too cumbersome to be taken along at the end of the lost war.

As noted previously, the Dutch government regards the comfort system primarily as "prostitution," while acknowledging an element of forced prostitution as well.[142] The Dutch interpretation of the Japanese military comfort system is only partially correct insofar as it represents the experiences of Dutch women residing in occupied Dutch East Indies. In another reckoning, Vera Mackie, an Australian feminist historian of modern Japan, has presented Japan's comfort system as enforced military prostitution, referring to *ianjo* as military brothels and *ianfu* as military prostitutes.[143] Although one may appreciate Mackie's transcending mere political correctness and the inflated blanket characterization of the system as sexual slavery,[144] hers is also a partial portrayal that glosses over multifarious criminal sexual behaviors committed by the military within the institutional framework discussed above.

To be sure, the intended purpose of the comfort system was to regulate military sexuality and discourage battlefield sex crimes. The comfort system, however, did not—and could not—prevent rapes, though it did help curb mass rape—especially in "pacified" areas in occupied territories. This curbing effect was acknowledged by none other than a Chinese prosecutor at the Tokyo War Crimes Trials and, more recently, by scholars of Japanese history.[145]

This chapter has demonstrated the complexities of the Japanese military comfort system, which was orchestrated by the paternalistic state and the military leadership to cater to what they—along with many other people in Japan and other patriarchal societies—regarded as the "normal" heterosexual needs of servicemen, as well as to forestall violent military hypermasculine sexual behaviors of wartime troops. In its operations it clearly straddled commercial and criminal sex. Although a statistical overview of the different categories of comfort stations may never be available, it is clear that some Japanese soldiers perpetrated collective acts of sexual violence and enslavement primarily against women of occupied enemy territories. At the same time many soldiers used the state-regulated and -endorsed concessionary or paramilitary *ianjo,* availing themselves of what they regarded as a form of licensed prostitution. In sum, both public sex and war crime sex were part of the fabric of imperial Japan's military comfort station system. This distinction more fully engages historical fact, but it in no way detracts from the overall oppression exercised in acting out a broader masculinist sexual culture in this historical institution during the more than decade-long and evolving phases of Japan's last war.

Part 2

Take as your time-span the course of human history, and locate within it the weeks, years, epochs you examine.

—C. Wright Mills, *The Sociological Imagination,* 1959

"What's Wrong with Prostitution?"

—Igor Primoratz, *Philosophy,* 1993

"Prostitution: Buying the Right to Rape"

—Evelina Giobbe, *Rape and Sexual Assault III,* 1991

PUBLIC SEX AND WOMEN'S LABOR

Chapter 4

Postwar/Postcolonial Public Memories of the Comfort Women

Well, you see, whatever we did in the military, we all dedicated ourselves to our country, or *gohōshi*. That's how I feel about the comfort women. It seems to me that the comfort women were a necessary evil. Particularly as we were fighting for so long. If we hadn't taken those women with us, there would have been a lot of trouble for the native women.

> —Ōmori Fumiko, a Japanese woman who served as a military nurse during the war, in Sekiguchi Noriko, *Sensō Daughters,* 1990

During the war everyone, yes everyone, had a hard time. Nevertheless, I feel nostalgic.... We all tried our best to help Japan win, and I felt bitter [about Japan's defeat]. Yes, that's true.

> —Pae Pong-gi, a Korean comfort woman survivor living in Okinawa, Japan, in Yamatani Tetsuo, *Okinawa no Harumoni,* 1979

A MAJOR CONSEQUENCE of the internationalization of the comfort women issue has been a full-fledged history war between Japan and Korea. History textbooks in particular emerged as the focus of the bilateral "war of memories" in the second half of the 1990s. Nationalistic representations of relations between the two countries over the past century have become an intractable obstruction to coming to terms with major historical facts—such as those surrounding the comfort women—about their shared past. The pitched political and psychological battles over what constitutes the "proper" inscription of the comfort women's story in history books are astounding in light of the total absence of the issue from both Japanese and Korean textbooks before the mid-1990s.[1]

By contrast, popular-culture "memory works"—works dealing with memories of historical events or life histories—on comfort women had been produced in the two countries before the start of the international redress movement. Suzuki Yūko, for example, listed in her 1991 booklet on Korean comfort women the titles of thirty books and pamphlets in Japanese on the comfort women issue, which she said represented those that were easily available.[2]

The contrast between these popular public memories of comfort women in postwar Japan and those of postliberation Korea prior to the formation of the Korean Council in 1990 forms an interesting and illuminating juxtaposition. Major nonfiction works in Japanese highlight Korean women's tragic stories with humanitarian sympathy, whereas Korean-language publications brim with postcolonial nationalist animosity against Japan.

COMFORT WOMEN IN THE POPULAR PUBLIC MEMORY

Many people, especially those outside Korea and Japan, appear to think the comfort women story was suppressed in these countries. For example, an American legal scholar claimed in 1995 that the story had remained a "long-kept dark secret" until the 1990s.[3] In fact, knowledge about comfort women was common in both Japan and Korea, especially among the older generations who lived through the war. Moreover, dozens of books on the subject were readily available at bookstores for postwar generations, especially in Japan. Some of the Japanese books highlighting the ordeals of Korean women in fact became best-sellers in the 1970s. Korean-language publications, by contrast, were very few in number, and none enjoyed the wide readership that certain Japanese works acquired before the start of the international redress movement. By and large, the books in Korean are written from a postcolonial nationalist perspective and denounce Japan for the forced mobilization of mostly "virgin" girls in the Chŏngsindae, who, most Koreans assert, were abused as comfort women. In comparison, the Japanese literature has encompassed a wider range of viewpoints, dealing not only with war veterans' intimate memoirs of their encounters at comfort facilities and the personal stories of former comfort women, but also with humanitarian and socially critical works sympathizing with the plight of the exploited women of colonial Korea.

Postwar Japan's Popular Public Memories

In postwar Japan, accounts about comfort women started to surface in the voluminous war-story literature from the late 1940s.[4] Between the early 1950s and 1989, the year in which Hirohito (posthumously referred to as Emperor Shōwa) died, more than two hundred Japanese documents concerning the comfort stations were published in a variety of formats, such as books, magazine articles, biographies, and memoirs.[5] Notably, they include the life stories of three former comfort women—two Japanese and one Korean.

The first and, at the time of this writing, only autobiography by a Japanese survivor was published in the summer of 1971 under the pseudonym Shirota Suzuko. The first documentary film and a resultant publication on Pae Pong-gi (a Korean survivor living in Okinawa, Japan), as discussed below, came out in Japanese in 1979. A complete biography of Pae was published eight years later.[6] The story of another Japanese survivor, Kikumaru-san, which was also initially published in the summer of 1971, was first reported in a popular magazine.

After Kikumaru-san's suicide in 1972, Hirota Kazuko discussed more of her life story in a nonfiction book that reported on the wartime experiences of several Japanese women in the battlegrounds of the South Pacific and Manchuria. Born in 1939 and a member of the Pacific War Research Group, the author's own personal memory of the war concerns the death of her younger sister right after the massive Tokyo air raid by the U.S. forces, which burned more than 80,000 persons to death in one night on March 10, 1945.[7] Published in 1975, Hirota's *Shōgen Kiroku Jūgun Ianfu/Kangofu: Senjō ni Ikita Onna no Dōkoku* (Testimonial Records of Military Comfort Women [and] Nurses: Lamentations of the Women Who Lived at the Front) discusses the testimonials of Japanese women who served the wartime military in their roles as comfort women and military nurses, respectively. The book is divided into two parts: the first half examines the lives of several comfort women through their recounting of their experiences at the paramilitary type of comfort station in Truk run by the navy. The second half of the book recounts the narratives of military nurses who cared for wounded soldiers in Manchuria and the Philippines. Some of the nurses offer vivid accounts of the horrible sexual ordeals their colleagues underwent in Manchuria when Soviet troops forced them to become comfort women after Japan's defeat.

Hirota's work is extremely valuable on two counts. First, it gives a voice to Japanese survivors' private memories of life as comfort women and its negative impact on their lives in postwar Japan. Second, it provides a young woman writer's critical insights into the complexity of the comfort women issue. Hirota identifies this wartime experience as an example of structural violence against "marginal women" whose lifelong difficulties were due not simply to the wartime demand for sexual labor, but also, and perhaps more, to their subsequent inability to return to mainstream social life in postwar Japan.

During her interviews with the geisha-turned-*ianfu* Kikumaru and other survivors, Hirota unexpectedly encountered the subjects' candid assessment that their days on Truk Island (known then as "Paradise of the South Pacific") were "happy" and even the "best" periods of their lives.[8] Taken aback to hear uniformly positive statements from the two survivors, regardless of their different positions (one was designated for officers and the other for enlisted men), Hirota went back and reread published reports on other former comfort women that she had remembered as being replete with dark melancholy. In her rereading, she discovered that it was not the wartime sexual labor itself but the humiliation of social stigma and isolation in their postwar lives that made these women despair. Kikumaru, for example, committed suicide in April 1972 at the age of forty-six, just months after the author first met her.[9] The two wills she left behind were addressed to a friend and to the editor of the weekly that had published her story in August 1971. She asked of the editor to sprinkle her ashes in the ocean around Truk Island.[10]

Mulling over Kikumaru's suicide, Hirota provides a psychological interpretation: One of thirty-three "elite" comfort women reserved for the officers on Truk Island, Kikumaru had felt a sense of pride about her life and work. That is, she believed that she was engaged in the performance of her duty as a gendered citizen under the wartime slogan "For the good of the country" (*Okuni no tameni*). When the war ended with Japan's defeat, however, the righteous justification of her life as a patriotic Japanese subject evaporated, turning her into an object of scorn.

The author further notes that realizing the true source of the survivors' sadness and depression was a "scary discovery," because she, too, is a gendered subject just like her informants. In summing up, she asks rhetorically, Where does the real "hell" lie for these women? Hirota remains critical of the prevailing teary-eyed humanitarian reports on comfort women, who are uniformly portrayed as pitiable and in need of sympathy. Having met a variety of former comfort women during her research, Hirota has vowed not to avert her eyes to the diversity of social reality in her future research on other marginalized women.

Between 1973 and 1983, works on the topic by three male authors of the older generation—two Japanese (Senda Kakō and Yoshida Seiji) and one Korean living in Japan (Kim Il-myŏn)—significantly contributed to the construction of a sympathetic Japanese popular memory of the wartime plight of Korean comfort women, especially among progressives. These critical works, discussed below, served as the foundations of the paradigmatic story developed by activists in the 1990s.

A reporter for the *Mainichi Shimbun* (a major national daily newspaper in Japan), Senda Kakō, first saw pictures of Korean comfort women in 1964 when he was working on a photographic book, *Nihon no Senreki* (Japan's War Chronicle), which was published by the *Mainichi* in 1967. In the process of selecting photographs for the book from more than twenty thousand taken by *Mainichi* photojournalists who reported on the Japanese military during the Fifteen-Year War, Senda came across a number of strange pictures of women marching together with the troops. Some of them showed the women carrying trunks on top of their heads, which Senda recognized as a traditional manner of carrying things among Korean women.[11] One picture taken right after Japan's defeat showed the women wearing kimonos, while another showed one woman with a Japanese hairstyle being stared at contemptuously by a Chinese. The explanations attached to the negatives of these pictures did not include the term *ianfu*. Senda, who was born and raised in Manchuria, pursued the identities of the women and came to learn, for the first time, about the existence of the so-called *jūgun ianfu*.

Senda's subsequent inquiries into factual details about the comfort women were met with either deception or requests for anonymity from those who had lived through the war. Senda was able to finally grasp the historical picture—so to speak—of the comfort women more clearly once he came to know Asō Tetsuo, a former army doctor, who was living in Fukuoka. Senda's trailblazing work *Jūgun Ianfu* (Military Comfort Women) was published in 1973. The book drew on his interviews with Japanese military veterans, Korean men, and others as well as relevant publications, including a book on the forced recruitment of Koreans authored by a Korean man in Japanese.[12]

Senda's book, which was quickly turned into a film by the major Japanese film studio Tōei,[13] provides many interesting anecdotes deriving from his personal encounters and data collected firsthand during his field research in Japan and Korea. The book, organized into seven chapters, considers a wide spectrum of issues that include the historical roots of the comfort women system, methods of recruitment, discrimination against Korean women, and the abandonment and "honorable deaths" (*gyokusai*) of comfort women in the final months of the war in the Pacific. He critically notes that comfort women who died on the battlefield were awarded neither medals nor pensions for their service.

Especially remarkable, in terms of the present study, is Senda's fourth chapter, in which he concentrates on the case of Korean women. Entitled, *Tsūkoku! "Teishintai"* (Lamentation! "Volunteers"), this chapter reports on

Senda's research trip to Korea, where he met several Koreans involved with or informed about the comfort system, including one journalist-turned-official at the Ministry of Education, Chŏng Tal-sŏn, who showed him a clipping from the *Seoul Sinmun* on the *chŏngsindae*. Through him and others, Senda learned that Koreans use the term *chŏngsindae* (*teishintai,* in Japanese) synonymously with "comfort women." Senda reported that when visiting a souvenir shop for Japanese tourists in a department store located in Myŏngdong in downtown Seoul, he was surprised by a middle-aged sales-woman who bowed her head to him in appreciation for his field research on the *chŏngsindae*. She had read about it in a magazine and expressed her "gratitude on behalf of Korean women" with tearful eyes.[14] While savoring an ice cream she offered him, the puzzled Senda asked her several questions, including why she thanked him for his research. After a brief silence, she answered, "I was pleased to learn that there is at least one Japanese who is thinking about the cases of those women."[15] Having learned that her father graduated from the prestigious Waseda University in Tokyo and that she had been divorced for several years and had two children of primary- and middle-school age, Senda wondered whether she might have a more personal reason to be sensitive about the *chŏngsindae* issue, but he could not confirm his suspicion owing to the woman's reluctance to offer any further details.

Through the introduction of a Korean journalist, Senda also met Kim Kyŏng-ae (pseudonym), a fifty-two-year-old woman who identified her-self as a former comfort woman. When Senda asked whether she went as *chŏngsindae* "that started in 1943," Kim stated that it was before that, in 1940.[16] Senda learned from her that a Japanese man accompanied by a po-liceman came to recruit Kim and that she was sent to battle zones in China. When asked where in China, Kim answered, "Here and there." When asked other questions about her hometown, life at the comfort stations, and the year she returned home, Kim maintained a stony silence. Sympathizing with her reluctance, Senda closed his notebook and stopped querying her. When he left the house, located on a hill crammed with little houses that looked like a village of refugees, the Korean journalist apologized to Senda and promised to find another survivor if he could spare more time. Senda replied, "No, that's enough. I heartily realize that the significance of silence for humans can be larger and weightier than speech."[17]

On his research trip to Korea, Senda was disturbed to encounter his fel-low Japanese men "crazed" over "*kisaeng* tourism" in Seoul. He could not help seeing—one might add, very perceptively—the phantom of imperial

Japanese soldiers brandishing their swords superimposed over the sight of contemporary Japanese sex tourists. Senda included his thoughts on sex tourism in *Zoku: Jūgun Ianfu* (Sequel: Military Comfort Women), published in 1974. The work describes both the arduous conditions and the atrocities committed during the hellish last weeks and days of the war and postdefeat stories involving comfort women. When a new publisher reissued the volume in 1978 in a "revised edition," however, Senda decided to remove the section on *kisaeng* tourism, regarding it as an unnecessary footnote to his report on comfort women.[18] The 1978 edition of both the main volume and the sequel, produced in a pocket edition, went through eleven printings by 1990 and 1992, respectively. They amply and critically informed Japanese readers of the sordid history of imperial Japan's military comfort system during the war and the mistreatment and predominance of Koreans among the victimized women.

Kim Il-myŏn (b. 1920), a first-generation *zainichi* (Korean resident in Japan) who writes in Japanese, published *Tennō no Guntai to Chōsenjin Ianfu* (The Emperor's Forces and Korean Comfort Women) in 1976, two years after Senda's sequel came out. The most comprehensive and pioneering work focusing on the plight of Korean comfort women, Kim's book is organized into thirteen chapters that present a historical overview of the structure and provenance of the comfort women system, the recruitment of the women, anecdotes of life at comfort stations across the region under Japanese occupation, the atrocities committed against the women toward the end of the war, and the Japanese women who became the "occupation forces' comfort women." The book, which had gone through thirteen printings by 1992, does not contain any primary-source data. Rather, it skillfully draws on the Japanese materials on the topic available as of the first half of the 1970s.

Underlining the paramount importance of women's chastity in Korean culture and using such terms as *sei no dorei* (sex slave) to describe the miserable lives of Korean women in the "sex hell" of the comfort stations,[19] Kim asserts that the forced recruitment and exploitation of Korean women amounts to an imperial Japanese policy of "genocide" (*minjok malsal,* in Korean) aimed at obliterating the Korean nation. His indignant criticism of the Japanese imperial forces, however, rests on the notion of the helpless Koreans' total victimhood and overlooks the political, economic, and social structural factors contributing to colonial Korea's collaboration in the operation of the comfort facilities, to say nothing of Korean recruitment of a large number of the young women. Nonetheless, Kim's ethnic nationalist perspective, coupled with paternalistic discourse regarding the traditional

Plate 4.1. Kim Il-myŏn holding up the author's autographed copy of Kim's *Tennō no Guntai to Chōsenjin Ianfu* during an interview in Tokyo, 1997. (Photo by the author.)

sexual mores for female chastity, has provided a solid framework for the Korean public discourse, greatly influencing works of collective memory published in postcolonial Korea.

Senda, as well as Kim, approached the comfort women issue from the perspective of humanitarian sympathy for the victims, criticizing Japan's racist treatment and colonial exploitation. Their informative works, however, did not lead to any serious collective social action or nationalist reactions. It is noteworthy here that Korean women researchers of the postcolonial generation who have interviewed and helped publish testimonials of Korean survivors critique both Kim and Senda for having taken a "commercial" (*sangŏpchŏk*) approach, greatly exaggerating their stories (for example, claims of comfort women serving "more than one hundred soldiers a day").[20] The charge of commercialism may also have to do with their dramatized depictions of soldiers' sexual behaviors at comfort stations and detailed descriptions of the physical ordeals the women suffered.

By contrast, it was Yoshida Seiji's two confessional books—although discredited since 1992 by activist historians of both the pro- and anti-redress camps—that provided the most potent ammunition for activists who argue that Korean women were forcibly recruited by agents of the Japanese state. Yoshida Seiji (b. 1913), who received a university education in Tokyo, served in the Yamaguchi Prefecture Patriotic Labor Service Association from 1942 until Japan's surrender.[21] As head of the mobilization department in Shimonoseki, a port city in Yamaguchi Prefecture with regular ferryboat services to Pusan, his main duty was to coordinate and control the flow of labor conscripts.

Yoshida described his role in the "hunting" of Korean laborers and comfort women in *Chōsenjin Ianfu to Nihonjin* (Korean Comfort Women and the Japanese, 1977) and *Watashi no Sensō Hanzai* (My War Crimes, 1983). The 1977 book describes how his office managed to recruit a hundred young Korean women under the guise of the Teishintai (Volunteer Labor Corps) and send them off to Hainan Island to be used as comfort women. The 1983 book, which had gone through five printings as of 1992 and whose Korean-language edition was published in 1989, further details how, over a period of a single week at the end of May 1943, he recruited 205 Korean women from Cheju Island by using deception (he promised them 30 yen per month for their work as Teishintai members) as well as physical force. Yoshida wrote that at the headquarters in Cheju he distributed to the women the Teishintai clothes, which had arrived in three sizes, small, medium, and large, from the Yamaguchi Police. He further stated that the conscripted women were kept in the military warehouse, where soldiers raped them before they boarded a ship.[22] Yoshida thus provided vividly detailed narratives of how Korean women were forcibly drafted by the agents of the Japanese state. These accounts have served in the 1996 U.N. report as uniquely valuable "evidence" of the "truth" of the paradigmatic story. Even after the history professor Hata Ikuhiko (b. 1932) discredited Yoshida's story in 1992, Yoshida's "confessions" continued to bolster Korean public discourse that comfort women were "deceived *chŏngsindae*."

During my interview in 1997, Hata described how he debunked Yoshida's story.[23] Hata first called Yoshida for telephone interviews, on March 13 and 16, 1992, and asked several questions about the story of the "slave hunting" but did not receive satisfactory answers. Having tried to locate Yoshida's wartime colleagues without success, Hata decided to go on a research trip to Cheju Island. There he talked with five old men who had worked at the button factory where Yoshida claimed his "hunting" took place. Hata confirmed that some male workers had been conscripted but concluded that no female workers had been drafted to be comfort women.

Further, during his research at a Cheju Island public library, Hata came across a review by Hŏ Yŏng-sŏn of the 1989 Korean edition of Yoshida's 1983 book in the August 14, 1989, issue of the *Cheju Sinmum*. Hŏ, a reporter at the newspaper, pointed out that there were no witnesses to support Yoshida's story and that the islanders, including a local historian who investigated the matter for several years after the book's original publication in 1983, dismissed it as a "fabrication" (*nalcho*). When Hata met Hŏ, she asked him, "Why would someone want to fabricate such a story?" Hata told me he was at a loss to answer her question.

Upon his return to Japan in 1992, Hata published his research findings in the April 30 issue of the national daily the *Sankei Shimbun* and in the May 1 issue of *Seiron,* a conservative monthly magazine. Supporters of the comfort women redress movement have criticized Hata for his "unscholarly approach" to the issue: instead of conducting comprehensive research on the issue of forced recruitment as a whole on Cheju Island, critics pointed out, Hata posed only specific questions that would refute Yoshida's story and based his conclusion on those answers. For instance, Uesugi Satoshi, a founding member and the director of the Center for Research and Documentation on Japan's War Responsibility, explained the negative reactions of the people on Cheju Island: the islanders have traditionally been discriminated against by fellow Koreans on the mainland, and people in small communities like Cheju feel a need to keep silent about the misfortunes of fellow villagers. Uesugi also wrote that Yun Chŏng-ok (of the Korean Council) found one villager who was willing to talk at first but then yielded to community pressure to keep silent. Nonetheless, Uesugi admitted that there *were* many problems with Yoshida's story, which appeared to be an amalgam of actions taken outside Cheju Island and thus cannot be considered a personal testimony. Uesugi wrote that he and his colleagues (such as Yoshimi Yoshiaki) have decided not to rely on Yoshida's story since 1992.[24]

Nevertheless, Yoshida's work served as a crucial resource for international human rights activists and the United Nations as they constructed the paradigmatic comfort women story. The United Nations special rapporteur Radhika Coomaraswamy, for example, redefined the comfort women system as a system of military sexual slavery. She quoted Yoshida's *Watashi no Sensō Hanzai* in her 1996 report for having confessed to "slave raids" in which he obtained "as many as 1,000 women" for comfort women duties.[25] Frustrated, Hata published a paper, "The Flawed U.N. Report on Comfort Women," and criticized the Coomaraswamy report for having "given Yoshida's long-discredited testimony a new lease on life" while also underscoring the credibility problem of survivors' life stories: "Nearly all evidence concerning the recruitment of 'comfort women' comes from the oral testimony of the victims themselves."[26]

What should we make of Yoshida-Hata controversy? For Hata, who is regarded as a reputable historian, the question of the credibility of the survivors' oral testimonials, given in a highly politicized context, is a legitimate scholarly issue. Indeed, conservative historians of the positivist tradition have tended to privilege the "objectivity" of documentary evidence over oral histories in the politics of history, an approach that activists and feminist scholars have lashed out against.[27] Nevertheless, it is important to remember here that even progressive historians and activists (such as Uesugi Satoshi) have decided against the truthfulness of Yoshida's story, which may belong to the genre of historical fiction rather than testimonial.

Despite the vividness of his account, Yoshida certainly is not the only one to exhibit symptoms of what some have called a "factitious disorder." There have been well-known cases of fabricated stories that were published as books or in prestigious newspapers and journals, some of which even garnered awards.[28] One might speculate that Yoshida, whose adopted son was Korean born,[29] may have been motivated to "confess" his war crime in part by his personal sympathy for Koreans and by his postwar feelings of repentance for his and his countrymen's wartime mistreatment of Koreans. In the fall of 1997, when I contacted Yoshida to request an interview, he let the phone ring about a dozen times before answering. I was momentarily quite taken aback to hear a loud, angry male voice yell at me: *"Dareda?"* (Who is it?). Quickly collecting myself, I identified myself, and Yoshida promptly apologized, saying that he had received many harassing phone calls. He expressed his regret for being unable to accommodate my request for an interview because of ill health.

In addition to the landmark books written by the authors of the older generation, men and women of the younger and postwar generation (introduced below) also produced, prior to the start of the redress movement, important works that advance our knowledge on the comfort women issue. One such person is Takasaki Sōji (b. 1944), a historian who began learning the Korean language in 1974. He visited South Korea the following year and wrote a short essay in 1976 for Japanese readers of the women's newsletter *Fujin Shinpō*, which presents Korean perspectives on comfort women.[30] His essay contains extensive direct quotations translated from Korean publications and suggests that comfort women and *kisaeng* tourism constitute interesting themes for Japan and Japanese women to consider "how Japan and Japanese women have conducted their colonial and postcolonial policies toward Korea and Korean women."[31] Takasaki concludes his essay by exhorting the readers to deepen their concern for these issues and extends the hope that they start learning the Korean language to that end.

Yamatani Tetsuo (b. 1947), an independent filmmaker and writer of the postwar generation, occupies a unique vantage point on the comfort women issue through his personal interviews with Pae Pong-gi, a Korean comfort woman survivor who remained in Okinawa after the war until her death in 1991. He produced the documentary *Okinawa no Harumoni* (A Grandmother, or an Old Lady, in Okinawa), subtitled *Shōgen: Jūgun Ianfu* (Testimony: Military Comfort Woman), in May 1979.[32]

Moved by unanticipated requests from his audiences and a contract offer from a publisher to publish a book, Yamatani compiled testimonials by one Korean and several Japanese war veterans as well as the Korean "Grandmother Pak" (Pae Pong-gi's pseudonym). Yamatani's *Okinawa no Harumoni: Dainippon Baishunshi* (Great Japan's Prostitution History) published in December 1979, includes Pae's life story, collected during a total of ten hours of interviews. Unlike most Korean ex–comfort women, Pae Pong-gie had been briefly married multiple times (at seven and at eight as a *minmyŏnŭri,* or adopted-daughter-in-law, respectively, and at seventeen and at nineteen).[33] Yamatani reports in the afterword that the ten years of her life as a divorced woman (from the time she left her hometown at nineteen until her recruitment in Pusan at age twenty-nine) remain puzzlingly unaccounted for. Yamatani was unable to learn details because Pae would say only that she had worked as a farm helper or cook in a variety of places. This decade remained blank even in a 1987 biography of Pae by the Japanese nonfiction writer Kawata Fumiko (b. 1943), who had known Pae Pong-gi since 1977.[34] The Korean-language edition of her book was published in the spring of 1992, about half a year after Pae's forlorn death in Okinawa in October 1991.[35]

Yamatani reflects on Pae's interesting observation that she had "wished Japan would win the war."[36] For Yamatani, this was also a most unexpected remark. He was further surprised when Pae stated that she was *kuyashikatta* ("disappointed" or "bitter") over Japan's defeat.[37] (One may note here, however, that Pae was not alone among Korean survivors in feeling disappointment at Japan's surrender.) It is, as Yamatani noted, only when one learns the details of the incredibly violent and tragic miseries Pae endured throughout her life, beginning with her childhood in Korea and continuing in postwar Okinawa, that one begins to understand why she looked upon her time as a comfort woman with nostalgia (*natsukashii*).[38] This—along with Japanese survivors' positive memories of their days as comfort women, discussed above—suggests important amendments or correctives to the multiple competing representations that have been assigned to comfort women in the historic context of a global paradigmatic shift to a postcolonial, transnational human rights perspective emphasizing women's victimhood in sexual slavery. Pae's unanticipated responses make one further wonder about the undeniable variability of the women's personal voices and of their views of their own lives.

It is interesting to note here that before producing the first documentary film about a Korean comfort woman survivor, Yamatani visited Korea to investigate the "women's volunteer corps."[39] In February 1978 he interviewed Choi Ch'ang-kyu (b. 1919), a Korean man who had served in the

Japanese army during the war before he escaped to join the Korean independence fighters in China. Choi testified that he had helped establish a military comfort station in China, but even with Choi's active cooperation Yamatani was unable to locate any former comfort women in Korea.[40] Back in Japan, Yamatani learned about Pae Pong-gi. He and his crew finally found her in August 1978. Despite her caretakers' efforts to persuade her, though, for seven days Pae refused to be interviewed. On the eighth day she finally agreed to meet them. Yamatani later learned that during the first week of his visit, Pae suffered one of the worst spells of the severe headaches that had plagued her since the war. The resultant eighty-six-minute film attracted more attention than Yamatani and his crew anticipated. Yamatani attributed its popular reception to the "boom in women's history" begun by Yamazaki Tomoko's 1971 *Sandakan Hachiban Shōkan,* which described the life stories of the *karayuki-san,* women of imperial Japan who labored as prostitutes overseas.[41]

Indeed, when an Okinawan businesswoman named Uehara Eiko (b. 1915) published a memoir of her life as a former prostitute in 1976, it went through nine printings in less than three months.[42] The memoir included very frank and engaging personal reflections on her "unforgettable memories" of an intense but brief sexual affair with a Japanese military officer who came from Osaka to fight in the war and committed suicide at the prisoner-of-war camp. Uehara, who was only four years old when her mother became ill and her stepfather sold her to a brothel in a red-light district called Tsuji, wrote that people took human trafficking for granted in those days. She noted, rather surprisingly, that her life after all had been that of a "happy woman" (*shiawasena onna datta*).[43] Her positive assessment of her own life as a woman, including twenty-five years of communal life in Tsuji (which she remembers warmly),[44] may have much to do with her personal achievements in the postwar years, when she became a successful businesswoman running a famous teahouse, married an American man working for the U.S. government, and became a mother. (Notably, Uehara was presented as one of two publicly known former Japanese comfort women at the Women's International War Crimes Tribunal held in Tokyo in December 2000, when Fujime Yuki argued that Japanese former comfort women must also be recognized as victims of military sexual slavery regardless of their prior occupation as licensed prostitutes.)[45]

Another important author of the postwar generation on the comfort women issue is Suzuki Yūko, who published *Feminizumu to Sensō* (Feminism and War) in 1986. She offers a critical rethinking of the roles Japanese women played in supporting the war effort, both as leaders of educated middle-class women's organizations and as members of volunteer labor corps (teishintai) at military supplies factories. She is especially critical in reflecting on the role that nationalistic women leaders played in passionately exhorting young unmarried women to work "for the good of the country." Four years later, in 1990, Suzuki courageously declared in an article in the February 1 issue of Mainichi Shimbun that the military comfort women policy was clearly Japan's "state crime" (kokka hanzai) and suggested that Japanese women demand that the state atone for the crime and accept responsibility for forging a new life for Japan as a "moral nation."[46] Since then, Suzuki has formed a strong alliance with the Korean Council, offering staunch support to the redress movement.

These major works by progressive writers were produced in postwar Japan and have contributed significantly to the construction of a humanitarian public memory of the comfort women by primarily spotlighting the Korean case. By contrast, in 1989 Sekiguchi Noriko, a Japanese woman filmmaker of the postwar generation, produced the documentary film Sensō Daughters (Daughters of War), which investigates the role women played in the Japanese Imperial Army's New Guinea campaign (1942–1945). Plagued by criticism and a lack of funding, it took five years for Sekiguchi to complete the documentary, its field research eventually supported by an Australian government fund.[47] The film was first screened at the Twelfth International Women's Film Festival, held in Paris from March 24 to April 2, 1990.[48] Four months later, in August, it was shown in Hiroshima and later in Tokyo.

Known as the "Forgotten War" in postwar Japan, the New Guinea campaign—in which 127,000 troops lost their lives, according to the official records, and only 11,000 men survived—had received no replacements or supplies, and the troops had to commandeer food from the local people.[49] The documentary begins with somber scenes of loyal Japanese citizens from all walks of life visiting the palace plaza in central Tokyo to offer get-well prayers for the gravely ill Emperor Hirohito in the autumn of 1988. Sekiguchi, as the narrator of the film, pronounces Hirohito to be "a barrier rather than a link" to Japan's past and notes that the film is a record of the southernmost battleground of what the Japanese used to call the "Great East Asian War" in New Guinea, today's Papua New Guinea. Sekiguchi interviews Papua New Guinea people as well as Japanese men and women of older generations, including Asō Tetsuo, Senda Kakō, former military nurses such as Ōmori Fumiko, and several military veterans who had served in the New Guinea campaign. Asō maintained that most of the Korean comfort women he examined in January 1938 were sexually inexperienced, while their Japanese counterparts were "professionals." He also showed Sekiguchi a photograph of an imposing building called the Cosmo-politan Hotel that had been used as a comfort station. The largest comfort station in the South Pacific, the hotel was located in Rabaul, which was the headquarters for the 100,000 troops of imperial Japan in the Pacific arena.

An elderly Papua New Guinean man who remembered the hotel—which had been demolished by the time of the filming—recounted that several hundred women had worked at the comfort station. He voiced his doubt that they had made it back to Japan because of the American bomb-ers. He further recalled that the wartime Japanese military was extremely strict: had a native person like himself touched even a finger of a comfort woman, the military would have punished him with decapitation. An old woman in New Ireland recounted how she was threatened into becoming the "wife" of the leader of a Japanese military unit. Another elderly woman, her daughter-in-law beside her, confessed that she, a married woman, was lured into having sex with a Japanese soldier named Kojima four times while her husband was away. As a result, she gave birth after the war to a baby boy with the lighter skin and "almond-shaped" eyes that are regarded as characteristic of the Japanese and other East Asians. After hearing the elderly woman's confession, her daughter-in-law commented that it finally confirmed her suspicion that her husband was half Japanese.

Postliberation Korea's Popular Public Memories

In South Korea the first mention of a former comfort woman, Kim Ch'un-hŭi, in the mass media apparently took place in 1964, nineteen years after Korea's liberation from Japanese colonial rule in 1945 and one year prior to the normalization of diplomatic relations between South Korea and Japan.[50] It is notable that the February 14, 1964, issue of the national daily *Han'guk Ilbo* used the term *wianbu*, not *chŏngsindae*, in the title of the article on Kim. Nevertheless, the text of the article, which used the term *kundae wi-anbu* (military comfort woman), equated comfort women with "members of the Patriotic Chŏngsindae" (*Aeguk Chŏngsindaewŏn*): "Kim Ch'un-hŭi was forcibly taken, during the period of imperial Japan, to the Southeast Asia as a so-called *Aeguk Chŏngsindaewŏn*, namely, as a *kundae wianbu*." Kim had died in 1963 at the age of forty-four, leaving a considerable amount of wealth in Vietnam. Kim's estate was estimated to be about US$200,000 (26 million wŏn in Korean currency) and included diamonds, cash in U.S. currency, and real estate, such as a café and a dairy farm. Numerous people attempted to claim Kim's estate by identifying themselves as her relatives, but not one of them actually was.[51]

In light of the terminology used in the 1964 media report on the late comfort woman, it is hard to find another example of such unpoliticized—one might say, in hindsight, "politically incorrect"—use of the term *kundae wianbu* in Korean public discourse on comfort women since then. Almost all Korean publications concerning the comfort women issue surfaced after the 1965 bilateral agreement was signed between South Korea and Japan. Nearly all have presented postcolonial nationalist perspectives, denouncing Japan for the forced mobilization of "virgins" as *chŏngsindae,* who, many Koreans have continued to assert, were abused as comfort women. Presumably the first work of fiction, little known even today, to depict comfort women as *chŏngsindae* was *Surado* (1969), by Kim Chŏng-han (b. 1908).[52]

It was with the commemoration of the quarter century since liberation that public discourse on the subject formally emerged in postcolonial Korea. In August 1970 the *Seoul Sinmun* ran a series of articles reviewing the twenty-five years since Korea's liberation. The sixth article in the series dealt with the Chŏngsindae, and its publication launched public discourse on the comfort women issue.[53] This article estimated that between 50,000 and 70,000 Korean women had been mobilized in the Chŏngsindae between 1943 and 1945. It quoted a former student-soldier (now a professor), who recounted his memory of running across about 200 *chŏngsindae* women in Singapore, from where they were to be shipped back home. He stated that far from being joyous about their survival, the women were weeping, perhaps out of sorrow for their lost youth (*chŏlmŭm*). For some comfort women survivors, however, the loss of savings and other possessions was an important source of unhappiness at the end of the war.[54] In any case, since 1970 Korean publications on comfort women have commonly referred to the women simply as *chŏngsindae,* dropping the term "patriotic" used in the 1964 media report.

Yim Chong-guk wrote an essay entitled "Joshi Teishintai" (in Japanese; Women's Volunteer Labor Corps) that was published in the March 1974 issue of the Japanese monthly *Ajia Kōron.*[55] The next year, the journalist-turned-researcher Kim Tae-sang published a book in pocket edition on the history of Koreans' forced mobilization during the war under imperial Japan. The book included a short chapter entitled "Yŏja Kŭllo Chŏngsindae" (Women's Volunteer Labor Corps).[56] The author noted that in contrast to other issues such as the forced labor mobilization, the failure to repatriate Koreans in Sakhalin, and the problem of Korean atomic bomb victims, all of which had been publicly debated, there existed no open concern or debate over the sacrifices of the *chŏngsindae.* These, Kim asserted, represented the most inhumane and tragic instance of Japan's mobilization of Korean human and natural resources for its war of aggression. He criticized the *Seoul*

Sinmun article for presenting the *chŏngsindae* issue only as a remembrance of the past and for failing to probe further into the matter. Kim Tae-sang wrote that the truth regarding the *chŏngsindae* mobilization should be clarified even if it meant reopening an old wound. He concluded the chapter by saying that Korean women's "lamentable history of suffering" (*t'onggok ŭi sunansa*) must be recorded, together with "the history of evil crimes" of Japanese militarism.[57]

It is interesting to note here that Senda's 1973 book *Jūgun Ianfu* was not only quickly translated and published in Korean (and is quoted in Kim Tae-sang's book), but was also made into a movie entitled *Yŏja Chŏngsindae* (Women's Volunteer Corps), even though the title of the Korean edition was *Chonggun Wianbu* (Military Comfort Women). The October 24, 1974, issue of the national daily *Dong-a Ilbo* carried an advertisement for the film at a movie house called the Sŭkara. The ad indicates that it is an "adult movie" (*sŏngin yŏnghwa*), expresses gratitude for the full house on the opening day, and declares, "Bold exposure!! Women worth three divisions were taken in like this! And they fought like this!"[58]

Nevertheless, it was not until 1981 that the first Korean-authored volume devoted to the topic of Korean comfort women was released to the general public. It helped fix Korean ethnonationalist discourse on "the comfort women as *chŏngsindae*" and motivated a fledgling novelist to fictionalize a Korean comfort woman's story. This was a Korean edition of Kim Il-myŏn's book, translated by Yim Chong-guk.

Strangely, however, Yim Chong-guk is identified as the *p'yŏnjŏja*, or editor-author. He does not disclose its provenance to be Kim's 1976 work *Tennō no Guntai to Chōsenjin Ianfu*, described above. Yim's "editorial" role extended only to changing a few of Kim's terms, as well as omitting a few paragraphs from and adding a new sentence to Kim's afterword. For example, in the Korean version, *Chŏngsindae Sillok* (True Records of the Chŏngsindae), Yim chose to translate *chōsenjin* (Korean) as *han'gukin* (people of the Republic of Korea, or South Koreans) instead of *chosŏnin* (Korean pronunciation of *chōsenjin*, or people of Chosŏn). Yim's translation of the term *chōsenjin* as *han'gukin* is problematic because the latter term did not exist during the colonial period and excludes the other half of the ethnic Koreans who live in the north as the people of the Democratic People's Republic of Korea, or North Koreans. Moreover, the phrase *chōsenjin ianfu*, in the title of Kim's chapter 3, is translated as *han'gukin chŏngsindae*. Most disturbing for me is that Yim Chong-guk put his own name and the date of June 1981 at the end of the afterword, instead of retaining Kim Il-myŏn's name and the original date of December 1975.

Plate 4.2. 1974 advertisement for *Yŏja Chŏngsindae*, the Korean film based on Senda Kakō's *Jūgun Ianfu*, screened at the Sŭkara Theater in Seoul. (Source: *Dong-a Ilbo*.)

A young woman novelist of the postliberation generation, Yun Chŏng-mo read Yim's book and was extremely shaken to learn about the comfort women. She refers to Yim Chong-guk as *sŏnsaengnim* (an honorific term for a teacher or a social elder) to show her respect for his work. She states with reverence that Yim Chong-guk dedicated his whole life to collecting resource materials on the history of imperial Japan's exploitation of Koreans.[59] Apparently not knowing that the true author was Kim Il-myŏn, the novelist credits Yim for having planted a "living volcano" in her heart to write about Korean women's ordeals. Remarkably, however, in place of the conventional usage of the euphemism *chŏngsindae,* Yun chose to adopt the term *Chōsen pi,* Japanese soldiers' sexualizing and objectifying slang for Korean comfort women, in the title of her novella, "Your Mother's Name Was *Chōsen Pi*" (*Emi Irŭm ŭn Chōsen Ppi Yŏtta*).[60] Published in 1982, this fictional account inspired the production of another "adult movie," whose title was—once again—*Yŏja Chŏngsindae* (Women's Volunteer Corps).

Yun's novella begins with a telegram that the narrator, Pae Mun-ha, a thirty-seven-year-old son and unmarried writer, has received telling him about the death of his long-estranged father. The first half of the novella reveals something of the father's unhappy personal history as recounted by Mun-ha's stepmother during his brief visit with her to make the funeral arrangements in Andong, North Kyŏngsang Province, in the southeastern region. The stories the stepmother remembers relay the suffering of Mun-ha's great-grandparents and uncles during the colonial period and describe his father's postliberation behavior, wallowing drunkenly in a sense of victimhood and completely rejecting his son from the very day Mun-ha was born. In the second half of the novella the son is back in Seoul, where he finally learns from his mother about her past and how his parents first met in the Philippines, just before the end of the war.

When she was eighteen, Mun-ha's mother, Sun-i, had volunteered to join the Chŏngsindae to prevent her older brother's being conscripted. She expected to work as a laundress for the military in Japan. Instead, she was among those selected to serve as comfort women and sent to Manila in the fall of 1943. She became a *pi* and was given the Japanese name Michiko. She was paid three wŏn for overnight service; however, all the money she earned—which came to about 2,000 wŏn, enough back then, according to Sun-i, to buy a small building—was in the form of the military vouchers that became worthless after Japan's defeat. One day toward the end of 1944, she found that the brothel manager and Japanese comfort women had disappeared and abandoned the Korean women. It was during the months of the retreat march with the soldiers that Sun-i met Pae Kwang-su, a wounded student-soldier from Korea. Pae Kwang-su owed his survival and recovery to the kindness of Sun-i, and they came to form a close bond. Conversations between the two directly address the delicate issues of women's sexuality and reveal their different, gendered perspectives. Pae Kwang-su once expressed a desire to remain in the Philippines with Sun-i and live there as farmers rather than returning home. He also told her, "Sun-i, I feel sad whenever I look at you. For no reason, I feel sad all the while. And I feel angry. I would offer you my life if you wanted, so why do I keep feeling angry? Sun-i, I've thought about it deeply. Maybe it's because you have lost the simple and unadorned beauty of the young unmarried women of our hometown."[61]

Sun-i felt that she fully understood Kwang-su's conflicted feelings about her. Yet, in her heart she wished that he would see her not as a comfort woman, but as a Korean woman who had encountered sudden disaster, just as he himself had. She knew that his anger derived from the fact that she had been spoiled by "countless Japs' semen." Outwardly, she remained calm, but inwardly she shouted, "The real gist of your conflict over your inability to forgive and forget is your own sense of victimization. You have to realize that by now!"[62] She screamed in her mind, "I am Sun-i now, and will be Sun-i until I die! Please let us forget. We must forget the past."[63]

Kwang-su then held her hand and asked, "If I married you, would my anger subside? If we lived together intimately, would my sadness disappear?"[64] Although others in their group regarded Kwang-su and Sun-i as a couple, Kwang-su had hardly ever touched Sun-i, even though they were together all the time. Once Kwang-su jokingly asked, "What would be the number of the soldiers you serviced? More than a few thousand? Anyway, after servicing so many Japanese men, would that thing of a woman turn into a Japanese style?" Stunned, Sun-i remained silent. Kwang-su rephrased his question. "What I meant was whether that would disable the woman's function." Sun-i replied, "The woman's function . . . it was finished long ago [for me]," thinking that was what Kwang-su wanted to hear. Kwang-su's question made Sun-i realize her situation. She thought she should let him go, and yet she could not help having some lingering affection for him, which, she said to her son, brought about the unhappy aftermath in their eventual lives together.

The two were detained separately at a prisoner-of-war camp. In October 1945 they were put on the same ship to return to Pusan, Korea, without knowing each other's whereabouts. Upon landing in Pusan, they ran into each other and then, prompted by Pae Kwang-su, began living together. This domestic arrangement did not last. A year later, when Sun-i gave birth to a baby boy, the husband left her without a word, returning only once or twice a year to demand money and beat her for displeasing him. He even referred to his son as a "whore's kid" (*kalbo saekki*) in the boy's presence, whereupon the mother fiercely confronted her husband and demanded—without success—that he recant. (Given the testimony of Kim Hak-sun, the first survivor to come out in Korea in 1991, about her husband's similar behavior of calling her names in front of their children, this fictional incident is remarkably prescient about the ordeals former comfort women continued to endure in their postwar lives.)

Whereas Yun Chŏng-mo's fictional account is supposed to tell the story of military sexual violence against women, the physical violence Sun-i suffered comes, ironically, from her husband back in postliberation Korea well after the war. Nevertheless, when recounting her life story to the son, Sun-i declares that the Japanese war was the source of her lifelong suffering. All the same, the author seems to criticize, in a roundabout way, the irresponsible and immature behavior of Korean men. The diffident son, whose estrangement from his father since birth seems to have negatively affected his sense of self, ends up raping a former high school friend, Ok-nim. Both Sun-i's husband and her son have arbitrarily imposed violence and suffering on women close to them. The underlying subplot highlighting men's customary violence against women is trenchant, even though it remains in backdrop and is never developed into a full-blown feminist critique of Korean sexual culture. In this regard, it is significant that the author attaches a "chronology" (*yŏnbo*) of her personal development into womanhood in the form of an appendix to the novella.[65]

Yun Chŏng-mo's own family background and private life history constitute the social and psychological context that has driven her to write. She was born in postliberation Korea in 1946; her parents were divorced the following year. Her mother remarried in 1948, and the family lived in Seoul until the Korean War broke out in 1950, when the mother left four-year-old Chŏng-mo at the household of her birth family in Kyŏngju. In the wake of her mother's departure, Chŏng-mo grew up under the care of her maternal grandmother and two teenaged maternal uncles. When she was in the fifth grade, her mother came to take her back with her to Pusan, where she was working in the entertainment business. Chŏng-mo then befriended several young women (including distant maternal relatives and former classmates) who worked in the so-called flower-and-willow world (*hwaryugye*)—the adult entertainment industry. She herself worked at a beer hall to pay her way through college.

In 1968, a year before she graduated from college, Yun Chŏng-mo published her first novel, which concerns the ordeals of a poverty-stricken female college student. Yun had gone through a decade of literary wandering when she came across Yim Chong-guk's *Chŏngsindae Sillok*. Like many of her generational cohorts (myself included), she was unaware of the *chŏngsindae* issue until she read Yim's book. Deeply shaken by the stories of the comfort women, she began to recall various stories she had heard from one of her friends in the adult entertainment industry. Of particular relevance to Yun Chŏng-mo's project was the statement that the female proprietor of the bar where her friend had worked had been a *chŏngsindae*. Yun immediately traveled to Pusan in search of the "*chŏngsindae* victim," only to find that she had passed away. She tried without success to locate a survivor from whom she could hear personal testimony. Nevertheless, the urge to write the "humiliating history of women's ordeal" remained, and she undertook a literature review for her book project, during which she also read Yoshida's book.

Not surprisingly, the phrases Yun uses—such as erroneously conflating the Korean *chŏngsindae* and comfort women and referring to life at comfort stations as "sex hell"—and the incidents she describes in her novella (such as the starving soldiers' cannibalism in the Philippines) echo those found in Yim Jong-guk's translation of Kim Il-myŏn's book. It is also remarkable that the author gives the amount of money saved by Sun-i as 2,000 wŏn because, after the redress movement began, it has become socially unacceptable and politically embarrassing to state that the women had been paid for their sexual service: many survivors have emphasized that they did not receive a cent, while some others have revealed in their testimonials that they had been paid and had saved their earnings. One might ask here whether Yun's fictional comfort woman's claim of receiving 2,000 wŏn is credible. As a reference point, the Japanese ex–comfort woman Kikumaru disclosed that, after she paid back her debt of 4,000 yen, she still had savings of about 10,000 yen at the end of her contract of a year and a half.[66]

Two years after the publication of Yun's novella, the mass media reported the dramatic story of No Su-bok, a sixty-three-year-old Korean comfort woman survivor who married a Thai and had resided in Thailand since the end of the war. Her *han*-filled life story was published in an eleven-part series entitled "Na nŭn Yŏja Chŏngsindae" (I Was a Woman *Chŏngsindae*) in the national daily the *JoongAng Ilbo* in March 1984. Two months later, with full financial support from Korean Airlines, she was able to travel to Korea with her three sons and nine other relatives for the first time in forty-two years.[67] She was reported to have brought her lifetime savings of US$1,600 to give to her siblings.[68] Her story was also reported in Japan in the November 2, 1984, issue of the national daily *Asahi Shimbun*. No Su-bok's life story in a nutshell is as follows:

> I was born to a very poor family in Andong County of North Kyŏngsang Province in 1921 and received no education. My parents arranged my marriage when I was fourteen. The bridegroom, whom I had never met, turned out to be a leper. After about a year of unhappy married life, I ran away and returned to the home of my birth. My enraged father refused to take me back, however, telling me that whether I lived or died, I should do so at my husband's place. I left home on foot and took a train to Taegu, where I worked as a live-in maid. A year later I returned to my parents' place with gifts purchased using my savings. My father once again angrily rejected me. I left again and worked as a maid in Pusan. There I met a man five years older than I, and he became my second husband. Missing my hometown, as a seventeen-year-old married woman accompanied by my new husband I paid a visit to my parents, but my father chased us away, saying that I brought shame to the family. I left my hometown for the last time. Four years later, I was forcibly recruited by Japanese policemen in 1942 and sent to Singapore, where I labored as a comfort woman for three years. Not wanting to return home after the war, I decided to escape from the British POW camp. It was during a sudden tropical downpour, or a squall, in an early afternoon in October 1945 that I ran away without being caught. Finally, I became a "liberated person of twenty-four" in Thailand.[69]

*   *   *

Four years after the media report of No's story—and after the death of Hirohito in January 1989—additional fictional accounts of comfort women by male Korean authors came out. They included a "*chŏngsindae* novella" serialized in a local newspaper in Pusan from August to October 1989 and a two-volume novel, *Chosŏn Yŏja Chŏngsindae* (Korean Women's Chŏngsindae).[70] *Yŏsŏng Sinmun,* a women's national weekly newspaper, published the life story of Pae Pong-gi in three installments in July 1989. Pae's life story had already been published in Japan in 1976 and 1987. Pae Pong-gi shared three things with No Su-bok: both came from very poor families, both married young, and both chose not to return to Korea after the war ended. In addition, Pae was a victim of severe domestic violence in her childhood. After her four marriages—including two childhood marriages, as noted earlier— failed, she was deceptively recruited at the age of twenty-nine to be a comfort woman in Okinawa.

In sum, Korean memoirs on the subject, whether fictional or nonfictional, have been extremely meager in number compared to the more than two hundred Japanese publications of this type that had been published by the late 1980s. The businesswoman and women's organization leader Kim Mun-suk felt frustrated when she started collecting data on the Chǒngsindae in 1990. She found a glaring lack of serious research by Koreans on the subjects of comfort women, forced labor mobilization, and Korean victims of the atomic bombs dropped in Hiroshima and Nagasaki. During her research trips to Japan, she was impressed by the sincerity of conscientious Japanese across the country who were conducting careful research on such topics. Kim wrote that she could not help but be angry at fellow Koreans who expediently use the Japanese materials or translate Japanese novels simply to make easy money.[71]

Korea went through tremendous political upheaval after liberation— with the unexpected division into the two Koreas and the ensuing traumatic fratricidal war from 1950 to 1953—which left Korean society in turmoil, with little energy to reflect on colonial injustices or to begin recognizing the needs of comfort women survivors. When asked by Senda Kakō about the lack of concern for the comfort women issue in Korea, his Korean counterpart gave an answer that seemed to sum up the Korean public sentiment of the early 1970s: "There are many important problems in Korea, and we have no time to turn our eyes to that [comfort women] issue."[72]

In addition, talking about the plight of military comfort women survivors must have been the last thing on the minds of those Koreans who, as labor brokers and managers or owners of military brothels, had actively pursued personal profit by participating in the criminal trafficking of compatriot women and girls. Furthermore, Korea's own masculinist sexual culture remained a major underlying sociopsychological factor that not only contributed to the absence of public discourse on the subject but also reinforced the survivors' self-censorship as they silently suffered from the stigma of having been sexually defiled, making them "ethically fallen" women. It is thus not surprising that neither Korean nor Japanese officials deemed the comfort women issue worthy of formal debate during the fourteen years of negotiations (1951–1965) that produced an agreement normalizing bilateral diplomatic relations.[73]

Nevertheless, by the time Yun Chǒng-ok published an article about her research visits to various places where Korean comfort women had labored (such as Hokkaido, Okinawa, Papua New Guinea, and Thailand), books and the personal tragic stories of three individual survivors reported in the news media had informed postliberation Korean society of imperial Japan's heinous system.

COMFORT WOMEN IN NATIONAL HISTORY TEXTBOOKS

The popular-culture memory works on comfort women I have discussed above were intended for adult readers. What and how have history textbooks in Japan and Korea taught their young citizens about the subject? Since textbooks "participate in creating what a society has recognized as legitimate and truthful,"[74] it behooves us to examine the formal narratives about comfort women in Japanese and Korean history textbooks.

Comfort Women in Japanese Textbooks

In Japan the first references to the comfort women issue appeared in all seven history textbooks that passed the government's screening process for adoption in the middle-school curriculum for the 1997 school year.[75] Using terms such as *ianfu* or *jūgun ianfu,* all of the texts mention comfort women in the context of wartime forced mobilization of Korean and Chinese laborers. A general description of the approximate number of forced laborers, the kinds of labor they performed, and the locations where the labor was done precedes a short sentence on the comfort women. Depending on the publisher, school textbooks mentioned the comfort women in a variety of ways, some relatively bland and others more incriminating: "Also, they made women serve as comfort women for the military and treated them badly" (Nihon Shoseki, publisher); "There were also many women who were forcibly sent to the battlefield as military comfort women" (Tokyo Shoseki); "Some of the women in Korea and Taiwan were made to labor at comfort facilities at the front line" (Shimizu Shoin); "They took young women from places such as Korea to serve as comfort women near the battlefield" (Ōsaka Shoseki); and "Many Korean women and others were also sent to the front line as military comfort women" (Kyōiku Shuppan).[76]

This unprecedented and unanimous mention of comfort women in the narration of the Asia Pacific War and Japan's postwar responsibility, in fact, constitutes one tangible result of the international redress movement. This was a clear response on Japan's part to international calls—such as that made by the special rapporteur Radhika Coomaraswamy in her 1996 report to the U.N. Commission on Human Rights—for the government of Japan to raise people's awareness of the comfort women issue by "amending educational curricula to reflect historical realities."[77]

Nevertheless, conservatives and neonationalists deeply resented this development and reacted by forming an organization called Atrashii Rekishi Kyōtasho o Tsukuru Kai (Society for History Textbook Reform; hereafter Tsukuru Kai) in December 1996. A leading proponent and founding member of Tsukuru Kai and a professor of education at the University of Tokyo, Fujioka Nobukatsu (b. 1943) regarded the mention of comfort women in middle-school textbooks as a "pathological symptom" of the masochistic view of the nation's history held by Japan's progressive intellectuals.[78] Guided by a sense of outrage, Fujioka committed himself to combating this view by helping found Tsukuru Kai and writing a new textbook from what he calls a "liberal" historical perspective (*jiyūshugishikan*) that is free of both "imperialist" and "masochistic" or "dark" views of history.[79]

One of the reasons Fujioka and his colleagues object to international pressure such as that brought to bear by the United Nations is that they regard it "unfair" to judge the military comfort facilities by today's standards without telling the whole truth surrounding them. Fujioka concedes that one might argue that the comfort women issue should be mentioned in textbooks from a perspective that regards prostitution itself as unforgivable evil. In that case, argues Fujioka, one must teach the fact that prostitution took place on the home front as well, and that not only the Japanese military but also the troops of other nations had the same institution, and that the American occupying army demanded that Japan offer similar facilities when it occupied the country.[80]

Fujioka asserts that there is no educational significance in raising the comfort women issue to middle-school students and revealing such a dark part of humanity to young adolescents. He further argues that all textbook descriptions of the comfort women issue violate one of the textbook screening standards concerning the appropriateness of the contents for the psychological and physical development of children and students. (The issue of whether discussions of the comfort women are appropriate for middle-school students, one might agree, is indeed a debatable question.) Fujioka notes that some middle-school students feel that Japan is the "most evil" country in the world after learning of this chapter of the country's history, and some are ashamed of being Japanese. Fujioka deplores such unbalanced, masochistic history lessons, maintaining that such an education is a serious crime.[81]

Tsukuru Kai's publication in 2001 of *The New History Textbook* (*Atarashii Rekishi Kyōkasho,* in Japanese; hereafter, *ARK*) and the Japanese government's certification of it triggered a whirlwind of controversy both domestically and internationally.[82] Not surprisingly, *ARK* does not mention comfort women. Instead, it simply describes the wartime labor mobilization, saying that it included students and unmarried women as members of Joshi Teishintai (Women's Volunteer Labor Corps) who were sent to work at factories.[83] Owing to a series of harsh criticisms and a vigorous citizens' movement led by lobbying organizations such as the Children and Textbooks Japan Network 21 (Kodomo to Kyōkasho Zenkoku Netto 21), only a tiny number (0.039 percent) of Japanese middle schools adopted Tsukuru Kai's *ARK*. Despite this abysmal proportion, Tsukuru Kai, with its neonationalist revisionist argument, has had significant impact on subsequent editions of other middle-school history textbooks, some of which omitted controversial topics such as the comfort women issue and the estimated number of the victims of the Nanking massacre.[84]

Comfort Women in Korean Textbooks

A review of middle- and high-school textbooks used from 1946 to 2002 shows that the first time the Chŏngsindae was mentioned in a Korean history textbook was in 1952, by Sin Sŏk-ho, who had personally witnessed the wartime mobilization system at the age of forty. Rhee Younghoon (Yi Yŏng-hun) has argued that Sin Sŏk-ho's use of the term *chŏngsindae* clearly refers to mobilized laborers, not *wianbu,* or comfort women.[85] It was in a textbook produced by the Ministry of Education in 1968 where Yŏja Chŏngsindae (Women's Volunteer Labor Corps) was first employed, albeit ambiguously: "even frail women were forcibly mobilized in the name of Yŏja Chŏngsindae."[86] This statement, however, was quickly excised, and no mention of either *chŏngsindae* or *wianbu* was made until 1978. The review shows that it is from the 1979 edition that mention of the forcible recruitment of women reappears in descriptions of Japan's wartime mobilization of Koreans.

From 1979 to 1982, textbooks read: "Even young women were forcibly taken to the industrial facilities and the front line." This, as Rhee Younghoon notes, sounds like a reference to the *chŏngsindae* mobilization but at the same time hints that the drafted women taken to the front served as comfort women. The revised edition used for the next fourteen years (1983–1996) states: "Even women of our country were sacrificed for [Japan's] war of invasion." This statement offers no clear explanation of how women might have been "sacrificed," but Rhee asserts that few middle-school students would miss the underlying meaning.[87]

Finally, the 1997 edition of the middle-school textbook *Kuksa* (National History) erroneously legitimated the glaring inaccuracy of conflating *chŏngsindae* with comfort women: "At that time, even women were drafted in the name of *chŏngsindae* and were sacrificed as comfort women of the Japanese military."[88] Thus, it continued an inaccurate statement that first appeared in high-school textbooks in 1996.[89]

One may be reminded here of the particular social context in which the new edition came out. The line in the 1996 and 1997 editions conflating *chŏngsindae* with comfort women was added at the height of the international redress movement, which had won the support of the United Nations. Nevertheless, the problem of this inaccurate construction of the national collective memory via history textbooks is its legitimization of the indiscriminate use of the term *chŏngsindae* for comfort women in public discourse and in the mass media. The latter especially have tended to blindly follow and support the strategic political use of the term by activist organizations such as the Korean Council. Remarkably, the government-authored 2002 edition of the middle-school textbook has corrected the error as follows:

> Imperial Japan exploited the labor force of even women by dragging them [into its war efforts] in the name of the Patriotic Labor Corps and the Women's Volunteer Labor Corps. Moreover, they forcibly mobilized a great number of women and sent them to the various regions in Asia where the Japanese military was stationed, turning them into military comfort women and subjecting them to inhumane lives.[90]

The middle-school textbook now distinguishes *chŏngsindae* and military comfort women as two separate categories of wartime mobilization. However, the error was allowed to stand in the high-school textbook.[91] Moreover, the mass media and the general public continue to conflate the terms *chŏngsindae* and "comfort women."

CONCLUSION

The comfort women story had been related to the general public in a variety of formats (including documentaries and movies) in both Japan and Korea well before the international redress movement began in the early 1990s. By and large, authors of both Japanese and Korean background have presented with deep sympathy very humanitarian portrayals of the ordeals of primarily Korean comfort women.

In addition, several survivors—both Japanese and Korean—have made their personal stories public since 1970s; however, none of their stories prompted social movements or legal action on the issue. In fact, the first-person narratives of former comfort women of both Japanese and Korean ethnicities have revealed some unexpectedly positive personal memories of their days as comfort women. This surprising fact can be better understood if we contextualize these memories in the personal lives of individual survivors, whose experiences of hardships encompassed not only their time at comfort stations but also the miserable family circumstances they endured prior to their recruitment and their postwar lives of social isolation and stigma as former comfort women.

At the governmental level, it is not surprising that no formal concern has been expressed about the comfort women issue in either Japan and Korea, given the fact that the government authorities and legislative leadership were represented by conservative men of the ruling class whose gender ideology and sexual behaviors were most likely to have been very conventional. Official state responses to the redress movement in the two countries were provisional and tentative until the mid-1990s. It took the 1996 U.N. report for the Japanese government to approve specific mention of the comfort women in national history textbooks aimed at middle-school students and for the South Korean government to include a brief sentence on the subject in the state-authored textbooks. The debate over the "proper" representation of the comfort women in middle-school textbooks has further elevated the comfort women issue into a formidable "condensation symbol," with potent emotional impact in the memory war waged within Japan as well as against Japan in its neighboring countries, most prominently in South Korea.[92]

Chapter 5

Private Memories of Public Sex

Even now, if there were two men proposing, one Korean and the other Japanese, I would rather marry the Japanese.

> —Pae Chok-kan, a Korean comfort woman survivor, in Dai Sil Kim-Gibson, *Silence Broken,* 1999a

Japanese soldiers enjoyed my singing. On my part, I was pleased to see the soldiers having a good time. Not just my sweetheart Yamada Ichirō but other soldiers as well comforted me; they would say: "I know it's a hard life here, but I hope you will survive it and return home safely and be a loving child to your parent." There were many good ones among the Japanese soldiers, and they all had a hard time, and I felt sorry for them.

> —Mun Ok-chu, a Korean comfort woman survivor, in Mun Ok-chu, *Mun Oku-chu: Biruma Sensen Tateshidan no "Ianfu" Datta Watashi,* 1996

Don't you know they say there is no national border in love?

> —Yamada Ichirō, a Japanese soldier, speaking to Mun Ok-chu, in Mun Ok-chu, *Mun Oku-chu: Biruma Sensen Tateshidan no "Ianfu" Datta Watashi,* 1996

She became my first love.

> —Motoyama, a Japanese soldier speaking of his encounter with a Korean *ianfu,* in Nishino Rumiko, *Jūgun Ianfu,* 1992

THANKS TO THE KOREAN comfort women movement, the 1990s saw an increase in the production of documentaries and an avalanche of publications on the subject in Japanese, including scholarly works, which—with such rare exceptions as those of Suzuki Yūko and Takasaki Sōji—had been conspicuously absent. In March 2000 the online database of the Japanese government–supported nonprofit organization Asian Women's Fund listed

2,708 Japanese publications, including 1,622 books on the comfort women. Some of these publications were written by people who view the transnational redress movement as ahistorical and an unfair imposition of a post–cold war human rights sensibility on customary sexual behaviors among men in patriarchal societies and among soldiers in war. Individual Japanese veterans have also recounted a variety of personal memories of their experiences of public sex at the comfort facilities as militarized masculine sexual subjects.

Human rights activists and supporters of the comfort women movement in the international community may regard the story of "Madam X" as a representative instance of horrific sexual violence committed by Japanese troops. She was a fifteen-year-old Chinese living in British Malaya in 1942 when three solders raped her in full view of her parents and brother. She was then taken by force and made a "comfort girl" at the *ianjo,* which was set up at the Tai Sun Hotel.[1] She stated that sex at the *ianjo* was "excruciating" and that she was paid half of the fee; the "mama-san" took the rest, as she did with all the comfort women.[2]

By contrast, as this chapter demonstrates, the private memories of a number of survivors of their lives at *ianjo* significantly complicate the categorical images, drawn by the lawyers for the 1994 International Commission of Jurists mission report, of a living hell. Although the vast majority of the countless wartime comfort women, who came from various ethnic and national backgrounds and social circumstances, will remain forever nameless and voiceless, some of the survivors have disclosed intimate private memories, revealing, in retrospect, a striking degree of self-possession as gendered sexual subjects. Most surprising have been the narratives of the women survivors and war veterans whose private and gendered memories of life at comfort stations unexpectedly run counter to, and complicate, the simplistic and ahistorical paradigmatic story of what Carol Gluck has called "transnational memories" purveyed by activists.[3]

Further, what deserves mention here is the powerful social and psychological effect of the masculinist sexual culture exerted differently on gendered lives of men and women after the end of the war. The gender factor is most poignantly underscored by a comparison between the patterns of personal lives of former comfort women of Korea and Japan and those of former soldiers in the two countries. In general, former soldiers and officers who had sex with comfort women had no problem reintegrating into family and marital life when they returned home after the war ended. Some Japanese men even wrote about their sexual experiences with women of varied ethnic backgrounds in their wartime memoirs.[4] By contrast, women survivors tried their best to conceal—as rape victims even today often do—from their families and friends their ordeals at comfort stations. Japanese as well as many Korean survivors have reported that they have been unable to lead conventional family lives. In addition to childlessness and chronic pain from past physical injuries or sexual abuse,[5] most Korean survivors reportedly have suffered low self-esteem and abiding psychological trauma over the loss of their virginity. Mun P'il-gi, the reader may recall, left home when her mother tried to arrange a marriage for her, not knowing about her daughter's past. Mun felt that her life as an ex–comfort woman disqualified her from married life. Testimonies of other survivors show that many more share Mun's sense of resignation and worthlessness.

COMMON DENIGRATION OF PROSTITUTES

Kim Hak-sun, who married a Korean man who helped her escape from a comfort station in China, as described in chapter 3, revealed during my interview with her in 1995 that her husband mistreated her for having been a comfort woman: "I had to suffer the hurt and indignity of being debased by my own husband who, when drunk, would abuse me in front of our son by calling me a 'dirty bitch' who prostituted herself for soldiers."[6]

The denigration of former comfort women as prostitutes even by family members as well as non-kin others was not limited to Korean cases. During my own field research in the Netherlands, I learned of a Dutch survivor who had suffered the indignity of being called names by her own family; it was her sisters, who apparently shared the masculinist conception of the comfort women as "whores," who hurt this woman the most. She died before receiving the "welfare" money paid by Japan's Asian Women's Fund (AWF). The representative of the Project Implementation Committee in the Netherlands (PICN)—a nongovernmental organization—whom I interviewed in The Hague in 2000 told me that her organization was determined to ensure that these sisters would not benefit from the AWF resources, which had been intended to improve the life of the dead sister they had abused.[7]

Jan Ruff-O'Herne thoughtfully reflected on her personal encounters with the Dutch "whores" who volunteered to work for the Japanese military. When O'Herne (I revert to her maiden name when speaking of her as an unmarried woman) and six other girls from the same prisoner-of-war camp (at Ambarawa) were taken against their will to a military brothel in

Semarang, they found two Dutch women (Dolly and Yvonne) there, whom the girls called "volunteers." When O'Herne asked them why they "volunteered to work in a brothel as prostitutes for the Japanese," the two women's answer was "simple and to the point":[8]

> When some young girls had been taken out of their prison camp, two of them only sixteen years old, Dolly and Yvonne felt sorry for them and suggested to the Japanese that they could go in their place. "Anyway," added Dolly, "I have no intention of dying of starvation. I want to get out of this war alive." My thought went to the two young girls who were spared because of Dolly and Yvonne. I learned a very important lesson that day—never to judge people![9]

It is also significant that when O'Herne and other women from the brothels in Semarang were taken back to a large women's prison camp in Batavia (Jakarta) and kept in isolated quarters away from the rest of the camp, the women in the other part called O'Herne's camp "*Hoeren* (Whores') Camp," assuming that they had been "voluntary workers in brothels for the Japanese."[10] O'Herne's camp, in fact, included a "volunteer worker" who gave birth to "a pair of gorgeous Japanese-looking twins!"

> At times, the women from the other part of the camp would shout abusive names at us through the fence and throw messages, written on paper and tied to a stone, over the fence. They addressed us as whores and traitors, or "konynen," meaning "rabbits." The only women who believed our stories were the Catholic nuns, with whom I had secretly made contact.
>
> One of the women in our camp was nicknamed "Blondie" because of her fair complexion and blonde hair. Blondie had been a volunteer worker in a brothel, and had been returned to the camp, pregnant. She had no idea who the father was, only that it had been the result of her time in the brothel. Blondie was a nice young woman, very joyful, and even proud of her pregnancy.[11]

It is striking to see the profoundly different attitudes O'Herne and Blondie held toward their experiences at the Japanese military brothels. One may wonder what sociological or psychological factors could explain their fundamentally different take on presumably similar sexual labor. My interviews with other Dutch survivors further deepened my puzzlement about the starkly different attitudes and private memories held by individual former comfort women about their lived experiences at the Japanese military comfort stations. Perhaps one might infer that personality characteristics are a significant factor underlying individual differences in the women's ability to cope with presumably similar situations at the Japanese military comfort station. This leaves out issues of gender socialization and the family's class status, as well as the extent of personal harm individuals and family members suffered. Based on my interviews with Dutch survivors, however, I would argue that equally, if not more, important are differences that had to do with the individual's willingness to recognize a generalized belief in normative heterosexual masculinity (which is embodied in the comfort station as an institution of public sex).

For example, in the case of Mrs. B, a Dutch survivor who was taken to the same concessionary brothel-type comfort station in Semarang as O'Herne, the forced-prostitution situation did not seem to have inflicted irreparable damage, either in physical or psychological terms. She met her future husband in the Netherlands after the war, and after half a year of dating she told him about her two-month experience of forced sexual labor. Mr. B was shocked but appreciated her candor. Afterward, they never discussed the matter again. (He emphasized during our interview that it did not affect their relationship.) Mrs. B was also fortunate not to experience any complications in her three pregnancies and childbirths after her marriage.

When I interviewed Mrs. B at her home on the outskirts of The Hague, she remembered her friend O'Herne's having been beaten for her acts of resistance but stated that she experienced no physical violence from Japanese military men. Her reminiscences during my interview included a serene image of herself sitting alone in her room during the day looking out onto the beautiful garden of the large residence of a Dutch colonist, which had been turned into a comfort station called the House of the Seven Seas.[12] She described her personality as "outgoing" and talked about being protected by angels, and she maintained she was "lucky." She also stated that her mother's motto, "You can always trust people," helped her cope with the situation:

> The Japanese officers were ordinary people . . . nice persons. When the officers saw the frightened girls, they informed Tokyo. After two months, they wrote a letter and the Japanese government stopped it.[13]
> I never had feelings of hatred [toward the Japanese men] but I had feelings of immense fear. I could understand, especially when I got

older, men in war, especially those who had good marriages, would want the comfort of women. That is why I could forgive, except for the part that I was forced.

By contrast, Ellen van der Ploeg (b. 1923), a Dutch survivor with painful memories of wartime suffering whom I first interviewed in The Hague in 1998, remembered, among other events, her father's death on a Japanese ship and stated that she could not forgive Japan. She, like Ruff-O'Herne, refused to accept money from the Japanese government fund disbursed by PICN in cooperation with AWF. A high school classmate of O'Herne, van der Ploeg was born to a Dutch father and an Indonesian mother. Her father was killed when the Japanese ship on which he was being transported was sunk by an Allied forces torpedo. She became a prominent plaintiff in the lawsuit against Japan that the nongovernmental organization Foundation for Japanese Honorary Debts filed on behalf of Dutch war victims seeking an apology and compensation from Japan. She was forced into prostitution for three months in 1944. After a three-day inspection by the Japanese, she was taken away from the internment camp to an area with large houses, where she found girls from other camps. She was forced to be with Japanese men every day, and on Sundays she and others were taken to army barracks, where they were to be with soldiers. She remembers that anything could lead to being hit very hard, a common occurrence. Although the men were ordered to use condoms, most did not. Because of malnutrition, she did not menstruate and therefore did not become pregnant. She did, however, contract several sexually transmitted diseases.[14]

Another Dutch survivor I interviewed in The Hague was Mrs. M, a petite and courteous elderly lady with a gentle, ingratiating smile who had been married (though childless) and was thirty-three years old when she was forced to become a comfort woman. She said that she "played the whore" for more than a year at a military comfort station managed by a Japanese civilian and two Indonesian women cooks. Apparently, a year's life as a comfort woman exerted little adverse effect on the course of her postwar life. Her husband, a pilot, was killed during the war, and in 1946 she remarried. She did not have children from the second marriage either. After her second husband, who she said loved her so much, died in 1960, Mrs. M never thought of remarrying—there could be "no replacement for him." As one of the oldest survivors, Mrs. M—along with nearly all the formally recognized Dutch survivors, including Mrs. B—chose to accept payment from the Japanese government's welfare fund for Dutch former comfort women offered through AWF.[15]

KOREAN SURVIVORS' PRIVATE COUNTERMEMORIES

When I first read Korean survivors' published testimonial narratives, I found it remarkable and quite surprising that a number of them revealed, often in passing and very briefly, private memories of genuine affection and personal compassion toward individual Japanese soldiers, who were sometimes referred to as "customers" in their narratives. I was quite struck by their candor, which awkwardly, but squarely, countered the movement activists' paradigmatic story now dominating the global discourse on the Japanese government's wartime comfort women. It appeared that those Korean survivors who revealed private memories of affection and compassion toward individual Japanese soldiers labored mostly at what I have called the concessionary types of *ianjo*. Their memories reveal undeniably human dimensions to the hideous institution of military comfort facilities. I must once again strongly emphasize that my intent is *not* to deny the dominant images of depersonalized sex slaves and violent rapists that have routinely been evoked in the activists' discourse and reported in the world mass media. Rather, my purpose here is to complicate the prevailing simplistic images by contrasting specific individual cases, which add glimpses of shared humanity between Korean comfort women and Japanese soldiers, and confounding the stereotyped portrayals of violent military hypermasculine sexuality in the dominant story.

Yuasa Ken, a medical doctor who not only served in the Japanese imperial army but also was held as a prisoner of war in China before his eventual return home, told me that the great majority of the soldiers felt no compunction about regarding non-Japanese comfort women as sex objects and sometimes exercising violence against them to release their tension.[16] He went on to add, though, that some men who developed close friendly relations with non-Japanese comfort women treated them with respect and compassion as fellow human beings. Testimonials from survivors amply support Yuasa's statements, about both the prevalence of abuse and the existence of relationships of romantic passion and affectionate care. Examples of the latter are introduced below, although detailed analysis of the two contrasting behavioral patterns of soldiers is beyond the scope of this work.

Yi Sun-ok, who left her home after persuading her parents to let her go abroad in search of a well-paying job but was delivered to a comfort station run by a middle-aged Korean woman in Guangdong, China, and later in Singapore, reminisced that among her *tan'gol* (regular customers or patrons, in Korean), one Japanese soldier named Haname had proposed marriage when she was making arrangements to return home. She rejected his proposal because she wanted desperately to go home. Before she returned in the winter of 1944, Haname took her shopping in downtown Singapore, saying that he wanted to buy her whatever she desired most as a parting gift.[17] Her return trip, however, was arranged with the help of another of her "regular customers" (*tan'gol sonnim*), a Korean man from Kwangju using the Japanese surname Fujiwara who was a civil engineer and was employed by the military.[18]

What should be noted here is that in Japan's long history of officially permitted organized prostitution (until the enactment of the 1956 Prostitution Prevention Law), it was not unusual for a male customer to marry a woman of the pleasure quarters.[19] In light of such historical practices, one should not be surprised to learn of marriage proposals and engagements between Japanese soldiers and Korean comfort women. For example, the reader may remember my earlier discussion of the *han*-filled testimonial of Song Sindo, a Korean survivor who spent seven years as a comfort woman in China and went to Japan after the end of the war with a Japanese soldier who had proposed to her. The 1944 U.S. military intelligence report on twenty Korean "comfort girls" who were captured in Burma also noted, "[T]here were numerous instances of proposals of marriage and in certain cases marriages actually took place."[20]

Much less common are stories of marriage proposals or connubial unions between Korean comfort women and Korean men, which was the case of Ha Yŏng-i (pseudonym; b. 1922), who left her sister's home in Ōsaka in 1936 after receiving a deceitful offer from a Korean female neighbor and trafficker to help her return to Korea. Ha, who labored for nearly ten years at Korean-owned *ianjo* in Taiwan, Kainanto, and Sumatra and had received marriage proposals from both a Japanese businessman in China and an army officer in Indonesia, chose to marry a Korean man named Yi Chongun, the owner of her *ianjo* in Sumatra, when he expressed his love for her. Ha added that when they announced their plans to other members of his *ianjo,* things quickly went awry. Other Korean comfort women, who apparently had secretly hoped to marry the bachelor-proprietor Yi, became very jealous of Ha and angry with her for forestalling their dreams of marriage. The women began fighting and refused to work hard. After a few months of hardship, Yi sold his business to another Korean and the couple moved to a new place near a huge oil field, where they prospered—Ha was very ashamed to confess—by running a comfort station employing local Indonesian women until Japan's defeat brought them unexpected personal disaster.[21]

Mun Ok-chu (1924–1996), the second South Korean survivor to come out after Kim Hak-sun in December 1991, came from a poor family in Taegu and had labored at multiple comfort stations. She was first taken to Manchuria in 1940 as a result of forcible recruitment by "a man in a Japanese military uniform" but was able to return home in about a year by obtaining a special travel permit from an officer who wanted to live with her by setting up a home outside the station. Taking advantage of the situation, she made up a story about her sick mother and asked him to let her go see her before she started living with him. After asking for and receiving several assurances from her that she intended to come back, he issued her the permit. Back in Taegu she spent about a year doing odd jobs and then left home in July 1942, without telling her family, with a friend who invited her to go with her and work in a restaurant for good wages. In Pusan they met a Korean man—with the Japanese name Matsumoto—who turned out to be the proprietor of a comfort station in Burma. The man took them to an inn where there were already about fifteen or sixteen women, one of whom was Kim Kye-hwa, who had been with Mun in Manchuria.[22]

Mun Ok-chu is one of the very few South Korean former comfort women whose fascinating life story has been made into a book by a Japanese woman writer, Morikawa Machiko. In *Mun Oku-chu: Biruma Sensen Tateshidan no "Ianfu" Datta Watashi* (Mun Ok-chu: I Was a "Comfort Woman" of the Shield Division on the Burma Front), published in Japanese in 1996, she reveals a much fuller story of her private life than she was able to narrate in the 1993 Korean publication. For example, she stated that as a young woman laboring in a comfort station in Burma she fell in love with Corporal Yamada Ichirō. She indicated that she was enormously popular with officers and that although she could have chosen to favor one of them, Yamada became her sweetheart, making her Korean colleagues wonder why she chose a corporal rather than an officer.

Here one might question whether Mun's compassionate reminiscence of the Japanese soldiers had to do at least in part with the fact that her life story was told to a Japanese writer. In any case, her positive attitude toward the troops certainly did not mean that her life at the comfort station was easy or sheltered by a high-ranking officer, as in the cases of a few luckier women. Nevertheless, the combination of her proficiency in Japanese, her musical talent, and her outgoing personality garnered for her high praise and generous tips from officers on special occasions such as birthday parties and farewell banquets, as well as after their overnight visits with her at the *ianjo*. She diligently saved her tips and was able to accumulate an astonishing sum of money. She deposited the tips she received from officers and soldiers into her savings account at the field post office, which handled the savings accounts of soldiers who deposited their salaries there.

The discovery of her savings account records at the Shimonoseki post office in 1992 revealed that it had a balance of 25,245 yen saved during her life as a comfort woman in Burma and Thailand from 1942 to 1945.[23] This was an enormous sum of money at the time; the monthly salary of a *myŏnjang* (the head of a township, a low-level civil servant) then was between 40 and 50 yen.[24] It would have taken anywhere from forty to more than fifty years of work for a *myŏnjang* to make the money Mun saved during a little more than three years. She once sent 5,000 yen from Thailand to her family in Taegu, Korea. Her brother received the huge sum, but all of the money was spent by the time she returned home in the spring of 1946.[25]

It is interesting to note from Mun's narrative that one of her close friends from her hometown, who labored at the same comfort station and was known by the Japanese name Hitomi, also saved her tips. Unlike Mun, Hitomi was able to withdraw all her savings from the Shimonoseki post office on her way home to Taegu. Hitomi then gave birth to a boy. When Mun met her for the first time back home, Hitomi showed up with her baby. Mun told Morikawa, "Since it was the child of her sweetheart, Hitomi was raising him with great care." She added that as of the summer of 1995, Hitomi was alive and well, but she did not come forward, most probably out of consideration of her grown-up son's position.[26]

The stories of Mun Ok-chu and her former colleague Hitomi again underscore the wide range of diversity in the life circumstances and personal experiences of individual comfort women, to which the National Archive pictures (of Korean comfort women captured in Burma in the last months of the war, discussed earlier) seem to graphically testify as well.

Like the Japanese veteran Yuasa Ken, Mun Ok-chu also noted (in the remark quoted in one of the epigraphs to this chapter) that soldiers who developed close friendly relations with Korean comfort women would "comfort" the women with words of sympathy for their hard life and treat them with respect and compassion, sometimes getting romantically involved with them. Private memories of other Korean former comfort women further corroborate the personal statements on the topic of both Mun Ok-chu and Yuasa Ken.[27]

A memorable example is seen in the testimonial narrative of Kim Sun-dŏk (1921–2004), who became one of the best-known survivors for her impressive paintings depicting life as comfort women and who traveled abroad multiple times to give testimony and personally grace the exhibits of the paintings produced by herself and other Korean survivors. Kim Sun-dŏk came from an indigent family in South Kyŏngsang Province. She started working as a housemaid at the age of twelve to help her widowed mother and her four siblings. In 1937 she met a Korean man who was recruiting women with false promises of well-paying jobs at a factory in Japan. The man took her and about thirty other women to a comfort station that he ran in Shanghai. As one of the "pretty and intelligent girls who were selected for very high-ranking officers and taken into the army unit by car,"[28] she met Izumi, a high-ranking officer in his fifties, with whom she developed a special relationship. Kim, whose father had died when she was a child, came to regard Izumi as her "father, husband, and family rolled into one."[29] She was able to return home safely in 1940, together with four of her colleagues, owing to Izumi's loving concern and care. He gave her 100 yen and an envelope containing official travel permits that entitled her and the others to travel by train, truck, and boat and to secure lodging and meals without difficulty.[30] Said Kim:

> After returning home, I received letters from Izumi constantly. I sent my replies to him and even sent care packages to him. He would write me thanking me for them, saying that he enjoyed the toasted grain powder, but the chili powder, he wrote, was so hot that it almost killed him, jokingly asking me whether I intended to kill him with it. He would also correct my Japanese spelling and write humorous letters as well. . . . After I moved to Seoul, I continued to receive his letters from Nanking until one or two years before the Liberation. I lost all the letters during the Korean War.[31]

Not surprisingly, Kim Sun-dŏk actively solicited help from Japanese supporters to find Izumi when she was taken to Japan to give public testimonials in the early 1990s. A representative of the Korean Council I interviewed in January 1995 acknowledged the embarrassment she and her colleagues felt about Kim's behavior and their decision not to include her on their subsequent business trips to Japan.

Pak Pok-sun, a plaintiff in the 1991 class-action lawsuit against Japan brought by Yujokhoe, whose unhappy relationship with the Korean Council leaders was discussed in chapter 2, provided a very sad life story that was published in Japan and included her undying love for her lost fiancé-soldier.[32] She was born out of wedlock to a Korean father and a Japanese mother in Tokyo. Immediately after her birth, her father returned with his baby girl to Korea, where she grew up. She was sixteen when she was deceptively recruited by a Japanese army civilian employee. She labored for seven years at several comfort stations of the paramilitary type in northern China and was freed to return home several months before the end of the war thanks to the intervention of a high-ranking Korean officer in the Japanese army. Despite her difficult life, she came to develop a loving relationship with a young man called "Sergeant S," to whom she was betrothed. When Pak gave public testimonials in various places in Japan, she continued to use her Japanese name, Kaneda Kimiko, which Sergeant S had created for her,[33] in the hope that some soldiers who knew her by that name—especially Sergeant S—would come forward. Pak and Sergeant S (who was in charge of hygiene administration) were secretly engaged. She had her picture taken at a photo studio in Tienjien, which the young man sent to his parents in Yokohama to introduce her as his future bride. In the picture, which she showed me during our meeting at her apartment in Puchŏn, Kyŏnggi Province, in April 2000 (she also allowed me to borrow it to make a photocopy at a neighborhood convenience store), Pak was wearing *hanbok* (traditional Korean dress).

Sergeant S also taught her a song:

Precious blood was shed.
At that mountain and at this river.
You are the flower in the sun.
You are a white orchid flower.

He promised her that he would teach her the second phrase of the song. Tragically, they could not meet each other again. "Perhaps, he killed himself when he learned that Japan was defeated, yes, I believe he died," she said to herself. Pak sang this song to herself for sixty years. For Pak, who never married, her relationship with Sergeant S was the one sweet, unforgettable memory she wished to cherish in her *han*-filled life.

Chang Ch'un-wŏl (b. 1919), whose father sold her twice to pay his debts and buy a house, had to leave home in 1936. She labored in China for nine years at three different comfort stations, all of which were run by Koreans.[34] She sent money home frequently, between 10 and 20 wŏn each time, for a few years until she heard that her beloved grandmother had died. She briefly recounted her memories of an officer, whose name she did not wish to reveal.

I was twenty-three then. He was about five years older and his work had to do with the railroad. About two years prior to the end of the

Plate 5.1. Pak Pok-sun during her days as a comfort woman, shown wearing *hanbok* (Korean dress) in a studio photograph taken in Tianjin, China, in the late 1930s or early 1940s. (Photo courtesy of the late Pak Pok-sun.)

war, the officer (whose rank was that of colonel) once took me with him to his home in Tokyo, where I stayed for about three months. His parents, who owned a general store and were rich, treated me cordially. We planned to return to Japan together after the war ended. After I returned to the comfort station, his mother sent me three dresses a year. When I moved to another town that was a four-hour train ride away, the colonel continued to visit me. He then gave me 500 wǒn and told me to return home. I was soon liberated by fully repaying my debt. I started a business, running a small general store using the money the colonel gave me. He visited me until March or April 1945, when he left for the battlefield, after which I never heard from him.[35]

Chang continued her business until September 1945. In less than a year she was able to earn 1,000 wǒn, more than doubling her business capital. After Japan's defeat, however, as she was leaving town, she lost everything. Chinese people beat her with a stick and robbed her of all her money and personal belongings. Chang's memory of that incident is still raw.[36]

Yi Yong-su, whose performances of thespian testimonials both at home and abroad were discussed in chapter 2,[37] labored under the Japanese name Toshiko at a comfort station in Taiwan for about eight months, during which time she came to know a young pilot intimately. Cherishing fond memories of the officer, who died on his *kamikaze* mission, Yi decided to visit Taiwan in 1998 to perform the rite of spirit marriage to the Japanese officer.[38] He was a member of Tokkōtai (Special Attack Corps, also known as the Kamikaze Corps).[39] Remembered Yi:

On the evening when he was scheduled to fly the combat mission, he gave me his photo and his toiletries (such as soap and a towel). He had come to me a couple of times before that evening and said he caught a venereal disease from me. He said he would take the disease as a present from me. He then taught me a song:

> With courage I take off. Departing from Sinzhu
> Golden waves and silver waves of the clouds I cross over
> With no one to see me off
> Toshiko alone cries for me.[40]

Fifty-three years later Yi returned to Taiwan and consummated her cherished love for him in the rite of spirit marriage. In her reminiscence, she recalled the last thing he said to her: "'I'll protect you even after my death so that you may return to your ancestral land safely.' These were his last words, which I could not forget."[41]

Pae Chok-kan, whose unhappy relationship with her mother was briefly described in chapter 2, also had some unforgettably bittersweet stories to tell the filmmaker and author Kim-Gibson when the latter interviewed her. In particular, Pae spoke to her at length and repeatedly of Ishikawa, the Japanese soldier who fell in love with her and asked her to marry him when the war was over:

> Ishikawa is the one who comes to my thoughts even now. . . . Once, he took off his undershirt, drew a Japanese flag on it, and then wrote his name and mine. Then, he inscribed it, "I will never forget you even if I die." You know what he wrote that with? With his own blood. The sight of the blood frightened me. When I told him that I didn't like it, he put his head down like a criminal and cried. . . . There were times when he made me detest him but his persistence moved my heart. He broke the rules many times because he could not help himself. He wanted to see me so much. So many times, he was punished. Sometimes, he would be kicked and thrown into the mud. His uniform would become muddy. I washed it, ironed it, and put it back on him. Sometimes, if I saw an officer coming, I would hide him.[42]
>
> He brought me all kinds of things—soap, candies, anything he could put his hands on. He was absolutely crazy about me. I believe he really loved me. Back then, I didn't know. I felt something for him but I said nothing to him. I didn't say I liked him. Now? I would hug him close to me, kiss him, and tell him that I love him. I would do that now, but not back then.[43]

Musing over her life as a comfort woman, Pae said, "Then, we were also soldiers. We were not prostitutes. We helped the soldiers to fight. Do you understand?" (Pae's statement is reminiscent of that of former Japanese comfort women, such as Kikumaru, who sincerely believed in their personal contribution to Japan's war project by laboring as comfort women so as to fulfill the wartime slogan of "for the good of the country.") When Kim-Gibson shook her head, Pae went on:

> You do know why the women were taken, don't you? If the men couldn't do that thing, they couldn't fight. That's why we were also soldiers. We helped them fight. Do I think what Japan did was evil?

Not really. After all, Japan was at war. They wanted to win the war. They could not have done that without doing evil things. Actually, I blame Korea most. The fact that our country was weak. Were we a strong country, it would not and could not have happened. So if I am to blame anything, anybody, it is Korea. . . . You keep pushing me to say that Japan was wrong, but I still say they did it for their country and we let it happen to us because we were not powerful enough. . . . Well, we should never let it happen again. Never.[44]

Pae also spoke of some other soldiers for whom she felt

human warmth, sympathy that bonded human beings together. . . . I remember the holidays when they made sticky, sweet Japanese rice cake. They stole those for me. I would fry them and eat them with soy sauce. It tasted so good. You should know that not all Japanese are bad. . . . When Japan was defeated, I was sad. Not only that, I was mad that Japan had been defeated. I couldn't understand how Japan could lose! . . . Thinking back, I was totally converted to be a loyal Japanese. . . . After all that, I don't blame Japan. Even now, if there were two men proposing, one Korean and the other Japanese, I would rather marry the Japanese. . . .

I can tell you [Kim-Gibson] still want to know the reasons for my feelings about the Japanese. Don't ask me the reasons. Can't you just accept some things without knowing the reasons? I had *chŏng* [human warmth or affection, in Korean] for the Japanese but not for the Koreans. True, I did have some feelings for my husband. He was handsome, learned, and proud. So I felt proud to be with him. He had no money but he himself was so presentable. And of course, I tasted what real sex was like with him. But I don't think it was love. I am frank about this. Most of the time, I just accepted him as part of my fate. He didn't buy me a pair of rubber shoes, not one dress. That's not all. Would you believe that he had other women? He would bother me at night but during the daytime, while I was doing bone crushing hard work, he would do that thing with other women.[45]

MULTIPLE PERSPECTIVES OF JAPANESE MILITARY VETERANS

It is remarkable that Japanese veterans of the Asia Pacific War described "nostalgically and with a certain fondness" their encounters with comfort women in published diaries and memoirs decades before the redress movement began.[46] These accounts express little sense of shame or remorse. Curiously, their reminiscences provide unanticipated counternarratives, albeit male-centered, to the grisly stories of sexual slavery that have dominated in the international media since the start of the comfort women redress movement. It is important to remember that the perspectives and attitudes of individual soldiers toward the comfort stations also varied.

Like Ichikawa Ichirō, a Mr. Honda (pseudonym; b. 1914),[47] a veteran who was called to military duty in 1939 and served in the army in China, did not know about the comfort women until he saw the sign "Army Special Comfort Station" in Hankow. Honda's first thought upon seeing the sign was whether he would be able to eat a great deal of *soba* (buckwheat noodles). "Would they let me drink?" he wondered. So, he asked, "Would you folks feed me some *soba* or something?" The answer he received, Honda recalled, was, "Mr. Soldier, this isn't that kind of place. You see the nameplates hung there. This is a place where we sell those women."[48]

Honda's private memories of public sex with comfort women, which he "confessed" to Nishino Rumiko, a Japanese activist and writer,[49] just before the international controversy over Japan's comfort women began to rage, included various aspects of life at several military comfort stations. He remembered, for example, a Korean proprietor who risked being punished for hiring Chinese women in his comfort station (where about thirty Korean women labored)—the authorities prohibited the use of Chinese women, fearing they might leak security information to the enemy. From among the many Korean comfort women Honda met, he could still remember one rebellious twenty-two- or twenty-three-year-old who drank heavily, broke dishes, and fought everyone. Wanting him to understand her state of mind, she told Honda that she had been deceived into sexual slavery, that her life was in danger with bullets flying around near her place, and that she wanted to return home but could not do so with her ruined body.[50]

Also memorable to Honda was the collective sense of righteousness among Korean comfort women, who abided by a moral code of justice and loyalty among themselves by refusing to offer service to men who they knew had been customers of their colleagues. Once when Honda wanted to choose a different woman, she refused him, saying, "You're Ms. So-and-so's customer." This strong moral code among the Korean women, Honda stated, made it impossible for him and other men to get to know all the women laboring at the same *ianjo*.[51] The Korean women he met, Honda remembered, spoke Japanese well and generally wore Western-style clothes such as blouses and skirts, though some were clad in kimonos tied with obis.

Honda further recalled situations in which Korean comfort women fell in love with Japanese soldiers. In such cases, according to Honda, the women did not accept money from the soldiers, who, in turn, would bring them gifts of special foods (such as *yōkan*) they saved from rations. Honda noted that only older Japanese women labored at the officers' club, which served as a restaurant as well. Soldiers could use the club until eight o'clock in the evening, while officers were allowed to stay from midnight until morning. The four hours between eight and midnight were reserved for noncommissioned officers.

Honda, who ruefully confessed to beheading dozens of Chinese prisoners of war, stated that "war" made people do all the things that are prohibited by civil law. As an aging veteran, Honda expressed his gratitude to the *ianfu* for having comforted (*nagusametekurete*) a great number of troops. Further, he stated that he now regards women as godly for the great role they play in producing posterity for humanity and that he felt sorry for what he did to women during his days as a soldier.

Although we will never get an accurate answer, we could ask at this point, What proportion of the Japanese soldiers availed themselves of the comfort facilities?[52] Matsui Yayori (1934–2002), a former *Asahi Shimbun* reporter turned feminist activist who played a pivotal leadership role in the comfort women redress movement, estimated that about 80 percent of the Japanese troops used the comfort stations. During my interview with her in Tokyo in June 1997, Matsui stated that her father, who served as a chaplain during the war, told her that he did not use the comfort facility.

Indeed, a small number of soldiers did not. Among more than a hundred people (including civilian employees of the military) who called the Tokyo Military Comfort Women Hotline in 1992, for example, twenty-two soldiers stated that they had never used the comfort station.[53] Twelve of the twenty-two respondents said that they were too young to do so. By contrast, a former civilian military employee who worked as an interpreter on an island in the Dutch East Indies said that he felt too sorry for the poor women enslaved at a "free comfort station." (The comfort station may have been of the criminal category described above.) Other reasons included "not having money," "fear for catching a disease," "no room for that because of bombings and hunger," "no leisure for an officer's underling [*shitappa*]," and, remarkably, "prohibited to a candidate for officer."

Here it is notable that the "War Journal, Independent Infantry, 15th Regiment Headquarter (January 8, 1945)"—which describes the standard operating procedure for the comfort facility called Yamato Center and its annex—lists, among other things, three categories of persons barred from entering the facilities: cadets, first-year soldiers in basic training, and any persons deemed inappropriate by commanders.[54] In general, Japanese men who refused to go to comfort stations were despised for their "weak," unmanly behavior.[55] Some officers regarded going to comfort stations as official business and reportedly cursed soldiers of conscience as "crazy" (*kichi-gai*). For their part, the latter laughed scornfully at the military authority, because they knew what comfort stations were about.[56]

When Matsui interviewed some veterans and asked why they went to comfort stations while others did not, they replied that they did so "lightheartedly" and that their behavior was a problem only when seen from a feminist perspective. Some veterans who called the Tokyo hotline reported that their visits were organized as a group activity coordinated by the unit and that they marched in an orderly fashion to the comfort station at an allotted time on a certain day of a given month.[57] Others said that they visited comfort stations because there was no place else to go. (In fact, the systemic lack of furloughs in the Japanese Imperial Army and the scarcity of cultural and sporting facilities for soldiers' recreation led the state to consider *ianjo* as a necessity for the periodic leisure or R & R [rest and recuperation] of the combat troops.)[58] The comfort stations were also sometimes used ritualistically, such as group visits before and after special battlefield operations and as an occasion to celebrate the completion of the six-month training for new soldiers.[59] The 1944 U.S. military intelligence report, however, noted: "The average Japanese soldier is embarrassed about being seen in a 'comfort house' according to one of the girls who said, 'When the place is packed he is apt to be ashamed if he has to wait in line for his turn.'"[60]

It should be remembered here that the Japanese troops included Korean men: about 187,000 soldiers and more than 22,000 sailors from colonial Korea.[61] They apparently also used the comfort facilities, as revealed in the testimonials of Korean victim-survivors. In addition, eyewitness accounts reveal that non-Japanese men who availed themselves of the comfort facilities included not only Korean but also Taiwanese soldiers and even Indonesian *heiho,* or paramilitary auxiliaries, trained by the Japanese who involved themselves in the Indonesian struggle for independence from Dutch colonial rule. They "regularly queued for service, from about 3 p.m. to 7 p.m." at two comfort stations run by a Japanese man and his German wife that employed about a hundred girls from nearby villages in northern Sulawesi, in occupied Dutch East Indies.[62]

Also significant is the fact that although soldiers who refused to join their colleagues in seeking sexual recreation at comfort stations were called names or sometimes forcibly taken to *ianjo*,[63] men whose patronage of the facility seemed too frequent were jeered or chided for their impropriety. A man named Yodi visited Jan O'Herne every night for two weeks at one of the Semarang military brothels. According to her, the "friendly looking, slightly built" Yodi was the only decent Japanese she met during wartime in occupied Dutch East Indies. At the request of her sister Aline, Yodi visited her at the military comfort station (of the house of prostitution type). Ashamed at what his fellow countrymen had done to her and others, and apologizing with humble gestures, Yodi told her not to fear and showed her the ticket he had bought for the whole night so as to give her a respite from sexual slavery. When he visited, he would often bring her letters and small parcels from her sister. They talked, played card games, and slept, O'Herne on her bed and Yodi on the floor. Yodi also told her that he was being "teased and laughed at by his friends because he visited the brothel every night and stayed all night."[64] Ruff-O'Herne wrote, "It must have been very hard on him, especially as he never once touched me." After helping her for two weeks, Yodi's visits stopped because he had to move out of Semarang with other troops.[65]

By contrast, some young soldiers apparently adopted a more positive outlook on their officially approved access to public sex at comfort stations. They seem to have tried to uphold their personal dignity by self-consciously engaging in sexual relations with comfort women as fellow human beings, not as a "supply" or a commodity.[66] A former soldier stationed in Harbin, China, between 1941 and 1944, a Mr. Motoyama (b. 1920), first visited a comfort station when a senior conscript decided to take him and another there for recreation. When Motoyama and his colleague submitted to the receptionist the same woman's name as their desired sexual partner, they decided to let the woman choose, and Motoyama, who never had sexual relations before, was selected. He then developed a steady and romantic relationship with the woman during his three-year duty in Harbin. He offered his private memories of public sex at the comfort station in terms of the sociopsychological significance of his visits to *ianjo* for personal and romantic relations with a young Korean girl:

> As a twenty-one-year-old bachelor, it was my first sexual experience. I really liked the teenage Korean girl working at the *ianjo,* where there were more than twenty such young Korean girls. I began to visit only her place, and she became my first love. When I received rations such

as dumplings, I would not eat them. Instead, I would bring them to her place. Sometimes I would take her out and we would go to the mountain together after obtaining special permission from the comfort station manager. When I went to her place, I always tried to prepare myself as best I could. . . . Some soldiers spoke of a "public toilet," but I wanted to develop a humane relationship with her despite the brief time I was allotted. For me, comfort women were not simply sex objects. My visit to their place seemed to restore humanity to my heart. I guess it served as evidence I was still alive.[67]

CONCLUSION

As Hegel noted long ago, the master is more dependent on the slave than the slave on the master in the everyday arts and chores of human existence.[68] In a similar vein, one can imagine how individual soldiers might have relied on comfort women to fulfill their needs and desires for the customary kind of care work—sexual and otherwise—that women provided and of which men were deprived during long military campaigns far from home. At the same time, the personal accounts of surviving Korean comfort women sometimes reveal private memories of sympathetic understanding of the soldiers' predicament and undying affection for the men they came to know intimately at comfort stations.

Most inconveniently for the prevailing paradigmatic story of forced recruitment and sexual violence, as some survivors have revealed the diverse circumstances of their recruitment, they have also candidly recalled both poignant and painful experiences at comfort stations. Though politically incorrect, their private memories include examples of genuine sexual intimacy with and human compassion toward individual Japanese soldiers, notwithstanding the unspeakable sexual ordeals, social denigration, and random violence they were forced to endure. Some even expressed nostalgia for the youthful days they had spent in tight-knit group settings. The full spectrum of the private memories of public sex recounted by Korean survivors and Japanese veterans seems to underscore, among other things, the complexities of the power dynamics in gendered human relations, especially in private sexual encounters.

Emanating from the Japanese and Korean cultural context, which normalized access to public sex as a male sex-right, such poignantly bittersweet private memories provide counternarratives that complicate and confound the paradigmatic story constructed by "transnational memory" activists, who tend to categorically represent public sex at the comfort station as nothing more than sexual slavery and violence against women. To represent the comfort women's story in *only* this blanket way—no matter how good the intentions—denies the personal truths of individual survivors and shortchanges the larger human history.

Chapter 6

Public Sex and the State

Not once, nowhere, not one word! The deaths of numerous young women who served as *ianfu,* or purveyors of sex, have never been consoled [mourned] in the forty years since the end of the war. I feel like saying [to my fellow Japanese], *you idiots [bakayarō], really!*

> —Mihara Yoshie, Japanese ex–comfort woman at sixty-four, in TBS radio interview, 1986

I wonder what interest the Korean or Japanese government would have in the miserable life of a woman like me whose death will end it all.

> —Kim Hak-sun, Korean ex–comfort woman at sixty-nine, in Han'guk Chŏngsindae-munje Taech'aek Hyŏpŭihoe and Chŏngsindae Yŏn'guhoe, *Chŭngŏnjip 1,* 1993

ON A HIGH HILL OVERLOOKING Tateyama Bay in Chiba Prefecture, a two-hour train ride from Tokyo and a fifteen-minute walk from the main house in Kanita Women's Village in Tateyama City, stands a simple monument dedicated to the memory of Japan's comfort women. To the best of my knowledge, this is the first (semi)public monument commemorating the wartime ordeals of Japan's military comfort women. The Japanese government established the village in 1965 as a women's rehabilitation center for former prostitutes who have had difficulty reclaiming their lives because of disability, social stigma, or a lack of family support. In July 2005, when I visited Kanita Women's Village and met its current director, Sister Amaha Michiko, I had the pleasure of running into Fukushima Mizuho, the woman leader of the Democratic Party of Japan, who was also visiting the place for the first time. Having interviewed her in 1997 when she served as a member of the attorney Takagi Ken'ichi's team of Japanese lawyers for the 1991 Yujokhoe class-action lawsuit (in which three former comfort women were included as plaintiffs), I appreciated the coincidence of our visits to the village to lay flowers in memory of Mihara Yoshie (also known by her pen name, Shirota Suzuko) and many other former comfort women.

Mihara Yoshie (1921–1993), who suffered from paralysis in her lower body as the result of syphilis, became the first resident of the facility. Having written an autobiography under the pseudonym Shirota Suzuko,[1] she let out her impassioned "cries of the stone" (*ishi no sakebi*) four decades after her repatriation from Palau, where she had worked as a comfort station manager. The epigraph that opens this chapter comes from a radio interview she gave to TBS in Japan that aired on January 19, 1986.[2] In speaking publicly, Yoshie-san became the first surviving comfort woman to directly and personally inform the public about the issue—more than five years before Kim Hak-sun did so in Korea. No other Japanese woman has followed her lead. The account below reveals a dimension of Yoshie-san's life story that is directly related to the comfort women issue:

> It was in 1938 that I received an advance of 2,500 yen for a three-year contract to work at a comfort station catering to the Japanese navy in Taiwan. After paying off my family's debt of 1,800 yen, I offered the remaining 700 yen to my weeping father before leaving for Taiwan. . . . During the last year of the war I became a staff member at a newly formed navy *ianjo* in Palau where all twenty of the *ianfu* stationed there came either from Korea or Okinawa. I witnessed the instantaneous deaths of three of the comfort women in an air-raid shelter during the bombing of the island by the Americans. I myself was injured and buried inside the shelter until men from the special restaurant (used as a comfort station) dug me out.[3]
>
> In 1984, an elderly woman in failing health, I was tormented by recurring nightmares of my harrowing memories of the deaths of the comfort women. As a way of dealing with my nightmares, I wrote to Fukazu Fumio, a Christian pastor and founder of Kanita Women's Village, and asked him to erect a monument to console and bring peace to the spirits of the dead women.[4]

After hesitating for a year, Fukazu bought a rectangular piece of wood for 7,000 yen and created a monument from it to observe the fortieth anniversary of the end of the war.[5] He initially thought of inscribing on it "Monument to bring peace to the spirits of military comfort women." In the end, he decided on the simple text "Monument to soothe the spirit" (*Chinkon no hi*).

Plate 6.1. Photograph of Mihara Yoshie displayed in the sanctuary of Kanita Women's Village. (Photo by the author.)

A tearful Yoshie-san thanked the pastor from her wheelchair and expressed her satisfaction with the location of the monument: she told the interviewer that the beautiful view of Tateyama Bay the monument commands from the hill resembled the vistas of Palau. She further commented that all wandering souls of deceased comfort women could now assemble there.

Having erected the monument in a small private ceremony attended by the residents of the facility, Fukazu learned to his surprise that the *Asahi Shimbun* had reported on it on August 19, 1985. He soon received sympathetic letters and support money from readers. Despite this outpouring of support, Fukazu was well aware of and could not ignore the silent animosity of those who objected to his opening up this old wound, which is why the radio broadcasters chose not to disclose Yoshie-san's full address when she summoned up the courage to go public about her past for the radio interview. She spoke scathingly of the "foolishness" of fellow Japanese, who

Plate 6.2. After laying bouquets, visitors from Tokyo posed in front of the Comfort Women Monument in Kanita Women's Village, Tateyama, Japan, July 2005. Fukushima Mizuho is flanked by Sister Amaha on the right and the author on the left; three local resident-activists stand next to her. (Photo by Tomizawa Yoshiko; source: the author.)

dutifully commemorate the deaths of unknown soldiers annually and repeatedly speak of the sufferings of civilians, including the victims of the atomic bomb, at commemorative events, yet never publicly acknowledge or make efforts to console the anguished souls of *ianfu* or the "purveyors of sex" (*sei no teikyōsha,* in Yoshie-san's own words), some of whom also perished anonymously near the battlefields.

Subsequently, private donations arrived from 166 people from across the country who had either read the newspaper report or listened to the radio interview. They wanted to help replace the impermanent wooden monument with a stone one, a wish Yoshie-san had expressed during her interview. Some of the donors were former comfort women themselves, but others were former soldiers who wished to thank the women. The inscription on the new stone monument simply reads, "O, Military Comfort Women" (*Aa! Jūgun Ianfu*), a phrase that connotes lamentation.

We might pause here to ask what would explain the complete lack of national-level recognition for the crucial duty that Japan's *ianfu* performed—that is, public-sex work—for military morale during the Fifteen-Year War? And why was there a similar lack of respect, even from redress movement activists, for Yoshie-san's courage in coming forward and calling public attention to the comfort women issue?

To address these questions from the primal angle, we must take into account the very long history of Japanese and Korean sexual cultural mores, which reveals the structurally embedded factors that cause societal denigration of, and indifference to, sex workers as well as habituation to the injustice and the social and personal suffering of these women in both countries. The problem cannot be considered without recovering and examining the deep-rooted traditional stigmatization of sexually "defiled" and "ethically fallen women" (*yullak yŏsŏng*, in Korean). Accordingly, I take the "genealogy" approach (inspired by the work of Michel Foucault)—which refers to "the 'coupling' together of scholarly erudition and local memories"—in my investigation of local institutional legacies that marked women's public-sex work as shameful but customary, gendered care work and reinforced dismissive and naturalizing attitudes toward men's public sex in Japanese and Korean societies.[6] I focus on the sociocultural and political economic aspects of prostitution and the integral role and structural power of states in shaping the contours of these national sexual landscapes. These state interventions have turned women's public-sex work into a core element of male sex-rights in Japanese and Korean histories.

My discussion in this chapter uncovers, with a focus on Korea, the centuries-old institutional roots of societal indifference to the plight of women laboring in the sex industry, euphemistically referred to as the "customary trade" in both Japan and Korea. I highlight the role of the state in the history of the major institutions of men's public sex and the continuing exploitation of women of the working class. In particular, I discuss the phenomena of (1) state-sanctioned military prostitution for the foreign forces in postwar Japan and postcolonial Korea, as well as the Korean Army's own "special comfort women" during the Korean War (1950–1953); and (2) state-condoned sex tourism in South Korea, euphemistically called "*kisaeng* tourism," which refers to the business of catering to the sexual desires of foreign civilian—primarily Japanese—men after the 1965 agreement to normalize diplomatic relations between South Korea and Japan.

WOMEN'S STIGMATIZED LABOR

Women's sexual labor is of course performed in the home as well as in marketplace for pay. When it is performed at home as part of the duties of a married woman, patriarchal societies ritualistically accord it proper respect as indispensable of reproduction, which helps ensure the continuity of the husband's patrilineage. When performed for pay outside the matrimonial sphere, by contrast, it is socially devalued and stigmatized, the shameful activity of immoral women even though it is offered in the form of a wide variety of commodified services—erotic dancing, bar hostessing, and barbershop or salon massage, not to mention outright prostitution—in today's capitalist consumer cultures. I argue that the subject of women's public-sex work deserves more scholarly attention as quintessentially *gendered customary care work*, whose economic contribution to the gross domestic product (GDP) has yet to be comprehensively acknowledged in accounts of the proverbial "economic miracles" of postwar Japan and postliberation Korea. Notably, research conducted by a government agency reported that in 2002 there were at least 330,000 South Korean women working full-time in prostitution—8 percent of employed women in their twenties and thirties; that 20 percent of South Korean adult men between the ages of twenty and sixty-four purchased a sexual service 9.2 times a year in 2001; and that the sex industry produced an estimated profit of 24 trillion wŏn, or 4.1 percent of the country's GDP, close to the 4.4 percent of the South Korean GDP contributed by the agriculture, forestry, and fishing industries combined.[7]

It is remarkable that scholarly works on the relationship between gender and work in East Asian economic development—including those written by female researchers—have routinely ignored the contribution of women's sexual labor to these countries' economies.[8] Theories dealing with "care work" also overlook the topic.[9] Jobs that offer personalized and interactive care work for pay—such as child care, nursing, and elder care—tend to be devalued and are often poorly rewarded. The general devaluation of care work, some have argued, is due to a bias against work associated with women. Others have shown that workers who provided a service or dealt with communication were paid less because these jobs require less education and thus are not as highly valued as others.[10] One may add here that, from the perspective of ordinary men as potential consumers, sexual services for pay have customarily been stigmatized care work provided by lower-class women with little education or occupational training.

Given this widespread devaluation of women's care work in general, and the centuries-old negative attitude toward women's sexual labor for pay in particular, it is hardly surprising that most Koreans and Japanese in postwar years have not considered the personal ordeals of the comfort women worthy of public debate or of a campaign for social justice. The silence—at both the personal and the official level—concerning ex–comfort women in postliberation Korea must be understood in light of these fundamental political economic, social, and cultural facts of power relations and sexual mores. On the personal level, the surviving victims were silent because as a group they hailed from lower-class families and lacked the political power to press for justice. Even if they had come from middle- or upper-class families, though, the masculinist sexual culture and their enculturation in it would have meant that initiating social or legal action was simply out of the question. Their one recourse was to do everything in their power to conceal their pasts. Testimonials of Korean survivors reveal their acute "shame" at having lost their virginity and engaged in sex with many men. Most thought they had forfeited their eligibility as proper marital candidates for future husbands.

It is not surprising that Korean government officials—whose perspectives on gender relations are steeped in the masculinist sexual culture—would not consider the comfort women issue worth broaching during the long years of bilateral negotiation between Korea and Japan. In fact, after signing the 1965 bilateral treaty with Japan, the Korean government condoned, even promoted, sex tourism for Japanese men—that is, the commercial exploitation of women's sexual labor—in the name of national economic development. This phenomenon also underscores how critical a factor unequal power relations between the states have been in the long, sorrowful history of women pressed into performing the incomparably stigmatized sexual labor for men of other states over the past millennium. In other words, the issue of redressing the comfort women's personal ordeals goes beyond the usual class-based exploitation of women in the sex industry and into the realm of international relations, in terms of the power disparity among nation-states.

WOMEN'S SEXUAL LABOR AND THE STATE IN HISTORY

Historically, Japan was not the first foreign power to exploit Korean women's sexual labor. In the mid-thirteenth century, the Koryŏ Dynasty (918–1392) on the Korean peninsula came under Mongol domination and was forced to send "tribute women" (*kongnyŏ*) to the Mongols.[11] For more than eighty years, the Mongol rulers of the Yuan Dynasty (1271–1368) in China compelled Korean officials to round up *kongnyŏ* from among Korea's female population.[12] This demand for Korean *kongnyŏ* did not stop with the demise of the Mongol Dynasty. Chinese rulers of the Ming Dynasty (1368–1662) continued to demand this "tribute" until around 1521.[13]

During the Chosŏn Dynasty (1392–1910) Korean women also suffered sexual abuse and unspeakable ordeals during both the Japanese and the Manchu invasions of the Korean peninsula. Sexual violence against Korean women was inflicted not only by the invading Japanese military, but also by the Chinese military when the Ming armies were dispatched to "rescue" Korea. Korean men also committed sexual crimes in the chaos of the fighting; they disguised themselves as Japanese soldiers and engaged in gang rapes of compatriot women.[14]

The two Japanese invasions of 1592 and 1597 gave rise to such egregious abuses that many women killed themselves after being raped, and some killed themselves to avoid rape. Their suicides were officially recognized as the honorable deeds of virtuous women. It is striking that after the Japanese had retreated, the awards conferred on "virtuous women" (*yŏllyŏ*) of Korea by King Sŏnjo (r. 1567–1608) numbered nearly five times that of the two male categories, "loyal subjects" (*ch'ungsin*) and "filial sons" (*hyoja*), combined.[15]

The reign of King Injo (r. 1623–1649) saw two Manchu invasions, in 1627 and 1636, when hundreds of thousands of Koreans were forcibly taken to China. Some of the captured women managed to return home, but they were regarded as defiled and were rejected even by their families.[16] Many of the returnee women hanged themselves, and their corpses littered the streets.[17] The term *hwanhyang-nyŏ* (literally, a home-coming woman) degenerated into *hwanyang-nyŏn,* or a promiscuous woman ("bitch" may be a better translation to convey the disparaging connotation of *nyŏn,* which is a term of opprobrium referring to women), and denoted a woman to be despised and ill-treated.[18] The painful ostracism that Korean women suffered after their return home from captivity several centuries ago still resonates deeply in the minds of today's comfort women survivors. (The derogatory term *hwanyang-nyŏn* is one of the first "dirty" words I recall having heard during my childhood when adult female relatives talked about certain "loose" women; only after conducting research for this study did I learn the origin of it in the old expression for returnee women, *hwanhyang-nyŏ.*)

After the Chosŏn Dynasty Korea signed the 1876 Kanghwa Treaty with Japan—which, as Bruce Cumings writes, was "diplomacy with a gun to the temple, an offer Korea couldn't refuse"[19]—Korean women of the lower classes began to engage in sexual labor as licensed prostitutes for civilians of both nationalities, a direct precursor to their comfort women role. At the end of World War II, American servicemen became the primary group of foreigners to whom poor Japanese and Korean women sold their sexual services. Since Korea and Japan normalized diplomatic relations in 1965, Japanese male tourists have emerged as a major group of foreigners in search of the sexual services of Korean women. Public-sex work may have been stigmatized in Korean society, but it has been seen by Korean government leaders as a significant source of foreign currency for the national economy. In the early 1970s, for example, the Korean minister of education, Min Kwan-sik, praised the contributions of the *kisaeng* to the country's economic development.[20]

Remarkably, the minister's comments echoed those of Fukuzawa Yukichi (1834–1901), a leading political theorist of prewar Japan. Fukuzawa recognized the contributions made by Japanese women working as overseas prostitutes (*karayuki-san*), who sent back foreign currency that helped forge Japan's modern free-enterprise economy.[21] In 1900, of a total one million yen sent to Japan by emigrant workers in Siberia, 630,000 yen came from *karayuki-san*.[22] This is quite astounding on two fronts: the significance of the monetary contribution made by *karayuki-san* and the candor of the Japanese government statistics.

Despite such public acknowledgment, sex workers who worked hard and made financial contributions to their families often returned home to cold treatment and sometimes outright rejection. Their siblings and even their own children avoided them because of the stigma attached to their status as former prostitutes.[23] Yamazaki Tomoko, author of a pioneering work on the *karayuki-san*, reported being moved by how one group of *karayuki-san* had expressed their collective grudge (or *han,* to use the Korean term) against Japan: when she visited their graves in Sandakan, North Borneo, in Indonesia, Yamazaki discovered that all the gravestones were deliberately set to face *away from* the direction of Japan, symbolizing a most poignant but firm rejection of their ancestral land.[24] This act silently and posthumously proclaimed their bitter resolve not to look toward Japan even after their death.

Nevertheless, as Yamazaki noted, we must also realize that, even in the face of being ostracized by their own people, the *karayuki-san* remained subjects of imperial Japan and constituted the vanguard of their nation's aggressive invasion of the Southeast Asia, first commercially and later militarily. From the perspective of Japanese society, they were morally culpable for engaging in the "indecent occupation" abroad that harmed the reputation of Japan as a country. From the perspective of the peoples of Southeast Asia, they were subjects of the Japanese empire and contributed to its ability to carry out acts of political and economic aggression.

In light of this, we can pursue why Yoshie-san's courageous coming out has gone largely unrecognized by both Japanese and transnational memory activists. If Japanese comfort women were exploited by their society, they were also positioned to exploit the situation created by their empire.[25] Placed at the top of the hierarchy among comfort women of different ethnicities, Japanese women enjoyed greater earning power and better living conditions than the other women. Even Koreans have had to confront the Janus-faced identity of victim and victimizer as a subject—albeit colonized—of the Japanese empire. For some Koreans living abroad, Japan's defeat in the war was a calamity that led to personal crises, further social injustices, and financial hardships.

A Korean woman named Yi, who ran a brothel in Taiwan, for instance, stated that she earned a lot of money there but was unable to bring it with her, and she returned home penniless at the end of the war. She added, "I feared the retaliation of the Taiwanese."[26] Chang Ch'un-wŏl, a Korean survivor in China who was able to liberate herself from a comfort station run by a fellow Korean master by paying back her debt, and who started her own business running a small store, stated that she still could not forget how the Chinese beat her and robbed her of all her money and personal possessions as she was leaving for home at the news of Japan's defeat.[27] Ha Yŏng-i, who married the Korean proprietor of her comfort station, suffered a similar personal crisis. Having labored at multiple comfort stations for more than eight years and helped her husband run a comfort station for about a year after marriage, Ha had accumulated a considerable amount of wealth by August 1945. She was far from pleased when Japan lost the war: she felt "dim and dizzy" instead of joyful at the news of Japan's defeat.[28] She was then robbed of all her personal possessions (including a lot of gold jewelry and new clothes) by angry Indonesians. From the perspective of Indonesians, who suffered under Japan's military occupation of their country, her Korean ethnicity was invisible: to them she was simply one of the hated Japanese who had occupied their country (which had been under a Western nation's colonial rule for centuries as Dutch East Indies). In her testimonial Ha reiterated her sense of "extreme injustice" at having returned from Indonesia penniless.[29] The injustices Ha experienced as a comfort woman again point to the multiple levels of structural violence at work in the military comfort system—from her fraudulent recruitment by a compatriot, to the exploitation of her sexuality as a Korean woman by the Japanese military, to her victimization by the Indonesians at the end of the war, a direct result of her identity and legal status as a colonial Japanese subject.

POSTWAR AND POSTLIBERATION MILITARY COMFORT WOMEN

Did the end of the war mean the end of military prostitution and sexual slavery for the working-class women of vanquished Japan and liberated Korea? The answer, unfortunately, is a resounding no. Women's public-sex work has continued to be exploited for the "comfort" of soldiers, especially foreign troops, in both Japan and Korea for the more than half a century since the end of the war in 1945. To be sure, forcible recruitments by state agents no longer prevail, and there are no colonial subjects to be exploited; however, pimps and other sex trade entrepreneurs continue their fraudulent and coercive methods to recruit poor and gullible young women. Published materials have shown that some survivors—both Japanese and Korean— found themselves selling sex to the foreign soldiers who landed in defeated Japan and liberated Korea.[30] In addition to military prostitution, the adult entertainment industry has prospered in both countries. In particular, the Korean adult entertainment business for civilian men has developed a new international public-sex institution by offering specialized sex work targeting foreign tourists, especially Japanese men.

National Policy Comfort Women

In defeated Japan women and women's bodies became a critical concern in the days immediately after its unconditional surrender.[31] To protect the nation's female population, Japan's fearful officials took the initiative to establish "special comfort facilities" for the Allied forces that were to occupy the country for seven years (1945–1952).[32] In Tokyo and the neighboring Kanagawa Prefecture, where the first units of the Allied forces were expected to land, people were in a panic amid rumors of rapes and castrations of prisoners taken for manual labor by the American military. The governor of Kanagawa Prefecture paid women civil servants three months' salary and advised them to hide in the countryside for a while. Young women were advised to wear *mompe* (baggy pantaloons) and have their hair cut short like men.[33]

That ordinary women in occupied Japan were in real danger of becoming victims of sex crimes is undisputed. From the first day of the occupation, rape and other crimes by U.S. soldiers were "rampant."[34] It is also worth noting here that Korean comfort women survivors, including Mun P'il-gi, recounted that on the road home from China, they put soot on their faces to make themselves unattractive, as a measure of protection from possible assaults by the advancing Soviet troops.[35]

In light of the widespread panic and masculinist cultural assumptions about human sexual behavior (including the random rapes committed by soldiers in occupied territories that underlay the official rationale for the comfort system), it is understandable that the Japanese government would issue an order to establish special comfort facilities for the dreaded Yankee libido. The officials emphasized the need to make the people understand that the purpose of this order was to "protect Japanese women."[36] Building comfort stations for the occupying forces—as "gifts" from the vanquished to the victors—was done out of fear of the demonized Other, not a matter of making money. The "national policy comfort women" project could not be left to brothel owners alone, and the government was willing to spend up to 100 million yen to get the project started; officials believed that this was a cheap price to pay for "the purpose of preserving the pure blood of the Japanese nation."[37]

Further, the government directive indicated that women who worked at these facilities as "gifts" or sanctioned "booty" for the victorious warriors should be recruited from among the geisha, already licensed or private prostitutes, waitresses, and habitual sex criminals.[38] Japanese police officers appealed to former prostitutes "to work again for the sake of the nation and for the [safety] of the Japanese people" when they recruited.[39] The unstated message was loud and clear: women who engaged in public-sex work would merit no protection by the government. Public announcements that appealed to women's patriotism like the one below drew destitute women into the comfort facilities:

> We are looking for women of the New Japan who will do their part in rebuilding our nation by doing the important deed of providing comforts for the American forces stationed in Japan. From ages 18 to 25. Shelter, food, and clothing provided.[40]

When the Allied forces—composed mainly of American soldiers—landed in Japan, the Japanese government was thus ready to offer these women as "gifts from the vanquished." The Special Comfort Facilities Association was formed on August 23, 1945, and was officially recognized five days later; it was renamed the Recreation and Amusement Association (RAA) about a month after that. The RAA guidance committee was composed of representatives from such agencies as the Departments of Internal Affairs, Foreign Affairs, Finance, and Transportation, as well as from the prefecture of Tokyo and the police.[41] "Comfort facilities," including houses of prostitution, cabarets, and dance halls, sprang up across Japan in a matter of two to three months. The association ran twenty-one comfort stations for the Allied forces, whose basic structures and the way they were operated closely resembled wartime comfort stations run for the Japanese military. An American writer wrote:

> The first U.S. Army ground reconnaissance patrol to enter Tokyo, on September 2, was intercepted by an RAA truck filled with prostitutes, bedecked in their best finery; a spokesman explained that the women were "volunteers" to satisfy the lust of the Occupation forces. By October, the RAA had opened what may have been the largest brothel of its type in the world: a long open-bay barracks divided into cubicles by sheets hanging from the ceiling and with futons on the floor serving as beds.[42]

This RAA brothel, nicknamed the "International Palace," was located in eastern Tokyo. Hundreds of GIs a day went through "an assembly-line operation so smooth that a soldier would leave his shoes at one end when he came in and pick them up, cleaned and shined, at the other end when he left."[43]

The treatment of the Japanese comfort women by the state contrasts sharply with the experience of their Korean counterparts, however. The paternalistic Japanese bureaucracy took care to monitor the material welfare of Japanese nationals laboring as comfort women for occupying foreign forces. The government provided excellent remuneration for their sex work, which included double the usual monetary reward—50 percent of the fee—as well as high-quality daily necessities, such as a decent kimono and a good supply of cosmetic products from the renowned cosmetics company Shiseidō, and free meals.

By December 1945, however, American officials of the Supreme Commander for the Allied Powers (SCAP) concluded that Japan's licensed prostitution system amounted to human trafficking and should be abolished. On January 12, 1946, the Japanese police office issued a notice regarding the abolishment of licensed prostitution, expressing its regret over the "recent social situation" that forced the closure of a system that had exercised a "considerable effect" on public (sexual) morality. The notice also assured licensed brothel owners that they would be allowed to operate as private entertainment businesses. The practice of advance payment (*maegari*) was now forbidden, because that could be interpreted as human trafficking. That same day four nongovernmental organizations, including the Women's Christian Temperance Union, submitted a joint petition to abolish licensed prostitution. The timing of the petition is reported to have been tied up with the American intention that the abolition not be seen a matter of one-sided moral pressure. The three-hundred-year history of the licensed prostitution system came to an end on February 20, 1946, as a result of the SCAP directive. Among the nearly two thousand prostitutes working in Tokyo, about four hundred were affected by the closure ordinance. By changing their working title from *kōshō* (licensed prostitute) to *settaifu* (hostess), however, they were able to continue laboring as private prostitutes.[44]

Soon afterward, though, more than five hundred "national policy comfort women" lost their jobs when the facilities of the RAA were closed at the end of March 1946, several weeks before the Tokyo tribunal began. These facilities had been plagued by rampant venereal disease, but sexual contact between Japanese women and Allied soldiers continued in the dance halls, beer halls, and the streets of occupied Japan throughout the Tokyo tribunal and beyond.[45] Some Japanese women, including those from outside the entertainment industry, became "war brides" who married Allied soldiers and emigrated to their husbands' home countries.[46]

During the Korean War (1950–1953), occupied Japan turned into a sexual comfort camp for the U.S. military. American soldiers fighting in Korea were flown to Japan for their R & R leaves of five days for every six weeks of combat duty.[47] It is said that R & R was referred to as "I & I" among the soldiers—intercourse and intoxication.[48] Not surprisingly, the peak year for military prostitution in postwar Japan happened to be 1952. In that year about 13,000 cases of trafficking were investigated by Japanese police, and more than 70,000 women worked as prostitutes serving U.S. soldiers.[49] In the military camp town of Yokosuka alone, the foreign currency these women earned for the year was said to have amounted to between 200 and 300 million yen.[50]

Even with the booming sex trade, however, many Japanese women suffered individual and gang rape by U.S. soldiers.[51] Moreover, some Japanese women working as maids, nurses, and typists on U.S. military bases were deceptively taken to Korea and made to serve as battlefield "comfort women" during the Korean War; many of them were killed.[52] Eight of fifteen Japanese nurses who were flown in from the Yokota Air Force Base hospital to Korea on July 27, 1950, for example, were gang raped by hundreds of U.S. soldiers after they had finished taking care of the wounded at the front line just outside Pusan.[53] They were then left behind, and "all died from American military bombing with napalm and rockets."[54]

Postoccupation Japan enacted the Prostitution Prevention Law in 1956, which went into effect in 1957; penal provisions were not enforced until 1958.[55] In the case of Okinawa, the law was not enforced until 1972, the year in which the American-occupied island was finally returned to Japan.[56] Even so, this law was meant only to curb rather than prohibit prostitution, as leaders of the Women's Christian Temperance Union lamented.[57] Today many women from developing countries migrate to Japan to work in the "customary trade" in adult entertainment. They are referred to as *Japayuki-san*,[58] or young migrant women from developing countries traveling to Japan for work, which, of course, is a play on the term *karayuki-san*—the women of prewar Japan who traveled overseas to work as prostitutes.[59] Many in Japan now avoid use of the term, preferring to use such terms as "immigrant workers."

Camp Town Comfort Women

After its liberation from Japanese rule in August 1945, the Korean peninsula was divided in two: Soviet troops occupied the northern half and the U.S. military, the southern half. The ongoing U.S. military presence in South Korea led to the formation and maintenance of *kijich'on*, or camp towns, around the military bases, a development that has had a striking social impact on Korean communities.[60] *Kijich'on* (literally, base or camp [*kiji*] village [*ch'on*]) refers to the civilian demimonde of residential buildings and commercial establishments that have sprung up around U.S. military bases and cater to the needs of American GIs. It is "a place where Koreans and Americans—mostly male military personnel—meet in an economic and emotional marriage of convenience."[61] As of the end of 1996, 37,000 American troops supported the economies of ninety-six *kijich'on*. The estimated number of *kijich'on* prostitutes over the more than four decades of the American presence ranges between 250,000 and 300,000.[62]

Kijich'on prostitution has evolved through four distinct phases. During the first phase (1945–1948) the American military government's elimination of licensed prostitution led to privatization of the sex trade. In the postliberation political chaos and economic destitution, many people, including prostitutes from the now-closed brothels, gathered near the American military bases. Koreans coined new terms such as *yang-galbo* (Western whore) and, more euphemistically, *yang-gongju* (Western princess) to refer to compatriot women who performed sex work for the American military. Interestingly, until the early 1990s the media routinely used the euphemistic term *wianbu* to refer to the prostitutes who serviced American troops.

The *kijich'on* sex trade consolidated and expanded during the second phase, which began with the Korean War. In her testimony, Pak Sun-i (pseudonym; b.1930), a Korean survivor who had labored at three different comfort stations in Japan from 1944 to the end of the war, recalled:

> At twenty-seven years of age, I was having a hard time making ends meet in Tongduch'ŏn [the largest *kijich'on* just outside Seoul].[63] I ended up cohabiting with a staff sergeant of the U.S. Army for about two years. . . . One of my friends from the days at a comfort station in Japan also worked as *yang-gongju,* but she passed away.[64]

An American veteran who served in Korea in the 1950s after the end of the Korean War recounted that on Friday nights half-ton trucks would bring into the base a few hundred women to stay for the night or weekend with the soldiers.[65]

The third phase of *kijich'on* prostitution started in 1971 as a result of two important events that brought to a head underlying tensions between the Korean and U.S. governments. (Katharine Moon has discussed these in detail in her study of the role military prostitution played in the strategic relationship between these two unequal states in the 1970s.)[66] First, the July 24, 1969, announcement of the Nixon Doctrine concerning the withdrawal of American troops resulted in the pullout of 20,000 U.S. troops from Korea by the end of 1971.[67] Second, a series of fights between black and white soldiers broke out in the summer of 1971 over racial discrimination practiced at local bars.[68] Soldiers also complained about "unhygienic *kijich'on* women" and demanded that they be treated better as "VIPs who came to rescue Korea."[69] The Korean government, under the general-turned-president Park Chung Hee, wished to prevent further withdrawals of U.S. troops and responded quickly and positively to the demands of the American military. To deal with the complaint of unhygienic conditions in the *kijich'on* sex industry, the Korean government started a clean-up campaign that included infrastructural improvements and enforced regular medical examinations of prostitutes; infected women were to be detained at special centers.[70] The government thus began active engagement in the surveillance and control of prostitutes servicing the U.S. military. *Kijich'on* prostitution, for all practical purposes, had taken on the characteristics of licensed prostitution.

In the 1980s, when Korean and U.S. troops regularly conducted major joint military exercises called "Team Spirit," *kijich'on* sex workers were dragged in by brothel owners, "just like the Japanese military comfort women," to serve the American soldiers.[71] Egged on by brothel owners who promised good money, and sarcastically referring to themselves as the "blanket squad" (*tamnyo pudae*), they followed the soldiers during exercises.[72] Each would engage in sexual labor with twenty to thirty soldiers a day on those occasions. In the 1990s these annual exercises were reduced to several small-scale joint exercises in such port cities as Pusan, P'ohang, and Chinhae. Each time an exercise took place, *kijich'on* women moved to the respective port.

From a nationalistic activist's point of view, these *kijich'on* women constituted "*che2ŭi chŏngsindae*," or second [generation] comfort women.[73] By contrast, Nan Hee, a thirty-three-year-old Korean "club woman" working in a camp town bar in 1989, maintained a rather businesslike approach to her life and seemed to possess a healthy self-respect. When interviewed by American researchers, she stated:

> I don't think there are good and bad businesses. There's an old saying: Earn like a dog and spend like the secretary of the treasury. I'm not ashamed of my work at all. I guess a person could be embarrassed by it, but I'm not like that. It doesn't matter what others say, if our hearts are clean. Some people may disdain us and call us evil, but I think such people are the evil ones. They are spitting in their own faces.[74]

In the fourth phase, since the late 1980s, the *kijich'on* sex industry has been reshaped by the development of industry-type prostitution (*sanŏp-hyŏng maech'un*) in the broader society. The growth of the adult entertainment industry has created a host of new types of sexual care work that offers prostitution as a by-product of legal personal care services at such places as massage parlors, bathhouses, and barbershops. These new types of sexual care work have spread to the *kijich'on* as well. Women in these businesses sometimes turn to the *kijich'on* on weekends to earn extra money or to meet prospective husbands among the American soldiers. In addition, some teenagers and college students visit the *kijich'on* looking for opportunities to practice their English and make friends with American servicemen. Some of these "wanderers" turn into *kijich'on* sex workers.[75]

Another notable feature of the international sex trade in Korea by the 1990s was an influx of foreign women from "third world" countries. Korea's economic success and the expansion of the domestic sex industry have made *kijich'on* sex work less attractive for young Korean women. To make up for the shortage of *kijich'on* workers, foreign women, mostly from the Philippines, have been brought in to work at the nightclubs.[76] Since the collapse of the Soviet Union, thousands of Russian women have also migrated to Korea to work as entertainers singing and dancing at nightclubs, but some of them have been forced into prostitution, not only for American soldiers but also for Korean civilian men.[77] The Korean public television network, KBS, reported on May 29, 2001, that about 4,000 Russian women were working in the Korean adult entertainment industry, and some of them were suffering financial exploitation and even human rights abuses.

A research report from 2003 found that foreign women outnumbered Korean women in the *kijich'on* clubs for the American military in northern Kyŏnggi Province. Filipino women were the most numerous, with the Russian women taking second place.[78] They are generally very young and able to speak English. Some have been "imported" as entertainers by Korean entrepreneurs, while others are illegal migrant workers. These foreign women are more easily controlled than Korean workers because some Korean sex workers have taken collective action to safeguard their threatened livelihood. Korean women criticize the business owners for the "unpatriotic" hiring of Filipino women, thereby losing foreign currency to them and robbing Korean sex workers of the opportunity to "help the national economy by earning foreign currency."[79] It is ironic that the rhetoric of patriotism started by male government officials has thus come full circle: now it is the sex workers themselves who resort to it to rally nationalist support against their foreign competitors.

Even though the cold war in Europe has ended, a large number of American servicemen will remain in Japan and Korea, and Japanese and Korean women will continue to engage in public-sex work in camp towns.[80] Because the division of the Korean peninsula has yet to be resolved, the American military is expected to have a continued presence in East Asia—as a stabilizing "guarantor" of the regional security—until at least 2015.[81] The atrocities of Japan's imperial army against women have been amply aired in recent years, but few people in the United States are aware of heinous sexual crimes committed by American military men, most of which go unpunished due to the unequal Status of the Forces Agreement (SOFA) between the superpower United States and Korea. One particularly gruesome case involving the murder of a Korean prostitute, Yun Kŭm-i, by an American soldier named Kenneth Markle prompted an unprecedented mass demonstration of 3,000 people in Tongduch'ŏn, the largest *kijich'on,* in 1992.[82] The barbarity of the crime mobilized enraged residents to stage a series of demonstrations that eventually led to the formation in 1993 of the

National Campaign for Eradication of Crime by U.S. Troops in Korea. According to statistics compiled by this organization, an average of two crimes per day were committed by U.S. troops from January 1993 to June 1996, and on average the Korean government exercised jurisdiction in 0.7 percent of cases. The case of Markle's murder of Yun Kŭm-i is one of the very few that resulted in the criminal serving his sentence in a Korean prison.

"Special Comfort Women"

The fact that Korean military also availed themselves of the "special comfort unit" during the Korean War has received little public attention, even since the Korean women's movement in support of the comfort women began in the 1990s. Until recently only piecemeal anecdotal materials on the Korean military's comfort women unit had come to light from memoirs written by retired generals and the testimony of soldiers who had fought in the war. Only in February 2002 did the first scholarly work appear presenting the embarrassing truth that the Korean military also created and operated its own comfort women system. Notably, this research—a paper focusing on military comfort women and military comfort stations during the Korean War by the Korean sociologist Kim Kwi-ok—was presented in Japan.[83] Kim's paper is based on her study of the official record of the military, *Hubang Chŏnsa* (War History on the Home Front), published by the Korean Army in 1956, as well as the memoirs of retired generals and testimonial narratives of those who had been involved in the system in one way or another.

It is still not clear exactly when the special comfort units were established. Kim estimates that they began in 1951. The closing date, by contrast, is specified as March 1954 in the army document that pointed out that the cessation of warfare eliminated the need for the units. Kim Kwi-ok argues that the Korean military ran its system through three types of "comfort" operations. First, they ran "special comfort units" called T'ŭksu Wiandae in seven locations—three in Seoul and four in Kangwŏn Province, including Ch'unch'ŏn. It is not clear how many women were kept at these stations, but on the basis of partial figures disclosed in *Hubang Chŏnsa*, Kim could only surmise that the number of comfort women was about 120.[84] Second, the military also operated mobile units that visited the barracks, and, third, they hired women working in private brothels to service the soldiers.

Characterizing the Korean military comfort system as an "unfortunate offspring" of the Japanese colonial legacy, Kim Kwi-ok called for victimized women, civic organizations, and scholars to come together and confront the unresolved issues of this historical injustice. The media reports of

Kim's work, however, have generated virtually no societal response. There has been no audible public outcry regarding the Korean military's use of comfort women during the Korean War or its violation of women's human rights. Koreans' silence on these issues is reminiscent of the earlier societal indifference toward survivors of imperial Japan's comfort system. It mirrors the reticence of many Japanese to come to terms with the history of their own country's wartime comfort system. As in the case of Japan, many in Korea, including retired military leaders, seem to regard women's sexual labor simply as the performance of customary sexual care work to meet the needs of fighting men.

That Korea's army leadership was trained by imperial Japanese forces may also have contributed to the creation of the special comfort units. It is notable that Korean records refer to the women as "fifth category supplies"—an addition to the four normal supply categories, reminiscent of the Japanese classification of comfort women as "military supplies." Retired General Kim Hŭi-o, for example, describes an instance of using prostitutes as "comfort" in his 2000 memoir, *In'gan ŭi Hyanggi* (The Aroma of Humanity). As his company was preparing for nighttime combat training, he received instructions regarding the "fifth supply" of six comfort women. According to his recollection, they were brought in from Chongsam, the then famed red-light district in Seoul. The women were sent to his company, to be employed for eight hours during the day. He remembers his ambivalence about the arrangement, which led to soldiers forming long queues in front of the tented barracks. Two women were allocated to his platoon, and one of them was first sent to him, the platoon leader. He wrote that after exchanging small talk with the woman, he gave her a bundle of ration biscuits he had accumulated and handed her over to a first sergeant.[85]

It is noteworthy that military authorities have acknowledged that the system of special comfort units contradicts the national policy of banning licensed prostitution. Nonetheless, they have insisted that the special units were created to further an important social goal. Although it is not clear how the recruitment process worked for women in the South, some women from the North were kidnapped by South Korean agents.[86] The general operational methods of the Korean army comfort system were reminiscent of the Japanese system. All the women had to undergo regular medical examinations by army doctors to combat sexually transmitted diseases. The similarities in the pattern of operations include soldiers lining up in front of the tents, the women being classified according to the ranks of the men they served, and a hierarchical order of access to their sexual service. Nearly identical pictures emerge of wartime military sexual behaviors both for Japanese soldiers and for their postcolonial Korean counterparts. Given the much shorter period of warfare, however, the Korean military used far fewer women than the Japanese. Another difference of political significance for the Koreans is that the men and women were of the same nationality.

In light of Japan's and Korea's long history of similar masculinist sexual mores, it is both significant and unsurprising that the rationale cited by the Korean army for establishing comfort units should mirror that of Japan's imperial forces. Like the Japanese, the Korean military argued that these units were critical to raising morale and preventing servicemen from forcing unwanted sex on the civilian population. In other words, the Korean military regarded its comfort system as a kind of necessary social evil. This very masculinist perspective, in fact, was advanced in defense of the *kisaeng* system of the Chosŏn Dynasty by its high officials.[87] It is clear that both the imperial Japanese military and the postcolonial Korean army leadership shared the belief in men's uncontrollable need for, and therefore right to, women's bodies outside marriage, whether in war or peace.

INSTITUTIONS OF PUBLIC SEX AND THE STATE IN KOREAN HISTORY

Licensed prostitution was officially abolished in southern Korea in November 1947 under the U.S. military government in Korea. However, a private system of sexual labor has continued to prosper in a variety of manners and places in Korea in the form of customary care labor. The international sex trade prospers in the capitalist economies of Japan and Korea despite endless incidents of criminal abuse of women by both foreigners and compatriots.

As discussed above, the U.S. military in Japan and Korea has had easy access to the sexual services of postwar comfort women residing individually in the numerous local camp towns in the two countries since 1945. In addition, Japanese civilian men have also traveled to Korea in pursuit of sex tourism since the mid-1960s. In 1961, when General Park Chung Hee took power in a military coup, his regime legislated the Prostitution Prevention Law as part of its social purification drive. The government, in fact, took a compromise position, allowing 104 special districts for prostitution nationwide in 1962. By the early 1970s prostitution catering to foreign men had received semiofficial support, as exemplified in the *kijich'on* sex trade serving the U.S. military and in the development of so-called *kisaeng* tourism, which targeted Japanese visitors.

The traditional *kisaeng* system no longer exists as a formal institution, but the tourism industry began to appropriate the term *kisaeng* euphemistically, using it to refer to women sex workers catering to foreign—primarily Japanese—tourists. Before we further discuss the postliberation phenomenon of *kisaeng* tourism in South Korea, however, it is imperative that we take a brief overview of Korea's very long history of the state-supported institution of *kisaeng,* which helped legitimate the male right to public recreational sex for over a millennium.

The Institution of *Kisaeng/Kinyŏ*

Although a system of licensed prostitution began under Japanese colonial rule,[88] Korea already had the institution of *kisaeng* or *kinyŏ* for men's entertainment, which had originated in the Koryŏ Dynasty (918–1392) and continued until the end of the Chosŏn.[89] *Kinyŏ* (literally, skilled woman) referred to young females of lowborn social status who were trained to serve the state by their skill in medicine, needlework, music, and dance. It is believed that most of the Koryŏ-era *kinyŏ* were in fact government slaves,[90] who had been trained to entertain men at court feasts and other parties with songs, dances, and witty banter.[91] Following the Tang Chinese model, a training institute, Kyobang, was established for *kinyŏ* in the early Koryŏ period.[92] These women were classified into three types: official *kinyŏ* (*kwanki*),[93] household *kinyŏ* (*kagi*), and private *kinyŏ* (*sagi*). The *kwanki* were mostly slaves and lowborn young females who acquired superior skills in the arts of literature, music, and dance. They were in turn ranked into three groups, with the top-ranking group serving at official ceremonies and occasions at the palace.[94] In exceptional cases, these *kwanki* could enjoy wealth and power by attracting the attention of kings and high officials and becoming their concubines.[95] In general, however, they were despised because of their status outside regular society.[96] The *kagi* were nongovernmental slaves who played the role of skilled women for households. The *sagi* were young girls who were bought and trained by old retired *kinyŏ* as a means for the latter to earn a living. They apparently served primarily commoners and outcasts (such as butchers). It appears that women whose occupation was prostitution also existed in Koryŏ Dynasty, and a scholar of late Koryŏ has recorded the existence of a "market in females" (*kyejip sijang*) offering public sex in the back alleys of Seoul.[97]

By the time of King Sejong (r. 1418–1450) of the Chosŏn Dynasty, sex work had come to dominate the life of *kinyŏ.* High-level Confucian scholar-officials in the Chosŏn Dynasty tried repeatedly to have the institution abolished, but opponents successfully argued that sex crimes were likely to increase if that happened.[98] It is not surprising that such a biologically determinist argument should have won the debate with relative ease in Korea's masculinist sexual culture and continued to rally support for both *kinyŏ* and the practice of acquiring *ch'ŏp* (concubines). Notably, by the middle of the Chosŏn Dynasty, in the seventeenth century, the *kwanki* (official or government *kisaeng*) in Seoul, most of whom came from the provinces, were permitted to have a husband (*kibu*) who worked at a low-level law-enforcement job such as a warrior or palace security guard. Urban *kisaeng* with *kibu* lived in public housing and practiced their skills but apparently did not engage in prostitution.[99] Rural *kisaeng,* however, did not have husbands; instead they had "mothers," who functioned as their masters (*chuin*).[100]

When a *kisaeng* became a concubine, or a woman from a poor family was taken as a concubine by an upper-class (*yangban*) man, the woman suffered legal and social discrimination. She could not participate in any formal family events. Her children were labeled *sŏja* (illegitimate offspring) in contrast to the *chŏkcha* (legitimate children) born of the lawful wife. Koryŏ society further recognized the lawful wife posthumously if she had been a "virtuous woman" who did not show jealousy toward her husband's *kich'ŏp* or *kisaeng*-turned-*ch'ŏp* (concubine): posthumous praise for her good conduct was inscribed on her tombstone.[101] The Korean practice of concubinage, one may argue, essentially functioned as a stabilized form of prostitution for men of wealth and power in Chosŏn society and beyond.[102] It enabled the ruling elites to maintain façades of being morally upright married men espousing Confucian virtues while enjoying institutionalized proprietary access to recreational sex.

What should be noted here is that this behavior continues among married men in Korea today. All three of the men who have served as presidents of the Republic of Korea since 1990—Kim Young-sam, Kim Dae-jung, and Roh Moo-hyun—have been rumored to have illegitimate daughters.[103] Given the traditional "son preference," it is not surprising that children not accepted into their father's family registry are all daughters. Illegitimate sons are typically taken into the main family and entered in the family registry in due time. Examples of this social practice include not only the story that the survivor Mun P'il-gi tells about her younger half-brother (see chapter 2), but also, most dramatically, the case of one prominent candidate in the 1997 presidential campaign who was born of a mistress to the founder of a leading *chaebŏl* (business conglomerate) company.

Kinyŏ as Wianbu in Chosŏn Korea (1392–1910)

It is striking to note that in the social history of Korean women's public-sex work, a native conception of *kinyŏ* as *wianbu* for soldiers developed in the Chosŏn Dynasty, several centuries prior to the emergence of imperial

Japan's wartime military *ianfu* system. In the fifteenth and sixteenth centuries, for instance, Korean kings recognized the need to maintain the *kinyŏ* system "to comfort" (*wian-hada*) soldiers stationed far away in the northwestern region near the border.[104]

The role and functions of *kinyŏ* gradually transformed into those of prostitutes or *wianbu* by the latter period of the Chosŏn Dynasty.[105] Without an understanding of this historical transformation, the apparently nonchalant use of the term *wianbu* in *Han'guk Yŏsŏngsa* (History of Korean Women)— published by Ewha Womans [Women's] University in 1972—to mean "*kinyŏ* as *wianbu*" would be astounding to nationalist Koreans, given the political implications the term has acquired in the 1990s owing to the international redress movement for surviving comfort women.

Toward the end of the Chosŏn Dynasty, the *kisaeng* system began to disintegrate. Around the reign of Kojong (1864–1907), *kinyŏ* were classified into three ranks.[106] The top rank, Ilp'ae, was called *kisaeng* and played the role of official *kinyŏ*, serving upper-class society and the state. The Ilp'ae had to retire when they reached thirty years of age. The middle rank, Ip'ae, was called "the secretive one" (*ŭnkŭnja*) to denote its private, stealthy engagement in prostitution. The bottom rank, Samp'ae, was engaged primarily in prostitution. The Samp'ae resided in Sidong in the southern part of Seoul during the rule of Kwangmu (1897–1907). In 1908, with the support of a high official, the Samp'ae formed their own union and began to refer to themselves as *kisaeng*.[107] Because they lacked the singing skills expected of trained *kinyŏ*, they were pejoratively called *pŏng'ŏri* (mute) *kisaeng*. Nevertheless, they were welcomed by the "deaf playboys" of the times so long as they were pretty and coquettish.[108] The term *kisaeng* thus evolved into a synonym for courtesan and whore (*kalbo*) by the last years of Chosŏn.

Korean *Kisaeng* Tourism

It is not clear exactly when and how *kisaeng* tourism began in South Korea, but what is clear and undeniable is that the economic development policies of the state, especially after normalization of diplomatic relations with Japan in 1965, have helped it prosper.[109] The state-led economic development plans emphasized growth through exports; they kept wages low and working hours long. The state launched a series of five-year economic plans to help achieve a "miracle on the Han" by exploiting, among other things, the labor of working-class people, especially young women employed at manufactories. In 1985 the average wage of women workers, for example, was less than half—46.7 percent—that of men.[110]

Further, in an effort to earn foreign currency, the Korean government condoned, if not formally facilitated, the commodification of sexual services by young Korean women billed as *kisaeng*. After the 1965 normalization of relations, the number of Japanese visitors to Korea rapidly increased, and *kisaeng* tours became enormously popular among predominantly Japanese male visitors to Korea in the late 1960s.[111] By the end of the decade, the state began to see foreign-currency-earning prostitutes as an important human resource in its national economic development.

Tourism thus emerged as a strategic industry. The Tourism Promotion Law was promulgated in 1971, and since that time the number of Japanese tourists has exceeded that of American visitors. In 1972, with the formation of the Korea International Tourism Association, the special districts for prostitution set up in 1962 were abolished.[112] Further, the Prostitution Prevention Law no longer applied to prostitutes serving foreign visitors in specially designated tourist hotels, nor to prostitutes serving American servicemen in the *kijich'on*.[113] In the 1970s Korean women who wished to work formally for foreign tourists at the specified hotels had to acquire a license certifying their health status and the completion of a required orientation. The orientation lectures given by university professors were a peacetime version of those for imperial Japan's wartime Women's Volunteer Corps (Yǒja Chǒngsindae); they emphasized the importance of this "patriotic" work, which helped earn precious foreign currency for the nation's economic development.[114]

In 1973 the number of Japanese tourists to Korea was more than double that of the previous year, approaching half a million. Then as now the great majority of them were men. The dramatic increase in 1973 was primarily due to Japan's normalization of diplomatic relations with the People's Republic of China in 1972, which resulted in Japan's severance of its formal relations with Taiwan. Many Japanese men who had gone to Taiwan for sex tourism turned to Korea after September 1973. By the time Korea reached its goal of attracting a million tourists in 1978, more than 60 percent of them came from Japan. In 1979, 649,707 Japanese tourists visited Korea, and an estimated 100,000 Korean women worked as tourism *kisaeng*.[115]

The commercially organized *kisaeng* tours became ready sources of income for young Korean women; their earnings contributed to increasing foreign currency income for the nation (Table 6.1). The majority of Japanese men who visited Korea to attend *kisaeng* parties came from the lower classes to enjoy sexual entertainment at one-fifth the cost of comparable services in Japan.[116] The euphemistic term "*kisaeng* party" masked the fact of mass

Table 6.1 Foreign visitors to South Korea, 1964–1966 and 1968–1978

Year	Total number of visitors	Japanese	American	Contribution to annual gross national product (in thousands of U.S. dollars)
1964	24,935	2,280	11,530	15,704
1965	33,464	5,110	14,152	20,798
1966	67,965	19,740	39,274	33,817
1968[a]	102,749	25,219	41,823	35,454
1969	126,686	31,821	49,606	32,809
1970	173,335	51,711	55,352	46,772
1971	232,795	96,531	58,003	52,383
1972	370,656	217,287	63,578	83,011
1973	679,221	436,405	N/A	269,000
1974	518,000	326,340[b]	N/A	159,000
1975	633,000	411,450[b]	N/A	141,000
1976	834,000	398,790[b]	83,400[c]	275,000
1977	950,000	570,000[b]	95,000[c]	370,000
1978	1,079,000	667,319	107,900[c]	408,000

Source: Adapted from KCWU 1983: 7.

[a] The data for 1967 are missing from the original source.

[b] The figures for 1974, 1975, 1976, and 1977 (Japanese visitors) are calculated from the approximate percentages (63 percent, 65 percent, 63 percent, and 60 percent) given in the original source.

[c] The figures for 1976, 1977, and 1978 (American visitors) are calculated from the approximate percentages (10 percent, 10 percent, and 10 percent) given in the original source.

prostitution. Typically, planeloads of men were transported in buses to special *kisaeng* houses/restaurants called *yojŏng* (*ryōtei,* in Japanese) ensconced in buildings designed in the grand style of traditional Korean architecture. There, impatient tourists could sometimes pick their partners by barging into the women's standby room. One Japanese tourist who attended a *kisaeng* party and contributed an essay to a Japanese magazine compared his experience to "picking out a slave in the slave market."[117] At "tourist *yojŏng*" the tourists were fed and entertained by attentive *kisaeng,* in imitation of the way wealthy business people and powerful officials used to hold their exclusive parties. Clad in traditional garments of *ch'ima* (long skirt) and *chŏgori* (short jacket) and sitting next to a sex tourist, a *kisaeng* would feed the tourist with chopsticks and fill his glass with beer or other alcoholic drinks. At the end of such party almost all men take their partners back to their hotels for sexual intercourse.[118] Some Japanese men have made fraudulent marriage proposals to young Korean women whose dreams of becoming a "Japanese princess" resulted in cruel violations of their human rights.[119]

More than a quarter of a century after women in Korea and Japan began fighting against sex tourism, Japanese sex tours to Korea continue, albeit less conspicuously, in smaller groups and without reference to the term *kisaeng*.[120] Every single day during my research trip to Korea in January 2000, I observed several examples of a particular type of couple—middle-aged Japanese men in casual clothing accompanied by fashionably dressed and fully made up young Korean women—eating breakfast together at a downtown hotel restaurant in Seoul. Prosperous middle-class Korean men, meanwhile, have embarked on their own international quest for sexual adventure. This has been dubbed "Don't-Ask Tourism" (*mutchima kwankwang*), which takes them to the less developed countries of Southeast Asia.

CONCLUSION

Mulling over the Korean outcry at Japan's wartime exploitation of Korean women, and remembering the sordid history of sexual violence and prostitution involving the U.S. military in postliberation Korea, the historian Bruce Cumings posed the following questions in 1992, the year in which the comfort women issue was first brought to the attention of the United Nations.

> Does it make much difference that American soldiers paid cash for the half-ton-truck girls, instead of giving them room and board as did the Japanese? Or perhaps the half-tonners "wanted" to do what they did and "freely chose" it in the marketplace of a Korea with a per-capita income of $100, as opposed to the evil Japanese who "kidnapped" the women?[121]

His ruminations continue:

> What, then, do you make of top-secret internal North Korean eyewitness reports, captured by the U.S. and recently declassified, that speak of some three hundred politically suspect Korean women

(party members and people's committee leaders, mainly) confined to a warehouse and used at will by American forces in wartime Seoul in the fall of 1950?[122]

The questions Cumings has raised are crucial to an overall and comparative understanding of the sociocultural patterns of military prostitution and sexual violence against women, especially during wartime. We must ask similar questions regarding the creation and operation of a "special comfort unit" by the South Korean Army during the Korean War, not to mention the egregious sexual crimes against women of Japan and Korea committed by the U.S. troops in postwar Japan and postcolonial Korea. The deep-rooted historical legacy of treating women's public-sex work as necessary but stigmatized and gendered customary care work, documented in this chapter, underscores the systemic nature of the exploitation of women of lower social classes. It sheds light on the social and political economic dimensions of the sexual cultures and the role of the "state as pimp" (to borrow John Lie's phrase)[123] in instituting state-sanctioned military prostitution for the foreign forces stationed in postwar Japan and postliberation Korea, where most people long ignored the historical injustice and personal suffering inflicted on numerous survivors of Japan's wartime military comfort system.

Not surprisingly, the male-dominated Korean National Assembly from 1948 to 1989 concurred with the state's position regarding Korean women's sexual labor for the U.S. military at camp towns and for foreign sex tourists at urban hotels—it was necessary and positive for national security and for economic growth, respectively.[124]

But when it comes to the issue of Japan's wartime military comfort system, very few social critics or public intellectuals in Korea have dared to take the usual "customary trade" position publicly. There has been little critical public discourse on the legacies of that historical institution or on the social-structural dimension of the Korean comfort women phenomenon.[125] Few are willing to consider the unsavory fact that, accustomed to "customary" public institutions that grant men a sex-right to satisfy their carnal desires outside matrimony, few Koreans opposed, and many collaborated in, recruiting and running comfort stations by trafficking in girls and young women. Rather than dealing with the messy and unpleasant complications of the historical record, Korean public discourse has simply elevated the survivors to heroic symbols of national suffering under colonialism.

It is worth remembering here, however, that before the transnational redress movement took off in the 1990s, comfort women survivors had been socially marginalized and their sufferings culturally habituated and politically unproblematic in both Japan and Korea. By and large, survivors were perceived as sexually "defiled" women. As such, they simply did not merit encompassment in the postwar or postcolonial nationalist discourse on the social, cultural, and political category of "woman," which embodies feminine morality rooted in sexual purity and maternity.[126]

Epilogue | Truth, Justice, Reconciliation

Is reconciliation possible without some kind of powerful, tran-
scendental faith? Surely, as many have argued, a first step in the
politics of reconciliation and forgiveness is knowledge seeking,
learning exactly what happened to whom, by whom, and why.

—Nancy Scheper-Hughes, "Undoing," 2004

THE OVERARCHING THEME OF THIS STUDY has been the complex truth
about both Japan's military comfort women system and the sources of lifelong suffering of the Korean victim-survivors. Theoretically, it has aimed
to contribute to a deeper and more nuanced understanding of the comfort women phenomenon. To understand how and why women of colonial
Korea constituted the overwhelming majority in Japan's wartime military
comfort system and were later stigmatized for that role, I have gone beyond
the paradigmatic one-dimensional story of Japan's war crime by probing the
diversity and historicity of the women's lived experiences. I have examined
the specific sexual cultures and political-economic contexts of prewar and
wartime imperial Japan and colonial Korea, in which people, as self-serving
victimizers or victimized social actors, interacted in their everyday lives to
generate the particular behavioral manifestations of structural violence under study here. My analysis has underscored the historical conjuncture of
structural power (in colonialism, militarism, and capitalist statism), heterosexual mores (in masculinist sexual cultures), and customary violence against
women (under patriarchy, classism, racism, militarism, ethnic nationalism,
and cultural relativism). At the same time, my historical structural analysis
has encompassed a person-centered approach, whose perspective is not only
gendered but also pluralistic and thereby contributes to our uncovering the
subaltern voices of victim-survivors telling their versions of the truth.

By insisting on the necessity of examining both the structural conjuncture of power dynamics in the historical context and the disparate trajectories of personal lived experiences (as disclosed in testimonial narratives and

recounted during informal private conversations), and by adopting a critical anthropological lens that combines a "harsh light" with a "soft focus,"[1] the present study has revealed, among other things, the causal factors for the comfort women's lifelong suffering, included grave domestic abuse in their childhood and young adulthood and active local entrepreneurial collaboration in their recruitment as comfort women, in addition to their wartime ordeals at comfort stations and the social stigma they endured after returning to liberated Korea. The dual framework of structural analysis complemented by a person-centered perspective thus contributes to making my larger point about multiple personal truths and the significance of diverse underlying ideologies for competing narratives in the sexual and identity politics surrounding non-Japanese comfort women survivors.

Nationalist activists and elderly victim-survivors aside, the question at this point becomes, what portion of the general public really wants to know about the uncomfortable instances of gendered structural violence and is willing to see the larger sociohistorical picture of the comfort women tragedy? This problem of subjugated knowledge about a painful historical truth is especially tricky because such an introspective approach will likely complicate Korean demands for justice in the postcolonial politics of "settling the past" with Japan. Nevertheless, the Korean comfort women survivors' *han*-filled narratives of lifelong suffering analyzed in this study underscore the need to engage in political struggle for gender justice at the local level. Only such local political struggle, in conjunction with international campaigns for women's human rights, can help transform the dominant masculinist sexual culture and persistent structural violence.

A "GOOD-ENOUGH" TRUTH

Speaking of social suffering and the politics of remorse in South Africa, the anthropologist Nancy Scheper-Hughes reported:

> Those seeking truth in South Africa today do not want the partial, indeterminate, shifting truths of the postmodern. . . . Instead, they desire the single, sweet, "objective" truth of the moralist and, with it, a restored sense of wholeness and a taste of justice. Yet, . . . South Africans are willing to settle for an agreed-upon, a "good enough" truth.[2]

In the case of Japan's wartime comfort women, however, competing representations of them have created something like the bewildering confessional stories presented in Akira Kurosawa's (1910–1998) classic film *Rashomon*.[3] In this internationally acclaimed picture,[4] Kurosawa transformed the divergent accounts given by the actors implicated in crimes of theft, rape, and homicide into a meditation on truth and human nature. It powerfully illustrates the problem of finding "truth" amid multiple, contested, and subjective representations of criminal acts, because the characters in the film were motivated to present their own subjective versions—what may be called their "personal truth"—to uphold their own honor and dignity.

Similarly, what is fundamentally at stake in the comfort women controversy is the honor of members of the opposing camps. For Japanese conservatives and neonationalists, Japan's honor as a nation depends on the definition of the comfort system as a military version of licensed prostitution, which was not only legally available at the time but also socially tolerated as a customary practice. For human rights advocates, restoration of the honor and dignity of non-Japanese victim-survivors seems to hinge on the representation of the comfort system as military sexual slavery, a war crime, and a crime against humanity. Yet, testimonial narratives of Korean victim-survivors have revealed much more complex and varied lived experiences anchored to the painful sediment of their lifelong suffering than the paradigmatic, one-dimensional story of the Japanese military comfort system as war crime can satisfactorily explain.

Among the publications on the comfort women issue that have been authored by Koreans since the early 1990s, women activist researchers have produced the greatest number.[5] Some have drawn careful attention to a variety of sociological factors and political issues for the Korean comfort women cases by going beyond the prevailing postcolonial nationalist rhetoric. Kang Sŏn-mi and Yamashita Yŏngae, for example, have addressed the issue of sexual violence against women by focusing on the fascist state of imperial Japan that arose in the context of the emperor system, militarism, and a masculinist sexual culture that naturalized the existence of prostitutes.[6] Kim Eun-sil has offered a critical feminist analysis of the nationalistic public discourse that generalizes the particular aspects of individual women's experiences.[7] Yang Hyunah (Hyŏn-a) also critically analyzed, in an English-language publication, the Korean nationalist rhetoric on the comfort women.[8] An Yŏn-sŏn has reflected on multiple historiographic perspectives on the comfort women and analyzed the sexual and identity politics involving the makings of Korean women as "sex slaves" and the militarized masculinity of Japanese soldiers.[9]

More recently, Pak Yu-ha has offered critical reflections on the complexity of the comfort women issue and discussed the complicity and responsibility of Korean society for the lifelong suffering of the survivors.[10] In a similar vein, Rhee Younghoon has discussed the reality of the comfort women issue from a historical perspective and critically analyzed the process of the formulaic construction of collective memory through the use of novels, history textbooks, activist rhetoric, and the print media in Korea.[11]

In contrast, Chung Chin-sung continues to focus on ethnicity-based discrimination in the military comfort station "policy" of the Japanese state, asserting that imperial Japan "clearly planned to implement the system using the women of its colony, forcibly if needed."[12] Yun Myŏng-suk, who defines the military comfort women issue first and foremost as a war crime committed by the state, also emphasizes ethnicity-based discrimination by listing it as a major point in her historical study of the Japanese military comfort station system and Korean comfort women.[13]

Significantly, the official silence about the comfort women may have been broken, and the redress movement for the survivors has succeeded in gaining public support, but the general attitude regarding the proper place of the comfort women in the social landscape in both Korea and Japan has in fact not changed as much as one might expect. When Pusan ChŏngTaeHyŏp (the acronym of the nongovernmental organization Chŏngsindae-munje Taech'aek Hyŏpŭihoe) submitted a request to the city government of Pusan (South Korea's second-largest city) to build a memorial to the comfort women in Taech'ŏng Park in 1992, the petition was denied owing to strong opposition by the Association of the Widows of War Dead and Deceased Policemen. Offended, the group asserted that Taech'ŏng Park, with its Loyal Spirit Tower (Ch'unghon-t'ap), is a sacred area (sŏngyŏk). They adamantly objected to the placement of a memorial to "ugly comfort women" (ch'uhan wianbu) next to the tower dedicated to the memory of their husbands, who had died for the nation.[14]

Not surprisingly, similar negative sentiments also prevailed among Korean government officials and civic leaders when the Korean Council requested that a memorial to the Chŏngsindae be erected inside Independence Hall, arguing that it would serve as a national history lesson against allowing such humiliation to occur again.[15] In particular, members of the Kwangbok-hoe (Association of the Liberation [from Japanese colonialism]) were vehemently opposed to the idea, asking rhetorically how wianbu could be raised to the same level as those who had fought for the nation's independence.[16] These outright rejections of the very idea of erecting a memorial to deceased comfort women underscored how resolutely unsympathetic some Koreans are to the Korean Council's project. This rejection extended to the organization's elevation of victimized wianbu to the status of abused *chŏngsindae,* under which label the Korean Council leaders may have expected to memorialize the comfort women in the realm of publicly recognized fallen victim-heroes of the nation. The organization's founding corepresentative, Yun Chŏng-ok, wrote in 1994:

> What I cannot understand is the attitudes of the past governments of this nation and the men in this country. The government does not seem to possess historical consciousness and national pride. . . . During the war many girls became sex slaves to forestall the conscription of their brothers or fathers. However, very few men express strong interest in learning about the issue and endeavoring to resolve it.[17]

Despite the remarkable domestic and transnational success of the Korean redress movement since then, the Korean Council has been unable to obtain a positive response from the governments of Korea and Japan to its demand for the erection of a monument to comfort women. The Korean Council is now going ahead with its plan to create a War and Women's Human Rights Museum to commemorate the comfort women.[18] However, the organization's petition to place the museum in the historic Independence Park at the site of the old Sŏdaemun prison, where many independence fighters had been jailed during colonial rule, met once again with opposition from the Kwangbok-hoe, which regards the prison as a sacred site for Korea's independence movement.[19]

Aware of the international public relations dimension of the project, the Korean media have carefully refrained from "unnecessarily" reporting dissenting public views,[20] thereby lending indirect but nationalist support to the Korean Council's project. The Korean media, for instance, completely ignored the article "Statement of Recommendations to the Korean Council," published by Jee (Chi) Man-wŏn, a military analyst and conservative social critic (who holds a doctoral degree from the U.S. Naval Postgraduate School), on the home page of the System Club in December 2005, in which he charged the Korean Council with the "crime of distorting history" by referring to the comfort women issue as a Chŏngsindae issue. He has strongly urged that the Korean nongovernmental organization replace the term *chŏngsindae* with *wianbu* in its organizational name. Moreover, based on the information offered by the disgruntled former comfort woman Sim Mi-ja, whose relationship with the Korean Council has turned adversarial, he also raised the question of whether the organization had misappropriated support funds raised for the survivors. Several months earlier he had dared to challenge the Korean Council with uncomfortable questions such as the possibility of some survivors being fakes, enraging not only the Korean Council and the survivors, but also a large number of their supporters.[21] The Korean Council sued him, and he in turn countersued.[22] A notable consequence of Jee's public challenge regarding the Korean Council's misuse of the term *chŏngsindae* for the comfort women is that the Korean Council initiated a signature campaign on its Web site to help support the cause of the "true" *chŏngsindae* survivors.

"ENSLAVED PROSTITUTION"

> Every second, I feel as if I were being smothered. This is a hell, not fit for human life. If transmigration could occur, I wish to be born as a bird so I could be free to fly away.

So wrote a thirty-year-old woman in her diary. She had been held in what the Korean media dubbed "enslaved prostitution" (*noye maech'un*) for several years in a provincial town in postcolonial Korea before she was rescued in 2001. The police arrested the couple who owned the house and charged them with having forced thirteen women to labor for them as sex workers since 1987.[23] It should be pointed out that this is an especially egregious practice of the enforced prostitution still found in today's Korean society. An editorial in a major national daily lamented this sorry case and the prevalence of this sort of prostitution in Korean society.[24] It asked rhetorically, How is it possible for Korean society to overlook the phenomenon (of sexual enslavement) after the historical suffering of *chŏngsindae* women under imperial Japan?

Here again is another example of the twenty-first-century Korean media holding up the fallacious equivalency of the *wianbu* and *chŏngsindae*. By categorically referring to the comfort women (*wianbu*) of colonial Korea as abused members of the Volunteer Labor Corps (Chŏngsindae), the media conveniently not only help mask Korean society's collaboration in the historical recruitment of the young women to military prostitution but also ignore continued structural violence against women of the lower social classes.

The moral of the "enslaved prostitution" story, once again, in light of the Korean comfort women tragedy, is this: Activist struggle for gender justice must be fought, first and foremost, locally. This struggle can certainly be joined with the international campaigns for women's human rights to gain broader leverage, but in the end the goal must be to fundamentally transform the customary public-sex institutions and attitudes that not only underpinned imperial Japan's military comfort system but continue to pre-vail in today's Japan and Korea. This transformation must begin at home, by placing equal value on daughters and sons and by insisting on mutual respect between wives and husbands. In addition, legislators and policy makers must seriously address the need to protect the basic human rights of women working in the sex industry.

It took the tragic deaths of twenty prostitutes caught in two huge fires in September 2000 and January 2002 to forcefully rally feminist activists and the members of the Korean National Assembly to enact special anti-prostitution legislation, which went into effect in September 2004. The women, who were sleeping in locked brothels, could not escape the fires that engulfed the red-light district in Kunsan.[25] A U.S. government publi-cation listing Korea among the countries involved in international human trafficking was another factor spurring the Assembly into action.[26] The laws are intended to prevent prostitution, punish those involved in it, and protect victimized women. Its success will depend on the resolve of Korean society as a whole to respect and protect the basic human rights of women performing the stigmatized customary care work for men's public sex.

Indeed, men and women in Japan and Korea today need to confront the women's human rights issue in relation to everyday heterosexual behavior acted out in the public realms of the adult entertainment industry, where both local and foreign women continue to labor. Mongolians were recently added to the mix of foreign women deceptively recruited by Korean entre-preneurs when police arrested a group of men who were forcing Mongo-lian women to work under conditions of slavery out of a twenty-four-hour barbershop. Their passports had been taken away, and the women were kept under strict surveillance, beaten, and forced to engage in sexual labor even during their menstrual periods. Given the history of Korean "tribute women" offered to the Mongols of the Yuan dynasty, it is a real irony that more than seven centuries later Koreans are engaged in exploiting Mongo-lian women.[27] Meanwhile, in Uzbekistan, where prostitution is illegal, in recent years "Korean-style brothels" (what Koreans call "room salons") have reportedly mushroomed to cater to Korean tourists.[28]

In the United States, Korean women working at "bars" and "massage parlors" have led to the coinage of the term "Korean bar," meaning a place where "bar girls" (who may or may not be Korean) provide sexual services to male customers. These Korean women working abroad—who have been referred to as "international comfort women" by Korean Internet users—may well have been recruited deceptively, as were so many young women more than sixty years ago. Today, the conjunctural structure of women's victimhood as sex workers at home and abroad is embedded in the globalizing capitalist political economy, which obfuscates just which nation is the enemy in this fight.

By contrast, in cases of historical injustices and old crimes, how can fair settlement be made that "balances legal, psychological, and moral concerns"?[29] Moreover, among the past injustices that Koreans wish to settle, collective memories of Japan's colonial wrongdoings are perhaps the most intractable, for these two nation-states, which are of unequal political and economic power, disagree over the assessment of their past relationship as colonizer and colonized. One significant public demonstration of Korean activists' sentiment with respect to "settling the past" (*kwagŏ ch'ŏngsan*) with Japan took place when the Japanese prime minister, Koizumi Junichirō, came to Seoul as an invited guest for the inauguration of Korea's newly elected president, Roh Moo-hyun. The title of a newspaper article published on February 24, 2003, summed it up well: "Opposition to Koizumi's Visit to Korea without Settling the Past" ("Kwagŏ Ch'ŏngsan Ŏpnŭn Koizumi Panghan Pandae"). About sixty people representing civilian organizations, including the Korean Council, took to the streets to protest Koizumi's visit. Their opposition was based on the assertion that Japan has "not settled its past with Korea." But what did "settling the past" mean? This was their statement:

> We oppose Prime Minister Koizumi's visit to Korea because he has engaged in resurrecting the ghosts of Japan's imperialism with his visits to the Yasukuni Shrine while disregarding the demand of the Korean people to reveal the truth and repent of the crimes Japan committed. To reestablish the South Korea–Japan relationship, the Roh Moo-hyun administration must at once engage in the settlement of the history of [Japanese] invasion [as evidenced by] the military comfort women and victims of forced labor.[30]

It is in this sociopolitical context of historically rooted, ideologically constructed, and psychologically reinforced antipathy toward and mistrust of Japan that we should seek an understanding of South Korean activists' relentless politics of animosity toward the Japanese government over the comfort women issue for nearly two decades.

Dialogical Reflections

The various types of comfort stations that developed during the Asia Pacific War indicate that the comfort system accommodated the gamut of men's recreational public sex, ranging from commercial sex under licensed prostitution and indentured sexual labor, to wartime military rape, to battlefield abduction into sexual slavery. It is the reality of this widely divergent range of sexual activities—from conventional masculinist behaviors, legal or not, to grave crimes of sexual assault and enslavement—that resulted in the indisputable suffering of innumerable young girls and women, both inside and outside Japan. This mixture of socially condoned sexual activities and legally punishable sexual crimes makes it difficult to determine just what would constitute proper redress for the historical misdeeds committed by individual soldiers and their military and political leaders.

Nonetheless, comfort women's ordeals must be formally recognized, however belatedly, in history textbooks and other forms. The ultimate goals are to transform the prevailing culture of public sex (rooted in the customary practice of male sex-rights) and to ameliorate women's ongoing social penalization under continued structural violence. This formal recognition must occur, of course, both in Japan and in the afflicted nations. In addition, the international community, including the United States and other nations of the Allied forces, must acknowledge their complicity in allowing their troops to engage in similar acts and crimes against women in vanquished Japan and postliberation Korea.

There can be no question about Japan's official responsibility in masterminding the military comfort system. The antagonistic nationalists in Japan and their counterparts in Korea must be shown the need to rise above blind ethnonational and identity politics and to recognize the complex historical truth of the comfort system. They should recognize and reflect on the historical conjuncture of the system's basic organizational features and the participants' personal circumstances in the era of imperial aggression and colonial exploitation. It was the conflation of masculinist sexual culture and structural violence under consumer capitalism, realized in the system of licensed prostitution (exploiting the pauperized working-class population under colonial rule), that constituted one major conjuncture, which facilitated in wartime (and still facilitates) trafficking in women of lower socioeconomic origins, often with the tacit collaboration of authorities and little overt protest on the part of local residents or community leaders.[31]

Categorically defining the Japanese comfort stations as "rape centers"—as the United Nations special rapporteur Gay McDougall did—is a political act in support of the redress movement. This partisan prejudice, which overlooks historical incidents of sex crimes committed by other conquering armies, has in fact mischaracterized the nature of the Japanese comfort system. Similarly sweeping characterizations offered by progressive Japanese historians, such as "officially recognized sexual violence" and "a systematic and comprehensive structure of military sexual slavery," are in line with the paradigmatic story advanced by contemporary feminist and human rights discourse.[32]

Unquestionably, the Japanese state deserves censure for its active role in setting up and maintaining a system that led to the sexual violation of numerous women. In spite of this heinous past, we must note that definitions such as those given above do not offer an accurate view of the comfort system: they simplistically conflate the diverse categories of *ianjo* discussed in this study into one, and this conflation in fact has reduced the persuasiveness of their meticulous research among the general public in Japan. It has in fact prompted reactions such as the rise of historical revisionism and neonationalist activism against the comfort women redress movement. It is tempting, and quite understandable, for progressive scholars and their supporters to want to categorically define the comfort system as sexual slavery and war crime in recognition of the undisputable degradation of countless women and the horrendous ordeals of sexual violence recounted by many victim-survivors. However, such a one-dimensional representation would mean overlooking some aspects of the factual truth concerning the comfort system as history. In their conscientious support of the transnational human rights discourse, progressive intellectuals and grassroots activists have completely ignored the popular public memories that are rooted in the personal lived experiences of many military veterans and their supporters. The controversy surrounding NHK television's coverage of the 2000 Women's International War Crimes Tribunal, which resurfaced in the spring of 2005,[33] unequivocally underscores the deep divisions in Japanese society over the publicly acceptable narrative of the comfort women issue. Moreover, so long as the lawsuits over the issue are decided on a case-by-case basis, it is necessary to examine each case of the surviving comfort woman regarding the method of recruitment and the life at a particular type of *ianjo* in a specific locale and time period. If some cases apparently belong to the conventional case of licensed prostitution, others may clearly be defined as criminal sexual slavery. It should be reiterated here that many prostitutes indeed lived then, and continue to live, in slavery-like conditions today.

Beyond Ethnic Nationalisms

As I have attempted to demonstrate throughout this study, the tragedy of Korean comfort women is not simply a matter of war crimes but also a prominent example of gendered structural violence that has operated insidiously through the less obvious mechanisms of class and "race" exploitation in combination with the institutional legacies of public sex under colonial capitalism and imperial Japan's war of aggression. Most regrettably, the activists' master narrative has glossed over the more complex, wider-reaching narratives of women's oppression and has thereby failed to generate a sense of societal responsibility among Koreans for their compatriots' lifelong suffering. For more than a decade and a half, since the start of the Korean comfort women movement, there has been little room for critical self-reflection in South Korean public discourse on the victim-survivors. Questions of enduring social inequality and the sexual exploitation suffered by lower-class women simply are not broached. When I mentioned the tone of nationalism that seemed to override the recognition of the socioeconomic status or class factor in the Korean public debate on the comfort women issue, a Korean Council staff member retorted, "One cannot be *not* nationalist [in this matter]."[34] This is not entirely surprising, because in Korea's modern history feminism has generally been subordinated to nationalism.[35]

Although researchers and academics of the younger generation have published critical analyses of the Korean nationalist discourse on the comfort women issue, no socially prominent Korean feminist scholar outside the movement activist circle has risked a self-critical public debate on nationalist identity politics over the comfort women issue. By contrast, one nationally and internationally known Japanese feminist scholar has discerningly problematized, from the mid-1990s, the nationalistic discourses in Japan and Korea that, respectively, represent comfort women either as "willing prostitutes" or "forcibly conscripted virgins," and she has persistently stressed the need for feminism to transcend nationalism.[36] Such a postmodernist call, coming from a Japanese perspective, however, will not convince many Koreans, who may suspect her of taking this position for ulterior motives.

*　　*　　*

To come to terms with their dark history, Koreans must acknowledge their share in the suffering of compatriot women by their silent collaboration in wartime recruitment and the social stigmatization of survivors in liberated Korea in the postcolonial years. Still, few Koreans have been willing to acknowledge in public their complicity in the deceitful or forcible recruitment of young girls and women for their own profit in the colonial social and economic contexts. Those in a position to make the sordid story better-known have been reluctant to do so, because of the historically rooted antipathy toward Japan and the likely repercussions of being branded *ch'inilp'a,* or pro-Japan collaborators. In the spring of 2001 the Korean translators of Bruce Cumings's 1997 *Korea's Place in the Sun* contacted the author more than once to express their grave concern with his statement regarding the role Korean men played in the mobilization of compatriot women to serve as military sex slaves.[37] They wished to confirm that Cumings wanted his original statement to remain in the translated version. During my interview with Cumings,[38] he related how he told the translators that Korean collaboration was a historical fact that other writers, such as George Hicks, had already pointed out.[39]

This reluctance to grapple with factors contributing to the suffering of comfort women in late colonial Korea and in postliberation Korean society has persisted. It is only since 2004 that one has been able to find encouraging signs of critical self-reflection on the topic. A public debate on the government-led "settlement of history" project televised in September 2004 is a case in point. The debate unexpectedly generated a nationwide furor over passing comments on the comfort women issue made by Rhee Younghoon, a professor of economic history at Seoul National University.[40] The gist of his statement—that the comfort women issue is rooted in the historical institution of licensed prostitution—met with strong objections from Song Yŏng-gil, a member of the National Assembly who belonged to the ruling Uri Party and a copanelist. Song offered such inflammatory and distorting rhetorical questions as "Is Professor Rhee arguing the Japanese right wing's 'licensed prostitution theory'?" The following day, the online newspaper *OhmyNews,* which has characterized itself as a guerrilla-style critical medium that enlists numerous "citizen reporters," misquoted Rhee as having equated Korean comfort women with prostitutes.[41]

Predictably, Rhee was severely censured for his alleged remarks by the Korean Council and its supporters, most of whom did not watch the televised debate itself but only read misrepresentations of the event reported in the media. The Korean Council demanded not only an apology but also Rhee's immediate resignation *and* his dismissal from the university. The strength of nationalist fury was registered in severe critiques posted on media Web sites as well as angry individual denouncements that flooded the Web site of the University School of Economic Studies, which forced Rhee, among other things, to issue an explanatory statement. Facing the threat of a demonstration on the university campus by activist survivors, members of the nongovernmental organization's staff, and their supporters, Rhee then visited the House of Sharing to meet several former comfort women and apologize to them in person. There some of the irate survivors denounced him, saying that his "faulty" perspective rendered him unqualified for the position of professor. Their personal attacks included both verbal and physical abuse. My informant, a mild-mannered resident of the House of Sharing, told me that one of the more militant women expressed her anger by throwing water over the professor.[42]

The level of furor at scholarly commentary on a sensitive topic once again underscores two salient facts about contemporary Korean society: (1) the dramatically forceful role of the self-righteous and populist media, backed by the freewheeling power of Internet users, who can be extremely aggressive in making their emotional, moralistic, and often very nationalistic voices heard; and (2) the blinding effect of nationalist history education, which has contributed to blocking a deeper and more critical understanding of Korea's turbulent modern history, including the Korean comfort women issue.

In Japan, conservatives and neonationalists would do well to remember the late Yoshie-san and reflect on the significance of her voluntary public disclosure of painful private memories and her heartfelt plea for a memorial to the deceased comfort women. Ten years after the comfort women monument was erected in Kanita Women's Village, increasing pressure from the international community led the Japanese government, under Prime Minister Murayama, to establish the Asian Women's Fund (AWF) to atone in some small part for its brutal exploitation of women during the war. Although South Korean activists have scornfully dismissed the AWF's atonement project as a "second rape," it is undeniable that the fund has offered substantive help to those who were willing to accept it. For individual recipients, including the plaintiffs in the class-action lawsuit, the AWF projects apparently did contribute, both symbolically and materially, to a formal reckoning with personal suffering, as the testimonials of Filipina and Dutch victims clearly reveal.[43]

The atonement projects had offered some financial and psychological solace to a total of 364 elderly survivors by the time the AWF was dissolved in March 2007 (after fulfilling its government-mandated ten-year project). This number includes most of the formally recognized survivors in the Philippines, the Netherlands, and Taiwan. In South Korea, the Korean Council, which had rejected the AWF project from the start, has continued its battle relentlessly for its several itemized demands, including formal apologies and state compensation. As a result, the majority of Korean survivors, it is believed,[44] have received neither atonement money nor letters of apology from either the Japanese prime minister or the AWF president.

The comfort women issue has by now become thoroughly politicized, and political issues require diplomatic negotiations if they are to be formally settled. The governments of Japan and South Korea have been negligent in pursing resolution for more than a decade, hiding behind the AWF and the Korean Council, respectively. Because it is clear by now that nongovernmental organizations alone cannot solve the problem, it is incumbent upon the two governments to deal with the matter diplomatically. In view of the deep internal divisions in Japanese society and the transnational prevalence of partial truths about the comfort women issue, however, people must engage in a process of "reconciliation at home" first, in both Japan and Korea, before diplomacy can work. For true reconciliation, both sides must acknowledge that the Japanese military comfort system accommodated a gamut of diverse masculine sexual behaviors straddling both commercial and criminal sex. Japanese soldiers did perpetrate collective criminal acts against women of occupied enemy territories, while many others used the state-regulated and -endorsed sexual services offered by indentured prostitutes and other young women often fraudulently recruited by both Japanese and Korean entrepreneurs and human traffickers.

Finally, when we remember and write about the contested memories of wartime comfort system and the lives of tens of thousands of women who labored there, we must move beyond the political correctness of well-intentioned progressive academics, the litigious courtroom arguments, and the competing discourses of ethnic nationalists and ahistorical memory activists if we are to obtain a fully contextualized understanding of the system and its victims. The victimization of colonial Korean women as Japan's military comfort women is a prominent example of long-standing structural violence (intersecting with class, ethnicity, and nationality factors) embedded in the still-prevalent masculinist sexual cultures of the two countries. Only honest reflections on this conjuncture can lead to earnest, healing dialogue about a tragic chapter in the inextricably tangled histories of Japan and Korea. Reflective dialogue may, in turn, help pave the difficult road toward genuine reconciliation between the two neighbors. As a consequence, we may even realize collaborative commitment, at both the national and the international levels, to combat sexual exploitation and violence against women in war and in peace.

Appendix | Doing "Expatriate Anthropology"

THE IDEA FOR THIS BOOK germinated in my mind during one of my annual trips to Korea, in July 1992, when I paid a courtesy visit to Professor Lee Hyo-chae, a leading sociologist and activist scholar who had just retired from Ewha Womans University and cofounded the Korean Council for Women Drafted for Military Sexual Slavery by Japan. Handing me copies of various documents on the council's activities to bring the world's attention to the historical injustice committed against compatriot women under Japanese colonial rule (1910–1945), Professor Lee urged me to conduct research on the topic, adding that people—myself included—who are native-born Korean scholars working abroad should help the movement by publishing on the comfort women issue in English to disseminate more widely knowledge about this hitherto largely ignored problem.

Upon my return home to San Marcos, Texas, I began with a sense of obligation to work on my first paper on the comfort women issue, using primarily the materials I received from Professor Lee. When I presented the paper, "Korean 'Comfort Women' for the Japanese Imperial Army: Sexism, Paternalism, and Nationalism," at the annual conference of the Western Social Science Association, Corpus Christi, Texas, in April 1993, I was surprised to find a charged atmosphere in the conference room—with standing room only—which seemed to indicate a high level of interest in the topic in the academic community.[1]

The first opportunity for me to conduct ethnographic field research on the comfort women issue came in 1995, right after I moved to California to accept a faculty appointment at San Francisco State University, a great urban public institution whose strong progressive bent has proved a welcoming environment in which this project in its incipient phase firmly took root. In the thick of a harsh, wintry January that witnessed, among other things, the disastrous earthquake in Kobe, Japan, I spent the month in Korea, interviewing the council leaders as well as victim-survivors in South Korea. I also observed the weekly demonstrations held in front of the Japanese embassy in the heart of Seoul. In hindsight, I had just taken the first step in my very long and arduous journey to produce this book.

Back in the United States, as a board member of the Association for Asian Studies Committee of Women in Asian Studies, in April 1995 I helped draft a resolution calling on the Japanese government to reach a fair solution of the comfort women issue. As I continued my study of the issue, however, I became acutely aware of the need to move beyond the postcolonial ethnonationalist and post–cold war activist rhetoric and broaden the scope of the project by incorporating a historical and comparative perspective. I therefore undertook additional field research in order to contextualize Korea's comfort women tragedy through a supranational, cross-cultural comparative lens. As a result, what began as a modest proposal to write about the stories of Korean comfort women has gradually developed into a long-term, multi-site ethnographic research project that included multiple research trips not only to South Korea but also to Japan and the Netherlands, where I met with a variety of subjects and informants of diverse ethnic and nationality backgrounds. Seeking a more comprehensive understanding of the complexities surrounding Japan's military comfort women issue, I also traveled to the National Archives in Washington, D.C., to consult archival materials and to New York City to interview a Korean American activist lawyer representing a Korean survivor.

For this study of the controversy surrounding the true nature of imperial Japan's wartime military comfort system and the lifelong social injustice suffered by Korean victim-survivors, I adopt the lens of cross-cultural, critical anthropology using both a "harsh light" and a "soft focus."[2] An important ingredient in my comparative and pluralistic approach is the use of feminist political-economic perspective to analyze multiple tiers of power relations at the heart of comfort women's suffering, both within society and beyond the national border. I painfully remember the evening when I began recounting to my spouse some of the heart-wrenching life stories of Korea's comfort women survivors after returning from my January 1995 field research. While talking about the life story of Mun P'il-gi, one of the key subjects of my study, I was overwhelmed with emotion and unexpectedly broke into tears. I found myself sobbing and unable to continue my talk. After I regained my composure, when I brooded over the implications of Mun's life story, I felt my deep sorrow and sympathy—for her and other victim-survivors I interviewed—being overtaken by intense anger, recognizing the familiar patterns of women's suffering and their victimhood rooted in structural violence, especially among the poor.

As I immersed myself in analytical reflections on their personal life trajectories, I became strongly, and at the same time dishearteningly, struck by the "banality of evil": from my perspective, it was the structural violence of Korean patriarchy (with its masculinist sexual culture and the political economy of capitalist colonial modernity and postcolonial political economic development), *in tandem* with the military comfort system and imperialist aggression of wartime Japan, that loomed large as a fundamental source of my subjects' lifelong social and psychological suffering.

In retrospect, my research project has helped me acquire a great deal of new knowledge about the topic of the comfort women and related aspects of Korea's twentieth-century colonial history under imperial Japan, about which I was taught very little during my formal education in Korea. Having sojourned with my family in Japan for a year during my adolescence, I am especially interested in comparative studies of the cultures of Korea and Japan. My intellectual commitment in this project has been to research and write against prevailing adversarial ethnic nationalisms and ahistorical international feminisms, with a view to helping the two neighboring countries move forward toward more amicable bilateral relations by shedding a critical light on the sexual cultures of these two patriarchal societies and the political economies of nation-states of unequal power regarding heterosexual men's "needs" and desires. Toward that goal, I strive to offer a balanced, multilayered analysis of Japan's comfort women in terms of sexual violence and postcolonial/postwar memory in Korea and Japan surrounding the comfort women issue—an issue that was culturally muted, socially shunned, and academically unexamined until the transnational human rights discourse of "military sexual slavery" spread in the 1990s.

The theoretical attention of the book primarily focuses on three fronts: (1) the ideological underpinnings of the identity politics that inform contentious representations of comfort women by both domestic and international supporters of the survivors and by ethnic nationalists of opposing camps in the transnational redress movement; (2) the history of masculinist sexual culture and structural violence against women in a patriarchal society under one capitalist colonial regime; (3) and, most of all, the fractured and partial "truth" concerning personal life stories, official discourses, private counternarratives, and public memories of the comfort women recovered from the sociopolitical matrix of adversarial ethnic nationalisms and shared cultural legacies in Korea and Japan, where women's public-sex work is a stigmatized but "customary" form of paid care work. Here the political-economy perspective, using the notion of structural power,[3] is especially helpful for understanding the class- and ethnicity-based exploitation of female sexuality in Korea's colonial capitalist modernity; an emblematic representation of this structural violence is the implementation of the Japanese licensed prostitution system in colonial Korea.

I also take seriously the theoretical criticisms and methodological issues concerning the representation of the "other" that postmodernism and feminism have raised against conventional ethnography.[4] Korean comfort women have been multiply "othered,"[5] not only by Japan but also by their own colonized and postcolonial patriarchal society: they were often devalued as daughters at home prior to their deceptive recruitment into military prostitution, and later, after their return home, they were stigmatized as sexually impure women.

While retaining the "executive, editorial position" of the author,[6] I have endeavored to incorporate multiple competing voices and different vantage points on the comfort women controversy. For example, I draw into my discussion hitherto subjugated knowledge and personal memories of intimate encounters between Korean comfort women and Japanese soldiers as I build up a comparative perspective, working from postcolonial, postmodern sensitivity to the partiality of "truth" in representations of the other. This genealogical approach couples local, discontinuous, and subjugated knowledges with the paradigmatic story of the comfort women that dominates the transnational discourse of Japan's comfort women issue;[7] it thus risks incurring strong displeasure from activists of both international feminist and ethnic nationalist stripes (and from progressive academics as well),[8] but it is especially called for in this research.

Out of concern with structural violence as a persistent part of the human condition, I have adopted the methodology of an anthropological "processual holism" that endeavors to capture the overall condition suffered by the comfort women.[9] I must emphasize, however, that this holistic methodology is not intended to condone the comfort system as a valid Japanese historical institution in the name of cultural relativism. On the contrary, it aims to offer a critical genealogical synthesis out of competing narratives on the comfort women issue, from a historically and culturally nuanced social-structural, supranational, and comparative anthropological pluralism.

Here I should also point out that cultural relativism has reigned as a disciplinary credo among anthropologists seeking to understand people of other cultures from the natives' standpoint ever since Franz Boas and his colleagues helped found American anthropology as an academic discipline more than a century ago. In particular, as my research expanded beyond South Korea and turned transnational in scope, I became acutely aware of the special tension between anthropological respect for "native" perspectives and feminist humanitarian faith in the universal concept of human rights. In this study I take the viewpoints of both "natives" and the expatriate researcher to inform its comparisons and adopt both synchronic and diachronic lenses through which to observe the historical legacies of masculinist institutions of public sex that are evident not only in the wartime practices of the military comfort system but also in postwar military prostitution and international sex tourism. My methodological strategy has led me to take up what has been called "experimental" forms of ethnographic writing,[10] which include juxtaposing and contrasting contradictory discourses of universalistic advocacy of women's human rights, on the one hand, and cultural relativism supplemented by personal counternarratives, on the other.

The techniques I used to collect my ethnographic data included observations of courtroom hearings, events organized by civic groups, staff meetings of activist groups and research organizations, questionnaires, and informal as well as semistructured interviews with informants such as survivors, activists, nongovernmental organization members and leaders, students, and taxi drivers, as well as such professionals as lawyers, researchers, and government officials. In Japan the activists I interviewed included both advocates and critics of the redress movement. Moreover, in Japan I was able to meet with and interview non-Japanese victim-survivors and several representatives of the redress movement organizations from the Netherlands, the Philippines, and Taiwan. The focus of this study, however, is the sociohistorical context of the Korean comfort women phenomenon and competing representations of Japan's wartime military comfort women in the contemporary redress movement. This focus has necessitated that I uncover the legacies of masculinist institutions of public sex in Korea and Japan not only during colonial rule and the war of aggression, but also in postcolonial and postwar everyday life.

*　　*　　*

The main intent of my research is to present, from my social position of an insider-outsider as an expatriate anthropologist, a nuanced ethnographic analysis of complex issues involving the historical injustices suffered by numerous former comfort women of Korea. Born into the postliberation generation, I have no lived experiences of colonial injustice nor any personal axes to grind. I was educated in South Korea, Japan, and the United Kingdom before coming to the United States for graduate school. Nevertheless, when I conducted ethnographic fieldwork on women in Korean politics as a graduate student in the mid-1980s and subsequently published my research findings in the United States as *The Chosen Women in Korean Politics,* I regarded my work as a piece of "native anthropology."[11] Having lived abroad for the majority of my adult life by now, however, I would assert that my present work belongs to a genre I call "expatriate anthropology."[12]

As a Korean-born expatriate anthropologist residing in the United States, I have situated myself as a concerned observer rather than an active participant in the comfort women redress movement in order that I may maintain a reasonably objective scholarly position. As a supporter of feminist humanitarian efforts to promote gender equity worldwide, and as an expatriate anthropologist who has chosen to engage in multiple layers of "border crossings," I strive to rise above the activists' competing rhetoric on the comfort women issue and address from the middle ground the international controversy that has been fueled by the parallel political dynamics of ethnic nationalisms and transnational feminist human rights activism. Had I resided in Korea, it would have been extremely difficult for me to stake the methodological standpoint delineated here. Lacking any formal affiliation with Korean academia, I have worked in solitude most of the time and with a considerable amount of anxiety over the painstaking task of fairly representing the multiple and contentious actors in the international comfort women controversy. As I have engaged in the transnational and multidisciplinary border-crossings that have led me to locate myself at the controversy's center, my primary concern has remained the daunting objective of presenting a nuanced picture of it.

Accordingly, I have tried to sustain the special anthropological tension of simultaneous engagement and detachment. I have kept a conscious professional distance from the competing social organizations and political actors, even while I obtained from several of them valuable data for my study.[13] My methodological stance has precluded direct personal involvement in the activities of advocacy groups, and I believe it has significantly contributed to the achievement of a more integrated perspective on the comfort women issue. For one thing, it has led me to consider, theoretically as well as practically, critical questions regarding the meaning of "women's human rights" in the everyday lives of the surviving comfort women. In one of my articles,[14] for example, I attempted to give voice to a silenced minority of dissenting victim-survivors who suffered name calling and ostracism stemming from their personal decisions to accept the atonement project of Japan's national Asian Women's Fund. (Their decisions defied the hard line taken by the Korean Council leaders, who categorically rejected the fund.)

Unsurprisingly, my methodological stance displeased some militant advocates seriously enough that I sustained personal attacks. The first episode took place in an Indonesian restaurant in a suburb of The Hague in May 2000. I had been invited to attend a dinner party cohosted by a Dutch law professor whom I had interviewed about his involvement in a Dutch citizens' organization seeking legal compensation from Japan for wartime suffering and a Chinese-born activist historian from a college in Minnesota who was then representing the Global Alliance for Preserving the History of WWII in Asia (formed in 1994). The twenty-one attendees included European war victims turned activists and litigants against Japan (a majority of whom were members of the Dutch nongovernmental organization called Foundation of Japanese Honorary Debts), two Chinese-born activists from North America (the cohost and a woman from Canada), and two men from Japan, a reporter for the Japan Communist Party newspaper (*Akahata*) and the activist historian Arai Shin'ichi representing the Center for Research and Documentation on Japan's War Responsibility. The Chinese woman activist from Vancouver, British Columbia, Canada, whom I first met in Tokyo and last saw in The Hague, sat next to me and during the dinner asked me to explain the Asian Women's Fund. I gave her a detailed response, but toward the end of my explanation she unexpectedly burst into an impassioned verbal assault on me in piercing tones. (A Japanese activist who knows her and heard about the incident from his colleague at the party compared—during my meeting with him in Tokyo several months later—her zealous behavior to that seen in popularized dramatic scenes of verbal badgering that took place during the heyday of China's Cultural Revolution. I was surprised to hear his comments for two reasons: first, the imagery his comments conjured up corresponded to mine, and second, his colleague talked to him about the incident, because the two Japanese men at the party had remained completely mute during the incident, although they expressed sympathy to me for my social and psychological ordeal when we shared a ride back to the same hotel.)

In any case, the woman activist's sudden rant stunned the party into a dead silence for a few seconds before Dutch friends of hers and the compatriot cohost of the dinner rushed to her side, asking what the matter was. (Then the Dutch cohost posed a similar question to me, trying to sort things out.) What I gathered from her angry pronouncements and disparaging remarks about scholarly work she made to her solicitous friends was that she suspected the motives in my research and objected to my addressing the meaning of "human rights" for victim-survivors in terms of their individual right to decide on acceptable forms of apology and compensation for their wartime ordeals against the formal platform formulated by the leadership. Obviously she had been offended by some of my papers that have been posted on the Web site of the Institute for Corean-American Studies, which she seemed to have (mis)read. She has never responded to repeated e-mail invitations by the institute's executive director to formally express her rebuttal on its Web site. Several years later I came across a perceptive reader's comments on the potential distress that might befall those who try to take the middle ground in the comfort women issue. They hit home for me because of the incident I have described. I quote below "Reader Jack" of San Diego, California, who claims to have done some research on the subject and wrote his review of Yoshimi Yoshiaki's *Comfort Women* on the Amazon Web site on which the book was advertised:

> Frankly, I find it difficult to take sides. This book, unfortunately, has not helped. . . . Anyway, I advise potential readers to approach this topic with caution. No matter which side you take, there will be people who will hysterically hate you for it. Trying to take the middle ground will make you the enemy of people on both sides, because each side believes that EVERYTHING they believe is the TRUTH, even when it is patently not. Trying to sift the facts from the overblown accusations is a frustrating enterprise. In the end, it gets very political and very race oriented. And it will ruin your day many times over.[15]

I now see the disconcerting public verbal assault I endured in The Hague as my first personal encounter with what the anthropologist Lila Abu-Lughod called the "Rushdie effect"[16]—the result of living in a global age when the subjects of ethnographic studies—as well as their advocates—begin to read anthropologists' works, take offense at them, and strike back in rage.

My work on the comfort women issue had been published only in English until February 2006, when my *Critical Asian Studies* article was translated and included as an invited chapter in a two-volume Korean-language collection of selected academic articles previously published in Korea, Japan, and the United States since the 1980s.[17] The collection received much attention from the South Korean print media, television news programs, and Internet users for its critical reinterpretations of modern Korean history surrounding the years prior to and after liberation from Japan's colonial rule, which seriously challenged the dominant nationalist understandings of the subject.

Ten months later, when I visited the office of the Korean Council in December 2006, I found myself subjected to another unsettling Rushdie-effect experience. The young staff member in charge of the Korean Council's War and Women's Human Rights Museum project, who had politely sat with me to answer my questions, abandoned her politeness in favor of hostility when she returned from answering a phone call from her supervisor (who now heads the Korean Council as a corepresentative): she told me that she no longer wanted to talk with me. She did not explain why, and I did not argue with her. Instead, I then indicated that I wanted to take a look at the documents and reference materials displayed in the several bookshelves lining the walls of the office, which I used to do routinely during my previous visits to the Korean Council office since 1995. My request was flatly denied, and I had to leave the office thwarted. The sudden and unexplained cold shoulder I received from the Korean Council, I could surmise, was probably because of the activists' displeasure with my critical feminist analysis of the Korean comfort women phenomenon, which they now learned about from my article in the aforementioned Korean-language edited volume.

Notwithstanding these unfortunate incidents of angry activists' seemingly outright rejections of my works, I strongly uphold a methodological stance of expatriate anthropology that is predicated on intellectual flexibility and perspectival pluralism, which will help present a larger, more holistic picture of the complicated truth about the comfort women phenomenon than ahistorically legalistic rhetoric and the transnational activists' "paradigmatic story" of violence against women in war would ever allow.

Notes

PROLOGUE

1. Kenan Professor of Anthropology at the University of North Carolina at Chapel Hill, James L. Peacock is a member of the American Academy of Arts and Sciences and a former President of the American Anthropological Association. The quotation is from Peacock 2001: 145.

2. For further discussions of the androcentric euphemism "comfort women" and the feminist criticism against its use to refer to the victims, see chapter 1.

3. Yoshimi 1995: 79–80.

4. Chan and Su (2000: 81) have opined that Chinese women made up more than half of the estimated figure.

5. For a discussion of the tradition of cultural critique in anthropology, see Marcus and Fisher 1986: 111–136.

6. Robert Levy defines "person-centered anthropology" as investigations that focus on the problems of "examining and thinking about the relations of people and their contexts." See Levy 1994.

7. For further discussions of the concept of structural violence, see Galtung 1969; Bourgois 1995; Farmer, Connors, and Simmonds 1996; Farmer 2002; Scheper-Hughes and Bourgois 2004.

8. For further discussion of my use of the term holism in this study, see the appendix.

9. The quotation is from Marcus and Fisher 1986: 133.

10. For Foucault's notion of "subjugated knowledge," see Mahon 1992: 120–121; see also Foucault 2003: 7–8.

11. Foucault 1980: 62.

12. Cowan 2006.

13. Examples of nuanced ethnographic works on controversial human rights issues include Ginsburg 1989; Cowan 2001; Gruenbaum 2001; Montgomery 2001.

14. See "The Worst U.N. Scandal," editorial, *New York Times,* October 24, 2005.

INTRODUCTION

1. The Korean term *ch'ŏnyŏ* refers to young, unmarried women generally and also connotes sexual purity. The term *kongch'ul* in colonial Korea referred to the people's

obligatory contribution of various resources (including the rice and the hardware) to the government for its wartime projects. After the Second Sino-Japanese War broke out in July 1937, an alarming rumor about *chŏnyŏ kongch'ul* in colonial Korea led many parents to worry that the authorities might require them to provide their daughters for war-related labor service. In rural areas where most people had no daily access to radio and newspapers, groundless—yet very effective— rumors spread spontaneously and widely (S-w. Park 2003). Some concerned families chose to arrange early marriages for young daughters to avoid the onus of *chŏnyŏ kongch'ul*. These "evil" rumors illustrate James Scott's argument about the "weapons of the weak" in various forms of "real and effective" resistances carried out by people with very little power over their lives. See Scott 1990.

2. She survived six years of life as a comfort woman in China and Singapore. For more details of her story, see HCTH and CY 1993: 167–180.

3. E. Wolf 1994: 219.

4. For a discussion of my research methodology, see the appendix.

5. For the purpose of pinpointing the *sexual* behavior of men as men, I choose to use the term "masculinist," rather than "patriarchal," since the latter connotes men as fathers. I reserve the use of the term "patriarchal" for the social organization of gendered hierarchical relationships modeled on the patrilineal kinship system. In this study, the term "masculinist" refers to those men or women who uphold the ideology of male superiority by, for example, conceding to men, and only men, the "natural" right to seek sexual comfort inside and outside marriage.

6. The "three obediences" are obedience to the father in childhood, to the husband during marriage, and to the son in old age. See Y-C. Kim 1979: 44.

7. In theorizing the social hierarchy, Pierre Bourdieu speaks of different structures of assets, such as economic capital, cultural capital, and social capital, which characterize differences among classes. "Cultural capital" is measured primarily by educational qualifications. See Bourdieu 1984.

8. Y-C. Kim 1979: 153–155.

9. For the poignant memoirs of her life, see Hyegyŏnggung Hong Ssi 1996.

10. C-ŏ. Kang 1999: 90. See also Deuchler 2003.

11. C-ŏ. Kang 1999: 89.

12. Y-C. Kim 1979: 153–161, quotation on 161. For a historical overview of the institution of *kisaeng,* see chapter 6.

13. See Y-C. Kim 1979: 218–219.

14. See K-b. Lee 1984, chapter 13.

15. Y-C. Kim 1979: 215–216.

16. For details on women's education in prewar Japan, see Mackie 2003: 25–27.

17. Tsurumi 1984.

18. Y-C. Kim 1979: 225, 230.

19. Mackie 2003: 26.

20. See Y-C. Kim 1979: 276; Y-H. Kim 1994b; Y-s. Sin 1999; B-y. Yi 1999; Y-H. Kim 2002; O-p. Mun et al. 2003. See also Nah 2004 for an insider's portrayal of the fascinating and tragic life of her paternal aunt, Na Hye-sŏk, Korea's first woman painter with a literary talent, whose progressive feminist ideas and individualistic actions were too far ahead of her time to be tolerated in Korean society.

21. Hiratsuka Raichō (1878–1942) was a prime mover in the birth of *Seitō* (Bluestocking), a literary magazine created by women alone as an outlet for their art in 1911. For further details about the Bluestocking women, see Sievers 1983:163–188; Mackie 2003: 45–49. See also O-p. Mun et al. 2003 for some comparative perspectives on the "new woman" in Korea and Japan.

22. Tsurumi 1984: 305.

23. For an introduction and analysis of the *manmun-manhwa* ("commentary cartoons") in colonial Korea, see M-j. Sin 2003 and 2004.

24. For recent revisionist historical studies of colonial modernity in Korea in the English language, see Shin and Robinson 1999.

25. For a collection of recent critical anthropological discussions of the concept of modernity, see Knauft 2002.

26. Y. Yamashita 1992b:139.

27. C-g. Yim 2004: 23.

28. C-g. Yim 2004: 26.

29. In the 1920s the *kisaeng*'s hourly fee was 1 wŏn/yen and 30 chŏn/sen, of which the *kisaeng* received 97 chŏn 5 ri; the remainder was divided between the restaurant and the *kwŏnbŏn. Kisaeng,* all of whom were members of the *kwŏnbŏn,* had to pay 5 wŏn sales tax to the Kyŏngsŏng local government (C-g. Yim 2004: 24–25).

30. HCTH and CY 1993: 164.

31. Y. Yamashita 1992a: 45.

32. Y. Yamashita 1992a; Yu 1999.

33. N-h. Yi 1992: 439.

34. Y. Yamashita 1992a: 50–51.

35. Yu 1999: 297.

36. They tended to have worked as domestic servants (19 percent), housewives (15 percent), or farmers (10 percent) before becoming prostitutes (Y. Yamashita 1992a: 62).

37. Song 1997: 189.

38. Song 1997: 191.

39. One Japanese man who visited the pleasure quarters in Seoul and Inchŏn in 1926 found, to his surprise, that Japanese women cost between six and seven yen, while the fee for Korean prostitutes was only three yen. See Yu 1999: 296.

40. Only after prostitutes engaged in numerous strikes in the 1930s did the colonial government amend the regulations to improve working conditions, including per-

mission for a one-day leave that took effect in 1935. Yu 1999: 298 does not indicate how often the one-day leave was permitted.

41. Yu 1999: 298.

42. C-s. Pak 1996: 58–75.

43. C-o. Yun 2000.

44. *Dong-a Ilbo,* September 2, 1927, quoted in Yu 1999: 297.

45. See Yu 1999: 297.

46. Song 1997: 202.

47. Song 1997: 203.

48. Yu 1999.

49. For her full testimony, see Y-k. Kang 2000: 325–330. Kim Sun-ok was able to pay off her debt in about four years (Y-k. Kang 2000: 332).

50. In contrast to the Korean term *modan* (meaning "short-haired"), which renders the hairstyle an icon for the "new woman," the term *modan* in *modan gaaru* (the Japanese transliteration of "modern girl") is a Japanese-English word for "modern." In Japan, the "new woman" emerged earlier than in Korea, around the turn of the twentieth century (see Rodd 1991; Mackie 2003; Sato 2003). A 1932 Korean magazine essay, "'Miss Korea,' Please Cut Your Hair," for example, argues that short hair (*tanbal*) is a symbol of modernity and progress and recommends that Korean women cut their hair short (C-s. Kim 2004/1999: 242–243). For a recent discussion of the "new woman" and "modern girl" in colonial Korea, see Y-s. Sin 1999; O-p. Mun et al. 2003. This was during the decade known as the Jazz Age in the United States, when young American women ("flappers") broke away from the Victorian image of womanhood and created the "new" or "modern" woman by wearing heavy makeup, bobbing their hair, smoking, drinking, and dancing in public. See Douglas 1986; Fass 1977.

51. J. Kim 2007: 86.

52. Barraclough 2006: 345.

53. For more nuanced discussion of the depictions of "factory girls as sexual victims of capitalism," see Barraclough 2006, quotation on 350.

54. So 2005: 13–14.

55. For further discussion of "modern working women" in colonial Korea, see Y-C. Kim 1979: 271–276. See also J. Kim 2007: 86, who notes, "While factory work yielded little reward for some, others, through their experiences of wage work, eventually attained laudable degrees of economic and social independence."

56. For a study of *ero guro nansensu* as expressions of the vitality of the mass culture in Japan from the 1920s into the 1940s, see Silverberg 2006.

57. The intellectuals of the day theorized that the *ero gŭro nŏnsensŭ* boom developed due to the popularity of jazz. Recent studies also state that the birth of jazz and the

subsequent formation of mass culture in the United States resulted in the global spread of the full-scale capitalist commodification of sexuality. See, for example, So 2005: 16.

58. So 2005: 36–48.

59. For further discussion of modern women's fashions in colonial Korea, see C-r. Kim 2005.

60. HCTH and HCY 1997: 170.

61. According to Yi's testimonial, the Japanese recruiter transported her and five young unmarried women, first north by train and then south by ship from the Chinese port city Dairen [Luda] to the comfort station he owned in Taiwan, arriving several days after the New Year's Day in 1945. For her full story, see HCTH and CY 1993: 123–132, quotations on 123 and 124.

62. See Cumings 1984b. The history of Korean capitalism is a very sensitive topic on the part of contemporary Koreans. Postliberation nationalist historiography has sought to demonstrate the "sprouts" (*maenga*) of capitalism in Chosŏn dynasty, referring to increasing commercialization and the existence of private artisans and hired labor in seventeenth- and eighteenth-century Korea. It is only very recently that serious revisionist voices began to be heard from among South Korean scholars regarding the need to "deconstruct" *kuksa* (national history). For recent collections of revisionist or nonnationalistic essays see Yim and Yi 2004; Pak, Kim, Kim, and Rhee 2006. Earlier works in English on capitalist development in Korea tended to side with the general position of nationalist historiography. McNamara 1990, for example, characterized the development of "native enterprise" with limited autonomy under colonial rule as "benign capitalism," stressing the difficulty of Korea's transition from an agrarian to a commercial and industrial economy. Similarly, Shin 1996 discussed Korean agricultural "growth without development" under colonialism. For a revisionist perspective of the "rise of Korean capitalism" under Japanese colonial rule and the role of the Japanese in Korea as both agents of modern socioeconomic change and political oppressors, see Eckert 1991. For a collection of more recent revisionist works in English, see Shin and Robinson 1999.

63. Cumings 1984b: 487.

64. See chapter 2 for Yi's testimonial narrative.

65. Cumings 1984b: 489. See also M-y. Yi 1997 for a discussion of the relationship of historical background of colonial Korea to the formation of the Japanese military comfort women policy.

66. S-w. Park 2003.

67. Cumings 1984b: 490. About 2.3 million Koreans were residing in Manchuria at the time of Japan's defeat in August 1945. Seventy-nine percent of the population of Yanbian in Jilin Province, China, for example, was Korean, over 90 percent of them

farmers (C-s. Kim 2004). For a sociological study of the nature of the Korean peasantry and the role of Koreans and capitalism in the extension of Japanese empire in Manchuria from the 1920s to the 1940s, see H. O. Park 2005.

68. S-w. Park 2003. For comparable wartime experiences of "doubling expectations" of Japanese women, see Miyake 1991.

69. *Maeil Sinbo,* June 3, 1943, quoted in Ahn 2003.

70. S-w. Park 2003.

71. For the developmental history of licensed prostitution in colonial Korea, see chapter 6.

For the emergence of the working class in colonial Korea, see S-w. Park 1999.

72. See Y-k. Kang 2000: 328.

73. Barraclough 2006: 345–346.

74. Senda 1990a: 64–65.

75. Ha 1998: 324.

76. A naturalized American citizen, Richard E. Kim was born in northern Korea and served in the South Korean military before leaving in 1955 for the United States to pursue a college education and graduate school training in writing and Asian studies.

77. See R. Kim 1998: author's note.

78. The author notes that this is a "happy predicament" for him: on one hand, his fiction is not accepted as such; on the other, he has realized "the dream of every fiction writer" by creating a fiction that appears "real" (R. Kim 1998: 198).

79. Ha 1998: 238; see also Moon 2005 for a reassessment of the Ilchinhoe as a Korean populist reformist group.

80. Ha 1998: 279.

81. Havens 1975, quotation on 921.

82. Havens 1975: 918.

83. See Miyake 1991.

84. The estimates vary regarding the number of Koreans forcibly recruited during the war. According to a South Korean NGO, the Association of Pacific War Victims and Bereaved Families (APWVBF 1993: 7–14), over 7.5 million Koreans were conscripted to work as laborers in Japanese factories, construction projects, and mines and as members of the "volunteer army" between 1938 and August 1945. The figure that a North Korean government representative claimed at the United Nations Human Rights Committee meeting in April 2005 was 8.4 million. Rhee Younghoon criticized that these are "imaginary numbers" (*hŏsu*) and pointed out that according to the 1940 national census, the total number of males aged between twenty and forty was 3.21 million—less than half of the conjectural numbers quoted above. See Rhee 2005; see also Ahn and Rhee 2007: 217–220.

85. Seok-heung Chang 2004: 9.

86. Cumings 1997: 177.

87. Cumings 1997: 177 notes: "[T]he dirtiest work was in the pits—where Koreans, including women, who were forced to work bare-breasted, formed 60 to 70 percent of the pit force [in the mines in Japan], working twelve-hour days from dawn to dusk."

88. The number of overseas Koreans at the time of Japan's defeat in 1945 reached some 5 million in Japan, China, and Russia, accounting for 20 percent of the total Korean population. Of these, "1.2 million is generally accepted as the total number of Koreans forced to migrate overseas during the colonial period" (Seok-heung Chang 2004: 7).

89. With the expansion of battle, male students "volunteered" as soldiers when the regulations concerning the temporary mobilization of special volunteer soldiers for the army were passed in October 1943. Starting in April 1944, physical examinations were given to new recruits (of college age and above), and a total of 206,000 Korean men (94.2 percent of the recruits) passed the physical test. Chung Hye-Kyung (H-K. Chung 2004: 43–45) states that the total number of Koreans employed as soldiers and civilian military employees is estimated to be more than 600,000.

90. I thank Professor Nah Yong-gyun for responding to my inquiry by contributing this story by e-mail, March 10, 2006.

91. I first interviewed Professor Takasaki in December 1997 and met him several more times at international workshops and conferences held in Japan on the comfort women issue.

92. See Takasaki 2000: 7.

93. C-o. Yun 1981.

94. T-s. Kim 1970.

95. Dutch Government 1994: 1, 2. As Stoler 2002: 6 has noted, one was classified as "European" in the Dutch colony on the basis "not [of] skin color alone but [of] tenuously balanced assessments of who was judged to act with reason, affective appropriateness, and a sense of morality." Dutch Government 1994: 3 also acknowledges that "the term European referred not only to the 'totoks,' or full-blood[ed] Dutch, and other persons of European origin, such as Germans, Italians, Hungarians, Russians, Belgians, British etc., but also to Persons of Eurasian and, since the Japanese Act of the early 1900s, Japanese origin living in the Dutch East Indies. In addition to approximately seventy million Indonesians, there were thus approximately three hundred and sixty thousand Europeans in the Dutch East Indies, most of whom lived on the island of Java." Although more than 150,000 Europeans were interned either as prisoners of war or civilian internees, those of Indo-Dutch origin living on Java—who constituted more than half of the "European" population (approximately 220,000) in the Dutch East Indies—stayed out of the camps, according to the Dutch government report. One of the Dutch comfort women survivors, whom

I first met in The Hague in 1998, for example, is a daughter of a Dutch man and an Indonesian woman.

96. Dutch Government 1994: 14.

97. Dutch Government 1994: 8.

98. Dutch Government 1994: 15. For more details, see Yoshimi 2000: 171.

99. For a description of the preparation of the opening night and the operation of one of the four Semarang comfort stations, see Ruff-O'Herne 1994.

100. Dutch Government 1994: 18, 16.

101. In 1925 Japan became a signatory to three treaties: the International Agreement for the Suppression of White Slave Traffic (1904); the International Convention for the Suppression of White Slave Traffic (1910); and the International Convention for the Suppression of Traffic in Women and Children (1921). For details on the treaties, see Yoshimi 1995: 163–166.

102. For the case of Indonesian women, for example, see Y. Tanaka 2002.

103. See Yoshimi 1995: 186–188.

104. For further discussions of the Dutch colonial discourses of sexuality in the production of class and racial power, see Stoler 1997 and 2002.

105. Piccigallo 1979: 161.

106. Dutch Government 1994: 24.

107. See, for example, C-s. Chung 1993: 29.

108. The other three concern the Yasukuni Shrine, Japanese history textbooks, and the competing territorial claims over the rocky islet called Tokdo in Korean and Takeshima in Japanese.

109. See Haraway 1991; Mohanty 1991; D. Wolf 1996.

110. See Yoshimi 1995 and 2000.

111. I further discuss in chapter 2 South Korean feminist researchers' initial shock over Kil's case and their eventual decision to include it in a publication that presents twelve Korean survivors' life stories (HCTH-CYSY 2004).

CHAPTER 1

1. See Dolgopol and Paranjape 1994: back cover.

2. Antonio Gramsci has noted the need to "distinguish between historically organic ideologies" that are necessary to a given structure, and "ideologies that are arbitrary, rationalistic, 'willed'" (Forgacs 2000: 199). I am using "ideology" here as Williams 1977, Comaroff and Comaroff 1991, and others do, to refer to the "worldview" of any social groupings in general and to the ideas and beliefs concerning the comfort women issue in particular.

3. See, for example, Cook 1994; Binion 1995; Peters and Wolper 1995; Naples and Desai 2002.

4. The Chinese word is romanized as *pi* in the old Wade-Giles system, but *bi* (even tone) in the modern pinyin system. It is transliterated as *pi* (ピ) in Japanese.

5. See, for example, Stiglmayer 1994.

6. See *Hankyoreh,* February 17, 1993.

7. For a Japanese nationalist perspective, see, for example, Fujioka 1996 and 1997; Hata 1999.

8. United States Office of War Information 1944: 1.

9. Quotation from the letter (dated September 28, 2006) sent to the members of the United States House of Representatives in protest against House Resolution 759 (concerning Japan's comfort women) by Kase Hideaki, chairman of the Society for the Dissemination of Historical Fact (in Japan). See also Kase and Ogata 2007: 10.

10. United States Office of War Information 1944: 2–3.

11. United States Office of War Information 1944: 3.

12. United States Office of War Information 1944: 2. For a discussion of "comfort bags" see chapter 3.

13. United States Office of War Information 1944: 3.

14. See http://www.hermuseum.go.kr.

15. For Pak's life story, see Nishino 2003.

16. I return to the periodization in the development of the military comfort system in chapter 3.

17. See Garon 1997.

18. For a fictional account of the humiliation that Koreans felt when forced to acquire "new names" in the Japanese style, see R. Kim 1988. For a comparative perspective on the *kōminka* processes in colonized Korea and Taiwan, see Chou 1996.

19. The existence of sizable Korean communities in China, the former Soviet Union, and Japan is a vivid legacy of Japanese colonial rule.

20. Asō 1993: 217.

21. See my discussion in chapter 5. See also, for example, HCTH and CY 1993: 53, 160.

22. Asō 1993: 41.

23. Ruff-O'Herne 1994: 79.

24. Anthropologist Fred Blake, private communication, February 2, 2002.

25. Nishino 1992:46.

26. Nishino 1992: 46.

27. HCTH and CY 1993: 161.

28. Asō 1993: 222.

29. Dalby 1998: 167; Garon 1993: 721.

30. Tanaka 1994 [1970]: 39–57.

31. For a further discussion of Tanaka Mitsu's article in the modern history of feminism in Japan, see Mackie 2003, quotation on 144. See also Kurihara 1993.

32. Vicinus 1982: 136.

33. For a similar agrarian metaphor in Turkey, see Delaney 1991.

34. Griffin 1990: 311. I thank Jerry Boucher for bringing this reference to my attention.

35. See, for example, Nishino 1992: 48, 52–53.

36. Copelon 1995.

37. MacKinnon 1993.

38. For discussions of systematic mass rapes committed by Serb forces, see, for example, Stiglmayer 1994.

39. See Soh 1996; Mackie 2000.

40. For a discussion of the emergence of a women's human rights movement, see Friedman 1995.

41. Barry 1995: 199.

42. Mackie 2003: 223 gives the figure for the participants as "over 5000," although the estimates I heard during the event were closer to 10,000.

43. For more details, see Fujime 2001.

44. For further discussion on the Women's Tribunal, see Matsui 2000. See also Mitsui 2007.

45. Yoshimi 1995: 5.

46. See Chŏngsindaemunje Silmu Taech'aekpan 1992.

47. An English version of the Kōno Statement is available at the Web site of the Ministry of Foreign Affairs of Japan, http://www.mofa.go.jp/policy/women/fund/state 9308.html.

48. For a detailed analysis of the controversy concerning the fund, see Soh 2003a.

49. Takagi Ken'ichi, interview by the author, Takagi's office, Tokyo, June 13, 1997.

50. I will return to the history textbook issue in chapter 4. For a collection of historical and comparative perspectives on the textbook controversy, see Hein and Selden 2000.

51. See Paul 1996.

52. The quotation is from an open letter dated May 2, 2007, and signed by Kase Hideaki, chairman of the Society for the Dissemination of Historical Fact, which I found in my office mailbox. It accompanied Hata Ikuhiko's 2007 *Shokun* essay translated into English, "No Organized or Forced Recruitment: Misconceptions about Comfort Women and the Japanese Military."

53. Chai 1993; Watanabe 1994.

54. They include Dolgopol and Paranjape 1994; Coomaraswamy 1996; McDougall 1998. Other works by individual legal scholars include Hsu 1993; Boling 1995; Totsuka 2001.

55. Dieng 1994: 7.

56. Dolgopol and Paranjape 1994: 205.

57. Coomaraswamy 1996: 5.

58. McDougall 1998.

59. Hicks 1995; Howard 1995.

60. Sancho 1998.

61. See Watanabe 1994; Soh 1996; Lie 1997.

62. C. Choi 1997.

63. Yoshimi 2000; Ueno 2001 and 2004.

64. When I inquired about this in 2006 and 2007, neither the translator nor the editor at Columbia University Press could tell me clearly how the subtitle came to be added.

65. Yoshimi 2000: 29.

66. Tanaka 1998: 80.

67. I return to the topic of military prostitution in postwar occupation Japan in chapter 6.

68. Kim-Gibson 1999a; Schellstede 2000.

69. Kim-Gibson 1999b. For a review of it and another video on Korean comfort women, see Soh 2001a.

70. For a critical analysis of the Japanese biological warfare plans and experiments on POWs, see, for example, chapter 5 of Tanaka 1998.

71. Stetz and Oh 2001.

72. Schmidt 2000: v.

73. Schmidt 2000: vi.

74. Soh 2000a; Soh 2000b; Hein 1999; M-s. Kim 2001; Soh 2001b; Soh 2003a; Min 2003 and Soh 2004b; Soh 2006a; Soh 2007; Mitsui 2007.

75. For a discussion of the South Korean case, see H. Yang 1998.

76. Keller 1997; Lee 1999; T. Park 1997.

77. T. Park 1997: 20.

78. The quotation is from Amazon's Web page for this book, http://www.amazon.com/Gift-Emperor-Therese-S-Park/dp/0595350054/ref=sr_1_1?ie=UTF8&s=books&qid=1219170664&sr=1-1 (accessed February 25, 2006).

79. The quotations are from Amazon's Web page for this book, http://www.amazon.com/Gift-Emperor-Therese-S-Park/dp/0595350054/ref=sr_1_1?ie=UTF8&s=books&qid=1219170664&sr=1-1 (accessed February 25, 2006).

80. Keller 1997: 19.

81. For a critical literary analysis of *Comfort Woman* by an Asian American researcher, see Chuh 2003.

82. S-j. Yang 1997.

83. The quotations are from Amazon's Web page for this book, http://www.amazon.com/review/product/0140263357/ref=cm_cr_dp_all_helpful?%5Fencoding=

UTF8&coliid=&showViewpoints=1&colid=&sortBy=bySubmissionDateDescending (accessed February 25, 2006).

84. S-j. Yang 1997.

85. Keller 1997: 17.

86. Keller 1997: 16.

87. Keller 1997: 175–176.

88. Keller 1997: 176.

89. Keller 1997: 15.

90. The reviewer is identified as "A reader" on Amazon's Web page for this book, http://www.amazon.com/review/product/0140263357/ref=cm_cr_dp_all_ helpful?%5Fencoding=UTF8&coliid=&showViewpoints=1&colid=&sortBy=by SubmissionDateDescending (accessed February 25, 2006).

91. All the comments on *Comfort Woman* quoted in this chapter are from the reviews of the book posted on Amazon's Web page for this book, http://www.amazon .com/review/product/0140263357/ref=cm_cr_dp_all_helpful?%5Fencoding= UTF8&coliid=&showViewpoints=1&colid=&sortBy=bySubmissionDateDescend ing (accessed February 25, 2006).

92. The reviewer is identified as "Lissa."

93. The reviewer is identified as "A reader."

94. The reviewer is identified as Fez Monkey (Santa Monica).

95. Chuh 2003: 18.

96. For a discussion of the phenomenon in terms of Korean American "feminist nationalism," see E. H. Kim 2003.

97. For a detailed critical literary analysis of *A Gesture Life* and *Comfort Woman* as examples of Asian American production of knowledge "about" comfort women, see Chuh 2003.

98. Lee 1999: 233.

99. Lee 1999: 163.

100. Lee 1999: 180.

101. The review quotations are from the multiple and conflicting commentaries on *The Gesture Life* posted by the readers of the book at http://www.amazon.com (accessed February 16, 2000).

102. Chongshindae is an alternative transcription for Chŏngsindae. The Institute has translated its English name in various ways, including "Korean Institute for the Women Drafted for Military Sexual Slavery by Japan" and "Korea Chongshindae's Institute."

103. For a summary of the background and activities of the Korean Council up to the mid-1990s, see Soh 1997a.

104. See Soh 1997c for a biographical sketch of Yun.

105. Chŏngsin (挺身) in the sense of "volunteering, or offering one's body" should not be confused with its homonym *chŏngsin* (精神, mind, spirit), which is a much more commonly used term. An anonymous reviewer of my article submitted to a scholarly journal, for example, erroneously used the Chinese characters for the "spirit" to comment on the Chŏngsindae. See the *Essence Korean-English Dictionary* (Seoul: Minjungseorim, 1984), 1293.

106. See the Institute's Web site, http://www.truetruth.org.

107. M-g. Kang 1997b: 13–14.

108. I have examined more than one hundred Korean testimonial narratives. They include the seventy-nine cases whose stories have been coedited by the Korean Council and Korean Research Institute on Chŏngsindae in the six volumes of "collections of testimonies" between 1993 and 2004 (HCTH and CY 1993; HCTH and HCY 1997 and 2001; HCY and HCTH 1999; HCTH 2001; HCTH-CYSY 2004) and the ten cases of Korean survivor-residents in China published in two separate volumes (CY and HCTH 1995; Pak and Liu 1995). In addition, I have studied seventeen more cases described below. A statistical analysis of various dimensions of these diverse testimonial narratives, however, is unavailable for methodological reasons, discussed below.

After the first two volumes, which present the interview data on South Korean survivors in biographical frames (albeit formulaic), the narrative style in the multivolume series changed in an effort to record the survivors' stories in their own colloquial words and dialects. The latter format allows the reader to hear vividly the voice of each individual survivor and also helps to give the reader a feel for her personality. At the same time, however, the individual storytelling format without common standard biographical frames presents a formidable challenge for any researcher trying to come up with a system for a comparative analytical overview of the life trajectories of the survivors as generational cohorts. The other important source of Korean survivors' testimonial narratives is Y-k. Kang 2000. A Korean researcher and permanent resident in the People's Republic of China, Kang (1944–1999) collected life stories of eight Korean comfort women survivors (in addition to forty-one former conscripts) living in northeast China between 1996 and 1998. (One of the survivors in Kang's book, Yi Ok-sŏn [b. 1927], has returned to Korea; her story has been included in the Korean Council's sixth volume, published in 2004.) Using the biographical format, Y-k. Kang 2000 revealed varying degrees of the individual survivors' agency and their astonishingly candid and extremely heartbreaking stories of their deplorable family circumstances prior to their recruitment. Their stories include most unflattering and "politically incorrect" details such as the advance payments the women or their families received from recruiters as well as several instances of liberation from indentured sexual labor performed as comfort women when they paid off their debts. Among the additional nine cases I examined, three were published in the Japanese language by Japanese nonfiction-writers-turned-activists (Kawata 1992; Song Sin-do v. Kuni 1993; Usuki 1996). Two other cases were included in an edited volume on Korean comfort women published in English in the United States (Schellstede 2000). Two more stories were published in South Korea, one in a national daily and another in a monthly magazine. The *JoongAng Ilbo* article on the life story of No Su-bok (serialized in the March 17–31, 1984, issues), which I will discuss in chapter 4, is reprinted in M-s. Kim 1990: 91–122. The story of Kim Su-hae (pseudonym) was published in the *Wŏlgan SinDonga,* May 2007. Finally, the cases of Yi Mak-tal and Sim Mi-ja are based on my interviews with them; the former came out only in 2005, while the story of the latter, who has been a vocal critic of the Korean Council (see below), has not been included in the multivolume series.

109. C. Chung 1993: 17.

110. For Kang's full story, see HCTH and CY 1993: 271–284.

111. See HCTH and HCY 1997: 237–250.

112. For their full testimonial narratives, see HCTH and HCY 1997: 84–99 for Kim, 225–236 for Pak.

113. See C. Chung 1997: 10.

114. For more of Ms. K's story, see Schellstede 2000: 102–105.

115. See, for example, C. Chung 2004.

116. C. Chung 1999: 12. Chung wrote that 6 of 175 officially registered survivors as of December 1993 (plus, later, 2 additional survivors) testified to have been recruited as "*kŭllo* (labor) *chŏngsindae*" but that they became comfort women (C. Chung 2004: 19, 70). Despite the varying degrees of clarity and credibility of their statement, however, she has asserted that the eight testimonials provide a "sufficient" (*ch'ungbunhada*) hint that clear, institutionalized distinctions did not exist in the recruitments of *chŏngsindae* and military comfort women in colonial Korea (C. Chung 2004: 20–21).

117. You 2001.

118. Ienaga 1978: 158.

119. Y-s. Kim 1995.

120. Kim Mun-suk, interview by the author, Kim's office, Pusan, December 17–18, 2004. See M-s. Kim 1990; 1992; 1994; 2001.

121. Nah 2004.

122. M-g. Kang 1997b: 13–14.

123. C. Chung 2004: 25–26.

124. I met Kim Yun-sim twice during my field research trip in December 2004 and observed the session held at KRIC.

125. HCTH-CYSY 2004: 348.

126. The Korean name, Yŏsŏngbu, literally means Ministry of Women. In June 2005, to add the issues concerning the family, its name was revised to Yŏsŏngkajokbu, known in English as the Ministry of Gender Equality and Family.

127. See HCTH and Yŏsŏngbu 2002: 32.

128. Zhu Delan, interview by the author, Tokyo, March 1, 2001.

129. For more details on the origin and the development of the Korean comfort women movement, see Soh 1996.

130. Executive Committee for the International Public Hearing 1993: vi.

131. Executive Committee for the International Public Hearing 1993: 67.

132. I obtained the double-sided flyer "The Center for Research and Documentation on Japan's War Responsibility" during my visit to JWRC in Tokyo in the fall of 1997.

133. JWRC flyer.

134. Totsuka 2001: 66.

135. Suzuki 1997.

136. Skelton 1996.

137. For a discussion of the role of *manga* (cartoons) and cyberspace in Japanese history debates, see Morris-Suzuki and Rimmer 2002.

138. I discuss the history textbook issue further in chapter 4.

139. Hata 2007.

140. See the video "Comfort Women and Kōno Statement," in Japanese with English subtitles, at http://www.youtube.com.user/TAMAGAWABOAT (accessed April 28, 2007).

141. Hata 2007: 2.

142. Hata 2007: 12.

143. Hata 2007: 14.

144. According to a Korean newspaper, there was strong criticism and a backlash following the *Washington Post* advertisement. The U.S. vice president reportedly found it very upsetting and ordered his staff to investigate its details. See the June 18, 2007, issue of *Dong-a Ilbo Daily English,* "U.S. House to Present Resolution on Comfort Women."

145. See, for example, Onishi 2007.

146. Amnesty International, for example, issued a welcoming public statement, "European Parliament Adopts Resolution on Comfort Women," on December 14, 2007, International Secretariat, London.

147. Personal communication with Marguerite Hamer, July 10, 2005.

148. Ienaga 1978.

149. Shin 1996.

150. The term can be written using three Chinese characters, 慰安婦. I will discuss traditional Korean masculinist sexual culture in chapter 6.

151. Yoshimi and Hayashi 1997.

152. See Yoshimi and Hayashi 1997: iv.

153. I-m. Kim 1976: 284.

154. I will return to the topic of camp town military prostitution in South Korea in chapter 6.

155. The sociologist Chizuko Ueno has referred to this modern phenomenon of incorporating women into the national political-economic life scheme in imperial Japan as the "nationalization of women." See Ueno 2004.

156. Ruff-O'Herne 1994: 136–137.

157. Personal communication with Marguerite Hamer, July 10, 2005.

158. I received a copy of the letter during my interview with Lee in July 1992.

159. I-m. Kim 1976: 98. I discuss his work and its impact on the Korean public discourse and popular memories of the comfort women further in chapter 4.

160. For more details on the House of Sharing, see chapter 2.

161. For a full description of the discussions at the meeting, see Dōshisha Daigaku Asano Ken'ichi Zemi 1999: 44–62.

162. Sŏ 1997.

163. Kim-Gibson 1999a: 11.

164. I will return to the topic of "overseas prostitute" in chapter 3.

165. Yamazaki 1999: 197.

166. The Korean kinship terminology system, for instance, has a conceptual term, *ch'on,* that measures the degree of relatedness between two kin. One's father and mother are both one degree, or *ch'on,* removed from oneself, whereas one's grandparents are two *ch'on* removed. Hence, a Korean may argue that addressing someone as *ŏmŏni,* rather than *halmŏni,* connotes a closer kin relationship and conveys primordial affect toward the addressee.

167. *Yonhap News,* April 29, 2007.

168. HCTH and CY 1993: 128.

169. See Lee and Harvey 1973 for an analysis of Korean kinship terminology and its usage in the daily life in South Korea. For a perceptive discussion of gender and traditional naming practices in Chinese society, see Watson 1986.

170. Chuh 2003: 21.

CHAPTER 2

1. For a collection of critical discussions on the genre *testimonio,* see Arias 2001.

2. Kondo 1990 is an important reference for the theoretical perspective of this chapter. As she notes, "crafting selves" implies a concept of agency and connotes a lifelong creative process (48), but the analytical lens of this chapter is focused retrospectively on the early formative years of certain surviving comfort women as they valiantly struggled to craft modern gendered selves in the context of colonial Korea.

3. *Han'guk Ilbo*, December 17, 1997.

4. The Chinese ideograph for the term *han* under discussion is 恨 It should not be confused, for example, with the homonym *han* (韓) in *han'guk* (Korea).

5. See H-g. Choi 1991; C. S. Kim 1992; J. H. Lee 1994.

6. Kendall 1985; C. S. Kim 1992; and Lie 1998, respectively. Derived from French *ressentir*, to be angry, *ressentiment*, which seems closest to conveying the sense of the Korean term *han*, refers to a "generalized feeling of resentment and often hostility harbored by one individual or group against another, especially chronically and with no means of direct expression" (see the *American Heritage Dictionary of the English Language*, 3rd ed., 1992).

7. See Bourdieu 1990.

8. For one recent introduction to Korea's modern history, see Cumings 1997

9. See Y-k. Kim 1981; J. H. Lee 1994. See also Grinker 1998, chapter 5.

10. This does not mean, however, that Korean culture constructs the emotion of *han* "as female." Cf. Lutz 1988.

11. Hence, some people perform a rite of "ghost or spirit marriage" (*yŏnghon kyŏrhonsik*) for such cases, as exemplified in the case of one Korean survivor (see chapter 5). The lyrics of a shaman's song addressing the spirits of unmarried decedents among former comfort women are given at the end of this chapter.

12. Y-H. Kim 1994a; see also Y. Lee 2002.

13. The Korean Council began the weekly demonstration in January 1992 and has continued to stage the event up to the time of writing in order to publicize their demands (see Soh 1996).

14. A note on the composite and crafted nature of the reported first-person narratives: Mun's voice in this book is, unavoidably and necessarily, a result of my analytical distillations of the published materials as well as my ethnographic fieldwork. I translated my interviews and fragmented conversations with her from colloquial Korean into English and arranged it in a chronologically ordered first-person narrative supplemented by her published testimonial. This note on the crafted nature of the reported first-person narratives applies to the life stories of other survivors in this study as well when given as first-person narratives.

15. In Korean folklore and slang expressions, a sly or manipulative woman is metaphorically referred to as a "fox" (*yŏu*).

16. The traditional strict distinction between primary and secondary wives dates back to a law enacted in 1413, which elevated a primary wife's position within her husband's descent group and thus institutionalized "a special kind of female inequality" in the domestic sphere (Deuchler 2003: 143). For further discussion of institutionalized discrimination, see chapter 6.

17. Most surviving comfort women, in fact, had shared this anxiety all their postwar lives, and some used pseudonyms when they decided to come out.

18. For an ethnographic study of ancestor worship in Korean society, see Janelli and Janelli 1982.

19. When I met Mun in December 2004, I confirmed her bitter resolve never to visit her father's gravesite.

20. See HCTH and CY 1993: 181–196, 197–211.

21. For Yi Sang-ok's full testimonial, see HCTH and CY 1993: 181–196.

22. For Yi Tŭk-nam's full testimonial, see HCTH and CY 1993: 197–211.

23. Given the rule of "three obediences," it is not surprising that Kim's father did not obey his mother.

24. The factory work experience of Kim Ok-sil (identified by her formal name, Kim Ŭn-rye) is included in J. Kim 2007.

25. I first met Kim Ok-sil in Seoul in January 1995; my last meeting with her was at the Women's International War Crimes Tribunal on Japan's Military Sexual Slavery held in The Hague in December 2001. Her full testimonial, under the name of Kim Ŭn-rye, is included in HCY and HCTH 1999: 119–139.

26. See HCY and HCTH 1999: 139.

27. This information is revealed in Kim-Gibson 1999b.

28. For Pae's testimonial, see HCTH and HCY 1997: 168–183, quotations on 169–170.

29. For more information, see http://nanum.org.

30. *Han'guk Ilbo,* June 8, 1996.

31. See Hyejin 1997.

32. The incident, I suggest, underscores the deep-seated problem of masculinist sexual culture ingrained in Korean society, discussed further in chapter 6.

33. This paragraph draws on my review of the documentary. For a fuller discussion, see Soh 2001b.

34. See H-c. Yi 1997: 342.

35. Hyejin, interview by the author, San Francisco, CA, November 14, 2000.

36. For a detailed analysis of the controversy surrounding the Japanese "atonement project" for the surviving comfort women, see Soh 2000b and 2003a.

37. I discuss Pak's life story in more detail in chapter 5.

38. See HCTH and HCY 2001: 122.

39. I met Sim Mi-ja together with Rhee Younghoon at Sim's home in Kwangju, Kyŏnggi Province, in December 2004.

40. For further discussions of the nature of colonial memories, see Stoler and Strassler 2000.

41. Jeffery 1999: 69.

42. See, for example, Wilson 2001.

43. *Digital Chosun,* February 17, 2004; http://www.chosun.com/w21data/html/news/200402/200402170445.html (accessed February 17, 2004).

44. Burgos-Debray 1984.

45. Stoll 1999.

46. For competing arguments and critical analyses from both sides, see Arias 2001.

47. Douglass 2003: 56.

48. For example, see Hata 1999, chapter 6.

49. For scholarly debates in Japan, especially between Yoshimi Yoshiaki and Ueno Chizuko, on the value of oral histories for historiographical research, see Ueno 1998, 2001.

50. HCTH and HCY 2001: 16–17; see also Oka 2001 for a discussion of the difficult process of bearing testimony as a singular "event" for both narrator and listener.

51. HCTH and CY 1993: 124.

52. HCTH and CY 1993: 124.

53. See HCTH and CY 1993: 127–128. Notably, an Internet site on the "sex slaves" quotes Yi as having said she was "raped, electrocuted and beaten with a wooden bat." See http://thechrysanthemums.com (accessed November 19, 2007).

54. For a list of differing versions of Yi's account of her "kidnapping," see Hata 2007.

55. The 1993 version of Yi's testimonial states that she left home in the fall of 1944, when she was sixteen, and arrived at a comfort station in Taiwan in January 1945 (HTCH and CY 1993: 123–127). For Yi's FCCJ press conference statement, see Y. S. Lee 2007.

56. See HCY and HCTH 1999: 7, 78.

57. Y-h. Pak 2005: 78.

58. HCTH-CYSY 2004: 352–353.

59. For a methodological discussion of the multivolume series, see chapter 1.

60. See Ahn 1993: 8–10.

61. See also Ahn and Rhee 2007.

62. M-g. Kang 1997a: 4.

63. Ahn and Rhee 2007: 237–238.

64. See, for example, the criticism by Je Sŏng-ho, the spokesperson of the conservative group, Newright Union, dated December 7, 2006, and posted at www.newright.net (accessed December 7, 2006).

65. See M-h. Kim 2004.

66. Ueno 2004: 105.

67. HCTH-CYSY 2004: 8, 345.

68. For a discussion of the everyday life of Korean colonial modernity and the lure of modern urban life from the 1920s, see M-j. Sin 2004. For women's social mobility stories in postliberation South Korea, see Abelmann 2003.

69. Wieviorka 2006: xii.

70. Kase and Ogata 2007: 10.

71. See Y-k. Kim 1981; H-g. Choi 1991. See Kendall's (1985) ethnographic research on Korean shamanism for a description of the *kut*.

72. A women's organization, Alternative Culture (Ttohana ŭi Munhwa), organized the event, in which nine women shamans performed the *kut* on the compound of the Christian Academy House in Seoul. *JoongAng Ilbo,* July 18, 1990.

73. *Yŏnji* and *konji* symbolize the bridal makeup for the traditional wedding ceremony.

CHAPTER 3

1. See, for example, C-s. Chung 1993: 29.

2. Chuter 2003: 3.

3. As a leading convener Matsui (2000) explained why they organized the Tribunal. For details of the Tribunal, visit the Web site of VAWW-NET Japan (Violence against Women in War-Network Japan) at http://www.jca.apc.org/vaww-net-japan/.

4. See Gluck 2002.

5. Barry 1995: 198.

6. See, for example, Lerner 1986b.

7. Lerner 1986a: 132.

8. Jacques Rossiaud and Leah Otis quoted in Shrage 1994: 114–115.

9. For a historical study of the interplay between sexuality, scientific knowledge, social control, and empire building in modern Japan, see Frühstück 2003. Quote from Foucault 1990: 11.

10. Y-o. Song 1997: 172.

11. For a concise summary in English of Japanese history of prostitution, see Colligan-Taylor 1999. For more detailed information, see, e.g., I-m. Kim 1997.

12. I-m. Kim 1997:13.

13. I-m. Kim 1997.

14. The Yoshiwara the American invaders visited was, in fact, the Shin (New) Yoshiwara built after the great fire of 1657. It was relocated from a central district in the city to the very outskirts of Edo. The Shin Yoshiwara was twice as large as the old one, about 18 acres of ground rectangular in shape and surrounded by a shallow canal. The main street was lined by teahouses whose primary function was to arrange appointments with courtesans in the more prestigious brothels. The brothels were on the quieter side streets. See Longstreet and Longstreet 1970.

15. Jenkins 1993: 16.

16. Jenkins 1993: 18. It was said that paying for the services of high-ranking courtesans for more than three days a month would ruin a client financially (see I-m. Kim 1997).

17. It has also been suggested that this rule was meant to prevent the women from ending their miserable lives, should they manage to get hold of such weapons (Longstreet and Longstreet 1970: 15).

18. Jenkins 1993: 18.

19. Fairbank, Reischauer, and Craig 1989, chapter 17; Jansen 1995.

20. I-m. Kim 1997: 83. Even during the Tokugawa period, a red-light district existed in Nagasaki to serve foreign (white) customers (Fujime 1997: 164).

21. The new pleasure quarters that opened in November of the same year included 130 brothels, 1,724 prostitutes, 92 brothel geishas, and 109 independent geishas (I-m. Kim 1997: 84). The business of licensed prostitution prospered. By the beginning of the twentieth century, the Yoshiwara was no longer exclusive and privileged: It had become only one of six licensed quarters in Tokyo (Longstreet and Longstreet 1970: 19).

22. I-m. Kim 1997: 82–83.

23. Fairbank, Reischauer, and Craig 1989: 503–504. For a discussion of the Japanese appropriation of Western sexology as part of their modernization project, see Frühstück 2003.

24. For a list of such laws and ordinances of the 1870s, see Fujime 1997: 137–138. In the nineteenth century many continental European governments, for example, sought to control prostitution through a system of compulsory registration, licensed brothels, and medical inspection of prostitutes. This system was challenged by feminists. See Corbin 1990; Shrage 1994; Offen 2000.

25. I-m. Kim 1997: 93.

26. For details on the Meiji policy of licensing prostitution to control the spread of syphilis, see Burns 1998.

27. Fujime 1997.

28. For details, see Offen 2000.

29. Fujime 1997: 139.

30. Fujime 1997: 141.

31. Burns 1998: 4.

32. I-m. Kim 1997: 88–98.

33. The reading of the Chinese character for Ōe's given name is differently rendered in I.-m. Kim 1997 (Suguru) versus Fujime 1997 (Taku).

34. Four months later, in February 1873, the Peruvian government lodged a complaint against Japan's handling of the Maria Luz incident and demanded an apology and compensation of 481,718 piasters for damages the captain incurred. To resolve the dispute, the minister of the U.S. diplomatic delegation recommended that it be mediated by a third-country court. The two countries accepted the American proposal and agreed to ask the Russian government to be the judge. The court was held in St. Petersburg, where they examined the documents submitted by Japan and Peru. The verdict, given under the name of Alexander II on February 19, 1875, found that the action taken by the Japanese government was appropriate and therefore it was not liable for compensation (I-m. Kim 1997: 97–98).

35. I-m. Kim 1997: 98.

36. I-m. Kim 1997: 98–100.

37. Fujime 1997: 149–150.

38. Fujime 1997; Burns 1998.

39. Fujime 1997: 163.

40. The term *karayuki-san,* which was coined by the people of northern Kyūshū, has three components: *Kara* is an archaic word for China; yuki, from the verb *yuku* (to go), means "going" or "one who goes"; and *san* is an honorific suffix one attaches to both personal and family names, as well as to professions, to show respect or courtesy. Mihalopoulos 1993; Mackie 1998.

41. Fujime 1997: 159, 164.

42. Kurahashi Masanao, cited in Colligan-Taylor 1999.

43. See Shiga-Fujime 1993 for the details of the severe economic conditions and their impact on women's lives in prewar Japan.

44. Mihalopoulos 1993; Warren 2003. For life stories of the *karayuki-san,* see Yamazaki 1999; Warren 2003.

45. Ramseyer 1991: 93.

46. Ramseyer 1991: 90.

47. Ramseyer 1991: 94–95.

48. Ramseyer 1991: 113.

49. See I-m. Kim 1997 for a detailed discussion of the genealogy of sex workers in the Japanese women's history.

50. During Allied bombings in Burma, for example, the comfort houses were bombed and "several of the girls were wounded and killed" (United States Office of War Information 1944: 5).

51. Sahlins 2000: 272.

52. Sahlins 2000: 271. Generally speaking, the anthropological notion of "culture" encompasses three dimensions of human social life: ideational, behavioral, and material. That is to say, culture exerts a hegemonic hold on the manner in which people think, behave, and make a living. For the purpose of this study, I use "culture" to refer to socially learned and generally shared values, attitudes, and goals that are manifest in the behavioral patterns of the members of a societal community in specific historical periods. As such, cultures adapt and change.

53. Herdt 1997: 11.

54. Connell 1995: 123.

55. See chapter 6 for more discussions of the *kisaeng.*

56. Rich 1980: 645; see also Pateman 1988: 2.

57. See Yoshimi 1995: 74.

58. Tanaka 2002: 18–19.

59. Following Raymond Firth, who distinguished "social structure" (as a set of ideal principles and norms of behavior) from "social organization," I use the term "or-

ganizational" to refer to "the processes of ordering of action and of relations in reference to given social ends, in terms of adjustments resulting from the exercise of choices of members of the society" (Firth 1954: 10).

60. Nakasone 1978.

61. For more details, see Yoshimi 1995 and 2000, chapter 1.

62. Testimonials of Chinese women, however, reveal that this type existed in China in 1940. See Terazawa 2005.

63. No information is available on other nonnormative sexual behaviors (such as homosexuality) practiced by the Japanese military, except for the testimonial narratives by male Dutch survivors of pedophilia.

64. The May 7, 1998, issue of the North Korean newspaper *Rodong Sinmun* reported the existence of the two *ianjo* (*wianso,* in Korean) buildings (used as Ŭnwŏllu and P'unghaeru) and the discovery of the grave of a Korean woman murdered at an *ianjo*. See Ito 1999: 24.

65. See Shirota 1971 for details.

66. See Hata 1999: 411–414.

67. See Cumings 1997, chapter 3, for details of the policy.

68. See Tanaka 2002: 54.

69. The building has been preserved in China as an historical relic (Y-k. Kang 2000: 393).

70. Y-k. Kang 2000: 389. She labored for nearly a decade from 1936.

71. Comfort women were normally required to wear makeup. One survivor recalled that all her cosmetics were made in Japan (HCY and HCTH 1999: 281).

72. See Y-k. Kang 2000: 387–388.

73. Y-k. Kang 2000: 325–333.

74. The Korean *kisaeng,* like the Japanese geisha, received formal training in the arts of singing, dancing, and playing traditional musical instruments. They differed from licensed prostitutes in that their primary function was to entertain men with their artistic and social skills without necessarily engaging in prostitution. I return to the subject in chapter 6. For a study of the institution of *kisaeng* in English, see McCarthy 1991.

75. Yoshimi 2000: 90.

76. Quoted in Nishino 1992: 18.

77. Ichikawa Ichirō, interview by the author, Tokyo, December 12, 1997.

78. To prevent espionage, Chinese women were not to be used at military *ianjo* located in China. A Mr. Honda, a Japanese war veteran who fought in central China, remembered one *ianjo* run by a Korean man who employed Chinese women, risking punishment if discovered by the military police (Nishino 1992: 15).

79. See Dalby 1998: 67–68.

80 For her full testimony, see HCTH and CY 1993: 45–57.

81. See HCTH and CY 1993: 121–132 for her full testimony.

82. See Ruff-O'Herne 1994.

83. HCY and HCTH 1999: 279–288. I provide more of Ha's story in chapter 6.

84. Variant forms of *harimise* are practiced in today's sex industries across national borders, including South Korea and the famed alleys in Amsterdam, allowing potential customers to engage in window shopping to locate a desirable prostitute.

85. An official document of the Foreign Ministry (dated February 1939) revealed, for instance, there were twenty military *ianjo* in Hankow (M-s. Yun 1995).

86. Y-k. Kang 2000: 314–320.

87. CY and HCTH 1995: 34–35.

88. See chapter 5 for more of Kim Sun-dŏk's life story.

89. Linguistically, the Chinese character–based Japanese term *jōshi* (娘子; pronounced *nangja,* in Korean) in *jōshigun* (娘子軍; *nangjagun,* in Korean) is an antiquated term meaning "maiden" or "young unmarried female," and is distinct from the more generally used contemporary term *joshi* (女子), meaning simply "female," "girl," or "female child." According to Suzuki 1993: 78, the *jōshigun* was another name for the *karayuki-san* (see also Yoshimi 1995: 21).

90. Yoshimi 1995: 71–72.

91. Quoted in Yoshimi 2000: 48.

92. HCTH and CY 1993.

93. See HCTH and HCY 1997: 184–196.

94. Yoshimi 1995: 19.

95. For examples of such documents, see Yoshimi 1995: 35–38.

96. HCTH and HCY 1997: 193–194. Around the time Ch'oe left the comfort station, a soldier she knew helped her send the money to Seoul. He gave her a blue ticket and told her to use it to claim the money in Seoul. Because she was illiterate, she could not tell whether it was a bank or a post office and whether her name was listed as Ch'oe Il-rye or as Haruko. She then lost the ticket and thus all chance of getting her money back (HCTH and HCY 1997: 191). Mun Ok-chu, a Korean victim-survivor, stated that one could buy a small house for 1,000 yen in Taegu in the mid-1940s. See O-c. Mun 1996: 76.

97. Yoshimi 2000: 51.

98. See, for example, Hicks 1995: 189; Fujioka 1997: 135.

99. Yun Chŏng-ok, interview by the author, Tokyo, November 5, 1997. I have kept the information to myself until now out of respect. Now that more than a decade has passed since Kim's death, I have decided to reveal it here as part of our search for truth.

100. Kim Hak-sun, interview by the author, September 1, 1995. Kim's testimonial narrative is available in both Korean and English. See HCTH and CY 1993: 31–44; Howard 1995: 32–40.

101. See Sancho 1998.

102. For a discussion of the English translation of "Rules for Authorized Restaurants and Houses of Prostitution in Manila" for the Japanese military in the Philippines, see Hicks 1995: 88–90.

103. See Henson 1996.

104. Henson 1996: 60.

105. For a cautionary commentary against the Korean Council's assertion of Japan's use of Korean comfort women as a genocidal act, see C. Choi 1997: ix.

106. See Stiglmayer 1994.

107. Stiglmayer 1994: 115.

108. See MacKinnon 1994.

109. Henson 1996: 72.

110. Notably, sexual crimes are euphemistically referred to as *fūzokuhanzai,* or "customary" crimes. Moreover, the term *fūzoku* is a slang for "prostitute" in contemporary Japan. I thank Wada Masumi for this information.

111. The Japanese official records, for example, noted that Korean "lower-level prostitutes" increased in numbers in Shanghai in 1931 (see Fujinaga 2006: 350). For a historical study of prostitution and modernity in twentieth-century Shanghai, see Hershatter 1997.

112. Yoshimi 1993: 125. See also Fujinaga 2006: 351.

113. For the names and home provinces of the Koreans, see Fujinaga 2006: 357, table 5–2.

114. For more details on Korean participation in the running of military comfort stations in Shanghai, see Fujinaga 2006: 351–359.

115. See Yoshimi 1995: 43–56. The estimated number of Chinese women raped ranges between 20,000 and 80,000 (I. Chang 1997: 6).

116. Asō 1993: 217.

117. Iritani 1991: 124.

118. Quoted in Iritani 1991: 124–125. The woman learned later that "many soldiers were illiterate and had to ask other soldiers to write for them" (Iritani 1991: 125).

119. APWK v. Japan 1992: 32.

120. United States Office of War Information 1944: 4. Research Report No. 120 of Allied Translation and Interpreter Section of the Supreme Commander for the Allied Powers, dated November 15, 1945, noted that there were two types of comfort bags, which were gratuitous issue to troops: those issued by the Army and those from civilian charity organizations (Supreme Commander for the Allied Powers 1945:27). As the photo shows, however, families and friends could purchase the comfort bags that were sold at department stores and send them to soldiers stationed in China.

121. Hata 1999: 105.

122. Hata 1999: 103.

123. See, for example, Ruff-O'Herne 1994; Goos 1995; Henson 1996.

124. For a discussion of incentives for relationships of collaboration between Japanese agents and local elites in wartime China, see Brook 2005.

125. Senda 1990a: 103.

126. See HCTH and Yŏsŏngbu 2002: 25. Pak Sun-ae (pseudonym), for example, was married, but her husband sold her to an employment agency, where she encountered many women who had just run away from home, leaving all their personal effects behind (*maenmomŭro*). The agency fed and clothed them and would charge a large sum if any of the family showed up to take them home (HCTH and CY 1993: 242).

127. Senda 1990a: 113.

128. Depending on the decade, about 40 to 50 percent of the police force in colonial Korea was Korean (Cumings 1997: 153).

129. See HCTH and Yŏsŏngbu 2002: 34.

130. HCTH and Yŏsŏngbu 2002: 26.

131. HCTH and Yŏsŏngbu 2002: 27, 46.

132. Senda 1990a: 111–113.

133. Senda 1990a: 113.

134. See Yoshimi 1995: 43–47, quotation on 36.

135. Yoshimi 1995: 62.

136. See HCTH and CY 1993: 114.

137. HCTH and CY 1993: 190.

138. See Yoshimi 1993: 92.

139. Tanaka 2002: 54.

140. Ueno 1993.

141. I-m. Kim 1976: 20–21.

142. See Dutch Government 1994.

143. Mackie 2000: 38, 46.

144. When I gave a paper at the International Conference on Gender and Labour in Korea and Japan, held at the University of Sydney, July 10–12, 2006, Mackie stated that she was against the use of the term "sexual slavery" because the term conjured up pornographic images. Hence, she uses phrases such as "survivors of military prostitution" and "women subjected to enforced military prostitution" rather than "sex slaves" when she refers to the surviving comfort women.

145. For details, see Wakabayashi 2003: 246–247.

CHAPTER 4

1. For discussions of the 2001 textbook controversy in Japan and Korea, see Hamada 2002; Nelson 2002; Soh 2003b.

2. See Suzuki 1991: 62–63. Of the thirty, the majority (twenty-four) were published

between 1965 and 1988, before the leaders of Korean women's organizations started speaking publicly about the comfort women issue.

3. Boling 1995: 590.

4. For example, the list of references in I-m. Kim 1976 contains two publications from the late 1940s.

5. See, for example, the comprehensive bibliography in AWF 1997: 1–24.

6. See Kawata 1992.

7. Ienaga 1978: 199.

8. Hirota 1975: 25, 38.

9. Kikumaru-san's suicide note may be found in Hirota 1975: 13–14. Kim Il-myŏn also reported on her suicide and partially quoted the note originally published in *Shūkan Asahi Geinō* (Weekly Asahi Entertainment, August 2, 1973). See I-m. Kim 1976: 270–271.

10. Hirota 1975: 13.

11. Senda 1990a: 219.

12. For details on his references, see Senda 1990a: 224.

13. Senda 1990b: 12.

14. Senda 1990a: 129.

15. Senda 1990a: 130.

16. Senda 1990a: 122.

17. Senda 1990a: 124.

18. Other than that, there is no revision, except for several rephrasings. Senda 1990a: 10–11.

19. I-m. Kim 1976: 98.

20. HCY and HCTH 1999: 341.

21. Yoshida 1983: 3.

22. Yoshida 1983: 100–151.

23. Hata Ikuhiko, interview by the author at Hata's residence, Tokyo, October 29, 1997. For details of his field trip, see Hata 1999: 229–248.

24. Uesugi 1997: 139–140; see also Yoshimi and Kawata 1997: 26–27.

25. Coomaraswamy 1996: 8.

26. Hata 1996: 70.

27. For example, see Ueno 1998 for a feminist sociologist's critique of the positivist historiography.

28. One infamous example is the article by an American journalist, Janet Cooke, that appeared in the *Washington Post* on September 29, 1980. Cooke wrote a heartrending story of Jimmy, a boy who had become a heroin addict. After Cooke won a Pulitzer Prize for her story in April 1981, she admitted that her story was fictitious. For a detailed account of how and why it came to be published by the *Washington Post,* see the article "Janet's World," by Bill Green, then the newspaper's reader ombuds-

man, published in the *Post* on April 19, 1981. See also Bradlee 1995, an autobiography of a former editor of the *Post*. A more recent example concerns a fraudulent account of a young boy's survival in the Nazi death camps. Published as a memoir by Binjamin Wilkomirski in 1995, it was hailed as a literary masterpiece, was awarded numerous prizes, and was translated into twelve languages before it was eventually discredited. See Goldberg 2002 for a review of "As It Happened: Truth and Lies," a documentary that examines how an alleged Holocaust survivor's autobiography became a scandal. See also Geller 2002 for his thoughtful reflections on both the psychopathological and the criminal aspects of the Wilkomirski affair. I thank Joseph Parsons for alerting me to the Wilkomirski case as an example of the ongoing debate on the nature and function of memory and the veracity of truth-claims in both scholarship and creative writing.

29. Yoshida 1977; Hata 1999.

30. Since my first interview with him in Tokyo in the fall of 1997, I have met him several more times at various academic conferences. The newsletter was published by the Japan Christian Women's Temperance Union.

31. Takasaki 1976: 9.

32. *Harumoni* is the Japanese transliteration of the Korean term *halmŏni* or grandmother, which I discussed earlier.

33. Information on Pae's childhood marriage as a *minmyŏnŭri* (adopted daughter-in-law or child bride) is from Kawata 1992. Like the Chinese *sim-pua* marriage, *minmyŏnŭri* marriage was practiced only by impoverished families out of economic necessity. Even though the custom of *minmyŏnŭri* was regarded as a disguised form of slavery and the Chosŏn dynasty government attempted to ban it, the practice continued well into the "first third of the twentieth century" (Harvey 1983: 46).

34. Kawata 1992.

35. Kawata 1992.

36. Yamatani 1979: 37.

37. Yamatani 1979: 121.

38. Yamatani 1979: 37.

39. Yamatani 1979: 21.

40. A Japanese woman writer and supporter of the comfort women redress movement, Usuki Keiko, also went to Korea and made similar unsuccessful efforts to meet Korean former comfort women in 1982. Usuki 1983: 8.

41. Yamatani 1979: 6. Since the comfort women movement began, several more documentaries have been produced by women of various nationalities, including Japanese, Korean, Taiwanese, and Korean American, and shown on television and in theaters in Japan and elsewhere.

42. See Uehara 1976.

43. Uehara 1976: 3.

44. See Uehara 1976: 2.

45. Fujime 2001: 93–97. For my discussion of the Women's Tribunal, see chapter 1.

46. Suzuki 1990.

47. M-s. Kim 1990: 67.

48. M-s. Kim 1990: 60.

49. See Sekiguchi 1990.

50. *Han'guk Ilbo,* February 14, 1964, cited in I-m. Kim 1976: 273.

51. The Korean prosecutor's office, which conducted an eight-month investigation in response to the Vietnamese government's request, concluded on February 13, 1964 that no heir existed in Korea. If her estate were returned to Korea, it would go into the national coffers. Quoted in I-m. Kim 1976: 273. See also Yim 1981: 299.

52. For a critical analysis of Kim's novel for incorrectly identifying *chŏngsindae* as comfort women, see Rhee 2007: 118–121.

53. See Tŏk-sŏng Kim 1970.

54. For instance, see the cases of Kim Kkŭt-sun and Ha Yŏng-i (both pseudonyms) in HCY and HCTH 1999.

55. Takasaki 1976: 9.

56. See Tae-sang Kim 1975: 115–129.

57. Tae-sang Kim 1975: 129.

58. *Dong-a Ilbo,* October 24, 1974, cited in Takasaki 1976: 9.

59. C-m. Yun 1997: 213.

60. See chapter 1 on the use of the term *pi.* For its Korean version, I transliterate it as *ppi* to reflect the Korean orthography (삐).

61. C-m. Yun 1997: 178.

62. C-m. Yun 1997: 179.

63. C-m. Yun 1997: 179.

64. C-m. Yun 1997: 180.

65. See C-m. Yun 1997: 188–214.

66. See Hirota 1975: 24.

67. *Chosun Ilbo,* March 13, 1984; quoted in M-s. Kim 1990: 50.

68. M-s. Kim 1990: 50.

69. The *JoongAng Ilbo* article on the life story of No Su-bok (serialized in the March 17–31, 1984, issues) is reprinted in M-s. Kim 1990: 91–122.

70. The newspaper novella was written by Sŏng Pyŏng-o in *Kukje Sinmun.* For more on it, see M-s. Kim 1990: 33. The two-volume novel was written by Paek Wu-am (1989).

71. M-s. Kim 1990: 41.

72. Senda 1990a: 127–128.

73. For an excellent discussion of the bilateral negotiations, see C-s. Lee 1985.

74. Apple and Christian-Smith 1991: 4.

75. In Japan the school year starts in April.

76. See Tawara 1997: 338–341. For the excerpts from all seven, see Tawara 1997: 338–342.

77. Coomaraswamy 1996: 32.

78. For details see Fujioka 1997.

79. See Fujioka 1996 and 1997. For a critical discussion of Fujioka's *jiyūshugishikan* and the revisionist movement, see McCormack 2000.

80. Fujioka 1997: 24.

81. For more details, see Fujioka 1997.

82. For a detailed discussion of the new textbook controversy surrounding *ARK* and Tsukuru Kai, respectively, see Hamada 2002 and Nelson 2002. For an analysis of the Korean response to the 2001 textbook controversy, see Soh 2003b.

83. Nishio et al. 2001: 283.

84. For more details on Japan's history textbook debate, see Hein and Selden 2000; Orr 2001; Nozaki 2002; Saaler 2005; Bukh 2007.

85. Rhee 2004.

86. The 1968 Ministry of Education textbook, p. 173. Quoted in Rhee 2004: 73.

87. Rhee 2004: 74.

88. Korean Ministry of Education and Human Resources 2002b/1997: 151.

89. Korean Ministry of Education and Human Resources 2002a/1996: 136.

90. Korean Ministry of Education and Human Resources 2002c: 262.

91. Rhee 2004: 74.

92. For a critical analysis of the symbolic dimension of politics and "condensation symbols" that serve as the focus of psychological tensions in politics, see Edelman 1985. I thank Joseph Parsons for alerting me to this reference.

CHAPTER 5

1. Hicks 1995: 12–13.

2. Hicks 1995: 92–93.

3. Gluck 2002.

4. See I-m. Kim 1976; Ueno 2001.

5. For an analysis of the impact of sexual labor on the survivors' impaired fertility, see Soh 2006a.

6. For a further discussion of her story, see chapter 3; also Soh 1997b.

7. For a discussion of the AWF atonement project, see Soh 2003a.

8. Ruff-O'Herne 1994: 87.

9. Ruff-O'Herne 1994: 87.

10. Ruff-O'Herne 1994: 115.

11. Ruff-O'Herne 1994: 115–116.

12. For a detailed description of the house, see Ruff-O'Herne 1994.

13. For a more accurate account of the closure of Semarang comfort stations using Dutch women, see Y. Tanaka 2002; Yoshimi 1995 and 2000.

14. For more details on her life story, see Goos 1995.

15. For discussions of diverse responses to the AWF project by different survivors, see Soh 2003a.

16. Yuasa Ken, interview by the author, at Yuasa's clinic in Tokyo, November 1997.

17. HCTH and CY 1993: 178.

18. HCTH and CY 1993: 177–178.

19. I-m. Kim 1997.

20. United States Office of War Information 1944: 4.

21. For more details, see HCY and HCTH 1999: 277–292.

22. A concise version of Mun's life story is available in HCTH and CY 1993: 147–165.

23. See O-c. Mun 1996: 153. Supported by activists in Japan, Mun energetically but unsuccessfully sought to claim her savings until her death in 1996.

24. Y-s. Kim 1995: 355.

25. O-c. Mun 1996: 150.

26. O-c. Mun 1996: 152.

27. Yuasa Ken, interview by the author, Tokyo coffee shop, September 1997.

28. Howard 1995: 46. See also HCTH and CY 1993.

29. Howard 1995: 47. See also HCTH and CY 1993.

30. See HCTH and CY 1993.

31. See HCTH and CY 1993: 55.

32. Kaneda 1996.

33. About the name Kaneda Kimiko, see Usuki 1996: 15–16.

34. For more details of her story, see CY and HCTH 1995: 111–122.

35. CY and HCTH 1995: 117–118.

36. CY and HCTH 1995: 118–119.

37. For her full testimonial, see HCTH and CY 1993: 121–132.

38. This refers to the postmortem wedding practice that has been a Korean marriage custom since the Chosŏn Dynasty (1392–1910). The rite is generally performed by bereaved families of young people who died unmarried from accidents or illness. See S-m. An 2002 for further contemporary examples.

39. All Tokkōtai, which is an abbreviation for Tokubetsu Kōgekitai (Special Attack Corps), were young men about nineteen or twenty years of age, according to Yi's testimonial. When Yi asked the officer what the Tokkōtai did, he told her that two Tokkōtai men rode in one airplane to attack the enemy's ship or base. For a native-born anthropologist's perspective on the Kamikaze, see Ohnuki-Tierney 2006 for her study of diaries and correspondence of several highly educated young Tokkōtai.

40. HCTH and CY 1993: 130.

41. Yi, quoted in S-m. An 2002.

42. Kim-Gibson 1999a: 91.

43. Kim-Gibson 1999a: 88.

44. Kim-Gibson 1999a: 80–81.

45. Kim-Gibson 1999a: 93–94.

46. Ueno 2001: 304. For a list of publications on comfort women, including magazine articles, that were published in postwar Japan up to the mid-1970s, see I-m. Kim 1976: 281–284.

47. For details of his reminiscences, see Nishino 1992: 13–19.

48. Nishino 1992: 17–18.

49. Currently Nishino serves as the director of the Women's Active Museum on War and Peace, Tokyo, Japan.

50. Nishino 1992: 16–17.

51. Nishino 1992: 18.

52. Information reported in this section was gathered on July 17, 2000, during a group discussion at the International Workshop on the Comfort Women Issue organized by the activist organization Citizens for Redress (CFR-Tokyo) in Japan. See also Jūgun Ianfu 110 Ban Henshūiinkai 1992.

53. Jūgun Ianfu 110 Ban Henshūiinkai 1992: 136.

54. The English-language Web site of the South Korean Ministry of Gender Equality and Family (MOGEF) provides the contents of the "War Journal, Independent Infantry, 15th Regiment Headquarter (January 8, 1945)" as evidence of what MOGEF calls "the victims' system." http://www.mogef.go.kr/english/victims/evidence/evidence _05_ (accessed September 7, 2006).

55. In this regard, it is interesting to learn of General George S. Patton's dictum "A man who won't fuck, won't fight" (Mondschein 2006). It strikes me that although Japanese soldiers' disdain for their colleagues who refused to participate in the sexual activities at *ianjo* seems to point to their commonly held notion of normative masculine heterosexuality, Patton's comment seems to underscore the notion of military hypermasculinity that connects the sex act in men to aggression and violence.

56. For further discussion of sexual behaviors of the Japanese troops by First Lieutenant and psychiatrist Hayao Torao in a 1939 report, see Yoshimi 1995: 45–47.

57. See Jūgun Ianfu 110 Ban Henshūiinkai 1992: 135.

58. For further discussions of the reasons why the Japanese military authorities saw the need to establish comfort stations, see Yoshimi 1993: 86–88; Y. Tanaka 2002: 23–30.

59. Jūgun Ianfu 110 Ban Henshūiinkai 1992: 135.

60. United States Office of War Information 1944: 4.

61. Ienaga 1978: 158. According to historian Utsumi Aiko, who discusses the problems

of Korean "imperial soldiers" who were punished as Japanese at war trials and excluded from relief as foreigners, the total number of Korean soldiers in the Japanese military came to 130,723 (Utsumi 2001: 205).

62. Hicks 1995: 146.

63. Jūgun Ianfu 110 Ban Henshūiinkai 1992: 136.

64. Ruff-O'Herne 1994: 100.

65. Ruff-O'Herne 1994: 100–101, quotation on 100.

66. Nishino 1992: 55.

67. For more details, see Nishino 1992: 46–48.

68. Hegel 1977.

CHAPTER 6

1. Shirota 1971.

2. The TBS Radio interview was entitled "Ishi no sakebi." The interviewer addressed and referred to her as Yoshie-san, and I do the same hereafter.

3. For more details of her life as of 1970, see Shirota 1971.

4. Yoshie-san's statement during the TBS Radio interview "Ishi no sakebi."

5. For more details on Fukazu's story, see M-s. Kim 1990: 25–29.

6. For a further discussion of genealogy as a way of playing local discontinuous knowledges off against the unitary scientific knowledge, see Foucault 2003: 8–9.

7. Yŏsŏngbu (Ministry of Gender Equality) 2002.

8. One such example is Brinton 1993.

9. See, for example, England 2005 for a discussion of a variety of theories of carework that neglect women's public sexual carework.

10. For a survey of recent works on gender bias and the devaluation of carework, see England 2005: 382–385.

11. Some Koreans regard kongnyŏ as "Koryŏ's version of chŏngsindae." See I-h. Yi 1999: 208.

12. For details, see I-h. Yi 1999.

13. H-w. Kim 1999: 231.

14. O-g. Kim et al. 1972: 405; Y-C. Kim 1979: 105..

15. O-g. Kim et al. 1972: 401.

16. Y-C. Kim 1979: 107–110; H-w. Kim 1999: 234.

17. C-j. Mun 2001.

18. H-w. Kim 1999: 234–235.

19. Cumings 1997: 102.

20. See "Ilbonin Kwankwanggaek" (Japanese Tourists), Sin-Dong-a, January 1972. (More on the subject below.)

21. For a quote of Fukuzawa encouraging the emigration of women as prostitutes, see Warren 2003: 62.

22. *Hōjin Kaigai Hattenshi* [A History of Japanese Overseas Development] by Irie Toraji, quoted in Yamazaki 1999: 190.

23. On published examples of such mistreatment by family, see Yamazaki 1974.

24. Yamazaki 1974: 20–27.

25. It is also notable here that the postwar accounts of many Japanese emigrants in Manchuria have documented their suffering and victimization. Yet, despite their marginal and powerless status as ordinary emigrants, they were not simple victims: they both exploited and were exploited by their empire in complex ways. For a cogent discussion of "victims of empire," see Young 1998: 399–411. For a critical discussion of Koreans in Manchuria as both the colonized and colonizers, see H. O. Park 2005.

26. For more on her experience, see M-s. Kim 2001: 102–103.

27. CY and HCTH 1995: 119.

28. HCY and HCTH 1999: 289.

29. HCY and HCTH 1999: 291.

30. See, for example, Kawata 1987 and Shirota 1971 for postwar life stories of the sexual labor of Korean and Japanese comfort women survivors, respectively.

31. See Duus 1979, especially chapters 1 and 2.

32. Duus 1979; Y. Tanaka 2002.

33. Duus 1979: 18.

34. For a discussion of such crimes and official reports on sexual violence committed by the occupation forces against Japanese women, see Y. Tanaka 2002, chapter 5.

35. See, for example, Mun P'il-gi's story in HCTH and CY 1993: 117.

36. Duus 1979: 21–29; Shiga-Fujime 1993.

37. Duus 1979: 41.

38. Duus 1979: 27.

39. See Y. Tanaka 2002: 133–141, quotation on 135.

40. Shiga-Fujime 1993: 7.

41. Duus 1979: 40–41.

42. Whiting 1999: 13.

43. Whiting 1999: 14.

44. Duus 1979: 161–168.

45. Duus 1979, chapters 5 and 6.

46. See Nitta 1997 for stereotypes about war brides in Japan and the United States. See also Yuh 2002 for similar prejudices against Korean "military brides."

47. The current Rest and Recuperation Leave Program provides the opportunity for U.S. service members and Department of Defense civilians who are deployed in the combat theater on an unaccompanied tour for one year to take up to fifteen days of leave during their deployment. R & R leave periods are limited to one per

twelve-month period and are intended to provide respite from hostile fire and areas of imminent danger. See http://www.armyg1.army.mil/randr/faq.asp.

48. Duus 1979: 291.

49. Duus 1979: 292–293; Shiga-Fujime 1993: 7.

50. Duus 1979: 292.

51. See, for example, Y. Tanaka 2002, chapter 5.

52. For details of shocking but little-known stories of Japanese women's suffering of sexual violence and war crimes committed by the American military in the battlefields in Korea during the Korean War, see Fujime 1999.

53. I-m. Kim 1976: 267–268.

54. Fujime 1999: 128.

55. Shiga-Fujime 1993; Garon 1997: 202.

56. Tomimura 1982: 188.

57. Garon 1997: 202.

58. See Usuki 1983 for stories of Korean women as *Japayuki-san.* For an analysis of Southeast Asian women's experiences, see Mackie 1998..

59. In the 1980s the majority of *Japayuki-san* came from the Philippines and Taiwan, while in the 1990s women from Thailand became the latest newcomers to the multiethnic sex industry in Japan (Constantine 1993).

60. For an analysis of Korean fictional stories on *kijich'on,* see Fulton 1998.

61. Fulton 1998: 200.

62. H-s. Kim 1997: 14. For the life stories of sex workers for the U.S. military in Korea, Japan, and the Philippines, see Sturdevant and Stoltzfus 1992.

63. For a description of the bar system in Tongduch'on in the late 1980s, see Sturdevant and Stoltzfus 1992: 176–179.

64. For her life story, see HCTH and HCY 1997: 225–236, quotations on 233 and 235.

65. See Cumings 1992: 171. In 1958, five years after the armistice, the majority (59.1 percent) of about 300,000 prostitutes in Korea served American soldiers, according to a report in the August 11, 1958, issue of *Kyŏnghyang Sinmun* (quoted in H-j. Chŏng 1999: 300). The reliability of the figures is questionable. In any case, some of the women working at the U.S. military bases, like their Japanese counterparts, became "war brides" and emigrated to the United States as wives of U.S. servicemen. For more information on, and generalized bias against, Korean war brides, see Soh 1995; Yuh 2002.

66. Moon 1997.

67. H-s. Kim 1997; Moon 1997: 58–59.

68. See Moon 1997 for details, especially chapter 3.

69. H-s. Kim 1997: 15.

70. Moon 1997.

71. See H-s. Kim 1997, quotation on 22.

72. H-s. Kim 1997: 23.

73. H-s. Kim 1997: 24.

74. For her life story, see Sturdevant and Stoltzfus 1992: 180–207, quotation on 204.

75. H-s. Kim 1997: 19.

76. Cheng, n.d.

77. Korean men reportedly find Russian women exotic; having sex with them is referred to in their slang as riding on a "white horse" (*paengma*).

78. The research conducted by Durebang, an NGO for women's human rights, was reported in http://www.hani.co.kr (December 19, 2003).

79. H-j. Chŏng 1999: 352.

80. Some 100,000 American troops were stationed in Japan and Korea at the end of the twentieth century (Ch. Johnson 1999: 109).

81. Ch. Johnson 1999: 121. After one American brigade formerly based in South Korea deployed to Iraq in 2004, the American presence in Korea in 2007 was 28,000. South Korea fields 680,000 in its armed forces. See Shanker 2007.

82. Kenneth Markle, a twenty-year-old private in the U.S. Army stationed in South Korea, murdered Yun Kŭm-i, a twenty-six-year-old sex worker, by battering her with a Coke bottle and stuffing it into her vagina. He also shoved an umbrella into the anus of the bleeding, dying woman and stuffed matches into her mouth. He then sprinkled soap powder over her body, apparently in an attempt to destroy evidence of the murder. National Campaign for Eradication of Crime by U.S. Troops in Korea, n.d.

83. It was given at the Fifth International Symposium on Peace and Human Rights in East Asia held at Ritsumeikan University in Kyoto, Japan, February 22–25, 2002. A special report on it was published in the online newspaper *OhmyNews,* http://www.ohmynews.com (February 22, 2002).

84. According to the memoir of retired General Ch'ae Myŏng-sin, the South Korean Army ran three or four "comfort units" (*wianbudae*), each composed of about sixty women (Ch'ae 1994: 267, quoted in K-o. Kim 2002: 76).

85. H-o. Kim 2000: 70–80, quoted in K-o. Kim 2002: 77–78.

86. K-o. Kim 2002: 71.

87. See N-h. Yi 1992.

88. There are three basic views among researchers as to the origin of prostitution in Korean society. One is that there were prostitutes and prostitution from the Three Kingdoms period (57 BCE–668 CE). N-h. Yi 1992: 17–18, for example, states that prostitutes already existed in the Silla Dynasty (which began in 57 BCE, unified the Korean peninsula in 668 CE, and lasted until 935 CE) by the mid-sixth century. Another view is that prostitution started in the Chosŏn period (1392–1910). A third view is that prostitution as a profession began in colonized Korea. As Chin Yang-

gyo, a professor of urban planning, suggests, the diversity of the views hinges upon the definition of prostitution. See Chin 1998: 209–214.

89. Kwŏn 1999.

90. Y-C. Kim 1979: 55.

91. Y-C. Kim 1979: 139.

92. Y-C. Kim 1979 :54.

93. The term as well as the concept of *kwanki* as a historical legacy is still very much alive among men, especially bureaucrats and politicians, as demonstrated in an episode concerning the governor of North Ch'ungchŏng. In August 2007 the governor said to a major Korean presidential candidate—albeit in jest—that had this been in the old days, he would have arranged a *kwanki* to serve the candidate (who was staying overnight in the provincial capital in order to attend a political campaign event). The candidate's response, "Wasn't the one I had last night what you sent in?," playfully acknowledged the governor's metaphorical expression of his desire to provide hospitality to the visiting VIP. See http://www.unninet.net, a feminist Web site, which included the two men on its annual list of public speeches that denigrate women, posted on December 13, 2007 (accessed December 14, 2007).. See also *Hangyoreh,* December 13, 2007, which reported the annual feminist event.

94. Kwŏn 1999.

95. For anecdotes concerning the kings, members of the royal family, and government officials of Koryŏ and Chosŏn and their amorous relationships with *kisaeng,* see N-h. Yi 1992: 119–124.

96. Kwŏn 1999: 155–156.

97. Kwŏn 1999: 155.

98. S-k. Yi 1999: 215–216.

99. N-h. Yi 1992: 436–437.

100. N-h. Yi 1992: 439.

101. O-g. Kim et al. 1972: 277.

102. C-s. Pak 1996: 67 writes that the Korean system of concubinage was born as a social mechanism to supply "stable prostitutionalization" in Chosŏn society and continued throughout the colonial period.

103. In one case, a grown-up daughter, whose frustrated mother had committed suicide in 2000, was interviewed on a major television program on the SBS network and the subject of an article in the print media in April 2005. The one wish the daughter wanted to convey was that she be included in her father's family registry. Lawsuits have been filed in cases involving the "hidden daughters" of the other two presidents and were reported in 2005 and 2006, respectively. The lawsuits were reported on http://www.donga.com (September 28, 2005) and http://www.systemclub.co.kr (January 13, 2006), respectively.

104. Interestingly, King Yejong (r. 1468–1469) based his endorsment of *kinyŏ* in frontier

towns on the need for troops living away from home to get their torn and tattered clothing mended. See N-h. Yi 1992: 112–113.

105. O-g. Kim et al. 1972: 518–519, 521.

106. O-g. Kim et al. 1972: 522–523.

107. Yim 2004: 28.

108. Yim 2004: 27.

109. See, for example, Pyŏn and Hwang 1998. For a discussion of sex tourism in Asia as a reflection of political and economic inequality between men and women and between the underdeveloped countries of Asia and the industrialized nations of the West and Japan, see E. Kim 1987.

110. KWDI 1997.

111. KCWU 1983. See Japan Anti-Prostitution Association 1995.

112. The association changed its name to Korea National Tourism Corporation in 1984.

113. Pyŏn and Hwang 1998: 44.

114. KCWU 1983: 24.

115. KCWU 1983: 7.

116. For more details, see KCWU 1983.

117. KCWU 1983: 16.

118. KCWU 1983: 19.

119. KCWU 1983: 44.

120. I learned during my field research that Japanese male sex tourists have replaced the term *kisaeng* with the Japanese slang term *tachi* (a suffix that indicates the plurality of the noun, as in *onnatachi* [women]) to refer to Korean female sex workers.

121. Cumings 1992: 171.

122. Cumings 1992: 171–172.

123. Lie 1997.

124. Cho and Chang 1990.

125. A notable exception is the case of Rhee Younghoon, a professor of Korean economic history, whose critical public statement on the comfort women issue generated a fierce controversy in September 2004, which I will discuss in the epilogue.

126. For a South Korean feminist critique of the nationalist discourse on the comfort women, see E-s. Kim 1994.

EPILOGUE

1. For a discussion of the photographic metaphor, see the prologue and Peacock 2001.

2. Scheper-Hughes 2004: 460.

3. In the woods of the ancient city of Kyoto, a bandit raped a beautiful young woman and her samurai husband was killed. The bandit was later found with the dead man's horse. In a police court inquiry, the three characters each tell a completely different story of the rape and the death. The bandit claims to have killed the man

in a duel that was prompted by the raped woman. The violated woman tearfully confesses that she killed her husband out of shame, grief, and anger when she saw the cold contempt and hatred in her husband's eyes. Speaking through a medium, however, the dead samurai states that he killed himself using his wife's dagger. Akira Kurosawa created his film *Rashomon* by combining this story, entitled "In a Grove," by the modern Japanese writer Akutagawa Ryūnosuke, with another historical short story by the same author, entitled "Rashōmon," which depicts the social circumstances and the psychology of a destitute man committing his first act of thievery. For the two stories, see Akutagawa 1970.

4. *Rashomon* won the grand prize, the Golden Lion, at the 1951 Venice Film Festival, and consequently became the work that broke Japanese film into the western market. *Rashomon* has the claim of being the best known, most widely shown Japanese film of all time in the West. It also liberated young filmmakers through Kurosawa's flouting of the established rules of narrative cinema a full ten years before the French New Wave. For recent English-language publications on Kurosawa and his work, see Prince 1999; Yoshimoto 2000.

5. Chung Chin-sung, who has served as a corepresentative of the Korean Council, has also noted this phenomenon. See C-s. Chung 2004: 306.

6. Kang and Yamashita 1993.

7. E-s. Kim 1994.

8. H. Yang 1998.

9. Y-s. An 2003.

10. See Y-h. Pak 2005, in which she offers analyses of other bilateral issues and suggestions for reconciliation between Korea and Japan.

11. Rhee 2007, chapters 7 and 8.

12. C-s. Chung 2004: 306.

13. M-s. Yun 2003.

14. Kim Mun-suk, interview by the author, Pusan, December 2004. See also Y-s. An 2003: 216.

15. HCTH 1992: 51.

16. H-s. Sin 1994: 25.

17. C-o. Yun 1994: 12.

18. For details, see http://www.womenandwar.net and http://www.k-comfortwomen .com.

19. In support of the Korean Council, an editorial in the June 5, 2007, issue of *Seoul Sinmun* opined that it was not right to oppose the building of the "military comfort women museum" (*kunwianbu pangmulkwan*) in Independence Park because both the museum and the independence movement belong to the "history of liberation" (*kwangbok ŭi yŏksa*).

20. HCTH 1992: 134.

21. See *Korea Times*, April 15, 2005; *Hankyoreh*, April 29, 2005.

22. Their lawsuits were pending as of this writing in late 2007.

23. *Ilyo Sinmun*, March 4, 2001: 35.

24. *Han'guk Ilbo*, February 26, 2001.

25. In the September 2000 fire in Taemyŏngdong, Kunsan, five women who had been sleeping died, unable to get out of their locked room. In the January 2002 fire in Kaebokdong, Kunsan, fifteen died in a similar situation. In March 2005, six months after the special laws went into effect, a fire in the so-called Miari Texas brothel village in Seoul cost the lives of five more sleeping prostitutes. See http://www.Hani .co.kr/section-005000000/2005/03/ (accessed March 28, 2005).

26. The U.S. state department in 2001 assessed South Korea as belonging to the third-tier group of human rights violators for its involvement in international human trafficking. Subsequent government efforts at prevention resulted in improving its status: The state department reclassified it in the first-tier group in 2002 (*Hankyoreh*, June 6, 2002).

27. See http://www.donga.com, "Mongol yŏsŏng wijanggyŏrhon ipkuksikyŏ sŏngmae-mae" [Mongol Women Brought under Fraudulent Marriages and Forced into Prostitution] (accessed November 26, 2005). For a discussion of the Korean "tribute women" offered to the Mongols of the Yuan dynasty (1271–1368), see chapter 6.

28. "Uzbek Sex Clubs: Dark Side of 'Korean Wave,'" *Hankyoreh*, September 23, 2006, at http://www.hani.co.kr/arti/english_edition/e_international/159475.html (accessed October 31, 2006).

29. For a study that attempts to sort out which old crimes should be left to the past and which should not and provokes questions of responsibility and forgiveness, see Shuman and Smith 2000.

30. *Hankyoreh*, February 24, 2003.

31. South Koreans have yet to squarely confront the issue of Korean collaboration with the Japanese colonial state. For a detailed account of their failure to "purge pro-Japanese Koreans" during the Rhee administration, see Cheong 1991.

32. Yoshimi 2000: 66; Tanaka 2002: 173.

33. See *Asahi Shimbun*, January 12, 2005; *Japan Times*, July 30, 2005.

34. I met the young woman from the Korean Council on October 9, 2007, when she accompanied a comfort woman survivor from Korea, who gave her testimony at an event held at the University of California, Berkeley, and hosted by the Bay Area Coalition for Justice for "Comfort Women" and other Korean and Korean-American organizations.

35. For a feminist discussion of the relationship between gender and Korean nationalism, see E. H. Kim and Choi 1998. In particular, see H. Yang 1998 for her analysis of how the comfort women issue has been turned from the individual stories of victim-survivors to a public discourse of Korean national suffering under Japanese

colonial rule. See also E-s. Kim 1994; Y. Yamashita 1998. For a comparative perspective on the relationship between feminism and nationalism in developing countries, see Jayawardena 1986.

36. Ueno 2004.

37. See Cumings 1997: 179.

38. Bruce Cumings, interview by the author, Stanford University, June 6, 2001.

39. Hicks 1995: 4.

40. Rhee Younghoon, interview by the author, Seoul National University, December 2004.

41. See http://www.donga.com/fbin/news?f=print&n=200409030220 (accessed September 3, 2004); and http://www.hani.co.kr/section-005000000/2004/09/005000000 200409061312616.html (accessed September 5, 2004). *OhmyNews*, which is a hybrid between an online news site and a sophisticated blog, edits stories submitted by thousands of "citizen reporters" across the country. President Roh Moo-hyun granted his first domestic interview to *OhmyNews* against the conservative major national dailies that had supported his rival in the very close 2002 presidential race. For more details on this, see Hua 2005.

42. During my interview in December 2004, Rhee did not mention this incident, which I later confirmed with him.

43. See Soh 2003a: 228, 230–231.

44. The exact number of the Korean recipients is not known. After the severely criticized January 1997 event their privacy has been closely guarded by the AWF, which tried its best to keep offering its resources, in an undisclosed manner, to as many South Korean survivor-applicants as possible until the Korean project's conclusion in 2002. For more details, see Soh 2003a.

APPENDIX

1. See chapter 1 for my discussion of the international political context and the actions taken by the National Organization for Women in early 1993, which contributed to a surge of keen interest in the Korean comfort women issue among feminists and human rights activists in the United States.

2. I elaborated on James Peacock's photographic metaphor in the prologue. For his own discussion, see Peacock 2001.

3. For a discussion of Eric Wolf's notion of structural power, see the introduction.

4. See Clifford and Marcus 1986; Haraway 1988; Mascia-Lees, Sharpe, and Cohen 1989; Rosaldo 1989; Fox 1991; M. Wolf 1992; Behar and Gordon 1995; D. Wolf 1996.

5. In the lexicon of literary terms of colonial and postcolonial discourse theory, "othering" refers to "the process whereby the inhabitants of colonized countries are represented in negative and degrading ways and often generalized about as if they were all the same" (Mills 2004: 146).

6. Geertz 1983:140.

7. See Foucault 2003: 8–9 for his notion of genealogy, which refers to "the 'coupling' together of scholarly erudition and local memories."

8. This statement is based on my own experiences with anonymous readers and a journal editor regarding my manuscript in which I analyzed the nature of the Japanese comfort system and the complexity of Korean comfort women's victimization. Without divulging the details of the saga, I should like to indicate my concern with the culture war of political correctness being waged anonymously by some academics in the United States who self-righteously engage in politically motivated censorship on controversial issues.

9. Like "culture," "holism" is a term on whose meaning anthropologists do not agree. The approach of processual holism requires research data into both mental and behavioral activity, emic and etic analysis, the use of the comparative method, and the use of both diachronic and synchronic perspectives. Marvin Harris identified four kinds of holism: methodological, functionalist, laundry-list, and processual holism. In Harris's terms (1999: 133–139), methodological holism recognizes the "physical reality" of "both individual entities and distinctively supraindividual entities," while functionalist holism sees cultural elements "as interrelated and interdependent." Harris saw functionalist holism as the source of laundry-list holism, which attempts to view things "in the broadest possible context," and suggested that the escape from laundry lists can be achieved through processual holism, which implies a "commitment to a definite set of epistemological and methodological options."

10. See, for example, Clifford and Marcus 1986; Ginsburg 1989.

11. For a commentary on both advantages and disadvantages of "native" anthropologists, see Ohnuki-Tierney 1984. For a critique of the dichotomous paradigm of "regular" and "native" anthropologists, see Narayan 1997. For a critical discussion of the position of "natives" in the "world system" of anthropology from a Japanese perspective, see Kuwayama 2004.

12. A detailed theoretical discussion of the notion of "expatriate anthropology" will require a separate research paper.

13. For a detailed discussion of a similar methodological stance taken by a sociologist when she studied the underground movement groups in Japan, see Steinhoff 2003.

14. Soh 2000b.

15. Ten of eleven people, according to information on the Web site, found his quite lengthy review helpful. See http://www.Amazon.com/review/R117V2JZKZRHML/ref=cm_cr_pr_viewpnt#R117V2JZKZRHML (accessed May 25, 2006).

16. See Abu-Lughod 1991: 142.

17. Soh 2004b and 2006b.

Bibliography

Abelmann, Nancy. 2003. *The Melodrama of Mobility: Women, Talk, and Class in Contemporary South Korea.* Honolulu: University of Hawai'i Press.

Abu-Lughod, Lila. 1991. Writing against Culture. In *Recapturing Anthropology: Working in the Present,* ed. R. G. Fox. Pp. 137–162. Santa Fe, NM: School of American Research Press.

Ahn, Byung-jik. 1993. Chosa e Ch'amgahamyŏnsŏ (Participating in the Research). In *Chŭngŏnjip 1: Kangjero Kkŭllyŏgan Chosŏnin Kunwianpudŭl* (Collection of Testimonies 1: Forcibly Dragged Away Korean Military Comfort Women), ed. Han'guk Chŏngsindae-munje Taech'aek Hyŏpŭihoe and Chŏngsindae Yŏn'guhoe. Pp. 8–11. Seoul: Hanul.

Ahn, Byung-jik, and Rhee, Younghoon. 2007. *Taehanminkuk Yŏksa ŭi Kiro e Sŏda* (The Republic of Korea Stands at a Crossroads of History). Seoul: Kip'arang.

Ahn, Taeyoon. 2003. Mothering the Empire: The Mobilization of Women in Late Colonial Korea. Paper presented at the Association for Asian Studies annual conference, New York, March 27–30.

Akutagawa, Ryūnosuke. 1970. *Rashomon and Other Stories.* Trans. Takashi Kojima. New York: Liveright.

An, Sun-mo. 2002. Tugae ŭi Yŏngjŏng "Ch'oya" kkaji Ch'irŭnda (Two Portraits Even Observe the "First Night"). *Ilyo Sinmun,* January 6.

An, Yŏn-sŏn. 2003. *Sŏng Noye wa Pyŏngsa Mandŭlgi* (The Making of Sex Slaves and Soldiers). Seoul: Samin.

Apple, Michael, and Linda Christian-Smith. 1991. *The Politics of the Textbook.* London: Routledge.

APWK v. Japan. 1992. Asia T'aepyŏngyang Chŏnjaeng Han'gukin Hisaengja Posang Ch'ŏnggu Sakŏn Sojang (Asia Pacific War Korean Victim Compensation Request Case Written Complaint), 2nd ed. Tokyo: Hakkirikai.

APWVBF. *See* T'aepyŏngyang Chŏnjaeng Hisaengja Yujokhoe. *See also* Association of Pacific War Victims and Bereaved Families.

Arias, Arturo, ed. 2001. *The Rigoberta Menchú Controversy.* With a response by David Stoll. Minneapolis: University of Minnesota Press.

Asian Women's Fund. 1997. *"Ianfu" Kankei Bunken Mokuroku* (A Bibliography of Publications on the "Comfort Women" Issue). Tokyo: Gyōsei.

———. 2000. *Kankei Shiryō* (Related Material). Mimeographed document for an international workshop held in Tokyo, February 24–25.

Asō, Tetsuo. 1993. *Shanghai yori Shanghai e* (From Shanghai to Shanghai). Fukuoka: Sekifūsha.

Association of Pacific War Victims and Bereaved Families. 1993. *The Issue of Korean Human Rights during and after the Pacific War.* Seoul: The author.

AWF. *See* Asian Women's Fund.

Barraclough, Ruth. 2006. Tales of Seduction: Factory Girls in Korean Proletarian Literature. *positions: east asia cultures critique* 14 (2): 345–365.

Barry, Kathleen. 1995. *The Prostitution of Sexuality.* New York: New York University Press.

Behar, Ruth, and Deborah A. Gordon, eds. 1995. *Women Writing Culture.* Berkeley: University of California Press.

Bernstein, Gail Lee. 2005. *Isami's House: Three Centuries of a Japanese Family.* Berkeley University of California Press.

Binion, Gayle. 1995. Human Rights: A Feminist Perspective. *Human Rights Quarterly* 17 (3):509–526.

Boling, David Alan. 1995. Mass Rape, Enforced Prostitution and the Japanese Imperial Army: Japan Eschews International Legal Responsibility? *Columbia Journal of Transitional Law* 32 (3): 533–589.

Bourdieu, Pierre. 1984. *Distinction.* Trans. Richard Nice. Cambridge, MA: Harvard University Press.

———. 1990. *The Logic of Practice.* Trans. Richard Nice. Stanford, CA: Stanford University Press.

Bourgois, Philippe. 1995. *In Search of Respect: Selling Crack in El Barrio.* Cambridge: Cambridge University Press.

Bradlee, Benjamin C. 1995. *A Good Life: Newspapering and Other Adventures.* New York: Simon & Schuster.

Brinton, Mary C. 1993. *Women and the Economic Miracle: Gender and Work in Postwar Japan.* Berkeley: University of California Press.

Brook, Timothy. 2005. *Collaboration: Japanese Agents and Local Elites in Wartime China.* Cambridge, MA: Harvard University Press.

Bukh, Alexander. 2007. Japan's History Textbooks Debate: National Identity in Narratives of Victimhood and Victimization. *Asian Survey* 47 (5): 683–704.

Burgos-Debray, Elisabeth, ed. 1984. *I, Rigoberta Menchú: An Indian Woman in Guatemala.* Trans. Ann Wright. London: Verso.

Burns, Susan. 1998. Bodies and Borders: Syphilis, Prostitution, and the Nation in Japan, 1860–1890. *U.S.–Japan Women's Journal, English Supplement,* No. 15: 3–30.

Byun, Young-joo, dir. 1999. *Habitual Sadness: Korean Comfort Women Today*. 70 minutes. Distributed by Filmakers Library, New York.

Chai, Alice Y. 1993. Asian-Pacific Feminist Coalition Politics: The Chŏngsindae/Jugunianfu ("Comfort Women") Movement. *Korean Studies*. 17: 67–91.

Ch'ae, Myŏng-sin. 1994. *Sasŏnŭl Nŏmkonŏmŏ* (Repeatedly Traversing the Death Lines). Seoul: Maeilkyŏngje Sinmunsa.

Chan, Lihuei, and Su, Zhiliang. 2000. Chūgoku no Ianjo ni Kansuru Chōsahōkoku (Research Report on the Comfort Stations in China). In *"Ianfu": Senji Seibōryoku no Jittai II* ("Comfort Women": Actual Conditions of Wartime Sexual Violence II), ed. VAWW-NET Japan. Tokyo: Ryokufū Shuppan.

Chang, Iris. 1997. *The Rape of Nanking: The Forgotten Holocaust of World War II*. New York: Penguin Books.

Chang, Sa-hun. 1986. Women Entertainers of the Yi Dynasty. In *Women of the Yi Dynasty*, ed. Park Young-hai. Seoul: Research Center for Asian Women, Sookmyung Women's University.

Chang, Seok-heung. 2004. Overseas Migration of Koreans in the Colonial Period and the Historicality of Repatriation. *Korea Journal* 44 (4): 5–29.

Cheng, Sea-ling. N.d. Making Love and Money: Clubs around U.S. Army Camps in South Korea. Unpublished ms.

Cheong, Sung-hwa. 1991. *The Politics of Anti-Japanese Sentiment in Korea*. New York: Greenwood Press.

Chin, Yang-kyo. 1998. *Ch'ŏngnyangni ŭi Konggan kwa Ilsang: Ilkwa, Sijang Kŭrigo Yugwak* (Space and Life in Ch'ŏngnyangni: Daily Work, Market, and the Pleasure Quarters). Seoul: Seoulhak Yŏn'guso, Seoul City College.

Cho, Hyoung, and Chang Pil Wha. 1990. Perspectives on Prostitution in the Korean Legislature: 1948–1989. *Yŏsŏnghak Nonjip* (Journal of Women's Studies) 7: 109–111.

Choi, Chungmoo. 1997. Guest Editor's Introduction. *positions: east asia cultures critique* 5 (1): v–xiv. Special issue: The Comfort Women: Colonialism, War, and Sex.

Choi, Hong-gi. 1991. Yukyo wa Kajok (Confucianism and the Family). *Kajokhak Nonjip* (Journal of Family Studies) 3: 207–227.

Choi, Yu-ri. 1999. Manse Undong, Namnyŏ ga Ttaro Ŏpta (Independence Movement, There Is No Gender Difference). *Uri Nara Yŏsŏngdŭl ŭn Ŏttŏke Saratsŭlkka* (How Did Our Nation's Women Live Their Lives 2), ed. Yi Pae-yong et al. Pp. 144–153. Seoul: Chŏngnyŏnsa.

Chŏng, Hŭi-jin. 1999. Chugŏya Sanŭn Yŏsŏngdŭl ŭi Inkwŏn (Women's Human Rights Come Alive after Death). In *Han'guk Yŏsŏng Inkwŏn Undongsa* (A History of the Korean Women's Human Rights Movement), ed. Han'guk Yŏsŏng ŭi Chŏnhwa Yŏnhap (Korean Women's Telephone Association). Pp. 300–358. Seoul: Hanul.

Chŏng, Yŏn-t'ae. 1999. "Singminji Kŭndaehwaron" Nonjaeng ŭi Pip'an kwa Sinkŭndaesaron ŭi Mosaek (Criticism of the "Colonial Modernization Theory"

Debate and a Search for a New Theory of Modern History). *Ch'angjak kwa Pip'yŏng* 27 (1): 352–376.

Chŏngsindae Yŏn'guhoe and Han'guk Chŏngsindae-munje Taech'aek Hyŏpŭihoe, eds. 1995. *Chungguk ŭro Kkŭllyŏgan Chosŏnin Kunwianpudŭl: 50-nyŏn Hu ŭi Chŭngŏn* (Korean Military Comfort Women Dragged Away to China: Testimonies After 50 Years). Seoul: Hanul.

Chŏngsindae-munje Silmu Taech'aekpan. 1992. *Ilcheha Kundaewianbu Silt'aejosa Chungganpogosŏ* (Interim Report on the Investigation into the Military Comfort Women under Imperial Japan). Seoul: The author.

Chōsenjin Kyōsei Renkō Shinsō Chōsadan. 1974. *Chōsenjin Kyōsei Renkō: Kyōsei Rōdō no Kiroku* (Forced Conscription of the Koreans: A Record of Forced Labor). Tokyo: Gendaishi Shuppankai.

Chou, Wan-yao. 1996. The *Kōminka* Movement in Taiwan and Korea: Comparisons and Interpretations. In *The Japanese Wartime Empire, 1931–1945*, ed. Peter Duus, Ramon H. Myers, and Mark R. Peattie. Princeton, NJ: Princeton University Press.

Chuh, Kandice. 2003. Discomforting Knowledge, Or, Korean "Comfort Women" and Asian Americanist Critical Practice. *Journal of Asian American Studies* 6 (1): 5–23 (February).

Chung, Chin-sung. 1993. Haesŏl: Kunwianbu ŭi Silsang. In *Chŭngŏnjip 1: Kangjero Kkŭllyŏgan Chosŏnin Kunwianpudŭl* (Collection of Testimonies 1: Forcibly Dragged Away Korean Military Comfort Women), ed. Han'guk Chŏngsindae-munje Taech'aek Hyŏpŭihoe and Chŏngsindae Yŏn'guhoe. Pp. 15–29. Seoul: Hanul.

———. 1996. TongAsia Chŏngsindae-munje wa Yŏsŏng Inkwŏn (East Asian *Chŏngsindae* Issue and Women's Human Rights). *Sasang* (winter).

———. 1997. Sŏmun (Preface). In *Chŭngŏnjip 2: Kangjero Kkŭllyŏgan Chosŏnin Kunwianpudŭl* (Collection of Testimonies 2: Forcibly Dragged Away Korean Military Comfort Women), ed. Han'guk Chŏngsindae-munje Taech'aek Hyŏpŭihoe and Han'guk Chŏngsindae Yŏn'guhoe. Pp. 5–13. Seoul: Hanul.

———. 1999. Sŏmun: Sumŭn Yŏksa ŭi Palgul ŭn Kyesoktoeŏya Handa (Preface: Excavation of Hidden History Must Continue). In *Chŭngŏnjip: Kangjero Kkŭllyŏgan Chosŏnin Kunwianpudŭl 3* (Collection of Testimonies: Forcibly Dragged Away Korean Military Comfort Women 3), ed. Han'guk Chŏngsindae Yŏn'guso and Han'guk Chŏngsindae-munje Taech'aek Hyŏpŭihoe. Pp. 5–12. Seoul: Hanul.

———. 2004. *Ilbon'gun Sŏngnoyeje* (Japanese Military Sex Slavery). Seoul: Seoul National University Press.

Chung, Hye-Kyung. 2004. The Forcible Drafting of Koreans during the Final Phase of Colonial Rule and the Formation of the Korean Community in Japan. *Korea Journal* 44 (4): 30–59.

Chuter, David. 2003. *War Crimes: Confronting Atrocity in the Modern World*. Boulder and London: Lynne Rienner Publishers.

Clifford, James, and George E. Marcus, eds. 1986. *Writing Culture: The Poetics and Politics of Ethnography*. Berkeley: University of California Press.

Colligan-Taylor, Karen. 1999. Translator's Introduction. In *Sandakan Brothel No. 8: An Episode in the History of Lower-Class Japanese Women*, Tomoko Yamazaki. Pp. xiii–xxxix. Trans. Karen Colligan-Taylor. Armonk, NY: M. E. Sharpe.

Comaroff, Jean, and John Comaroff. 1991. *Of Revelation and Revolution*. Chicago: University of Chicago Press.

Connell, R. W. 1995. *Masculinities*. Berkeley: University of California Press.

Constantine, Peter. 1993. *Japan's Sex Trade: A Journey through Japan's Erotic Subcultures*. Tokyo: Yenbooks.

Cook, Rebecca J., ed. 1994. *Human Rights of Women: National and International Perspectives*. Philadelphia: University of Pennsylvania Press.

Coomaraswamy, Radhika. 1996. Report on the Mission to the Democratic People's Republic of Korea, the Republic of Korea and Japan on the Issue of Military Sexual Slavery in Wartime. U.N. Doc.E/CN.4/1996/53/Add.1, January 4.

Copelon, Rhonda. 1995. Gendered War Crimes: Reconceptualizing Rape in Time of War. In *Women's Rights, Human Rights: International Feminist Perspectives*, ed. Julie Peters and Andrea Wolper. Pp. 197–215. New York: Routledge.

Corbin, Alain. 1990. *Women for Hire: Prostitution and Sexuality in France after 1850*. Trans. Alan Sheridan. Cambridge, MA: Harvard University Press.

Cowan, Jane K. 2001. Ambiguities of an Emancipatory Discourse: The Making of a Macedonian Minority in Greece. In *Culture and Rights: Anthropological Perspectives*, ed. Jane K. Cowan, Marie-Benedicte Dembour and Richard A. Wilson. Pp. 152–176. Cambridge: Cambridge University Press.

———. 2006. An Obligation to "Support Human Rights" Unconditionally Is Misguided M oralism. *Anthropology News* 47 (7): 7.

Cumings, Bruce. 1984a. The Origins and Development of the Northeast Asian Political Economy: Industrial Sectors, Product Cycle and Political Consequence. *International Organization*: 1–40.

———. 1984b. The Legacy of Japanese Colonialism in Korea. In *The Japanese Colonial Empire, 1895–1945*, ed. Ramon H. Myers and Mark R. Peattie. Pp. 478–496. Princeton, NJ: Princeton University Press.

———. 1992. Silent but Deadly: Sexual Subordination in the U.S.-Korean Relationship. In *Let the Good Times Roll: Prostitution and the U.S. Military in Asia*, Saundra Pollock Sturdevant and Brenda Stoltzfus. Pp. 169–175. New York: New Press.

———. 1997. *Korea's Place in the Sun: A Modern History*. New York: W. W. Norton.

CY and HCTH. *See* Chŏngsindae Yŏn'guhoe and Han'guk Chŏngsindae-munje Taech'aek Hyŏpŭihoe.

Dalby, Liza. 1998/1983. *Geisha*. Berkeley: University of California Press.

Delaney, Carol Lowery. 1991. *The Seed and the Soil: Gender and Cosmology in Turkish Village Society.* Berkeley: University of California Press.

Deuchler, Martina. 2003. Propagating Female Virtues in Chosŏn Korea. In *Women and Confucian Cultures in Premodern China, Korea, and Japan,* ed. Dorothy Ko, Jahyun Kim Haboush, and Joan R. Piggott. Pp. 142–169. Berkeley: University of California Press.

Dieng, Adama. 1994. Preface to U. Dolgopol and S. Paranjape, *Comfort Women: An Unfinished Ordeal.* Pp. 7–9. Geneva, Switzerland: International Commission of Jurists.

Dolgopol, Ustinia, and Snehal Paranjape. 1994. *Comfort Women: An Unfinished Ordeal.* Report of a Mission. Geneva: International Commission of Jurists.

Dōshisha Daigaku Asano Ken'ichi Zemi, ed. 1999. *Nanumu no Ie o Tazunete: Nihongun Ianfu kara Mananda Sensō Sekinin* (Visiting the House of Sharing: War Responsibility Learned from Japanese Military Comfort Women). Tokyo: Gendaijinbunsha.

Douglas, George H. 1986. *Women of the 20s.* San Francisco: Saybrook.

Douglass, Ana. 2003. The Menchú Effect: Strategic Lies and Approximate Truths in Texts of Witness. In *Witness and Memory: The Discourse of Trauma,* ed. Ana Douglass and Thomas A. Vogler. Pp. 55–87. New York: Routledge.

Dutch Government. 1994. Report of a Study of Dutch Government Documents on the Forced Prostitution of Dutch Women in the Dutch East Indies during the Japanese Occupation (Verslag van de Resultaten van een Onderzoek in Nederlandse Overheidsarchieven naar Gedwongen Prostitutie van Nederlandse Vrouwen in Nederlands-Indie tijdens de Japanse Bezetting). The Hague: Dutch Government.

Duus, Masayo. 1979. *Haisha no Okurimono* (Gifts of the Vanquished). Tokyo: Kōdansha.

Eckert, Carter. 1991. *Offspring of Empire: The Koch'ang Kims and the Origins of Korean Capitalism.* Seattle: University of Washington Press.

Edelman, Murray. 1985. *The Symbolic Uses of Politics,* with a new afterword. Urbana and Chicago: University of Illinois Press.

Editorial Committee for the 1992 Kyoto "Teach Us! 'Comfort Women' Information Telephone" Report, ed. 1993. *Sei to Sinryaku* (Sex and Invasion). Tokyo: Shakaihyōronsha.

England, Paula. 2005. Emerging Theories of Care Work. *Annual Review of Sociology* 31: 381–399.

Executive Committee for the International Public Hearing. 1993. *War Victimization and Japan: International Public Hearing Report.* Osaka: Tōhō Shuppan.

Fairbank, John K., Edwin O. Reischauer, and Albert M. Craig. 1989. *East Asia: Tradition and Transformation.* Rev. ed. Boston: Houghton Mifflin.

Farmer, Paul. 2002. On Suffering and Structural Violence: A View from Below. *The Anthropology of Politics,* ed. Joan Vincent. Pp. 424–437. Oxford: Blackwell.

Farmer, Paul, Margaret Connors, and Janie Simmons, eds. 1996. *Women, Poverty, and AIDS: Sex, Drugs, and Structural Violence*. Monroe, ME: Common Courage Press.

Fass, Paula S. 1977. *The Damned and the Beautiful: American Youth in the 1920s*. New York: Oxford University Press.

Firth, Raymond. 1954. Social Organization and Social Change. *Journal of the Royal Anthropological Institute* 84: 1–20.

Fox, R. G., ed. *Recapturing Anthropology: Working in the Present*. Santa Fe, NM: School of American Research Press.

Forgacs, David, ed. 2000. *The Antonio Gramsci Reader: Selected Writings, 1916–1935*. New York: New York University Press.

Foucault, Michel. 1980. *Power/Knowledge: Selected Interviews and Other Writings, 1972–1977*. Ed. Colin Gordon. Trans. Colin Gordon, Leo Marchall, John Mepham, and Kate Soper. New York: Pantheon Books.

———. 1990. *The History of Sexuality*. Volume 1: An Introduction. Trans. Robert Hurley. New York: Vintage Books.

———. 2003. "Society Must Be Defended": Lectures at the Collège de France, 1975–1976. Ed. Mauro Bertani and Alessandro Fontana. Trans. David Macey. New York: Picador.

Friedman, Elizabeth. 1995. Women's Human Rights: The Emergence of a Movement. In *Women's Rights, Human Rights: International Perspectives,* ed. Julie Peters and Andrea Wolper. Pp. 18–35. New York: Routledge.

Frühstück, Sabine. 2003. *Colonizing Sex: Sexology and Social Control in Modern Japan*. Berkeley: University of California Press.

Fujime, Yuki. 1997. The Licensed Prostitution System and the Prostitution Abolition Movement in Modern Japan. *positions: east asia cultures critique* 5(1): 135–170.

———. 1999. Reisen Taisei Keiseiki no Beigun to Seibōryoku (The U.S. Military and Sexual Violence during the Formational Period of the Cold War System). In *Josei, Sensō, Jinken* 2: 116–138. Tokyo: Kōrosha.

———. 2001. Nihonjin "Ianfu" o Fukashi ni Surumono (The Thing That Renders Japanese "Comfort Women" Invisible). In *Sabakareta Senji Seibōryoku* (Wartime Sexual Violence Judged), ed. Nishino Rumiko and Kim Puja. Pp. 88–108. Tokyo: Hakutakusha.

Fujinaga, Takeshi. 2006. Sanghai ŭi Ilbon'gun Wianso wa Chosŏnin (Japanese Military Comfort Stations in Shanghai and Koreans). In *Haebangchŏnhusa ŭi Chaeinsik* (A New Understanding of the Pre- and Post-liberation History), ed. Pak Chi-hyang, Kim Chŏl, Kim Il-yŏng, and Rhee Younghoon. Pp. 295–386. Seoul: Ch'aeksesang.

Fujioka, Nobukatsu. 1996. *Ojoku no Kin'gendaishi: Ima, Kokufuku no Toki* (Shameful Modern History: Now, Time to Overcome). Tokyo: Tokuma Shoten.

———. 1997. *Jigyakushikan no Byōri* (An Analysis of Masochistic Historical Views in Japan. Tokyo: Bungeishunjū.

Fulton, Bruce. 1998. Kijich'on Fiction. In *Nationalism and the Construction of Korean Identity,* ed. Hyung Il Pai and Timothy R. Tangherlini. Pp. 198–213. Berkeley: Institute of East Asian Studies, University of California, Berkeley.

Galtung, J. 1969. Violence, Peace and Peace Research. *Journal of Peace Research* 167–191.

Garon, Sheldon. 1993. The World's Oldest Debate? Prostitution and the State in Imperial Japan, 1900–1945. *American Historical Review* 98 (3): 710–732.

———. 1997. *Molding Japanese Minds: The State in Everyday Life.* Princeton, NJ: Princeton University Press.

Geller, Jay. 2002. The Wilkomirski Case: *Fragments* or Figments? *American Imago* 59 (3): 343–365.

Geertz, Clifford. 1983. *Local Knowledge: Further Essays in Interpretive Anthropology.* New York: Basic Books.

Ginsburg, Faye D. 1989. *Contested Lives: The Abortion Debate in an American Community.* Berkeley: University of California Press.

Giobbe, Evelina. 1991. Prostitution: Buying the Right to Rape. In *Rape and Sexual Assault III: A Research Handbook,* ed. Ann W. Burgess. Pp. 143–160. New York: Garland.

Gluck, Carol. 2002. Kioku no Sayō (Operations of Memory). In *Kanjō, Kioku, Sensō* (Emotion, Memory, War). Tokyo: Iwanami Shoten.

Goldberg, Dan. 2002. Holocaust Fact or Fraud? *Australian Jewish News,* November 1.

Goos, Jos. 1995. *Gevoelloos op bevel* (On Command without Feeling). Utrecht: Het Spectrum.

Griffin, W. E. B. 1990. *Counterattack, The Corps,* Book III. New York: Jove ed., Berkeley Publishing Group.

Grinker, Roy Richard. 1998. *Korea and Its Futures: Unification and the Unfinished War.* New York: St. Martin's Press.

Gruenbaum, Ellen. 2001. *The Female Circumcision Controversy: An Anthropological Perspective.* Philadelphia: University of Pennsylvania Presss.

Gunther, John. *Inside Asia.* New York: Harper, 1938.

Ha, Il-sik. 1998. *Yŏnp'yo wa Sajin ŭro Ponŭn Han'guksa* (Korean History Seen through Chronological Tables and Pictures). Seoul: Ilpit.

Hakkiri-kai. *See* Nihon no Sengo Sekinin o Hakkiri Saseru Kai.

Hamada, Tomoko. 2002. Contested Memories of the Imperial Sun: History Textbook Controversy in Japan. *American Asian Review* 20 (4): 1–37.

Han'guk Chŏngsindae Yŏn'guso. 2000. *Halmŏni Kunwianbu ga Mwŏyeyo?* (Grandmother, What Are Military Comfort Women?). Seoul: Hangyŏre Sinmunsa.

Han'guk Chŏngsindae Yŏn'guso and Han'guk Chŏngsindae-munje Taech'aek Hyŏpǔihoe, eds. 1999. *Chǔngŏnjip: Kangjero Kkǔllyŏgan Chosŏnin Kunwianpudǔl*

3. (Collection of Testimonies: Forcibly Dragged Away Korean Military Comfort Women 3). Seoul: Hanul.

Han'guk Chŏngsindae-munje Taech'aek Hyŏpŭihoe. 1992. *Chŏngsindae Charyojip II* (Collection of Reference Materials on Chŏngsindae II). Seoul: The author.

————. 2001. *Kangjero Kkŭllyŏgan Chosŏnin Kunwianpudŭl 4: Kiŏk ŭro Tasi Ssŭnŭn Yŏksa*. (Forcibly Dragged Away Korean Military Comfort Women 4: History Rewritten with Memory). Seoul: P'ulpit.

Han'guk Chŏngsindae-munje Taech'aek Hyŏpŭihoe and Chŏngsindae Yŏn'guhoe, eds. 1993. *Chŭngŏnjip 1: Kangjero Kkŭllyŏgan Chosŏnin Kunwianpudŭl* (Collection of Testimonies 1: Forcibly Dragged Away Korean Military Comfort Women). Seoul: Hanul.

Han'guk Chŏngsindae-munje Taech'aek Hyŏpŭihoe and Han'guk Chŏngsindae Yŏn'guhoe, eds. 1997. *Chŭngŏnjip: Kangjero Kkŭllyŏgan Chosŏnin Kunwianpudŭl 2*. (Collection of Testimonies: Forcibly Dragged Away Korean Military Comfort Women 2). Seoul: Hanul.

————, eds. 2001. *Chŭngŏnjip: Kangje-ro Kkŭllyŏogan Chosŏnin Kunwianpudŭl 5*. (Collection of Testimonies: Forcibly Dragged Away Korean Military Comfort Women 5). Seoul: P'ulbit.

Han'guk Chŏngsindae-munje Taech'aek Hyŏpŭihoe and PCA Korea-Japan Lawyers' Group. 1995. *Ilbon'gun "Wianbu" Munje ŭi Kukjebŏpjŏk Haekyŏl ŭl Wihayŏ* (For the Resolution of Japanese Military "Comfort Women" Issue According to International Law). Seoul: The authors.

Han'guk Chŏngsindae-munje Taech'aek Hyŏpŭihoe and Yŏsŏngbu. 2002. *Ilbon'gun "Wianbu" Chŭngŏn T'onggye Charyojip* (Collection of Statistical Data from the Testimonials of the "Comfort Women" for the Japanese Military). Seoul: The authors.

Han'guk Chŏngsindae-munje Taech'aek Hyŏpŭihoe-pusŏl Chŏnjaeng kwa Yŏsŏnginkwŏn Sentŏ Yŏn'gutim. 2004. *Yŏksa rŭl Mandŭnŭn Iyagi: Ilbongun "Wianbu" Yŏsŏngdŭl ŭi Kyŏnghŏm kwa Kiŏk* (Stories That Make History: Experiences and Memories of Japanese Military *Wianbu* Women). Seoul: Yŏsŏng kwa Inkwŏn.

Han'guk Kyohoe Yŏsŏng Yŏnhaphoe, ed. 1983. *Kisaeng Kwankwang* (*Kisaeng*Tourism). Seoul: The author.

Han'guk Yŏsŏng Kaebalwŏn. 1997. *Yŏsŏng T'onggye Yŏnbo* (Annals of Statistics on Women). Seoul: The author.

Haraway, Donna. 1988. Situated Knowledge: The Science Question in Feminism and the Privilege of Partial Perspective. *Feminist Studies* 14: 575–599.

————. 1991. *Simians, Cyborgs, and Women: The Reinvention of Nature*. New York: Routledge.

Harris, Marvin. 1999. *Theories of Culture in Postmodern Times*. Walnut Creek, CA: Altamira Press.

Harootunian, Harry. 2000. *Overcome by Modernity: History, Culture, and Community in Interwar Japan.* Princeton, NJ: Princeton University Press.

Harumoni no Kaigaten Jikkō Iinkai, ed. 1999. *Harumoni no Kaigaten* (Harumoni's Painting Exhibition). Tokyo: Nashinokisha.

Harvey, Youngsook Kim. 1983. Minmyŏnŭri: The Daughter-in-Law Who Comes of Age in Her Mother-in-Law's Household. In *Korean Women: A View from the Inner Room,* ed. Laurel L. Kendall and Mark Peterson. Pp. 45–61. New Haven, CT: East Rock Press.

Hata, Ikuhiko. 1996. The Flawed U.N. Report on Comfort Women. *Japan Echo,* Autumn, 66–73.

———. 1999. *Ianfu to Senjō no Sei* (Comfort Women and Sex in the Battlefield). Tokyo: Shinchosha.

———. 2007. No Organized or Forced Recruitment: Misconceptions about Comfort Women and the Japanese Military. Revised English version of the essay first published in *Shokun,* May. Trans. Society for the Dissemination of Historical Fact, Tokyo.

Havens, Thomas R. 1975. Women and War in Japan, 1937–45. *American Historical Review* 80 (4): 913–934.

———. 1978. *Valley of Darkness: The Japanese People and World War Two.* New York: W. W. Norton.

HCTH. *See* Han'guk Chŏngsindae-munje Taech'aek Hyŏpŭihoe.

HCTH and CY. *See* Han'guk Chŏngsindae-munje Taech'aek Hyŏpŭihoe and Chŏngsindae Yŏn'guhoe.

HCTH and HCY. *See* Han'guk Chŏngsindae-munje Taech'aek Hyŏpŭihoe and Han'guk Chŏngsindae Yŏn'guhoe.

HCTH-CYSY. *See* Han'guk Chŏngsindae-munje Taech'aek Hyŏpŭihoe-pusŏl Chŏnjaeng kwa Yŏsŏnginkwŏn Sentŏ Yŏn'gutim.

HCTH and Yŏsŏngbu. *See* Han'guk Chŏngsindae-munje Taech'aek Hyŏpŭihoe and Yŏsŏngbu.

Hegel, Georg Wilhelm Friedrich. 1977. *Phenomenology of Spirit.* Trans. A. V. Miller. Oxford: Oxford University Press.

Hein, Laura. 1999. Savage Irony: The Imaginative Power of the "Military Comfort Women" in the 1990s. *Gender & History* 11 (2): 336–372.

Hein, Laura, and Mark Selden, eds. 2000. *Censoring History: Citizenship and Memory in Japan, Germany, and the United States.* Armonk, NY: M. E. Sharpe.

Henson, Maria Rosa. 1996. *Comfort Woman: Slave of Destiny,* with illustrations by the author. Ed. Sheila S. Coronel. Manila: Philippine Center for Investigative Journalism.

Herdt, Gilbert. 1997. *Same Sex, Different Cultures: Exploring Gay & Lesbian Lives.* Boulder, CO: Westview Press.

Hershatter, Gail. 1997. *Dangerous Pleasures: Prostitution and Modernity in Twentieth-century Shanghai*. Berkeley: University of California Press.

Hicks, George. 1995. *Wianbu: Ilbon'gundae ŭi Sŏngnoye ro Kkŭllyŏgan Yŏsŏngdŭl*. Trans. K. J. Chŏn and E. A. Sŏng. Seoul: Ch'angjak kwa Pip'yŏng. Published in English as *The Comfort Women: Japan's Brutal Regime of Enforced Prostitution in the Second World War* (New York: W. W. Norton, 1995).

Hirota, Kazuko. 1975. *Shōgen Kiroku: Jūgun Ianfu/Kangofu* (Testimonial Records: Military Comfort Women/Nurses). Tokyo: Shinjinbutsuōraisha.

HKJI. *See* Harumoni no Kaigaten Jikkō Iinkai.

Ho, Samuel Pao-San. 1987 Colonialism and Development: Korea, Taiwan, and Kwantung. In *The Japanese Colonial Empire, 1895–1945*, ed. Ramon H. Myers and Mark R. Peattie. Pp. 347–398. Princeton, NJ: Princeton University Press.

Howard, Keith, ed. 1995. *True Stories of the Korean Comfort Women*. London: Cassell.

Hsu, Yvonne Park. 1993. "Comfort Women" from Korea: Japan's World War II Sex Slaves and the Legitimacy of their Claims for Reparations. *Pacific Rim Law & Policy Journal* 2 (1): 97–129.

Hua, Vanessa. 2005. Korean Online Newspaper Enlists Army of "Citizen Reporters." *San Francisco Chronicle*, September 18.

Hyegyŏnggung Hong Ssi. 1996. *The Memoirs of Lady Hyegyŏng: The Autobiographical Writings of a Crown Princess of Eighteenth-Century Korea*. Trans. JaHyun Kim Haboush. Berkeley: University of California Press.

Hyejin. 1997. *Na Naeil Demo Kandei* (I'm Going to the Demonstration Tomorrow). Seoul: Taewŏnsa.

Ienaga, Saburo. 1978. *The Pacific War: World War II and the Japanese, 1931–1945*. Trans. Frank Baldwin. New York: Pantheon Books. Originally published as *Taiheiyō Sensō* (Tokyo: Iwanami Shoten, 1968).

Ilbon'gun "Wianbu" Munje Yŏn'gumoim. 1997. *Ilbon'gun "Wianbu" Munje ŭi Hyŏnhwang kwa Haegyŏlpang'an* (The Status and Resolution Measures for Japanese Military "Comfort Women" Issue). Seoul: The author.

Iritani, Toshiro. 1991. *Group Psychology of the Japanese in Wartime*. London and New York: Kegan Paul International.

Ito, Takashi. 1994. *Hin Otkorŭm Ip e Mulgo* (Holding a White Dress Ribbon in the Mouth). Seoul: Nunpit.

———. 1999. Nihonkaigun "Ianjo" no Rekishiteki Hakken (An Historic Discovery of the Comfort Station of the Japanese Navy). In *Kyōwakoku Chōsahōkokusho* (Report on the Investigation in the Republic). Pp. 24–35. Nagoya, Japan: Madang 21.

Janelli, Roger L., and Dawnhee Yim Janelli. 1982. *Ancestor Worship and Korean Society*. Stanford, CA: Stanford University Press.

Jansen, Marius B. 1995. *Japan and its World: Two Centuries of Change*. Princeton, NJ: Princeton University Press.

Japan Anti-Prostitution Association. 1995. *Against Prostitution and Sexual Exploitation in Japan*. Tokyo: The author.

Jayawardena, Kumari. 1986. *Feminism and Nationalism in the Third World*. London: Zed Books.

Jeffery, Anthea. 1999. *The Truth about the Truth Commission*. Johannesburg: South African Institute of Race Relations.

Jenkins, Donald, ed. 1993. *The Floating World Revisited*. Portland, OR: Portland Art Museum in Association with University of Hawai'i Press.

Johnson, Carol. 1996. Does Capitalism Really Need Patriarchy?: Some Old Issues Reconsidered. *Women's Studies International Forum* 19 (3): 193–202.

Johnson, Chalmers, ed. 1999. *Okinawa: Cold War Island*. Cardiff, CA: Japan Policy Research Institute.

———. 1999. The 1995 Rape Incident and the Rekindling of Okinawan Protest against the American Bases. In *Okinawa: Cold War Island,* ed. Chalmers Johnson. Pp. 109–129. Cardiff, CA: Japan Policy Research Institute.

Jūgun Ianfu 110 Ban Henshūiinkai, ed. 1992. *Jūgun Ianfu 110 Ban* (Military Comfort Women Hotline). Tokyo: Akashi Shoten.

Kaneda, Kimiko. 1996. *Ashiato Hitotsu Hitotsu ni Namida ga Nijimu* (Teardrops with Each Footstep). Tokyo: "Ianfu" Mondai o Kangaeru Tokōkyō Yūshi Nettowāku.

Kang, Chi-ŏn. 1999. Nae Ttal a, Irŏke Charadao (My Daughter, I Want You to Grow Up like This). In *Uri Nara Yŏsŏngdŭl ŭn Ŏttŏtke Saratsŭlkka 1* (How Did Our Nation's Women Live Their Lives 1), ed. Yi Pae-yong et al. Pp. 88–97. Seoul: Ch'ŏngnyŏnsa.

Kang, Man-gil. 1997a. Ch'aek ŭl Naemyŏnsŏ (Preface). In *Ilbon'gun "Wianbu" Munje ŭi Chinsang* (The Truth of the Japanese Military "Comfort Women" Problem), ed. Han'guk Chŏngsindaemunje Taech'aek Hyŏpŭihoe Chinsangchosa Yŏn'guhoe. Pp. 3–5. Seoul: Yŏksabip'yŏngsa.

———. 1997b. Ilbon'gun "Wianbu" ŭi Kaenyŏm kwa Hoch'ing Munje (The Problems of the Concept and Address Term for the Japanese Military "Comfort Women"). In *Ilbon'gun "Wianbu" Munje ŭi Chinsang* (The Truth of the Japanese Military "Comfort Women" Problem), ed. Han'guk Chŏngsindae-munje Taech'aek Hyŏpŭihoe Chinsangchosa Yŏn'guhoe. Pp. 11–36. Seoul: Yŏksabip'yŏngsa.

Kang, Sŏn-mi, and Yamashita Yŏngae. 1993. Ch'ŏnhwangje Kukka wa Sŏngp'ongnyŏk (The Emperor System State and Sexual Violence). *Han'guk Yŏsŏnghak* (Korean Women's Studies), vol. 9.

Kang, Yong-kwŏn. 2000. *Kangje Chingyongja wa Chonggunwianbu ŭi Chŭngŏn* (Testimonies of the Forced Conscripts and Military Comfort Women). Seoul: Haewadal.

Kase, Hideaki, and Ogata Yoshiaki. 2007. Arguing the Point: 2. *Number 1 Shimbun* 39 (5): 10.

Kawata, Fumiko. 1992. *Ppalgan Kiwajip: Chosŏn esŏ On Chonggunwianbu Iyagi* (House with a Red Tile Roof: The Story of a Military Comfort Woman from Korea). Trans. Han U-chŏng. Seoul: Maeilkyŏngje Sinmunsa.

——. 1997. *Indonesia no "Ianfu"* (Indonesian Comfort Women). Tokyo: Akashi Shoten.

KCWU. *See* Korean Church Women United.

Keller, Nora Okja. 1997. *Comfort Woman.* New York: Penguin Books.

Kendall, Laurel. 1985. *Shamans, Housewives, and Other Restless Spirits: Women in Korean Ritual Life.* Honolulu: University of Hawai'i Press.

Kim, Chin-song. 2004/1999. *Sŏul e Ttansŭhol ŭl Hŏhara* (Allow the Dance Hall in Seoul). Seoul: Hyŏnsilmunhwayŏn'gu.

Kim, Choong Soon. 1992. *The Culture of Korean Industry: An Ethnography of Poongsan Corporation.* Tucson: University of Arizona Press.

Kim, Chun-seon. 2004. The Settlement and Repatriation of Koreans in Northeast China after Liberation. *Korea Journal* 44 (4): 85–110.

Kim, Chu-ri. 2005. *Modŏn Gŏl, Yŏu Moktori rŭl Pŏryŏra* (Modern Girl, Discard the Fox-Fur Stole). Seoul: Sallim.

Kim, Elaine H. 1987. Sex Tourism in Asia: A Reflection of Political and Economic Inequality. In *Korean Women in Transition: At Home and Abroad,* ed. E-Y. Yu and E. H. Phillips. Pp. 127–144. Los Angeles: Center for Korean-American and Korean Studies, California State University–Los Angeles.

——. 2003. *Teumsae-eso:* Korean American Women between Feminism and Nationalism. In *Violence and the Body: Race, Gender, and the State,* ed. Arturo J. Aldama. Pp. 311–321. Bloomington: Indiana University Press.

Kim, Elaine H., and Chungmoo Choi, eds. 1998. *Dangerous Women: Gender and Korean Nationalism.* New York: Routledge.

Kim, Eun-sil. 1994. Minjok Tamnon kwa Yŏsŏng (Nationalist Discourse and Women). *Han'guk Yosŏnghak* (Korean Women's Studies) 9: 18–52.

Kim, Hŭi-o. 2000. *In'gan ŭi Hyanggi: Chayuminju/Taegongt'ujaeng kwa Hamkkehan Insaengyŏkchŏng* (The Aroma of Humanity: Life Trajectory That Accompanied the Liberal Democracy/Anti-Communism Struggle). Seoul: Wŏnmin.

Kim, Hye-su. 1999. Sijang e Kamyŏn Chŏnbu Yŏin Ppun Ida (In the Market All You See Are Women). In *Uri Nara Yŏsŏngdŭl ŭn Ŏttŏtke Saratsŭlkka 2* (How Did Our Nation's Women Live Their Lives 2), ed. Yi Pae-yong et al. Pp. 39–49. Seoul: Ch'ŏngnyŏnsa.

Kim, Hye-wŏn. 1999. Kongnyŏ wa Hwanhyangnyŏ. In *Uri Nara Yŏsŏngdŭl ŭn Ŏttŏtke Saratsŭlkka 1* (How Did Our Nation's Women Live Their Lives 1), ed. Yi Pae-yong et al. Pp. 226–236. Seoul: Ch'ŏngnyŏnsa.

Kim, Hyŏn-sŏn. 1997. *Kijich'on, Kijich'on Yŏsŏng, Honhyŏradong: Silt'ae wa Sarye* (Camp Town, Camp-Town Women, Mixed-Blood Children: Reality and Cases). Tongduch'ŏn, Kyŏnggi Province, ROK: Saeumt'ŏ.

Kim, Hyun Sook. 1997. History and Memory: The "Comfort Women" Controversy. *positions: east asia cultures critique* 5 (1): 73–106.

Kim, Il-myŏn. 1976. *Tenno no Guntai to Chōsenjin Ianfu* (The Emperor's Forces and Korean Comfort Women). Tokyo: San'ichi Shobō.

———. 1997. *Yūjo, Karayuki, Ianfu no Keibo* (The Genealogy of *Yūjo, Karayuki,* and Comfort Women). Tokyo: Yūzankaku Shuppan.

Kim, Janice. 2007. The Pacific War and Working Women in Late Colonial Korea. *Signs: Journal of Women in Culture and Society* 33 (1): 81–103.

Kim, Kwi-ok. 2002. Han'guk Chŏnjaeng kwa Yŏsŏng: Kunwianbu wa Kunwianso rŭl Chungsimŭro (The Korean War and Women: With a Focus on Military Comfort Women and Military Comfort Stations). Paper presented at the Fifth International Symposium on Peace and Human Rights in East Asia, February 22–25, Kyoto, Ritsumeikan University.

Kim, Mun-suk, ed. 1990. *Malsaldoen Myobi—Yŏja Chŏngsindae* (Extirpated Tombstones—Women's Volunteer Labor Corps). Pusan: Chipyŏng.

———. 1992. *Chōsenjin Guntai Ianfu* (Korean Military Comfort Women). Tokyo: Akashi Shoten.

———. 1994. *Ch'ŏnhwang ŭi Myŏnjoebu* (The Emperor's Acquittal). Pusan: Chipyŏng.

———, ed. 1997. *Ilbon eŭi Kyŏnggo* (Warning to Japan). Pusan: Sinan.

———. 2001. *Ssŭrŏjinja ŭi Kido* (Prayers of the Fallen). Pusan: Purŭnpyŏl.

Kim, Myŏng-hye. 2004. Sŏmun: Kiŏk ŭi Chŏngch'ihwa rŭl Sidohamyŏ (Preface: Attempting a Politicization of Memory). In *Yŏksa rŭl Mandŭnŭn Iyagi: Ilbon'gun "Wianbu" Yŏsŏngdŭl ŭi Kyŏnghŏm kwa Kiŏk* (Stories That Make History: Experiences and Memories of Japanese Military *Wianbu* Women), ed. HCTH-CYSY. Pp. 5–9. Seoul: Yŏsŏng kwa Inkwŏn.

Kim, Ok-gil et al. 1972. *Han'guk Yŏsŏngsa* (History of Korean Women). Seoul: Ewha Womans University Press.

Kim, Richard. 1998. *Lost Names: Scenes from a Korean Boyhood*. Berkeley and Los Angeles: Univerisity of California Press.

Kim, Tae-sang. 1975. *Ilcheha Kangje Illyŏk Sut'alsa* (A History of the Exploitation of Forced Labor under Imperial Japan). Seoul: Chŏngŭmsa.

Kim, Tŏk-sŏng. 1970. Migyŏl 25 Nyŏn: Chŏngsindae (Unresolved for 25 Years: The Volunteer Labor Corps). *Seoul Sinmun*, August 14.

Kim, Yŏl-kyu. 1981. *Hanmaek Wŏllyu* (The Ore of *Han,* the Stream of *Wŏn*). Seoul: Chuu.

Kim, Yong-su. 1995. *Hanil 50 Nyŏn ŭn Ch'ŏngsan Toeŏtnŭn'ga* (Has the 50-Year Korea-Japan Relationship Been Settled?). Seoul: Koryowŏn.

Kim, Yung-Chung, ed. & trans. 1979. *Women of Korea: A History from Ancient Times to 1945*. Seoul: Ewha Womans University Press.

Kim, Yung-Hee. 1994a. Women's Literature in the Chosŏn Period: *Han* and the Songs of Women. In *Korean Studies: New Pacific Currents*, ed. Dae-Sook Suh. Pp. 101–112. Honolulu: Center for Korean Studies, University of Hawai'i.

———. 1994b. Women's Issues in 1920s Korea. *Korean Culture* 15 (2): 27–33.

———. 2002. Creating New Paradigms of Womanhood in Modern Korean Literature: Na Hye-sŏk's "Kyŏnghŭi." *Korean Studies* 26 (1): 1–60.

Kim-Gibson, Dai Sil. 1999a. *Silence Broken: Korean Comfort Women*. Parkersburg, IA: Mid-Prairie Books.

———, prod. and dir. 1999b. *Silence Broken: Korean Comfort Women*. VHS/35mm film. Ho-Ho-Kus, NJ: Dai Sil Productions.

Knauft, Bruce M., ed. 2002. *Critically Modern: Alternatives, Alterities, Anthropologies*. Bloomington: Indiana University Press.

K.N.C. for UNESCO. 1983/1974. *Virtuous Women: Three Classic Korean Novels*. Trans. Richard Rutt and Chong-un Kim. Seoul: Royal Asiatic Society Korea Branch.

Kondo, Dorinne. 1990. *Crafting Selves: Power, Gender, and Discourses of Identity in a Japanese Workplace*. Chicago: University of Chicago Press.

Korean Church Women United (Han'guk Kyohoe Yŏsŏng Yŏnhaphoe). 1983. *Kisaeng Kwankwang* (*Kisaeng* Tourism). KCWU Research Material Issue No. 1. Seoul: The author.

Korean Ministry of Education and Human Resources. 2002a/1996. *Kodŭnghakkyo Kuksa (Ha)* (High-School National History, vol. 2). Seoul: Taehan Kyokwasŏ Chusikhoesa.

Korean Ministry of Education and Human Resources. 2002b/1997. *Chunghakkyo Kuksa (Ha)* (Middle-School National History, vol. 2). Seoul: Taehan Kyokwasŏ Chusikhoesa.

Korean Ministry of Education and Human Resources. 2002c. *Chunghakkyo Kuksa* (Middle-School National History). Seoul: Taehan Kyokwasŏ Chusikhoesa.

Kurihara, Nanako, prod. and dir. 1993. *Ripples of Change: Japanese Women's Search for Self*. VHS/16mm film. U.S./Japan.

Kuwayama, Takami. 2004. *Native Anthropology: The Japanese Challenge to Western Academic Hegemony*. Melbourne, Australia: Trans Pacific Press.

KWDI (Korea Women's Development Institute). *See* Han'guk Yŏsŏng Kaebalwŏn.

Kwŏn, Sun-hyŏng. 1999. Koryŏsidae Yŏsŏng ŭi Kyubŏm kwa Saenghwal (The Norms and Lives of Koryŏ Women). In *Uri Yŏsong ŭi Yŏksa* (Our Women's History), ed. Han'guk Yŏsŏngyŏn'guso Yŏsŏngsayŏn'gusil. Pp. 135–162. Seoul: Ch'ŏngnyŏnsa.

Lamont-Brown, Raymond. 1998. *Kempeitai: Japan's Dreaded Military Police*. United Kingdom: Sutton.

Lee, Chang-rae. 1999. *A Gesture Life*. New York: Riverhead Books.

Lee, Chong-sik. 1985. *Japan and Korea: The Political Dimension*. Stanford, CA: Hoover Institution Press, Stanford University.

Lee, Hyo-chae. 1997. Ilbon'gun "Wianbu" Munje Haegyŏl ŭl Wihan Undong ŭi Chŏn'gaekwajŏng (The Developmental Process of the Movement for the Resolution of the Japanese Military "Comfort Women" Issue). In *Ilbon'gun "Wianbu" Munje ŭi Chinsang* (The Truth of the Japanese Military "Comfort Women" Problem), ed. Han'guk Chŏngsindae-munje Taech'aek Hyŏpŭihoe Chinsangchosa Yŏn'guhoe. Pp. 311–358. Seoul: Yŏksabip'yŏngsa.

Lee, Jae Hoon. 1994. *The Exploration of the Inner Wounds: Han.* American Academy of Religion Academy Series No. 86. Atlanta, GA: Scholars Press.

Lee, Jin-sook. 1993. The Murder of Yoon Geum Yi. *Korea Report.* Pp. 16–17.

Lee, Ki-baik. 1984. *A New History of Korea.* Trans. Edward Wagner. Seoul: Ilchokak.

Lee, Kwang-kyu, and Youngsook Kim Harvey. 1973. Teknonymy and Geononymy in Korean Kinship Terminology. *Ethnology* 12 (1): 31–46.

Lee, Yong Soo. 2007. Former Sex Slave, Arguing the Point: 1. *Number 1 Shimbun* 39 (5): 8.

Lee, Younghee. 2002. *Ideology, Culture, and Han: Traditional and Early Modern Korean Women's Literature.* Edison, NJ: Jimoondang International.

Lerner, Gerda. 1986a. *The Creation of Patriarchy.* New York: Oxford University Press.

———. 1986b. The Origin of Prostitution in Ancient Mesopotamia. *Signs: Journal of Women in Culture and Society* 11 (2): 236–254.

Levy, Robert. 1994. Person-Centered Anthropology. In *Assessing Cultural Anthropology,* ed. Robert Borofsky. Pp. 180–187. New York: McGraw-Hill.

Lie, John. 1997. The State as Pimp: Prostitution and the Patriarchal State in Japan in the 1940s. *Sociological Quarterly* 38 (2): 251–263.

———. 1998. *Han Unbound: The Political Economy of South Korea.* Stanford, CA: Stanford University Press.

Longstreet, Stephen, and Ethel Longstreet. 1970. *Yoshiwara: City of the Senses.* New York: David McKay.

Lutz, Caterine. 1988. *Unnatural Emotions: Everyday Sentiments on a Micronesian Atoll and Their Challenge to Western Theory.* Chicago: University of Chicago.

Mackie, Vera. 1998. Japayuki Cinderella Girl: Containing the Immigrant Other. *Japanese Studies* 18 (1): 45–63.

———. 2000. Sexual Violence, Silence, and Human Rights Discourse: The Emergence of the Military Prostitution Issue. In *Human Rights and Gender Politics: Asia-Pacific Perspectives,* ed. Anne-Marie Hilsdon, Martha Macintyre, Vera Mackie and Maila Stivens. Pp. 37–59. New York: Routledge.

———. 2003. *Feminism in Modern Japan.* Cambridge: Cambridge University Press.

MacKinnon, Catharine. 1993. Crimes of War, Crimes of Peace. In *On Human Rights,* ed. S. Shute and S. Hurley. Pp. 83–109. New York: Basic Books.

———. 1994. Turning Rape into Pornography: Postmodern Genocide. In *Mass Rape:*

The War against Women in Bosnia-Herzegovina, ed. Alexandra Stiglmayer. Trans. Marion Faber. Pp. 73–81. Lincoln: University of Nebraska Press.

Mahon, Michael. 1992. *Foucault's Nietzchean Genealogy: Truth, Power, and the Subject.* Albany: State University of New York Press.

Marcus, George E. 1998/1995. Ethnography in/of the World System: The Emergence of Multi-Sited Ethnography. *Annual Review of Anthropology* 24: 95–117. Reprinted in *Ethnography through Thick & Thin* (1998): 79–104. Princeton, NJ: Princeton University Press.

Marcus, George E., and Michael M. Fischer. 1986. *Anthropology as Cultural Critique: An Experimental Moment in the Human Sciences.* Chicago: University of Chicago Press.

Mascia-Lees, Frances E., Patricia Sharpe, and Colleen B. Cohen. 1989. The Postmodernist Turn in Anthropology: Cautions from a Feminist Perspective. *Signs: Journal of Women in Culture and Society* 15 (1): 7–23.

Matsui, Yayori. 1977. Sexual Slavery in Korea. *Frontiers: Anthropological Journal of Women's Studies* 2 (1) 22–30.

———. 1984. Why I Oppose Kisaeng Tours. In *International Feminism: Networking Against Female Sexual Slavery,* ed. K. Barry, C. Bunch, and S. Castley. Pp. 64–72. New York: International Women's Tribune Center.

———. 2000. "Josei Kokusai Senpan Hōtei" o Naze Hirakunoka (Why Hold a "Women's International War Crimes Tribunal"?) *Sensō Sekinin Genkyū* 28: 52–57.

McCarthy, Kathleen Louise. 1991. Kisaeng in the Koryŏ Period. Ph.D. diss., Harvard University.

McCormack, Gavan. 2000. The Japanese Movement to "Correct" History. In *Censoring History: Citizenship and Memory in Japan, Germany, and the United States,* ed. Laura Hein and Mark Selden. Armonk, NY: M. E. Sharpe.

McDougall, Gay J. 1998. Contemporary Forms of Slavery: Systematic Rape, Sexual Slavery and Slavery-like Practices during Armed Conflict. Final report submitted. UN Doc. E/CN.4/Sub. 2/1998/13, June 22, 1998. Appendix: An Analysis of the Legal Liability of the Government of Japan for "Comfort Women Stations" Established during the Second World War.

McNamara, Dennis L. 1990. *The Colonial Origins of Korean Enterprise, 1910–1945.* Cambridge: Cambridge University Press.

Messer, Ellen. 1993. Anthropology and Human Rights. *Annual Review of Anthropology* 22:221–249.

Mihalopoulos, Bill. 1993. The Making of Prostitutes: The Karayuki-san. *Bulletin of Concerned Asian Scholars* 25 (1): 41–56.

Miller, James. 1993. *The Passion of Michel Foucault.* New York: Simon & Schuster.

Mills, C. Wright. 1959. *The Sociological Imagination.* New York: Oxford University Press.

Mills, Sara. 2004. *Discourse*. New York: Routledge.

Min, Pyong Gap. 2003. Korean "Comfort Women": The Intersection of Colonial Power, Gender, and Class. *Gender & Society* 17 (6): 938–957.

Mitsui, Hideko. 2007. The Resignification of the "Comfort Women" through NGO Trials. In *Rethinking Historical Injustice and Reconciliation in Northeast Asia: The Korean Experience,* ed. Gi-Wook Shin, Soon-Won Park, and Daqing Yang. Pp. 36–54. London and New York: Routledge.

Miyake, Yoshiko. 1991. Doubling Expectations: Motherhood and Women's Factory Work Under State Management in Japan in the 1930s and 1940s. In *Recreating Japanese Women, 1600–1945,* ed. Gail Lee Bernstein. Pp. 267–295. Berkeley: University of California Press.

Mohanty, Chandra Talpade. 1991. Under Western Eyes: Feminist Scholarship and Colonial Discourses. In *Third World Women and the Politics of Feminism,* ed. Chandra Talpade Mohanty, Ann Russo, and Lourdes Torres. Pp. 1–47. Bloomington: Indiana University Press.

Mondschein, Ken. 2006. A History of Single Life. http://www.nerve.com/regulars/singlelife, January 11 (accessed October 14, 2007).

Montgomery, Heather. 2001. *Modern Babylon? Prostituting Children in Thailand.* New York: Berghahn Books.

Moon, Katharine H. S. 1997. *Sex among Allies: Military Prostitution in U.S.–Korea Relations.* New York: Columbia University Press.

Moon, Yumi. 2005. The Populist Contest: The Ilchinhoe Movement and the Japanese Colonization of Korea, 1896–1910. Ph.D. diss., Harvard University.

Morris-Suzuki, Tessa, and Peter Rimmer. 2002. Virtual Memories: Japanese History Debates in *Manga* and Cyberspace. *Asian Studies Review* 26 (2): 147–164.

Mun, Ch'ang-jae. 2001. *Hoejŏlkang* (River of Revived Chastity). *Han'guk Ilbo,* January 27.

Mun, Ok-chu. 1996. *Mun Oku-chu: Biruma Sensen Tateshidan no "Ianfu" Datta Watashi* (Mun Ok-chu: I Was a "Comfort Woman" of the Shield Division on the Burma Front). As told to Morikawa Machiko. Tokyo: Nashinokisha.

Mun, Ok-p'yo, et al. 2003. *Sinyŏsŏng: Han'guk kwa Ilbon ŭi Kŭndae Yŏsŏngsang* (New Woman: Images of Modern Women in Korea and Japan). Seoul: Ch'ŏngnyŏnsa.

Nah, Yŏng-gyun. 2004. *Ilchesidae Uri Kajok ŭn* (My Family during the Era of Imperial Japan). Seoul: Hwangsojari.

Nagengast, Carole, and Terence Turner. 1997. Introduction: Universal Human Rights Versus Cultural Relativity. *Journal of Anthropological Research* 53 (3): 269–272.

Nakasone, Yasuhiro. 1978. Nijūsansai de Sanzennin no Sōshikikan (Commander of 3,000 Men at Age Twenty-Three). In *Owarinaki Kaigun* (Everlasting Navy), ed. Matsūra Takanori. Tokyo: Bunka Hōsō Kaihatsu Sentā Shuppanbu.

National Campaign for Eradication of Crime by U.S. Troops in Korea. N.d. Cases of Crimes Committed by U.S. Militarymen. Unpublished document.

Naples, Nancy A. and Manisha Desai, eds. 2002. *Women's Activism and Globalization: Linking Local Struggles and Transnational Politics.* New York: Routledge.

Narayan, Kirin. 1997. How Native Is a "Native" Anthropologist? In *Situated Lives: Gender and Culture in Everyday Life,* ed. Louise Lamphere, Helena Ragoné, and Patricia Zavella. Pp. 23–41. New York: Routledge.

Nelson, John K. 2002. Tempest in a Textbook: A Report on the New Middle-School History Textbook in Japan. *Critical Asian Studies* 34 (1): 129–148.

Nihon no Sengo Sekinin o Hakkiri Saseru Kai. 1995. *Watashitachi no Ikiteiru Ma ni!* (While We Are Alive!). Tokyo: The author.

Nishino, Rumiko. 1992. *Jūgun Ianfu: Moto Heishitachi no Shōgen* (Military Comfort Women: Testimonies of Former Soldiers). Tokyo: Akashi Shoten.

———. 2000. Nihonjin "Ianfu" (Japanese "Comfort Women"). In *"Ianfu" Senji Seibōryoku no Jittai II* (The Actual Conditions of Wartime Sexual Violence against "Comfort Women" II), ed. VAWW-NET Japan. Pp. 66–91. Tokyo: Ryokufū Shuppan.

———. 2003. *Senjō no "Ianfu"* ("Comfort Women" of the Battlefield). Tokyo: Akashi Shoten.

Nishio, Kanji, et al. 2001. *Atarashii Rekishi Kyōkasho* (The New History Textbook). Tokyo: Fusōsha.

Nitta, Fumiteru. 1997. Japanese Women Who Crossed the Oceans: War Brides Reconsidered. *Journal of Kibi International University* 7: 165–175.

Nozaki, Yoshiko. 2002. Japanese Politics and the History Textbook Controversy, 1982–2001. *International Journal of Educational Research* 37: 603–622.

Offen, Karen. 2000. *European Feminisms, 1700–1950: A Political History.* Stanford, CA: Stanford University Press.

Oh, Bonnie B. C. 2003. Why Should Comfort Women Matter to You? *News from Washington Coalition for Comfort Women Issues* 8, p. 3 (June).

Ohnuki-Tierney, Emiko. 1984. "Native" Anthropologists. *American Ethnologist* 11 (3): 584–586.

———. 2006. *Kamikaze Diaries: Reflections of Japanese Soldiers.* Chicago: University of Chicago Press.

Oka, Mari. 2001. Words of the Other. *Traces* 2: 383–397.

Okura, Yayoi. 1996. Promoting Prostitution. In *Voices from the Japanese Women's Movement,* ed. AMPO-Japan Asia Quarterly Review. Pp. 111–114. Armonk, NY: M. E. Sharpe.

Onishi, Norimitsu. 2007. Call by U.S. House Resolution for Sex Slavery Apology Angers Japan's Leader. *New York Times,* August 1.

Orr, James J. 2001. *The Victim as Hero: Ideologies of Peace and National Identity in Postwar Japan.* Honolulu: University of Hawai'i Press.

Paek, Wu-am. 1989. *Chosŏn Yŏja Chŏngsindae* (Korean Women Chŏngsindae). Seoul: Minsŏngsa.

Pak, Chi-hyang, Kim Chŏl, Kim Il-yŏng, and Rhee Younghoon, eds. 2006. *Haebangchŏnhusa ŭi Chaeinsik* (A Rethinking of the Pre- and Post-liberation History). Seoul: Ch'aeksesang.

Pak, Chong-sŏng. 1996. *Kwŏllŏk kwa Maech'un* (Power and Prostitution). Seoul: In'gansarang.

Pak, Sŏn-yŏng, and Liu Bao Ch'un. 1995. *Na nŭn Na rŭl Chukil Su Ŏpsŏtta* (I Could Not Kill Myself). Seoul: Kipŭnsarang.

Pak, Yu-ha. 2005. *Hwahae rŭl Wihaesŏ* (For Reconciliation). Seoul: Ppuriwaip'ari.

Pang, Sŏn-ju. 1992. Miguk Charyo e Nat'anan Hanin "Chonggunwianbu" ŭi Koch'al (A Study of the Korean "Military Comfort Women" Shown in the American Data). *Kuksakwan Nonch'ong* 37: 215–246.

Park, Hyun Ok. 2005. *Two Dreams in One Bed: Empire, Social Life, and the Origins of the North Korean Revolution in Manchuria.* Durham, NC: Duke University Press.

Park, Soon-Won. 1999. Colonial Industrial Growth and the Emergence of the Korean Working Class. In *Colonial Modernity in Korea,* ed. Gi-Wook Shin and Michael Robinson. Pp. 128–160. Cambridge: Harvard University Asia Center.

———. 2003. Colonial Home Front: World War II and Korean Rural Women. Paper presented at the Association for Asian Studies annual conference in New York, March 27–30.

Park, Therese. 1997. *A Gift of the Emperor.* Duluth, MN: Spinsters Ink.

Pateman, Carole. 1988. *The Sexual Contract.* Stanford, CA: Stanford University Press.

———. 1996. A Comment on Johnson's "Does Capitalism Really Need Patriarchy?" *Women's Studies International Forum* 19 (3): 203–205.

Patterson, Orlando. 1982. *Slavery and Social Death: A Comparative Study.* Cambridge, MA: Harvard University Press.

Paul, Christa. 1996. *Nachizumu to Kyōseibaishun* (Nazism and Forced Prostitution). Originally published in German as *Zwangsprostitution staatlich errichtete bordelle im nationalsozialismus.* Tokyo: Akashi Shoten.

Peacock, James L. 2001. *The Anthropological Lens: Harsh Light, Soft Focus.* 2nd ed. Cambridge: Cambridge University Press.

Peters, Julie, and Andrea Wolper, eds. 1995. *Women's Rights, Human Rights: International Feminist Perspectives.* New York: Routledge.

Piccigallo, Philip R. 1979. *The Japanese on Trial: Allied War Crimes Operations in the East, 1945–1951.* Austin: University of Texas Press.

Primoratz, Igor. 1993. What's Wrong with Prostitution? *Philosophy* 68 (264): 159–182.

Prince, Stephen. 1999. *The Warrior's Camera: The Cinema of Akira Kurosawa.* Princeton, NJ: Princeton University Press.

Pyŏn, Hwa-sun, and Hwang, Chŏng-im. 1998. *Sanŏphyŏng Maemaech'un e Kwanhan Yŏn'gu* (A Study of Industry-Type Prostitution). Seoul: Han'guk Yŏsŏng Kaebalwŏn.

Ramseyer, J. Mark. 1991. Indentured Prostitution in Imperial Japan: Credible Commitments in the Commercial Sex Industry. *Journal of Law, Economics, & Organization* 5 (1): 89–116.

Rawls, John. 2001. *Justice as Fairness: A Restatement.* Ed. Erin Kelly. Cambridge, MA: Belknap Press of Harvard University Press.

Rhee, Younghoon. 2004. Kuksa Kyokasŏ e Kŭryŏjin Ilche ŭi Sut'alsang kwa kŭ Sinhwasŏng (The Image of Imperial Japan's Exploitation Portrayed in the National History Textbooks and Its Mythical Nature). Paper presented at Han-Il Yŏndae 21 Inauguration Symposium, Seoul, November 19.

——. 2005. Pukhan Oegyogwan kwa Namhan ŭi Kyokwasŏ ga Ppajyŏ Innŭn Hŏsu ŭi Tŏt (The Trap of Imaginary Numbers into which the North Korean Diplomat and the South Korean Textbook Have Fallen).http://www.new-right.com (accessed April 26, 2005).

——. 2007. *Taehanminkuk Iyagi* (The Story of the Republic of Korea). Seoul: Kip'arang.

Rich, Adrienne. 1980. Compulsory Heterosexuality and Lesbian Existence. *Signs: Journal of Women in Culture and Society* 5 (4): 631–660.

Rodd, Laurel Rasplica. 1991. Yosano Akiko and the Taishō Debate over the "New Woman." In *Recreating Japanese Women, 1600–1945,* ed. Gail Lee Bernstein. Pp. 175–198. Berkeley: University of California Press.

Rosaldo, Renato. 1989. *Culture and Truth: The Remaking of Social Analysis.* Boston, MA: Beacon Press.

Ruff-O'Herne, Jan. 1994. *50 Years of Silence.* Sydney, Australia: ETT Imprint.

Rutt, Richard. 1983/1974. The Song of a Faithful Wife, Ch'unhyang. In *Virtuous Women: Three Classic Korean Novels.* Trans. Richard Rutt and Chong-un Kim. Pp. 235–333. Seoul: Royal Asiatic Society Korea Branch.

Saaler, Sven. 2005. *Politics, Memory and Public Opinion: The History Textbook Controversy and Japanese Society.* Munich: Iudicium Verlag.

Sahlins, Marshall. 2000. *Culture in Practice: Collected Essays.* New York: Zone Books.

Sancho, Nelia, ed. 1998. *War Crimes on Asian Women: Military Sexual Slavery by Japan during World War II; The Case of the Filipino Comfort Women.* Manila: Asian Women Human Rights Council.

Sato, Barbara. 2003. *The New Japanese Woman: Modernity, Media, and Women in Interwar Japan.* Durham, NC: Duke University Press.

Schellstede, Sangmie Choi, ed. 2000. *Comfort Women Speak: Testimony by Sex Slaves of the Japanese Military.* New York: Holmes & Meier.

Scheper-Hughes, Nancy. 2004. Undoing: Social Suffering and the Politics of Remorse in the New South Africa. In *Violence in War and Peace: An Anthology,* ed. Nancy Scheper-Hughes and Philippe Bourgois. Pp. 459–467. Oxford: Blackwell.

Scheper-Hughes, Nancy, and Philippe Bourgois. 2004. Introduction: Making Sense of Violence. In *Violence in War and Peace: An Anthology,* ed. Nancy Scheper-Hughes and Philippe Bourgois. Pp. 1–31. Oxford: Blackwell.

Schmidt, David. 2000. *Ianfu: The Comfort Women of the Japanese Imperial Army of the Pacific War.* Lewiston, NY: Edwin Mellen Press.

Scott, James. 1990. *Weapons of the Weak: Everyday Forms of Peasant Resistance.* New Haven, CT: Yale University Press.

Seigle, Cecilia Segawa. 1993. *Yoshiwara: The Glittering World of the Japanese Courtesan.* Honolulu: University of Hawai'i Press.

Sekiguchi, Noriko. 1990. *Sensō Daughters* (Daughters of War). Documentary (International Version). Tenchijin Productions, NSW 2000, Australia.

Senda, Kakō. 1990a. *Jūgun Ianfu: Seihen* (Military Comfort Women: The Main Edition). Tokyo: San'ichi Shobō.

———. 1990b. *Jūgun Ianfu: Zokuhen* (Military Comfort Women: The Sequel Edition). Tokyo: San'ichi Shobō.

Shanker, Thom. 2007. South Korean Says North Still Threat. *New York Times,* November 8.

Shiga-Fujime, Yuki. 1993. The Prostitutes' Union and the Impact of the 1956 Anti-Prostitution Law in Japan. *US–Japan Women's Journal English Supplement* 5:3–27.

Shin, Gi-Wook. 1996. *Peasant Protest & Social Change in Colonial Korea.* Seattle: University of Washington Press.

Shin, Gi-Wook, and Michael Robinson, eds. 1999. *Colonial Modernity in Korea.* Cambridge, MA: Harvard University Asia Center.

Shirota, Suzuko. 1971. *Maria no San'ka* (Maria's Song of Praise). Tokyo: Nihon Kirisuto Kyōdan Shuppankyoku.

Shrage, Laurie. 1994. *Moral Dilemmas of Feminism: Prostitution, Adultery, and Abortion.* New York: Routledge.

Shuman, Daniel W., and Alexander McCall Smith. 2000. *Justice and the Prosecution of Old Crimes: Balancing Legal, Psychological, and Moral Concerns.* Washington, DC: American Psychological Association.

Sievers, Sharon L. 1983. *Flowers in Salt: The Beginnings of Feminist Consciousness in Modern Japan.* Stanford, CA: Stanford University Press.

Silverberg, Miriam. 2006. *Erotic Grotesque Nonsense: The Mass Culture of Japanese Modern Times.* Berkeley: University of California Press.

Sin, Hye-su. 1994. Minjokjuǔi wa Peminijǔm (Nationalism and Feminism). In *Han'guk*

Yŏsŏnghak ŭi Chŏnmang kwa Kwaje (The Prospect and Tasks for Korean Women's Studies). Seoul: Korean Association of Women's Studies.

Sin, Myŏng-jik. 2003. *Modŏn Bboi, Kyŏngsŏng ŭl Kŏnilda* (Modern Boy, Sauntering in Kyŏngsŏng). Seoul: Hyŏnsilmunhwa Yŏn'gu.

———. 2004. Singminji Kŭndaedosi ŭi Ilsang kwa Manmun Manhwa (Everyday Life in a Colonial Modern City and Commentary Cartoons). In *Ilche ŭi Singmin Chibae wa Ilsangsaenhwal* (Imperial Japan's Colonial Domination and Everyday Life), ed. Yonsei University Korean Studies Center. Pp. 277–335. Seoul: Yonsei University.

Sin, Yŏng-suk. 1999. Yangjang ŭi Modangŏl (Short-Haired Girl in Western Clothes). In *Uri Nara Yŏsŏngdŭl ŭn Ŏttŏtke Saratsŭlkka 2* (How Did Our Nation's Women Live Their Lives 2), ed. Yi Pae-yong et al. Pp. 72–82. Seoul: Ch'ŏngnyŏnsa.

———. 2004. Ilche Sigi Yŏsŏngsa Yŏn'gu e Issŏ Minjok kwa Yŏsŏng Munje (Nation and the Woman Question in the Study of Women's History during the Japanese Colonial Period). In *Sŏngsin Yŏdae Nonjip*. http://truetruth.org (accessed January 2, 2004).

Skelton, Russell. 1996. Seisuke Okuno: "Comfort Women 'Did It for Money.'" *Sydney Morning Herald,* June 6.

Sŏ, Kyŏng-sik. 1997. Tŏ Isang Nae Ŏmŏni rūl Moyokhaji Mara (Do Not Humiliate My Mother Anymore). *Mal* (May): 144–148.

So, Rae-sŏp. 2005. *Ero Gŭro Nŏnsensŭ* (Eroticism, Grotesque, Nonsense). Seoul: Sallim.

Soh, Chunghee Sarah. 1993. *Women in Korean Politics.* Boulder, CO: Westview Press.

———. 1995. Korean War Brides. In *The Asian American Encyclopedia,* ed. Franklin Ng. Pp. 934–936. North Bellmore, NY: Marshall Cavendish.

———. 1996. Korean "Comfort Women": Movement for Redress. *Asian Survey* 36 (12): 1227–1240.

———. 1997a. The Korean Council for the Women Drafted for Military Sexual Slavery by Japan. In *The Historical Encyclopedia of World Slavery,* two vols., ed. Junius P. Rodriguez. Pp. 393–394. Santa Barbara, CA: ABC-CLIO Press.

———. 1997b. Kim Hak-sun. In *The Historical Encyclopedia of World Slavery,* two vols., ed. Junius P. Rodriguez. Pp. 390–391. Santa Barbara, CA: ABC-CLIO Press.

———. 1997c. Yun Chong-ok. In *The Historical Encyclopedia of World Slavery,* two vols., ed. Junius P. Rodriguez. P. 712. Santa Barbara, CA: ABC-CLIO Press.

———. 1998. Understanding the Concept of *Han.* Review of Jae Hoon Lee, *The Exploration of the Inner Wounds: Han. Korea Journal* 38 (3): 340–346.

———. 2000a. From Imperial Gifts to Sex Slaves: Theorizing Symbolic Representations of the "Comfort Women." *Social Science Japan Journal* 3 (1): 59–76.

———. 2000b. Human Rights and the "Comfort Women." *Peace Review* 12 (1): 123–129.

————. 2001a. Japan's Responsibility toward Comfort Women Survivors. JPRI Working Paper No. 77. Cardiff, CA: Japan Policy Research Institute.

————. 2001b. Centering the Korean "Comfort Women" Survivors. Video review. *Critical Asian Studies* 33 (4): 603–608.

————. 2003a. Japan's National/Asian Women's Fund for "Comfort Women." *Pacific Affairs* 76 (2): 209–233.

————. 2003b. Politics of the Victim/Victor Complex: Interpreting South Korea's National Furor Over Japanese History Textbooks. *American Asian Review* 21 (4): 145–178.

————. 2004a. Women's Sexual Labor and State in Korean History. *Journal of Women's History* 15 (4): 170–177.

————. 2004b. Aspiring to Craft Modern Gendered Selves: "Comfort Women" and Chŏngsindae in Late Colonial Korea. *Critical Asian Studies* 36 (2): 175–198.

————. 2006a. In/fertility among Korea's "Comfort Women" Survivors: A Comparative Perspective. *Women's Studies International Forum* 29 (1): 67–80.

————. 2006b. Kyoyukpatko Chariptoen Chaasilhyŏn ŭl Yŏlmanghaetkŏnman: Chosŏnin "Wianbu" wa Chŏngsindae e Kwanhan "Kaein Chungsim" ŭi Pip'an Illyuhakchŏk Koch'al. (Aspiring to Craft Modern Gendered Selves: "Comfort Women" and Chŏngsindae in Late Colonial Korea). Trans. of Soh 2004b. In *Haebang Chŏnhusa ŭi Chaeinsik 1* (A Rethinking of the Pre- and Post-liberation History 1), ed. Pak Chi-hyang, Kim Ch'ŏl, Kim Yŏng, and Rhee Younghoon. Pp. 434–476. Seoul: Chaeksesang.

————. 2007. The Korean "Comfort Women" Tragedy as Structural Violence. In *Rethinking Historical Injustice and Reconciliation in Northeast Asia: The Korean Experience,* ed. Gi-Wook Shin, Soon-Won Park, and Daqing Yang. Pp. 17–35. New York: Routledge.

Song Sin-do v. Kuni (Nation, i.e., Japan). 1993. Sojō (Complaint), filed at the Tokyo District Court, on 5 April. Tokyo: Zainichi no Ianfu Saiban o Sasaeru Kai.

Song, Youn-ok. 1997. Japanese Colonial Rule and State-Managed Prostitution: Korea's Licensed Prostitutes. *Positions: East Asia Cultures Critique* 5 (1), special issue, The Comfort Women. Pp. 171–217.

Steinhoff, Patricia G. 2003. New Notes from the Underground: Doing Fieldwork without a Site. In *Doing Fieldwork in Japan,* ed. Theodore C. Bestor, Patricia G. Steinhoff, and Victoria Lyon Bestor. Pp. 36–54. Honolulu: University of Hawai'i Press.

Stetz, Margaret, and Bonnie B. C. Oh, eds. 2001. *Legacies of the Comfort Women of World War II.* Armonk, New York: M. E. Sharpe.

Stiglmayer, Alexandra, ed. 1994. *Mass Rape: The War against Women in Bosnia-Herzegovina.* Trans. Marion Faber. Lincoln: University of Nebraska Press.

Stoler, Ann Laura. 1997. Educating Desire in Colonial Southeast Asia: Foucault,

Freud, and Imperial Sexualities. In *Sites of Desire, Economies of Pleasure: Sexualities in Asia and the Pacific,* ed. Lenore Manderson and Margaret Jolly. Pp. 27–47. Chicago: University of Chicago Press.

———. 2002. *Carnal Knowledge and Imperial Power: Race and the Intimate in Colonial Rule.* Berkeley: University of California Press.

Stoler, Ann Laura, and Karen Strassler. 2000. Castings for the Colonial: Memory Work in "New Order" Java. *Comparative Studies in Society and History* 42 (1): 4–48.

Stoll, David. 1999. *Rigoberta Menchú and the Story of All Poor Guatemalans.* Boulder, CO: Westview Press.

Sturdevant, Saundra Pollock, and Brenda Stoltzfus. 1992. *Let the Good Times Roll: Prostitution and the U.S. Military in Asia.* New York: New Press.

Supreme Commander for the Allied Powers, Allied Translator and Interpreter Section. 1945. Amenities in the Japanese Armed Forces. Research Report No. 120. November 15.

Suzuki, Yūko. 1986. *Feminizumu to Sensō* (Feminism and War). Tokyo: Marujusha

———. 1990. Imakoso "Jūgun Ianfu" ni Kodawaru (Now Is the Time to Focus on "Military Comfort Women"). *Mainichi Shimbun,* February 1.

———. 1991. *Chōsenjin Jūgun Ianfu* (Korean Military Comfort Women). Iwanami Booklet no. 229. Tokyo: Iwanami Shoten.

———. 1993. *"Jūgun Ianfu" Mondai to Seibōryoku* ("Military Comfort Women" Issue and Sexual Violence). Tokyo: Miraisha.

———. 1997. *Sensō Sekinin to Jendā* (War Responsibility and Gender). Tokyo: Miraisha.

T'aepyŏngyang Chŏnjaeng Hisaengja Yujokhoe (Association for the Pacific War Victims and Bereaved Families). 1996. *Hoebo* (Association News). Issue 2. Seoul: The author.

Takasaki, Sōji. 1976. Kankoku ni Okeru Jūgun Ianfu Kenkyū (Research on Military Comfort Women in Korea). *Fujin Shinpo* (October), 7–9.

———. 2000. Women's Voluntary Service Corps and "Comfort Women" in Korea. Paper presented at the International Round Table on the "Comfort Women" Issue, Tokyo, September 5.

Tanaka, Mitsu. 1994. Benjo kara no Kaihō (Liberation from the Toilet). In *Nihon no Feminizumu 1: Ribu to Feminizumu* (Japan's Feminism 1: Liberation and Feminism), ed. Inoue Teruko et al. Pp. 39–57. Tokyo: Iwanami Shoten.

Tanaka, Yuki. 1998. *Hidden Horrors: Japanese War Crimes in World War II.* Boulder, CO: Westview Press.

———. 2002. *Japan's Comfort Women: Sexual Slavery and Prostitution during World War II and the US Occupation.* New York: Routledge.

Tawara, Yoshifumi. 1997. *"Ianfu" Mondai to Kyōkasho Kōgeki.* (The "Comfort Women" Issue and Textbook Attack). Tokyo: Kōbunken.

Terazawa, Yuki. 2005. The Transnational Redress Campaign for Chinese Victims of Sexual Violence of the Japanese Military: Cases in Shanxi Province. Paper presented at the Association for Asian Studies conference, Chicago, March 31–April 3.

Tomimura, Junichi. 1982. *Mō Hitotsu no Himeyuri Butai* (One More *Himeyuri* Unit). Tokyo: JCA Shuppan.

Totsuka, Etsurō. 2001/1999. *"Wianbu" ga Anira "Sŏngnoye" Ida* (Not "Comfort Women" but "Sex Slaves"). Trans. Pak Hong-kyu. Seoul: Sonamu.

Tsurumi, E. Patricia. 1984. Colonial Education in Korea and Taiwan. In *The Japanese Colonial Empire, 1895–1945*, ed. Ramon H. Myers and Mark R. Peattie. Pp. 275–311. Princeton, NJ: Princeton University Press.

Uehara, Eiko. 1976. *Tsuji no Hana: Kuruwa no Onnatachi* (The Bloom of Tsuji: Women of the Pleasure Quarters). Tokyo: Jijitsūshinsha.

Ueno, Chizuko. 1993. Japan's Enduring Shame. *Korea Times*, Los Angeles ed., March 17.

———. 1998. Jendāshi to Rekishigaku no Hōhō (Gender History and Historiographical Method). In *Nashonarizumu to "Ianfu" Mondai* (Nationalism and the "Comfort Women" Issue), ed. Center for Research and Documentation on Japan's War Responsibility. Pp. 21–31. Tokyo: Aoki Shoten.

———. 2001. Narratives of the Past: Against Historical Revisionism on "Comfort Women." In *Approches critiques de la pensée japonaise du xxe siècle*, ed. Livia Monnet. Pp. 303–325. Montréal: Presses de l'Université de Montréal.

———. 2004. *Nationalism and Gender*. Trans. Beverley Yamamoto. Melbourne: Trans Pacific Press.

Uesugi, Satoshi. 1997. *Datsu Gōmanizumu Sengen: Kobayashi Yoshinori no "Ianfu" Mondai* (Abandon the Haughtiness Manifesto: Kobayashi Yoshinori's "Comfort Women" Problem). Tokyo: Tōhō Shuppansha.

United States Office of War Information. 1944. Japanese Prisoner of War Interrogation Report (No. 49). Psychological Warfare Team Attached to U.S. Army Forces India-Burma Theater. USNA Collection, RG 208, Box 226.

Usuki, Keiko. 1983. *Gendai no Ianfutachi: Guntai Ianfu kara Japayuki-san made* (Modern Comfort Women: From Military Comfort Women to the *Japayuki-san*). Tokyo: Gendaishi Shuppankai.

———. 1996. Kaneda Kimiko to Iu Namae (The Name of Kaneda Kimiko). In *Asiato Hitotsu Hitotsu ni Namida ga Nijimu* (Teardrops with Each Footstep). Tokyo: "Ianfu" Mondai o Kangaeru Tokōkyō Yūshi Nettowāku.

Utsumi, Aiko. 2001. Korean "Imperial Soldiers": Remembering Colonialism and Crimes against Allied POWs. Trans. Mie Kennedy. In *Perilous Memories: The Asia-Pacific War(s)*, ed. T. Fujitani, Geoffrey M. White, and Lisa Yoneyama. Pp. 199–217. Durham, NC: Duke University Press.

Vicinus, M. 1982. Sexuality and Power: A Review of Current Work in the History of Sexuality. *Feminist Studies* 8 (1): 133–156.

VAWW-NET (Violence against Women in War–Network) Japan. 2000. *"Ianfu": Senji Seibōryoku no Jittai II* ("Comfort Women": The Actual Conditions of Wartime Sexual Violence II). Tokyo: Ryokufū Shuppan.

Wakabayashi, Bob Tadashi. 2003. Comfort Women: Beyond Litigious Feminism. *Monumenta Nipponica* 58 (2): 223–258.

Warren, James Francis. 2003. *Ah Ku and Karayuki-san: Prostitution in Singapore, 1870–1940.* Singapore: Singapore University Press.

Watanabe, Kazuko. 1994. Militarism, Colonialism, and the Trafficking of Women: "Comfort Women" Forced into Sexual Labor for Japanese Soldiers. *Bulletin of Concerned Asian Scholars* 26 (4): 3–17.

Watson, Rubie S. 1986. The Named and the Nameless: Gender and Person in Chinese Society. *American Ethnologist* 13 (4): 619–631.

Whiting, Robert. 1999. *Tokyo Underworld: The Fast Times and Hard Life of an American Gangster in Japan.* New York: Pantheon Books.

Wieviorka, Annette. 2006. *The Era of Witness.* Trans. Jared Stark. Ithaca, NY: Cornell University Press.

Williams, Raymond. 1977. *Marxism and Literature.* London: Oxford University Press.

Wilson, Richard. 2001. *The Politics of Truth and Reconciliation in South Africa: Legitimizing the Post-Apartheid State.* Cambridge: Cambridge University Press.

Wolf, Diane L. 1996. Situating Feminist Dilemmas in Fieldwork. In *Feminist Dilemmas in Fieldwork,* ed. Diane L. Wolf. Pp. 1–55. Boulder, CO: Westview Press.

Wolf, Eric. 1994/1990. Facing Power: Old Insights, New Questions. In *Assessing Cultural Anthropology,* ed. Robert Borofsky. Pp. 218–228. New York: McGraw-Hill. Reprint of Distinguished Lecture: Facing Power; Old Insights, New Questions. *American Anthropologist* 92 (3): 586–596.

Wolf, Margery. 1992. *A Thrice Told Tale: Feminism, Postmodernism & Ethnographic Responsibility.* Stanford, CA: Stanford University Press.

Yamashita, Akiko. 2000. *Sengo Nihon no Feminizumu to "Ianfu Mondai"* (Postwar Japanese Feminism and the "Comfort Women Issue"). In *Nihongun Seidoreisei o Sabaku: 2000nen Josei Kokusai Senpan Hōtei no Kiroku* (Judging the Japanese Military Sexual Slavery System: Records of Women's International War Crimes Tribunal 2000), vol. 2, ed. VAWW-NET Japan. Pp. 264–288. Tokyo: Rokufū Shuppan.

Yamashita, Yŏngae. 1992a. Han'guk Gŭndae Kongch'angchedo Silsi e Kwanhan Yŏn'gu (A Study of the Implementation of the Licensed Prostitution System in Modern Korea). Master's thesis. Ewha Womans University.

———. 1992b. Chōsen ni Okeru Kōshōseido no Jisshi (The Implementation of the System of Licensed Prostitution in Korea). In Yun Chong-ok et al., *Chōsenjin Josei ga Mita Ianfu Mondai* (The Comfort Women Issue from Korean Women's Perspective). Pp.128–167. Tokyo: San'ichi Shobō.

————. 1998. Nationalism in Korean Women's Studies: Addressing the Nationalist Discourses Surrounding the "Comfort Women" Issue. *U.S.–Japan Women's Journal.* English supplement 15: 52–77.

Yamatani, Tetsuo. 1979. *Okinawa no Harumoni: Dainippon Baishunshi* (A "Grandmother" in Okinawa: A History of Prostitution in Great Japan). Tokyo: Banseisha.

Yamazaki, Tomoko. 1974. *Sandakan no Haka* (The Grave of Sandakan). Tokyo: Bungeishunjū.

————. 1999. *Sandakan Brothel No. 8: An Episode in the History of Lower-Class Japanese Women.* Trans. Karen Colligan-Taylor. Armonk, NY: M. E. Sharpe.

Yang, Hyunah. 1998. Re-membering the Korean Military Comfort Women: Nationalism, Sexuality, and Silencing. In *Dangerous Women: Gender and Korean Nationalism,* ed. Elaine H. Kim and Chungmoo Choi. Pp. 123–139. New York: Routledge.

Yang, Sung-jin. 1997. Keller Inspired by "Comfort Woman." *Korea Times,* August 30.

Yi, Bae-yong. 1999. Kaehwagi-Ilchesigi Kyŏrhonkwan ŭi Pyŏnhwa wa Yŏsŏng ŭi Chiwi (Changes in Views toward Marriage and Women's Status during the Period of Enlightenment under Imperial Japan). *Han'guk Kŭnhyŏndaesa Yŏn'gu* (Korean Modern History Research) 10: 214–245.

Yi, I-hwa. 1999. *Han'guksa Iyagi 7: Mongol ŭi Ch'imnyak kwa Samsimnyŏn Hangjaeng* (The Story of Korean History 7: The Mongol Invasion and the 30-Year Resistance). Seoul: Han'gilsa.

Yi, Man-yŏl. 1997. Ilbongun "Wianbu" Chŏngch'aek Hyŏngsŏng ŭi Chosŏnch'ŭk Yŏksajŏk Paegyŏng (Korean Historical Background to the Formation of the Japanese Military "Comfort Women" Policy). In *Ilbon'gun "Wianbu" Munje ŭi Chinsang* (The Truth of the Japanese Military "Comfort Women" Issue), ed. Han'guk Chŏngsindae-munje Taech'aek Hyŏpŭihoe Chinsangchosa Yŏn'guhoe. Pp. 69–97. Seoul: Yŏksabip'yŏngsa.

Yi, Nŭng-hwa. 1992. *Chosŏn Haeŏhwasa* (The History of Chosŏn *Kisaeng*). Seoul: Tongmunsŏn.

Yi, Sun-ku. 1999. Chosŏnsidae Yŏsŏng ŭi Il kwa Saenghwal (The Work and Lives of the Women of Chosŏn). In *Uri Yŏsong ŭi Yŏksa* (Our Women's History), ed. Han'guk Yŏsŏngyŏn'guso Yŏsŏngsayŏn'gusil. Pp. 191–224. Seoul: Ch'ŏngnyŏnsa.

Yim, Chi-hyŏn, and Yi Sŏng-si, eds. 2004. *Kuksa ŭi Sinhwa rŭl Nŏmŏsŏ* (Beyond the Myth of National History). Seoul: Humanist.

Yim, Chong-guk. 1981. *Chŏngsindae Sillok* (True Records of Chŏngsindae). Seoul: Ilwŏl Sŏgak.

————. 2004. *Pam ŭi Ilche Ch'imnyaksa* (History of Imperial Japan's Invasion in the Night). Seoul: Hanpitmunhwasa.

Yŏ, Sun-ju. 1994. Ilche Malgi Chosŏnin Yŏja Kŭllo Chŏngsindae e Kwanhan Silt'ae Yŏngu (A Study on the Actual Conditions of the Korean Women's Volunteer Labor

Corps in Late Japanese Colonial Period). Master's thesis, Ewha Womans University Graduate School.

Yoshida, Seiji. 1977. *Chōsenjin Ianfu to Nihonjin* (Korean Comfort Women and the Japanese). Tokyo: Shinjinbutsuōraisha.

———. 1983. *Watashi no Sensō Hanzai* (My War Crime). Tokyo: San'inchi Shobō.

Yoshimi, Yoshiaki. 1993. *Charyojip: Chonggun Wianbu* (Reference Materials: Military Comfort Women). Korean ed. Trans. Sun H. Kim. Seoul: Sŏmundang.

———. 1995. *Jūgun Ianfu* (Military Comfort Women). Tokyo: Iwanami Shoten.

———. 1997. Ianfu no Chōbo (Recruitment of the Comfort Women). In *"Jūgun Ianfu" o Meguru 30 no Uso to Shinjitsu* (30 Lies and Truths Surrounding the "Military Comfort Women"), ed. Yoshimi Yoshiaki and Kawata Fumiko. Tokyo: Ōtsuki Shoten.

———. 2000. *Comfort Women: Sexual Slavery in the Japanese Military during World War II.* Originally published as *Jūgun Ianfu.* Trans. Suzanne O'Brien. New York: Columbia University Press.

Yoshimi, Yoshiaki, and Hayashi, Hirofumi. 1997. Hajime ni (Preface). In *Nihon-gun Ianfu* (Japanese Military Comfort Women), ed. Yoshimi Yoshiaki and Hayashi Hirofumi. Tokyo: Ōtsuki Shoten.

Yoshimi, Yoshiaki, and Kawata, Fumiko, eds. 1997. *"Jūgun Ianfu" o Meguru 30 no Uso to Shinjitsu* (30 Lies and Truths Surrounding the "Military Comfort Women"). Tokyo: Ōtsuki Shoten.

Yoshimoto, Mitsuhiro. 2000. *Kurosawa: Film Studies and Japanese Cinema.* Durham, NC: Duke University Press.

Yŏsŏngbu (Ministry of Gender Equality). 2002. *Sŏngmaemae Silt'ae mit Kyŏngjekyumo e Kwanhan Chŏn'gukchosa (National Investigation into the Actual Condition of Prostitution and Its Economic Scale: A Research Report.* Seoul: The author.

You, Dongick. 2001. Nedŏllandŭ edo Chŏngsindae ga Issŏtta (The Netherlands Also Had Chŏngsindae). http://www.OhmyNews.com, November 21, (accessed July 4, 2002).

Young, Louise. 1998. *Japan's Total Empire: Manchuria and the Culture of Wartime Imperialism.* Berkeley: University of California Press.

Yu, Hae-jŏng. 1999. Ilche Singminjiha ŭi Yŏsŏng Chŏngch'aek (Policies for Women under Japanese Colonial Rule). In *Uri Yŏsong ŭi Yŏksa* (Our Women's History), ed. Han'guk Yŏsŏngyŏn'guso Yŏsŏngsayŏn'gusil. Pp. 275–300. Seoul: Ch'ŏngnyŏnsa.

Yuh, Ji-Yeon. 2002. *Beyond the Shadow of Camptown: Korean Military Brides in America.* New York: New York University Press.

Yun, Chŏng-mo. 1997. *Emi Irŭm ŭn Chōsen Ppi Yŏtta* (Your Mother's Name Was Korean *Ppi*). Seoul: Tangdae.

Yun, Chŏng-ok. 1981. Piun ŭi Wianbudŭl (Unlucky Comfort Women), *Han'guk Ilbo* August 29.

———. 1994. Kŭl Mŏri e: Chungguk Muhan Tapsa rŭl Tanyŏwasŏ (Preface: Upon Returning from the Field Research in Muhan, China). In *Chungguk ŭro Kkŭllyŏgan Chosŏnin Kunwianpudŭl: 50-Nyŏn Hu ŭi Chŭngŏn* (Korean Military Comfort Women Dragged Away to China: Testimonies after 50 Years), ed. CY and HCTH 1995. Pp. 3–13. Seoul: Hanul.

———. 2000. *Yŏnkkot ŭro Tasi T'aeŏnagop'a* (I Want to Be Born Again as a Lotus). In *Halmŏni Kunwianbu ga Mwŏyeyo?* (Grandmother, What Are Military Comfort Women?), Han'guk Chŏngsindae Yŏn'guso. Seoul: Hangyŏre Sinmunsa.

Yun, Myŏng-suk. 1995. Chōsen kara no Chōshū (The Levy from Korea). In *Nihon gun Ianfu* (Japanese Military Comfort Women), ed. Yoshimi Yoshiaki and Hayashi Hirofumi. Tokyo: Ōtsuki Shoten.

———. 2003. *Nihon no Guntai Ianjoseido to Chōsenjin Guntai Ianfu* (The Japanese Military Comfort Station System and Korean Military Comfort Women). Tokyo: Akashi Shoten.

Zatlin, Linda Gertner. 2001. "Comfort Women" and the Cultural Tradition of Prostitution in Japanese Erotic Art. In *Legacies of the Comfort Women of World War II*, ed. Margaret Stetz and Bonnie Oh. Pp. 26–41. Armonk, NY: M. E. Sharpe.

Zhu, Telan. 2001. Taiwan Ianfu Kankei Shiryō no Chōsa to Kenkyū (Investigation and Research on Data Concerning Taiwan Comfort Women). Paper presented at the International Roundtable on Comfort Women, Tokyo, March 1–2.

NEWSPAPERS

Asahi Shimbun
Chosun Ilbo
Dong-a Ilbo
Hankyoreh
Han'guk Ilbo
Ilyo Sinmun
Japan Times
JoongAng Ilbo
Korea Times
Kukje Sinmun
Mainichi Shimbun
New York Times
OhmyNews
Sankei Shimbun
Washington Post
Yonhap News
Yŏsŏng Sinmun

Index

Page references in italics refer to illustrations.

Bulletin of Concerned Asian Scholars, 46
Burgos-Debray, Elizabeth, 99
Burma, 8, 34–35, 39, 55, 121, 137, 182–84, 272n50
Burns, Susan, 111
Byun Young-joo, 93, 94

Café Asea, Shanghai. *See* Pak Il-sŏk (aka Arai Hakuseki)
capitalism: colonial, xii, 7, 237, 254n53, 256n67; consumer, 235; dynamics of, 115; history of Korean, 255n62. *See also* structural violence
"care work," gendered customary, 202
Center for Research and Documentation on Japan's War Responsibility (JWRC), Japan, 64–65, 154, 247
Chai, Alice Y., 46
Chan, Won Loy, Capt., U.S. Army, 35
Chang Ch'un-wŏl: memories of a Japanese colonel and his parents, 186, 188; memory of Japan's defeat, 188, 206; as small business owner, 188; sold by father, 186
Chang-rae Lee, *A Gesture Life,* 55–56
Chejudo, 139; Cheju Island, 153, 154
Cheju Sinmum, 153
Children and Textbooks Japan Network 21, 171
ch'ima, 83, 121, 222
China: Japanese military brothels in, 15, 17, 19, 55, 58, 59, 132, 133, 140, 157; Japanese sex workers in, 114; Korean comfort women survivors in, 93; Korean "tribute women" for, 203–4
Chinese war crimes tribunals, 22
ch'inilp'a, 238. *See also* collaboration
Chinnamp'o, Korea, 8
Ch'oe Il-rye: evidence of "maidens' aux-

iliary," 134; loss of savings, 274n96; uniquely significant testimonial of, 125–27
chŏgori, 83, 121, 223
Choi, Chungmoo, 48
Choi Ch'ang-kyu, 156–57
ch'on, 266n166
chŏng, 128, 190
chonggun wianbu (military comfort women), North Korean use of term, 62. *See also jūgun ianfu*
Ch'ŏngjin, Korea, 119
Chongsam (Seoul), 216
chŏngsin, defined, 57; homonym, 263n105
Chŏngsindae. *See* Teishintai (Volunteer Labor Corps); Women's Volunteer Labor Corps
chŏngsindae (Volunteer Labor Corps member), 18–20; documentary evidence of Korean women as, 58–59, 60–62; laboring in a factory, *19;* mobilization of, 58, 61; non-use of term in North Korean official discourse, 62; "real," 58, 60; South Korean conflation of, with comfort women, xv, 3, 22, 32, 45, 55, 57, 72, 106, 146, 150, 153, 159–61, 166, 172, 231–32; as South Korean "nationalist euphemism," 62, 106; use of term in colonial period, 58, 61. *See also teishintai,* colonial period use of term
"*chŏngsindae haewŏn kut,*" 106
chŏngsindae halmŏni ("grandmother") vs. *wianbu* (comfort women) *halmŏni,* 74
Chŏngsindae-munje Taech'aek Hyŏpŭihoe (aka ChŏngTaeHyŏp), 57. *See also* Korean Council for Women Drafted for Military Sexual Slavery by Japan (South Korea)

Comfort Women Monument (*Chinkon no hi*), Japan, 198–201, 239

"comfort women nude photographs," 98

"comfort women resolution." *See* Honda, Mike, U.S. congressman

Comfort Women Speak, 49

comparative and pluralistic approach, 242. *See also* anthropology

concessionary *ianjo*, 117–18, 131, 133, 134, 181; house of entertainment, 119–21; house of prostitution, 121–24. *See also* Japanese military comfort stations (*gun ianjo*)

"condensation symbol," 173

conjuncture: historical, xiii, xv, 2, 15, 235; structural, 105–6, 115, 227, 240

Connell, R. W., 116

Cooke, Janet, 277n28

Coomaraswamy Report, 48, 65, 66, 154, 169

Cosmopolitan Hotel, 159

countermemories: of Dutch comfort women survivors, 179–80; of Japanese ex-comfort women, 148, 157, 189; of Korean comfort women survivors, xv, 33, 156, 181–90, 195. *See also* Chang Ch'un-wŏl; Kikumaru; Kim Sun-dŏk (aka Kim Tŏk-chin); memories; Mun Ok-chu; Pae Chok-kan; Pae Pong-gi; Uehara Eiko

Cowan, Jane, xiv

"cries of the stone" (*ishi no sakebi*), 198, 283n2

criminal *ianjo*, 130–32, 133, 137; as anomaly, 119; as embodiment of violent military hypermasculinity, 132, 134; emergence of, 118–19; as "rape centers," 131. *See also* Japanese military comfort stations (*gun ianjo*);

war, sexual violence against women during

Critical Asian Studies, 248

critical feminist analysis, of comfort women discourse, 24, 229, 249. *See also* feminist humanitarian discourse; feminist scholarship

cultural capital, 252n7

cultural relativism: and concept of human rights, 244; and methodological strategy, 245

Cultural Revolution (China), 247

"culture," anthropological notion of, 272n52

Cumings, Bruce, 204, 223–24

"customary business or trade," 25, 116, 133, 134–35, 201, 211, 224

"customary" crimes, 275n110

"dealers in human trade" (*saram chang-sakkun*), 15

Democratic Party of Japan, 197

Democratic People's Republic of Korea (North Korea), 161

Dickens, F. V., 112

Dieng, Adama, 29, 30

Dolgopol, Ustinia, 47

Dolly, 178

domestic violence, 2, 4, 27, 104, 168. *See also* violence against women

Dong-a Ilbo, 10, 11, 161

Dong-a Ilbo Daily English, 265n144

Dongwoo Lee Hahm, 49

Dōshisha University, 73

Douglass, Ana, 99

Dutch Ad Hoc Military Court in Batavia (Jakarta), 22

Dutch comfort women, 67, 142; forcible recruitment, 20–22, 46; "volunteers" (*see* Blondie; Dolly; Yvonne)

"Forgotten War," 158

"For the good of the country" (*Okuni no tameni*), 148, 189

Foucault, Michel, 201, 292n7

Foundation for Japanese Honorary Debts, 180, 247

"free comfort station," 192

Fujime Yuki, 42, 111, 157

Fujin Shinpō, 155

Fujioka Nobukatsu, 170, 280n79

Fukazu Fumio, pastor and founder of Kanita Women's Village, 198, 199

Fukushima Mizuho, 197, *200*

Fukuzawa Yukichi, 205

geisha, 8, 116, 121, 131, 148, 208, 273n74; and *hikitejaya*, 110; s*homben*, 40

gender and Korean nationalism, relationship between, 237, 290n35

gender and violence. *See* patriarchal cultures; structural violence; violence against women; war, sexual violence against women during

gender discourse, "women's duty to comfort," 38

gendered structural violence, xii, xiv, xv, 228, 236. *See also* structural violence

gender ideology, Neo-Confucian, 4

gender justice, at the local level, 228, 232

genealogy approach. *See* Foucault, Michel

Geneva Convention, on wartime military rape, 41

"genocide" (*minjok malsal,* in Korean), 151

Giobbe, Evelina, 143

"girls' army" (*jōshigun*), 107, 124, 125, 274n89; as another name for the *karayuki-san,* 274n89

Global Alliance for Preserving the History of WWII in Asia, 247

global capitalist political economy, and women's victimhood as sex workers, xiii, 115–16, 234, 235, 243

Gluck, Carol, 176

gohōshi, 145. *See also* "For the good of the country" (*Okuni no tameni*)

Gramsci, Antonio, 258n2

"Grandmother Pak." *See* Pae Pong-gi

Greater East Asian War, 38

Greater Japan Women's Association in Korea, 15

Griffin, W. E. B., 40–41

"Guidebooks for womanhood," 5

Gumma Prefectural Assembly (imperial Japan), 113

"gutter language," 39. See also *"pi"* (vagina)

"gynocentric" discourse, of transnational women's human rights movement, 42

Habitual Sadness (Byun)*,* 94

Hague, The, 42, 64–65, 177, 179–80, 247–48, 258, 268

Hainan Island, 29, 62, 153

Hakkirikai (Association to Clarify Japan's War Responsibility), 96

halmŏni: as collective appellation for comfort women survivors, 73–76; nonuse of the term for women leaders, 75

han: concept of, 80–81, 267n4, 267n6, 267n10; narratives of, 80–92, 106, 130

Haname (Japanese soldier). *See* Yi Sun-ok

hanbok (Korean dress), 186–87

han'guk (South Korea), 267n4

Han'guk Ilbo, 19, 159

Han'guk Yŏsŏngsa (History of Korean Women), 220

Haraway, Donna, 23

harimise (sitting on public display), 110, 123, 124; variant forms of, 274n84

Harris, Marvin, 292n9

Harris, Townsend, 110

harsh light, xi, xii, 82, 115, 228, 242. *See also* Peacock, James L.; soft focus

Hata Ikuhiko, 23–24, 67; "The Flawed U.N. Report on Comfort Women," 154; on Yoshida's story, 153–54

Havens, Thomas, 17

Ha Yŏng-i (pseud.): marriage to Yi Chong-un, 182; and multiple levels of structural violence, 206–7; on raised fee for sexual labor, 123; returning home penniless, 206; running a comfort station, 182

healing or restorative truth, 98. *See also* truth

Hegel, Georg Wilhelm Friedrich, 195

heiho (paramilitary auxiliaries), Indonesian, 193

Henson, Maria Rosa, *Comfort Women,* 46–47, 131–32

"heterosexual sensibility," 116

Hibiscus Club. *See* Sim Mi-ja, and Hibiscus Club

Hicks, George, *The Comfort Women,* 48, 238

Hirabayashi, Sgt., U.S. Army, 35

Hiratsuka Raichō, 253n21

Hirohito, Emperor Shōwa, 42, 146, 158, 167

Hiroshima, 168

Hirota Kazuko, "Testimonial Records of Military Comfort Women (and) Nurses," 147–48

historical injustice, xvii, 215, 224, 234, 241; victims of, 98, 245

historical revisionism, and neonationalist activism, 236

history, positivist tradition, 154

history textbooks, as focus of bilateral "war of memories," 145. *See also* Japanese history textbooks, controversy over comfort women issue in; South Korean history textbooks

Hitomi (Korean comfort woman survivor), baby and savings of, 184

"*Hoeren* (Whores') Camp" (Dutch East Indies), 178

holism, 251n8; methodological, xi; processual, 244, 292n9

Honda, former infantryman, 121

Honda, Mike, U.S. congressman, 66, 68

Honda, Mr. (pseud.), Japanese war veteran, 191–92, 273n78

Honda, Robert, Tech. Sgt., U.S. Army, 35

Hong Kang-rim, 124

"honorable deaths" (*gyokusai*), 149

House of Councilors (Tokyo), 100

house of entertainment, 119–20, 133, 134. *See also* Japanese military comfort stations (*gun ianjo*)

house of prostitution, 122, 123, 133, 134, 135. *See also* Japanese military comfort stations (*gun ianjo*)

House of Sharing (South Korea), survivors as permanent residents of, 93–99

House of the Seven Seas, Java, 122–23

Howard, Keith, 48

Hŏ Yŏng-sŏn, 153

Hubang Chŏnsa (War History on the Home Front), 215

human rights: meaning of, for comfort

women survivors, 50; post–cold war politics of, 33, 41

human rights activism, 65, 246; unconditional support of, as "misguided moralism," xiv. *See also* feminist humanitarian discourse; international human rights activism

Hwang Kŭm-ju, 94, 96

hwanyang-nyŏn, 204

Hyegyŏng, Lady, 5, 252n9

Hyejin, 93, 94, 95; management style of, 94; *Na, Naeil Demo Kandei* (I'm Going to the Demonstration Tomorrow), 94; and sexual scandal, 94, 268n32

"hygiene sacks," 137

hypermasculinity, xvi, 119, 132, 282n55. *See also* sexuality

I Am Not a Comfort Woman, 72

ianfu (comfort women), xii, 38, 69, 70, 75, 77, 115, 121, 124, 142, 169, 198, 201; standard English translation of, 69. *See also* "comfort women"; feminist humanitarian discourse

ianjo. See Japanese military comfort stations (*gun ianjo*); *minkan ianjo* (private or civilian comfort stations)

Ichikawa Ichirō (former military policeman), about comfort women and *ianjo,* 121–22, 191

ICJ, 44, 47, 49. *See also* International Commission of Jurists

identity politics, surrounding the comfort women issue, xiii, xiv, xvii, 29, 46, 69, 228, 235, 237, 243

"ideology," 258n2. *See also* symbolic representations of comfort women

Ienaga Saburō, xxvii, 69

"I & I" (intercourse and intoxication), 210

Ilchinhoe (Unity and Progress Society), 16

imperial gifts, 30, 32, 37–39, 50, 135

Inchŏn, Korea, 8

Indai Sajor, 42

"indecent occupation," 113, 206

Independence Hall, 230

Independence Movement of 1919, 2, 53

Independence Park, Seoul, 231

"industrial comfort women," 10

Injo, King, 204

Institute for Corean-American Studies, 248

"international comfort women," South Korean women as, 233; in globalizing capitalist political economy, 234

International Commission of Jurists, 30–31, 176

international human rights activism: and definition of comfort system, xvii, 33, 48, 68, 229, 235–36; and definition of prostitution, 114; paradigmatic comfort women story, 33, 46–51, 68, 77, 154, 176. *See also* transnational redress movement

International Military Tribunal for the Far East (Tokyo, 1946), 42

"International Palace," 209, 210

International Public Hearing Concerning Japan's Postwar Compensation (1992), 64

international redress movement. *See* transnational redress movement

International Symposium on Comfort Women (1996), 50

International Symposium on Violence against Women in War and Armed Conflict (1995), 41

International Women's Film Festival, Twelfth (1990), 158

117; paramilitary *ianjo,* 118, 124–30, 134; quasi-brothels in China, 127, 128, 130; regulations for operation of, 119; service charges at, 141; three-phase evolutionary model of, 132–37; varieties of, xvii, 117–32; view of, as "hygienic public toilet," 40

Japanese military comfort system (*gun ianseido*), xiii, xv, xvii, 31, 115–17, 142, 236; characterization by human rights activists, 235–36; comfort women as military matériel, 38–39; on curbing effect on mass rape, 140, 142; deriving from, xiii, 115–16, 140; involvement of Koreans in, 135, 193; local sexual-cultural contexts of, 33; military version of licensed prostitution system, 31, 32, 114–15; as paternalistic state policy, 31; for prevention of venereal disease, 119. *See also* Dutch government

Japanese Military Comfort Women History Museum (South Korea), 93

Japanese Military Comfort Women Victims e-Museum, on South Korean Ministry of Gender Equality and Family Web site, 35

Japanese military nurses: as forced comfort women for Soviet troops, 147; in Manchuria and Philippines, 147

Japanese military veterans: multiple perspectives of, 190–95; and nonuse of comfort facilities, 192–93; personal memories of comfort facilities, 176

Japanese National Diet, 63, 64, 68

Japanese Navy hospital, 29–30

Japanese prime ministers: Abe Shinzō, 67, 68; Kaifu Toshiki, 63; Koizumi

Junichirō, 234; Miyazawa Kiichi, 44; Murayama Tomiich, 239; Tōjō Hideki, 18

"Japanese princess," 223

"Japanese Prisoner of War Interrogation Report No. 49," 34

Japanese progressive historians, 1, 51, 63, 65, 154, 170, 236

Japanese public discourse on comfort women: apology by Miyazawa, 44; books on comfort women, 146; Committee on Historical Facts, 68; conservative view, 31, 34, 46, 66, 68, 229; emergence of anti-redress camp, 24; on issue of comfort women as a war crime, 63–68; knowledge about comfort women, 146; "moral" versus "legal responsibility" for survivors, 44; nationalist perspective, 68; neonationalists' perspective, 229; pro- and anti-comfort women camps, 45; on wartime Japanese military involvement in comfort system, 44. *See also* Japanese National Diet

Japanese Red Cross, 29

Japanese sex tourists, 151; in Korea, 205, 207, 217–18. See also *kisaeng* tourism; South Korean men, "Don't-Ask Tourism"

Japanese sexual culture, 3, 227, 229; adult entertainment industry, 233; contemporary public-sex institutions and attitudes, 232–33, 235; *ianjo* rooted in, 132–33; mistress, 30; "toilet" as a sexual metaphor, 39–40. *See also* Korean sexual culture; masculinist sexual culture; pleasure quarters (*yūkaku*)

Japanese soldiers: barred from entering comfort facilities, 193; objectification and commodification of comfort women, 39, 181; personal relations with comfort women, 194–95; reasons for visiting comfort stations, 193; refusing to go to comfort stations, 194. *See also* Japanese war veterans, memoirs of encounters at comfort facilities

Japanese "war brides," 210

Japanese war veterans, memoirs of encounters at comfort facilities, 146. *See also* Japanese soldiers

Japanese women: middle-class women's organizations, 158; as "overseas prostitutes" in Korea, 8; rape by American soldiers, 210; servicing American servicemen (occupation Japan), 205; in volunteer labor corps, 158. *See also* Japanese comfort women

Japan Times, 100

Japayuki-san, 211, 285n59

Jee Man-wŏn, 231–32

Jenkins, Donald, *The Floating World Revisited*, 110

JoongAng Ilbo, 166, 263n108

jōshigun. *See* "girls' army" (*jōshigun*)

Joshi Teishintai (Women's Volunteer Labor Corps), 18, 160, 171

jūgun ianfu, 63, 70, 149, 169; implication of postwar Japanese term, 70, 124, 169

JWRC, 65, 68, 265. *See also* Center for Research and Documentation on Japan's War Responsibility (JWRC)

K, Ms., 59

Kabo Reform, 6

Kaifu Toshiki, 63

Kainansō, 30

Kakichi Shinji, 66

Kanagawa Prefecture, 207

Kaneda Kimiko, 97, 186. *See also* Pak Pok-sun (aka Kaneda Kimiko)

Kanghwa Treaty, 8

Kangjero Kkŭllyŏgan Chosŏnin Kunwianbudŭl ("Forcibly Dragged Away Korean Military Comfort Women"), 102. *See also* Korean Council for Women Drafted for Military Sexual Slavery by Japan (South Korea)

Kang Man-gil, 102–3

Kang Sŏn-mi, 229

Kang Tŏk-kyŏng: as "exceptional" case, 58; motivation to leave home, 58, 79; paintings, 96; as survivor, 93

Kangwŏn Province, 215

Kang Yong-kwŏn, 263n108

Kanita Women's Village, Tateyama City, Japan, 197, 239. *See also* Mihara Yoshie (aka Shirota Suzuko)

karayuki-san, 114, 115, 125, 157, 272n40; collective grudge against Japan, 205; contribution to Japanese economy (1900) by, 205

Kase Hideaki, 259n9, 260n52

Kawata Fumiko, and biography of Pae Pong-gi, 156

Kayama Mitsurō, 16

Keller, Nora Okja, *Comfort Woman*, 52–55

kempei (military policeman), 121

kibu (*kisaeng*'s husband), 9

kijich'on (camp town) prostitution: expansion during Korean War, 212; Filipino women in, 214; and joint military exercises with U.S. military, 213; phases of development, 211–13; rhetoric of patriotism by Korean women in, 214; and role of state, 212, 217; Russian women in, 214

Kikumaru: geisha-turned-*ianfu*, 148; and Japan's war project, 189; savings, 166; suicide, 147; suicide note, 277n9; wills, 148

Kil Wŏn-ok: *kisaeng* training, 8; "moral responsibility" to include testimonial of, 103; participation in redress movement, 103–4; sold to brothels, 24; and term *chŏngsindae*, 61

Kim, John, 76

Kim, Richard, *Lost Names*, 15–16

Kim Chŏng-han, *Surado*, 160

Kim Ch'un-hŭi, as *Aeguk Chŏngsindaewŏn* and as *kundae wianbu*, 159; death of, in 1963, 159; wealth in Vietnam, 159, 279n51

Kim Dae-jung, 16, 219

Kim Eun-sil, 229

Kim-Gibson, Dae Sil, 73, 189; *Silence Broken*, 49, 175

Kim Hak-sun: abusive husband, 130, 165, 177; born in Manchuria, 127; coming out, 91, 183, 198; critique of Korean and Japanese governments, 197; death of, 80, 274n99; escape from *ianjo*, 127, 130; father's death, 127; forced to *jūgun/chonggun*, 70, 124; foster father, 91, 127–28; *han*, 91, 130; historic significance of, 127; interviewed, *43*, 130, 177, 274n100; *kisaeng* training, 8, 91, 128; lawsuit against Japanese government, 43, 50, 96; marriage, 130; at quasi brothel, 127, 128–30; recruitment accounts,

127–28; remarried mother, 91, 130, 128; varying details in testimonial narratives of, 127, 274n99

Kim Hŭi-o, *In'gan ŭi Hyanggi*, 216

Kim Il-myŏn: description of Korean comfort women as "sex slaves," 72; ethnic nationalist perspective, 151; interviewed, *152;* on Kikumaru's suicide, 277n9; paternalistic discourse, 151–52; reference to term *jūgun ianfu*, 70; zainichi writer, 148, 151

Kim Kun-ja: recruitment story of, in testimony before U.S. House subcommittee, 101; "sold" by foster father, 67

Kim Kwi-ok, 215–16

Kim Kye-hwa, 183

Kim Kyŏng-ae (pseud.), 150

Kim Mun-suk, on Chŏngsindae, 60–61, 168

Kim Myŏng-hye, 103

Kim Ok-sil (aka Kim Ŭn-rye): domestic violence, 89; factory work, 89; *han,* 91; *kisaeng* training, 89; postwar life, 90–91; recruitment as comfort woman, 90

Kim Pok-tong, 58–59

Kim Su-hae (pseud.), 263n108

Kim Sun-dŏk (aka Kim Tŏk-chin), 88, 93 124; in Berkeley, *95;* paintings, 96; recruitment of, 185; relationship with Izumi, 122, 185

Kim Sun-ok, 11, 120, 254n49

Kim Tae-sang, 160–61

Kim Tŏk-sŏng, 19–20

Kim Young-sam, 219

Kim Yun-sim, xx, 264n124; on term *chŏngsindae*, 61

kinship terms, 76

224–25; role of nurses 125; their rates, 141; at time of Japan's defeat, 206; variations in sexual violence and abuse suffered, 30; victims of gendered structural violence, xii–xiii

"Korean 'Comfort Women' for the Japanese Imperial Army" (Soh), 241

Korean comfort women movement, 23, 33, 46, 48, 175, 237

Korean comfort women survivors: acute "shame," 203; complex and varied lived experiences, 229; countermemories of, toward individual Japanese soldiers, 181–90; denigration as prostitutes, 177–80; in foreign countries (*see* Chang Ch'un-wŏl; No Su-bok; Pae Pong-gi, Song Sin-do); *han* narratives, 80–96; lawsuit against the Japanese government, 43; lifelong suffering of, 227, 228; performative quality of bearing witness, 99–104; and postwar lives, 148, 177, 204; recollections of "modern girl" look, 12–13; registered, 92–99; reproductive health and infertility among, 50; "star," 95–96; subaltern voices of, 73, 103, 104, 227; subjectivity of, 103; as symbols of national suffering under Japanese colonialism, 223–24; testimonial narratives, 79, 263n108; at Women's Tribunal, 37. *See also* House of Sharing (South Korea), survivors as permanent residents of; South Korean public discourse on comfort women

Korean Council for Women Drafted for Military Sexual Slavery by Japan (South Korea), 57, 63; campaign abroad for resolutions on comfort women, 68; communal shelter Urijip

(Our House), 96; criticism of, 97; against Koizumi's visit to Korea, 234; and memorial to Chŏngsindae, 230–31; and NOW protest rally, 33; opposition to the AWF project, 96, 239; publication project titles, 102, 103; publication series of South Korean comfort women survivors' testimonials, 48; statistical data on Korean survivors, 139; Suzuki Yūko and, 158; use of term *chŏnsindae* for *wianbu*, 72, 74, 172, 231; War and Women's Human Rights Museum project, 231, 249; weekly demonstration, 267n13

Korean kinship terminology, 266n166

Korean patriarchy, and abuse and maltreatment of daughters and wives, xiii, xvi, 3

Korean Research Institute for Chŏng-s(h)indae (South Korea), 57, 99

Korean sexual culture: agrarian metaphor of sexual act, 40; and anti-prostitution legislation (2004) in South Korea, 233; contemporary public-sex institutions and attitudes in South Korea, 232–33; masculinist, 3, 105, 168, 203, 219, 227; origin of prostitution in, 286n88; stigmatization of sex workers, 201; women's chastity in, 151. *See also* adult entertainment industry; licensed prostitution (colonial Korea)

Korean Studies, 46

Korean victims of atomic bombs, 168

Korean War (1950–53), xvi, 43, 90, 165, 201, 210–11, 212, 215, 216, 224, 285n52

Korea's Place in the Sun (Cumings), 238

Koryŏ Dynasty (918–1392), 203, 218, 219, 283n11, 287n95

Manchuria, *14,* 132; invasion of, xii; Korean comfort women in, 139; Koreans in, 284n25; regulated prostitution in, 113

Manchurian Incident, 125–27, 134

"marginal women," 147

Maria Luz, 112, 271n34

Markle, Kenneth, 214, 215, 286n82

marriage proposals: to comfort women, 92, 182; to kisaeng, 223

"masculinist," 252n5

masculinist sexism, 31, 32, 39, 77

masculinist sexual culture: categories of women in, 40; comfort women as prostitutes in, 32; concept of, 3, 31, 77, 252n5; in Korea and Japan, 240; and *pi,* 39–46; social and psychological effect of, on postwar lives, 176; and violence against women, 88, 164, 227, 235. *See also* Japanese sexual culture; Korean sexual culture

Matsui Yayori, 42, 192, 270n3

McDougall, Gay J., 48, 235

Meiji state (imperial Japan): birth of, 110–11; education system, 6; and modern prostitution system, 111–13

memoir (1976), of former prostitute and businesswoman (Okinawa). *See* Uehara Eiko

memoir (1994), of Ch'ae Myŏng-sin, retired general (South Korea), 286n84

memorial to comfort women, objection to erection of, 230–31

memories: childhood, of comfort women survivors, xiii, xvi, 3, 4, 82, 91, 104, 130; collective, of comfort women in Japan, 114, 146–59, 234; collective, of comfort women in South Korea,

159–69, 198, 234; comfort women survivors', of wartime experiences, 97, 146–49, 178–80, 198, 239; of Dutch comfort women survivors, 178–80; ethnic nationalism and, 43–46; Japanese military veterans', of comfort facilities, 160, 176, 190–95; Japanese public, of Asia Pacific War, 66; nostalgic, 63, 145, 190; South Korean, of colonial occupation, 15; South Korean collective, of comfort women, 152, 159–69; war of, 145; works on the politics of, 48. *See also* countermemories; Dutch comfort women survivors; Japanese public discourse on comfort women; Korean comfort women survivors; South Korean public discourse on comfort women

memory and truth-claims, in scholarship and creative writing, 277–78n28

"memory works," 145–46

Menchú, Rigoberta, 99. *See also* "thespian truth"

Mihara Yoshie (aka Shirota Suzuko): and comfort women monument, 198–201; coming out, 201, 206; on family debt and work at comfort stations, 198; radio interview of, 198; significance of, 239

Military Center, Manchuria, 120

"military comfort women museum," opposition to building of, 289n19

military hypermasculinity, xvi, 115, 132, 134. *See also* Patton, George S.

Mills, C. Wright, *The Sociological Imagination,* 143

Ming Dynasty (China), demand for Korean "tribute women" (*kongnyŏ*), 204

Ministry of Gender Equality, 139.
See also South Korean Ministry of
Gender Equality (Yŏsŏngbu); South
Korean Ministry of Gender Equality
and Family (Yŏsŏngkajokbu)
Ministry of War (imperial Japan), 21, 137
minkan ianjo (private or civilian comfort
stations), 121
Min Kwan-sik, 205
minmyŏnŭri (adopted-daughter-in-law),
156, 278n33
"misguided moralism," xiv
Mitsubishi, 18
Mitsukoshi (today's Sinsegye) Department Store (Seoul), 18
Mitsukoshi Department Store (Tokyo),
135, 136
Miyazawa Kiichi, and public apology for
the comfort women issue, 44
modan. See "modern girl"
"modern girl," 11; *modan gaaru,* 254n50;
short hair, as symbol of modernity,
254n50. *See also* "new woman" (*atarashii onna/sin yŏsŏng*)
mompe (baggy pantaloons), 207
Mongolian women, 233
Mongols. *See* Yuan dynasty (China)
"Monument to soothe the spirit,"
198–201, 239
Moon, Katharine, 212
Morikawa Machiko, 183
Motooka Shōji, 63
Motoyama, Mr., 194–95
Mun Myŏng-gŭm, 120
Mun Ok-chu: *Chōsen pi,* 39; claiming
her savings, 281n23; and Hitomi, 184;
memories of Yamada Ichirō, 183;
money sent to family, 184, 274n96; on
multiple recruitments, 183; *Mun Oku-
chu,* 175, 183; as nurse, 125; postwar

kisaeng training, 8; reminiscences of
Japanese soldiers, 175, 183; tips saved,
183–84
Mun P'il-gi: abusive father, 83; aspirations and agency of, 3; deceitful
recruitment, 140; exercise of agency
leading to tragedy, 82; and father's
gravesite, 85; fear of Soviet troops,
208; half-brother, 219; interviewed,
84–85; Japanese name of, 123; lack of
education as *han,* 79, 80; life story of,
82–84, 242, 284n35; as participant in
redress movement, 94; postwar self-
concept, 177; pursuit of autonomy,
86, 88; recollecting life as comfort
woman, 123; runaway daughter, 79; at
school-age and elementary education
in colonial Korea, 7
Murayama Tomiichi, 239
Murmuring, The (Byun), 93
myŏnjang, 86, 140, 184

Na, Naeil Demo Kandei (Hyejin), 94
Naehun, 5
Nagasaki, 168; red-light district,
271n20
Na Hye-sŏk, 6, 253n20
Nah Young-gyun, *As to My Family in the
Era of Japanese Empire,* 61
naisen ittai policy, 141
Nakasone Yasuhiro, 118
Nakayama Tadanao, 107, 125
Nakazato Chiyo, 29–30
names: change of Koreans' to Japanese
style (colonial Korea), 15–16, 37;
given to comfort women, 39, 74,
123; in identity politics, 69; political
symbolism, 69–72; women's after
marriage, 76. *See also* Kim, Richard,
Lost Names

Nan Hee, 213

Nanking (Nanjing) massacre, 37, 125, 134, 135, 140, 171

Nanum ŭi Chip, 93–99

National Campaign for Eradication of Crime by United States Troops in Korea, 215

National Organization for Women (U.S.), 33, 291n1

New Guinea campaign, Japanese Imperial Army, 158

New History Textbook, The (Tsukuru Kai), 170–71

"new woman" (*atarashii onna/sin yŏsŏng*): aspiring to become, 82; comparative perspectives on, 253n21; criticism of, 6–7; education and, 4–6; emergence of, 6; *modan,* 254n50; and new lifestyles, 7–8; working-class, 11–13, 15, 254n55. *See also* "colonial modernity"; "modern girl"

New York City, 76

New York Times, 67, 101

NHK, television coverage of 2000 Women's Tribunal, 236

Nihon no Senreki, 149

Nishino Rumiko, 175, 191, 282n49

Nixon Doctrine, 212

nongovernmental organizations, role in "resignification" of the comfort women, 50

normative heterosexual masculinity, 116, 133, 179, 282n55

North Hamkyŏng Province, 119

North Korea: ICJ mission to, 47; official discourse on comfort women, 62; report on *ianjo* buildings, 273n64; UN mission to, 48

North Korean comfort women survivors, 36, 37, 42, 64

"No. 606," 122

No Su-bok: life story of, as Korean comfort woman survivor in Thailand, 166–67; "Na nŭn Yŏja Chŏngsindae" (I Was a Woman *Chŏngsindae*), 166, 264n108

NOW, 33, 291n1

Nŭngkwang, 94

"O, Military Comfort Women" (*Aa! Jūgun Ianfu*), 200–201

Odajima Tadashi, 20–22

Ogawa Shinsuke Award, 93

Oh, Bonnie, 50

O'Herne, Jan. *See* Ruff-O'Herne, Jan

OhmyNews, 238, 291n41

Okinawa, Korean comfort woman survivor in, 147, 155; Korean comfort women in, 141, 145, 168, 169, 198; Prostitution Prevention Law (1956) and, 211; red-light district in, 157

Okinawa no Harumoni (Yamatani), 155–56. *See also* Pae Pong-gi

okiya (geisha house), 8

Okuno Seisuke, 66, 68

ŏmŏni (mother), 73

Ōmori Fumiko, 145, 158

Osaka, 10, 157, 182

Osaki, 73–74

Pacific Islands, 133

Pacific War Research Group (Japan), 147

Pae Chok-kan: childhood abuse, 92; *chŏng* for the Japanese, 175, 190; comfort women as "soldiers," 189; husband, 189; and "modern girl" look, 12; relationship with mother, 92, 189; remembrances of Ishikawa, 189

Pae Pong-gi, 99; documentary and publications on, 147, 155; interviews of, 155, 157; life story of, in *Yŏsŏng Sinmun,* 167; multiple marriages of, 156; nostalgia for time as a comfort woman, 145, 156

Pagoda Park, 53

Pak Chong-sŏng, 9–10

Pak Il-sŏk (aka Arai Hakuseki), officer in Shanghai Korean Association, 135; owner of comfort station in Shanghai,135

Pak Ok-nyŏn (aka Pak Sun-ae), 93; sold by husband, 276n126

Pak Pok-sun (aka Kaneda Kimiko): born out of wedlock, 185; charges of survivors' "untruthful" testimonies, 97, 123; death of (2005), 96; interviewed, 97; and the Korean Council, 185; memories of Sergeant S, 186; photograph of, *187;* and Usuki Keiko, 96

Pak Sun-i (pseud.): fraudulently recruited, 58–59; in postwar *kijich'on* sex trade, 212

Pak Tu-ri, 93, 94

Pak Yŏng-sim, as "Japanese" prisoner of war, 35–*36,* 49; as North Korean survivor, 36–37

Pak Yu-ha, 229–30

Palau, 69, 87, 198

"paradigmatic story," of comfort women, 24, 29, 31, 33, 46–47; activists', 100–102, 227, 229, 236, 244, 249; construction of, 105, 148, 154; defined, xi; emergence of, 77; in "the era of the survivor," 64; ethnic nationalisms and, 50–51; feminist humanitarian, xiv–xv; interfering with activists', xiii, 176, 181, 195; Japanese reactions to, 68; as master narrative, xiv;

media representations of, 51; and UN reports, 48, 153–54

paradigm shift, regarding comfort women, 41, 156

"Paradise of the South Pacific," 148

parallel political dynamics, 246

paramilitary *ianjo,* 124–30, 133, 134; "maidens' auxiliary," 124, 125–27; "quasi-brothel," 124, 127–30; run by Japanese military, 118. *See also* Japanese military comfort stations (*gun ianjo*)

Paranjape, Snehal, 47

Park, Therese, *A Gift of the Emperor,* 51–52

Park Chung Hee, 16, 212, 217

patriarchal cultures: customary practices in, 88; structural violence against women in, xii, xiii, xvi, 3–4, 105. *See also* gendered structural violence; violence against women

Patriotic Chŏngsindae, 159

Patriotic Labor Service Association, Yamaguchi Prefecture (Japan), 152

Patton, George S., 282n55

Paul, Christa, 46

payment: advance *(maegari),* 112–13, 210, 263; of comfort women, 123, 126; of tips, 126, 183–84

Peacock, James L., xi, xv, 251n1

Pearl Harbor attack, 38, 43, 60, 134, 137

pedophilia, 273n63

People's Republic of China: Japan's normalization of relations with, 221; Korean researcher in (*see* Kang Yong-kwŏn); survivors from, traveling to Japan, 42, 64

Perry, Matthew C., 110

Philippines, 42, 64, 239; comfort women,

xii, xvii, 1, 48, 104, 130, 137, 147, 239; *kijich'on* workers from, 214; redress movement in, 245

photographic metaphor: of anthropological approach, xi; synchronic and diachronic lenses, 245. *See also* harsh light; Peacock, James L.; soft focus

"*pi*" (vagina): Chinese slang, 53; *Chōsen*, 163; commercial and communal, 32; connotations of, 39; in private informalism, 77

pimping, feminist definition of, 109

pleasure quarters (*yūkaku*): establishments in, 119; ethnicity-based fees, in colonial Korea (1926), 253n39; for foreign men (imperial Japan), 110; forerunner of, 109; formation and spread of, in colonial Korea, 8–10; government policies concerning, 122; *harimise* in, 123; licensed prostitution in, 109; marriage of women of, 182; new, 271n21; "prostitutes liberation law" and, 112; as "public latrine," 40; syphilis clinic in, 111

p'oju (master of brothel), 9

political correctness, 142, 240; culture war of, 292n8

political economy: colonial Korea, 15, 151, 203, 227; global capitalist, and women as sex workers, xiii, 115–16, 234, 235, 243; and Japanese comfort system, 108, 204, 242; of prostitution, 201

positions, east asia cultures critique, 48

positivism, 154

postcolonial Korea. *See* South Korea

postmodernism, 244

power dynamics, 105–6, 195, 227. *See also* structural power

Primoratz, Igor, 143

prisoner-of-war camps, Southeast Asia, 64

"Prisoners of War—Japanese women," United States War Department photo, 35–36

Project Implementation Committee in the Netherlands (PICN), 177, 180. *See also* Asian Women's Fund (AWF)

prostitution: in both preindustrial and industrial societies, 109; as commercial sex versus sexual slavery, 114; indentured, xiv; regarding of comfort system as, 32, 141. *See also* Japanese sexual culture; Korean sexual culture; licensed prostitution (imperial Japan); Manchuria

"Prostitution" (Giobbe), 143

prostitution abolitionists, 113, 210

"public sex," xii

"public toilet," 39–40, 195

Puch'ŏn, 186

"Pure Japan," 113

"purveyors of sex," 200

Pusan (Korea): comfort women sent to, 8, 61, 83, 87, 156, 213; on memorial to comfort women in, 230

P'yŏngyang, 126; Kim Ok-sil and, 88, 90; *kisaeng*, 84, 87, 89; *kwŏnbŏn* in, 8; procurers in, 11

quasi-brothels, 124, 127–30, 133, 134, 135. *See also* Japanese military comfort stations (*gun ianjo*); paramilitary *ianjo*

RAA, 208–9

Rabaul, 159

Ramseyer, J. Mark, 114

rape: by the military in wartime, 33, 140, 207–8, 210; as a war crime, 41, 131

"rape centers," xvii–xviii, 131, 133

Society for History Textbook Reform, 66, 170. *See also* Tsukuru Kai (Society for History Textbook Reform)

soft focus, xi, xiii, 82, 228, 242. *See also* photographic metaphor

Soh, C. Sarah: on anthropological engagement in controversial issues, xiv–xv; ethnographic research methodology, 241–45, 263n108, 267n14; methodological stance of, as expatriate anthropologist, 246; as native anthropologist, 245–46; and "Rushdie effect," 247–49

Sohye, Queen, 5

Sŏk Pok-sun (pseud.), 97

Sŏ Kyŏng-sik, 73

Song Pyŏng-jun (aka Noda Heijirō), 16

Song Sin-do: and employment agency (*sogaeso*), 91; lawsuit against Japan, 91, 92; proposal from Japanese soldier, 182; resentment toward mother, 91; supporters of, in Japan, 91, 92

Song Yŏng-gil, 238

Song Youn-ok, 9, 10

Sŏnjo, King, 204

South Africa, 228

Southeast Asian countries, under Western colonial rule, 133

South Korea: abolishment of licensed prostitution in, 217; bilateral agreement with Japan, 160; camp towns for U.S. military, 211–15, 224; comfort women survivors in, xii; ethnonationalism, xiii, 2; foreign visitors to, 222; human rights violations of women, 1–2; knowledge about comfort women, 146; "miracle on the Han," 220; nationalism, 57–63, 100, 237; political upheaval after liberation, 168; Prostitution Prevention Law

(1961), 217; role of populist media, 239; "settlement of history" project, 238; social stigmatization of comfort women survivors, 224–25, 237–38; special anti-prostitution legislation (2004), 233; Tourism Promotion Law, 221; unequal diplomatic relations with Japan and with the United States, 106. *See also* South Korean public discourse on comfort women

South Korean activists: antipathy and distrust of Japan, 234; feminist, 233; rhetoric of "forcible recruitment," 102; "settling the past" with Japan, 234

South Korean Army: comfort stations during the Korean War, xvi; "special comfort unit," 215–16, 224; "special comfort women," 201, 215–17

South Korean Association of the Pacific War Victims and Bereaved Families, lawsuit against Japan, 43, 96

South Korean critical feminist researchers, 24; and "moral responsibility" to include Kil Wŏn-ok's story, 103, 258n111

South Korean historians, and comfort women issue, 102

South Korean history textbooks: comfort women issue in, 145, 171–72; conflation of *chŏngsindae* with comfort women in, 171; effect of nationalist education, 239

South Korean men, "Don't-Ask Tourism," 223

South Korean Ministry of Education, 171

South Korean Ministry of Gender Equality (Yŏsŏngbu), 62, 92, 139

South Korean Ministry of Gender Equality and Family (Yŏsŏngkajokbu), 35, 265n126; Web site, 35, 282n54

South Korean National Assembly: anti-prostitution legislation (2004), 233; on prostitution for American troops and foreign sex tourists, 224

South Korean presidents: Kim Dae-jung, 16, 219; Kim Young-sam, 219; Park Chung Hee, 16, 212, 217; Roh Moo-hyun, 219, 234, 291n41; Roh Tae Woo, 63

South Korean public discourse on comfort women, 45; comfort women as abused *chŏngsindae*, xv, 55, 57, 58, 59, 72, 153, 160, 161; comfort women as "sex slaves," xi, xiii, xiv, 1, 3, 22, 32–33, 41–46, 47, 50, 71–72, 229, 231; and feminist humanitarian perspective, 46; Japanese comfort system as war crime, 22, 79, 107; lack of concern about comfort women issue, 173, 203; media's equivalency of *wianbu* and *chŏngsindae,* 232; postcolonial nationalist perspectives, 146, 160; survivors as *chŏngsindae halmŏni,* 74; survivors as heroic symbols, 224, 237; use of term "military comfort women under Imperial Japan" *(ilcheha kundae wianbu),* 70–71, 74; use of term *kundae wianbu* (military comfort women) (1964), 160

South Korean redress movement, xvii, 231. *See also* Korean comfort women movement

South Korean sex industry, 202; adult entertainment business, 207; Filipino women in, 214; and international human trafficking, 233, 290n26; Russian women in, 214; as source of foreign currency, 205. *See also kijich'on* prostitution; *kisaeng* tourism

South Korean women researchers: of the postcolonial generations, 152; publications on comfort women issue, 229–30

Special Comfort Facilities Association, 208

"special comfort unit" (T'ŭksu Wian-dae), 215–16, 224

"special comfort women," 201, 215–17

"special personnel," 70, 125

"special platoon," 125

special restaurant, 8, 119, 121, 131, 134, 198, 222, 253n29, 275n102

Special Student Volunteer Soldiers, 60

"speech errors," fear of making, 101

"spirit marriage," 188, 267n11; postmortem wedding rite, 281n38

"state-as-pimp," 48, 224

"Statement of Recommendations to the Korean Council" (Jee), 231

Status of the Forces Agreement (SOFA), 214

Stetz, Margaret, 50

Stoll, David, 99

"Stories That Make History," 99, 103

structural power, 3, 201, 227, 235, 243, 291n3

structural violence, xii–xiii, 27, 139; under consumer capitalism, xiii, 115–16, 234, 235, 243; gendered, 237, 240; against "marginal women," 147; and masculinist sexual culture, xiii, 115–16, 234, 235, 243; in patriarchal cultures, xii; power dynamics of, against comfort women, 50, 105–6; and victimization of Korean women, xii, xiv, xv, 38, 50, 236–37, 240

subaltern voices, 73, 103, 104, 227

Tokyo tribunal, 42

Tokyo War Crimes Trials, 142. *See also*
International Military Tribunal for
the Far East (Tokyo, 1946)

Tongduch'ŏn, 212, 214, 285n63

Tongnyŏnghyŏnsŏng, 120

Totsuka Etsurō, 64, 66, 68; *Nihon ga
Shiranai Sensō Sekinin,* 72

Toyama (Japan), xxii, 58; Prefecture,
58, 59

Toyotomi Hideyoshi, 109

traffic in women and girls, international
treaties banning, 21–22

"transnational memory," 108, 176, 195.
See also memories

transnational redress movement, 6, 19,
44, 230, 231; and comfort women in
Japanese textbooks, 169; criticism of
Hata, 154; effect on survivors, 94, 96;
human rights discourse, 156, 176, 236;
neonationalist activism against, 236;
and partial truths, 240; and postcolonial ethnic nationalism, 22–23; and
silencing some survivors' voices, 79;
ultranationalist critics of, 70; and use
of term "comfort women," 71; and
use of term *jūgun,* 70; use of term
"military sexual slavery," 108

"tribute women" (*kongnyŏ*), 203–4, 233,
290n27; as Koryŏ's *chŏngsindae,*
283n11

troostmeisje ("comfort girl"), 69; as "victims of forced prostitution," 72

*True Stories of Korean Comfort
Women,* 49

Truk Island, 119, 147, 148

truth: "approximate," xvii; four different kinds of, 97–98; "good-enough,"
228; healing or restorative, 98; partial,
xvii, xviii, 240; personal or narrative,
98; "personal truth," 229; social or
dialogue, 98

"Truth about Comfort Women, The"
(2007), newspaper advertisement, 68

Truth and Reconciliation Commission
(TRC), South Africa's, 97–98

Tsuji, red-light district in Okinawa, 157

Tsukuru Kai (Society for History Textbook Reform), 66, 68, 170

Uehara Eiko: as "happy woman," 157; as
victim of sexual slavery, 157

Ueno Chizuko, 266n155; *Nationalism and
Gender,* 48

Uesugi Satoshi, 154

ultranationalist critics, of comfort
women redress movement, 70

United Nations: Commission on Human
Rights (UNCHR), 65, 72; Coomaraswamy Report, 48, 153, 154; debates
on the comfort women issue, 33; Economic and Social Council, 30; reports
on the comfort women issue, 49

United Nations peacekeeping missions,
and sexual abuse of women and girls,
xvii

United States Army, G-2 Myitkyina
Task Force, 35

United States House of Representatives:
resolution on the comfort women
issue, 68; subcommittee on Asia, the
Pacific, and the Global Environment
public hearing, 67, 100

United States Justice Department, 49

United States military, 207–8, 235; sex
crimes against women in Japan and
Korea, 207–8, 235; wartime report on
Korean "comfort girls," 34

United States National Archives, 35–36,
242